Real Sadhus Sing to God

AAR
AMERICAN ACADEMY OF RELIGION

RELIGION, CULTURE, AND HISTORY

SERIES EDITOR
Robert A. Yelle, University of Memphis

A Publication Series of
The American Academy of Religion
and
Oxford University Press

ANTI-JUDAISM IN FEMINIST RELIGIOUS WRITINGS
Katharina von Kellenbach

CROSS-CULTURAL CONVERSATION
(*Initiation*)
Edited by Anindita Niyogi Balslev

ON DECONSTRUCTING LIFE-WORLDS
Buddhism, Christianity, Culture
Robert Magliola

THE GREAT WHITE FLOOD
Racism in Australia
Anne Pattel-Gray

IMAG(IN)ING OTHERNESS
Filmic Visions of Living Together
Edited by S. Brent Plate and David Jasper

CULTURAL OTHERNESS
Correspondence with Richard Rorty, Second Edition
Anindita Niyogi Balslev

FEMINIST POETICS OF THE SACRED
Creative Suspicions
Edited by Frances Devlin-Glass and Lyn McCredden

PARABLES FOR OUR TIME
Rereading New Testament Scholarship after the Holocaust
Tania Oldenhage

MOSES IN AMERICA
The Cultural Uses of Biblical Narrative
Melanie Jane Wright

INTERSECTING PATHWAYS
Modern Jewish Theologians in Conversation with Christianity
Marc A. Krell

ASCETICISM AND ITS CRITICS
Historical Accounts and Comparative Perspectives
Edited by Oliver Freiberger

VIRTUOUS BODIES
The Physical Dimensions of Morality in Buddhist Ethics
Susanne Mrozik

IMAGINING THE FETUS
The Unborn in Myth, Religion, and Culture
Edited by Vanessa R. Sasson and Jane Marie Law

VICTORIAN REFORMATION
The Fight over Idolatry in the Church of England, 1840–1860
Dominic Janes

SCHLEIERMACHER ON RELIGION AND THE NATURAL ORDER
Andrew C. Dole

MUSLIMS AND OTHERS IN SACRED SPACE
Edited by Margaret Cormack

LITTLE BUDDHAS
Children and Childhoods in Buddhist Texts and Traditions
Edited by Vanessa R. Sasson

REAL SADHUS SING TO GOD
Gender, Asceticism, and Vernacular Religion in Rajasthan
Antoinette E. DeNapoli

AAR
AMERICAN ACADEMY OF RELIGION

REAL SADHUS SING TO GOD

Gender, Asceticism, and Vernacular Religion in Rajasthan

ANTOINETTE ELIZABETH DENAPOLI

OXFORD
UNIVERSITY PRESS

OXFORD
UNIVERSITY PRESS

Oxford University Press is a department of the University of Oxford. It furthers the University's objective of excellence in research, scholarship, and education by publishing worldwide.

Oxford New York
Auckland Cape Town Dar es Salaam Hong Kong Karachi
Kuala Lumpur Madrid Melbourne Mexico City Nairobi
New Delhi Shanghai Taipei Toronto

With offices in
Argentina Austria Brazil Chile Czech Republic France Greece
Guatemala Hungary Italy Japan Poland Portugal Singapore
South Korea Switzerland Thailand Turkey Ukraine Vietnam

Published in the United States of America by
Oxford University Press
198 Madison Avenue, New York, NY 10016

Library of Congress Cataloging-in-Publication Data

DeNapoli, Antoinette Elizabeth.
Real sadhus sing to God : gender, asceticism, and vernacular religion in Rajasthan / Antoinette Elizabeth DeNapoli.
pages cm
Includes bibliographical references and index.
ISBN 978–0–19–994001–1 (cloth : alk. paper) — ISBN 978–0–19–994003–5 (pbk. : alk. paper) 1. Women sadhus—India—Rajasthan. 2. Asceticism—Hinduism. 3. Women in Hinduism—India—Rajasthan. I. Title.
BL1241.53.D46 2014
294.5'6108209544—dc23
2013039009

1 3 5 7 9 8 6 4 2
Printed in the United States of America
on acid-free paper

Contents

Acknowledgments

AN ACCOMPLISHMENT AS priceless as a first book represents the dedication of many people, not only the author herself. There are no words adequate enough to express the unbelievable sense of gratitude I feel to the sadhus of Rajasthan. These brave women and men allowed me into their lives and taught me about their worlds. Without their support and blessings, this book would not have been possible. The sadhu Ganga Giri Maharaj deserves special mention. The oldest and most respected female sadhu in the region of Rajasthan where I worked, Ganga Giri's enduring kindness and acceptance of me, especially in the beginning stages of fieldwork, inspired the other female sadhus to work with me and teach me about their religious practices. Thanks are also due to Manvendra Singh Ashiya, my indefatigable field associate, and his family for their help and hospitality. Manvendra's sisters, Divya and Rajmani, helped me in transcribing hundreds of tapes and explaining the ideas discussed in them. Enormous thanks go to Jagdish Chander Sanadhya and his family, and especially to his daughter Kalpana, for opening their hearts and home during a critical period of research. Finally, thanks to Sohan Lal Chechani ("Dadaji") and his family for introducing me to many of the sadhus of Rajasthan. Dadaji infused much humor and happiness into my research and made fieldwork an enjoyable challenge.

Heartfelt thanks go to Joyce Burkhalter Flueckiger and Laurie L. Patton, my co-advisors at Emory University, for their strength, brilliance, and passion for their work and their students. Their courage and compassion have been inspirational, and I am the scholar I am today because of their examples. They read numerous drafts of this book and encouraged me in so many ways, big and small. I thank them for being model teachers and mentors. I also wish to thank here other academics who have played a signal role in my development as a scholar-teacher and in the development of this book: Paul Courtright, Corinne Dempsey, Kathleen Erndl, Ann Gold, Lindsey Harlan, Jack Hawley, Ramdas Lamb, Jeffrey Long, Philip Lutgendorf, P. Pratap Kumar, June

McDaniel, Karen Pechilis, Jennifer Saunders, Rita D. Sherma, Perundevi Srinivasan, Susan Wadley, and Kate Zubko. These colleagues read the manuscript, or parts of it, during various stages of writing. The conversations I had with Jack Hawley, Ann Gold, and Lindsey Harlan during the final stages of the writing of the book were inspirational. Susan Wadley helped in organizing the American Institute of Indian Studies' (AIIS) three-day seminar on turning the dissertation into a book, in which I participated in November 2010. In that context, I received the astute comments and encouragement from Sue and Corinne Dempsey that pushed me forward in pursuing this book's publication with Oxford. I thank Philip Lutgendorf for inviting me to give a presentation on my research with female sadhus when I was teaching as a visiting assistant professor at Grinnell College in Iowa during the 2009–2010 academic year. That presentation helped me to clarify the ideas developed in Chapter 8 of this book. The collegiality and friendship of June McDaniel and Karen Pechilis have been precious gifts. They have been gracious mentors, showing their kindness and sharing their insights, and have been paragons of intellectual generosity in academia. Thanks are due to the anonymous readers of the manuscript who made many valuable and encouraging suggestions. Finally, the support of my colleagues at the University of Wyoming—Paul V. M. Flesher, Caroline McCracken-Flesher, Mary Keller, Neely Mahapatra, Quincy Newell, Kristine T. Utterback, Seth Ward, Susan Dewey, and Bonnie Zare—has been vital and sustaining. Each of these colleagues provided critical feedback on chapters of the book and, in several cases, in preparing the manuscript for publication. They have made me feel like an integral part of this university's intellectual community, and so have my UW students.

Individual funding agencies have made it possible for me to conduct research and advanced language study in India. A Hindi Language Fellowship and a Junior Research Fellowship from the American Institute of Indian Studies allowed me to study and live in India for several years. Thanks to Pradeep Mehendiratta and Purnima Mehta of the AIIS Delhi headquarters, and to all the Hindi language teachers at the AIIS institute in Jaipur, Rajasthan, for their endless support, immediate help in times of visa troubles, and hard work for making the lives of students and scholars run a whole lot smoother. Thanks to Elise Auerbach of AIIS Chicago for her steady stream of support over the years. A Basic Research Grant and an International Travel Grant from the University of Wyoming enabled me to spend three months in Rajasthan in the summer of 2011 and conduct follow-up research to the field research I carried out in the years between 2004 and 2006 through AIIS funding. A pre-dissertation research grant through Emory University's Funds for Internalization enabled me to spend enough time in India to put together a research proposal, and a dissertation grant through the same program two years later allowed me to purchase much-needed equipment for my 2004 research trip. Thanks to Emory University's Graduate Division of Religion and the Graduate School for funds that allowed me to attend and present at academic conferences. A teaching fellowship from the Andrew W. Mellon Foundation allowed me to teach at Dillard University in New Orleans between 2007 and 2008. Thanks to Danille Taylor, Dean of the Division of Humanities at Dillard; to Regina Werum and Rudloph Byrd, codirectors of the Emory Mellon program, for their constant support; to my Dillard mentor Mona Lisa Saloy for her "red beans and ricely yours" kindness; and to Marylin Mell of Dillard, with whom everyday conversations turned into earth-shattering revelations.

Several chapters, or parts thereof, have benefited substantially from the valuable comments provided by the anonymous reviewers of previously published articles on which those chapters are based. The Introduction draws on "Vernacular Hinduism in Rajasthan," in *Contemporary Hinduism*, edited by P. Pratap Kumar (Bristol, CT: Acumen Publishing, 2013); Chapter 1 draws on "Performing Materiality through Song: Hindu Female Renouncers' Embodying Practices in Rajasthan," *Nidan: International Journal for the Study of Hinduism* 23 (2011): 5–36; Chapter 2 draws on "By the Sweetness of the Tongue: Duty, Destiny, and Devotion in the Oral Life Narratives of Female Sadhus in Rajasthan," *Asian Ethnology* 68, no. 1 (2009): 81–109; Chapter 7 draws on "Write the Text Letter-by-Letter in the Heart: Non-Literacy, Religious Authority, and Female Sadhus' Performance of Asceticism through Sacred Texts," *Postscripts: The Journal of Sacred Texts and Contemporary Worlds* 4, no. 3 (2008): 3–40; and Chapter 8 draws on "'Crossing over the Ocean of Existence': Performing 'Mysticism' and Exerting Agency by Female *Sadhus* of Rajasthan," *The Journal of Hindu Studies* 3, no. 3 (October 2010): 298–336.

I thank Cynthia Read and Marcela Maxfield at Oxford University Press for their support, time, and commitment to this book before and during its production; Robert Yelle, acquisition editor for the AAR/Religion, Culture, and History series, for his genius in seeing this book through to publication; and Jacob Kinnard, who was the previous editor of the series before Robert came on board, for his help and kindness in the early, yet critical, stages of the publication process. I further thank Saranya Prabuthass for her dedicated assistance in managing the book through to publication, and Kristen Holt-Browning for her astute copyediting of the manuscript.

Perhaps there is no greater debt of thanks than the one I owe to my absolutely awesome parents, Rocco DeNapoli and Helena de Jesus Caballero

DeNapoli. They are my rock and have walked this long and difficult journey with me, supporting me in ways I can never repay. Without their enduring love, patience, guidance, and confidence in me, this project would not have been possible.

This book is dedicated to them and to Ganga Giri.

A Note on Transliteration and Translation

THIS BOOK CONTAINS names and terms in the Sanskrit, Hindi, and Rajasthani (i.e., Mewari) languages. There is considerable variation in the spelling and pronunciation of words in Hindi and in Rajasthani. To avoid confusion, I have used the standard Hindi form of a word, which traditionally drops the spelling (and pronunciation) of the final "a" vowel. So, Sanskritic words such as *karma, dharma, yoga, sannyāsa,* and *mokṣa,* for instance, appear in both standard modern Hindi and in everyday conversational Hindi as *dharm, karm, yog, sannyās,* and *mokṣ.* In instances in which a word or name is more familiar in its Sanskritic context, I use the Sanskrit form of the word, such as *Purāṇa* and *Veda,* instead of *Purān* and *Ved.* Many of the sadhus and householders I knew in Rajasthan switched between Mewari, Hindi, and occasionally, Gujarati in everyday speech contexts, and in the performance contexts described in this book. I indicate in the text the Rajasthani and/or Gujarati forms of the words that were used by my collaborators.

I have used the conventional transliteration system, with one exception. To indicate the symbol "ṛh" for the "tongue-flap" Hindi consonant, I have used "ḍh." Hence, *anpaṛh* appears as *anpaḍh,* and *paṛhnā,* as *paḍhnā.* I have also used diacritical marks for the transliterated terms; however, terms which have become integrated into American English, such as guru, chai, and sari, appear without diacritics (and are not italicized). In addition, place names (e.g., Rajasthan), names of languages (e.g., Hindi), the names of the sadhus, and the names of the various deities mentioned in this book appear without diacritics. This is to create ease of reading. In the spirit of making the term *sādhu* more user-friendly for American English speakers, I have left out the diacritics and do not italicize this word, which are now standard practices in most academic studies on sadhus.

All translations of stories, songs, and texts that I recorded from the field are my own. Either Manvendra Singh, my field associate, or Kalpana Chander Sanadhya, my Brahmin host sister, assisted me with these translations, especially with those performances which had occurred in Rajasthani (or Gujarati). All translations of the Rajasthani sadhus' oral traditions were made from performances recorded by me and transcribed either by me or by Manvendra's sisters, Rajmani and Divya; and by Kalpana Sanadhya and her sister-in-law, Jaya Sanadhya.

Real Sadhus Sing to God

Introduction

Orienting Metaphors

SINGING *BHAJANS* AS DEVOTIONAL ASCETICISM

Real sadhus sing to God.

—GANGA GIRI MAHARAJ

THE GARDEN BUSTLES with activity on this warm April afternoon in 2005. Mrinalini Tara,[1] a widowed sixty-three-year-old householder, has invited Ganga Giri, a ninety-five-year-old sadhu, or female Hindu renouncer, to her home, which is located in a middle-class and mixed-caste colony in Udaipur city, Rajasthan, for a *satsang*, or devotional gathering. Many of Tara's neighbors have come to listen to Ganga Giri's teachings and prepare food for the event. As a sadhu, Ganga Giri has renounced, or left behind, the normative societal expectations of marriage and family (i.e., householding), the ritual ties to her family, and the economic security characteristic of the lives of householders, in order to devote herself permanently and purposefully to the worship of the divine. Her unconventional way of life is known as *sannyās* (renunciation); it evokes respect and reverence from other sadhus and householders alike. Walking with a wooden cane, Ganga Giri makes her way into Tara's garden, and the householders line up to touch her feet. She blesses them by putting her right hand[2] on their heads and telling them to "live long and happy lives." Several of the people attending this *satsang* consist of members of my Brahmin host family, with whom I have been staying since my arrival in the city in January 2005. Only two months prior to today, I introduced Tara to Ganga Giri at the latter's ashram, and Tara, a deeply religious woman who has taken an interest in my research on sadhus, immediately bonded with Ganga Giri and became her newest devotee. Seated on a chair under the shade of a large *rudrākṣ* tree,[3] with the neighborhood children gathered by her feet, and the mostly Brahmin-caste adults taking their places on a large cotton blanket on the ground, Ganga Giri runs this *satsang* much like she runs the *satsangs* that occur at her ashram every day: by singing devotional songs (*bhajans*), telling religious stories (*kahāniyān*), and reciting in a literary dialect of Hindi (Avadhi) memorized verses from sacred texts (*pāṭh*), such as the *Rāmcaritmānas*.[4] On this occasion, Ganga Giri shares a story from her large narrative repertoire, one which I hear for the first time since our initial collaboration in the summer of 2001, and which brings to light her idea of renunciation as the performance of songs, stories, and sacred texts. Here is the story she narrated at this gathering:

> [The rule of] Lord Mordhvaj [a king] took place before that of Lord Ramchandraji.[5] Ram's [rule] was afterwards. So, when we go to Limva, now there's a road. But before, there was no road there. It was made in front of me [i.e., she remembers when the road was made]. At that time, people used to walk to get into the temple. So, the laborers were working over there. They were building the road and they started digging into the cave of some sadhus. They dug this much [gestures a large space with her hands]. They dug the cave this much. Inside the cave, a holy flame was lit. Those sadhus were sitting next to each other, but not with one in front of the other. If they had sat with one in front of the other, they would have died. Those sadhus had scary faces. Their eyes were closed. They didn't open their eyes; they didn't sit with one in front of the other. So that cave was dug with a shovel. When the laborers opened the cave, the sadhus asked, "Is it the reign of Mordhvaj or Ramchandraji's?"
>
> This is how we [sadhus] talk about time, by asking which god has taken incarnation [in which cosmic era].[6] We say like this that Ramchandraji will take incarnation at King Dasharath's place. We used to talk like that. [Laughs]. Those sadhus were waiting for the reign of Ram. That's why they asked if it was Mordhvaj's or Ram's reign. When the laborers saw this, they ran from there. They went to their officers and told them what had happened. "We have seen sadhus with scary faces. We dug the cave, and we saw them." The officers came with boots on their feet. The sadhus were talking, "*bharang bharang*." They were speaking loudly. They kept asking, "Is it the reign of Mordhvaj or Ram's?" "It is the reign of the ones who wear the hats [*topī*]," the officers said. [An audience member interjects: "It was the rule of the Britishers."] It was the rule of Congress [i.e., after Indian Independence[7]]. Earlier they didn't use to wear hats. They wore turbans [*sāfā*]. It was the time of Congress. So, those sadhus said, "You run from here, or you will be finished." The laborers made the road from the other side, and closed the caves of those sadhus. They made the road from somewhere down there.

> This thing happened during my lifetime, when I was not too old. [Another audience member interjects: "Those sadhus were so old."] Those sadhus were so old. They sat in that cave during Mordhvaj's time. While singing *bhajans*, the time just passed. How many eons passed by singing *bhajans*! Those sadhus spent all those eons [from the time of Mordhvaj's reign to the time of India's Congress Party] singing *bhajans* to God [*bhagwān*]. Lakhs and crores [literally, "millions"] of years elapsed just by singing *bhajans*. *Bhajan* is such a thing! There are many mysterious qualities in God's name. You can't see God's name. There is a lot of attraction in God's name, but you can't see it. You make a phone call, you call Mumbai from here. You talk, et cetera. In this way, there's attraction. But God's name has much more attraction than that. Never leave the name of God. Do everything, farming, business, everything. But always keep the name of God.

The narrative that Ganga Giri tells teaches her audience about the ultimate power of remembering God, through recitation of the divine name,[8] in their lives, regardless of whether they work in "farming" or "business." Her narrative performance reminds them to keep God close to them by keeping God in their heart-minds (*man*), and to develop an "attraction" to the practice of singing *bhajans*, by which their precious time on this earth will "pass" productively. In this way, Ganga Giri's story "performs," or constructs, several overlapping messages: that singing *bhajans* creates and sustains connection to the divine in one's daily life; it helps to create a better rebirth in the endless cycle of reincarnation (*sansār*)[9] ; it helps to release one from that cycle altogether; and it further transforms one's health by helping one live longer. That is, singing *bhajans* creates immortality. As the story makes explicit, the sadhus "with scary faces" increased the length of their lives by "lakhs and crores" of years (i.e., many eons of cosmic time), just by singing to God. "*Bhajan*," as Ganga Giri emphasizes, "is such a thing!"

But just as significant, Ganga Giri's narrative performs a message about the religious role of sadhus like herself, an elite class of religious virtuosi: namely, that sadhus sing to God, tell religious stories, and recite (or read) sacred texts. In performing this idea, Ganga Giri is not saying anything new. The freedom of movement that *sannyās* provides sadhus makes it possible for them to travel the entire countryside, transmitting religious teachings and traditions through their expressive practices. Kirin Narayan's (1989) ethnography of the storytelling practices of Swamiji, a male sadhu with whom she worked in the hill station of Nasik, India (Maharashtra State), brought to light that sadhus (and householders) perceive these practices as illustrative of the classic renunciant role (cf. Khandelwal 2004; Gross 2001; Henry 1988; 1991; 1995). In twenty-first-century India, sadhus' use of their expressive traditions extends well beyond transmitting traditional religious teachings. Lisa I. Knight (2011) shows that Bauls in East India and Bangladesh—religious specialists[10] with renunciant-like worldviews known for their socially progressive attitudes—are hired by government organizations and NGOs alike to teach about AIDS, leprosy, and the mistreatment of daughters through their song performances (129–131).

What Ganga Giri suggests that *is* unique, especially in regard to what is typically known about sadhus in South Asia from the available academic and popular literature on the subject, concerns her idea that "singing *bhajans*" is synonymous with *sannyās*. Not only is it a practice in which sadhus engage; it also *creates* their renunciation. For the sadhus with whom I worked, singing *bhajans* performs a view of *sannyās* as these female sadhus interpret, experience, and practice it, in Rajasthan and wherever they move and settle in the subcontinent. That is, the sadhus not only live their *sannyās* by singing *bhajans*, but also construct it as they sing. Singing *bhajans* represents a paradigmatic idiom, or to use Thomas Tweed's words (2006), an "orienting metaphor," for the sadhus' singing, storytelling, and sacred text performances, which I characterize as the "rhetoric of renunciation," and engenders what I term "devotional asceticism" as an alternative to the dominant view of *sannyās*. Singing *bhajans* embodies asceticism as relational and celebratory, and establishes a female way of being a sadhu in the world. This book proposes singing *bhajans* as a new analytic model for thinking about renunciation in South Asia.

In narrating her story, Ganga Giri further performs specific definitional parameters for identifying (and contesting) what she believes to constitute the lives and practices of sadhus, and, therefore, for distinguishing between genuine and fraudulent sadhus on the basis of those conceptual boundaries. By performing her songs, stories, and sacred texts, Ganga Giri, in turn, constructs herself as an authentic sadhu to her interlocutors (such as householders like Tara), other sadhus, and an American anthropologist like myself. Associating singing *bhajans* with legitimacy is not exclusive to Ganga Giri, but rather is shared among most of the sadhus I collaborated with in Rajasthan. They, too, insist that "real" sadhus "sing to God." The title of this book describes their individual interpretations, and not my own. I make no claims concerning who "real" sadhus are, or what "real" *sannyās* is all about. Instead, I document the views of the sadhus who themselves made such hard claims, and explain their rationales and implications.

The emphasis that the Rajasthani sadhus place on differentiating between real and fake sadhus in our meetings signals a foremost theme in my fieldwork experiences with these sadhus. During three years of field research (which I conducted over a period spanning ten years in the summers of 2001 and 2003, between 2004 and 2006, and in the summer of 2011) in the former princely state of Mewar, south Rajasthan, the sadhus consistently asked me if the other sadhus whom I had talked to, both men and women, (they were aware, as I had told them, that my field study consisted of many sadhus), sang *bhajans*. A conversation I had with Ganga Giri in July of 2003 at her hermitage demonstrates this point. On that day, she asked me where I had gone and whom I had visited. We had not seen each other for almost a week. After I had informed her about my visit to the ashram of another female sadhu in the area, Ganga Giri matter-of-factly asked me, "Did she sing a *bhajan* for you?" I admit that, at the time, I found her question a little odd. I replied, "No, *māī rām* [a title for female sadhus; literally, "holy mother"], she did not." In response Ganga Giri said, "If she didn't sing a *bhajan*, she's not a real sadhu. Real sadhus sing to God."

The Female Sadhus of Rajasthan: Traditions, Aesthetic Styles, and Practices

The extraordinary and witty women whose practices of singing to God constitute the focus of this book are celibate renouncers (*sannyāsinīs* and/or *yoginīs*). As a class of religious women, they are atypical in India (constituting less than 10% of the Hindu renouncer population),[11] and their unusual way of life affords them a freedom of movement and capacity to interact with others that is uncommon for most Indian women. *Sannyāsinī* translates as "female renouncer"; it signifies the gendered feminine linguistic equivalent of *sannyāsī* (lit., "male renouncer") (Khandelwal 2001; 2004). *Yoginī* is the feminine equivalent of *yogī* (practitioner of yoga and/or an ascetic). Of the different terms used to describe Indian renouncers (or ascetics) I have chosen the word *sādhu*, which is a generic and a grammatically gendered masculine term for holy persons (the feminine form is *sādhvī*), and which the sadhus used in addition to that of *māī* and/or *mātā* ("mother"), but in lieu of *sādhvī* and/or *sannyāsinī*/*yoginī*, to describe themselves. In this book, when I employ "sadhu," I describe renouncers who have undergone initiation into *sannyās*. Meena Khandelwal (2004) notes the ambiguity inherent in the term *sādhvī*, which denotes either "a virtuous wife" or "a female ascetic" (7), discouraged the female sadhus whom she worked with in North India from using it in their self-representations. The sadhus Khandelwal talks about preferred to call themselves (and be called) sadhus, and not *sādhvīs*. The Rajasthani female sadhus similarly seemed aware of the terminological fuzziness implied in *sādhvī*. But their reasons for not using it, as they said, stemmed from their shared perceptions that a *sādhvī* describes a married woman who becomes possessed by the Goddess and then heals people afflicted with physical or mental ailments through her power.

The sadhus have taken formal (i.e., legal) initiation as renouncers into either the Dashanami (lit., "ten names") or the Nath traditions of renunciation, which represent two Shaiva forms of *sannyās*, meaning that sadhus in these pan-Indian traditions often, but not always, perceive the god Shiva as their patron deity and as the mythic exemplar for their way of life.[12] *Sannyāsinīs* are initiates of the Dashanami tradition, and *yoginīs* of the Nath tradition. Shaiva sadhus distinguish themselves in their styles of dress from other (i.e., Vaishnava) sadhus by wearing the distinctive colors of *bhagwā* (lit., "God's color"): namely ochre, orange, saffron, or salmon (Vaishnavas tend to wear white clothing). As illustrated in Figure 0.1, clothing for females tends to consist of a blouse and long piece of fabric wrapped around the waist that typically

FIGURE 0.1 Female sadhus in Rajasthan.
Photo taken by A. DeNapoli.

falls below the ankles. Those with whom I worked frequently wore oversized blouses and shapeless skirts that cloak overt signs of female form from (male) view. Unlike most (rural) Indian women, the sadhus do not practice the cultural custom of veiling, but their conservative comportment indicates that they, too, are concerned with female modesty (*lajjā*). Other distinguishing symbols are the three horizontal white (or ash-colored) lines drawn on the forehead with a red dot in the middle, and the dark brown beads made from the seed of a *rudrākṣ* tree, which sadhus use for their daily religious practices (prayer, meditation, singing), and which they wear as a bracelet or necklace.

Most of the sadhus in this study are postmenopausal and have been sadhus for a quarter of a century or more. Their average age is sixty-eight years; their ages ranged from thirty to ninety-five years. They come from different caste backgrounds, though the majority comes from the upper castes. They are primarily nonliterate, live mostly independently in ashrams or temples in rural, multi-caste villages, and are mainly Rajasthani by birth. Apart from using the nonsectarian word "sadhu" for themselves and other sadhus, whether Shaiva or Vaishnava, another term on which they draw is *sant* ("good person"). They use these terms interchangeably and equate *sant* with sadhu. Both terms carry the same connotations to these sadhus: a (renunciant) lover of God. By the same token, the sadhus neither strictly follow mainstream Shaiva approaches to *sannyās*, which stress the path of knowledge and the combined practices of meditation, yoga, and scriptural study (Khandelwal 2004; Gross 2001; Dazey 1993), nor do they uphold the dominant Shaiva goal of *mokṣ*, defined as union with a formless and nameless Absolute.[13] Instead, their practice of *sannyās* is generally eclectic:[14] it parallels the nonsectarian attitude featured in their self-representations and, more importantly, draws on an integrated system of thought and practice characteristic of the lives of the *bhakti* (devotional) poet-saints, and Mira Bai's life in particular (see below). Use of Mira Bai's model provides a powerful means for the sadhus to validate their renunciation.

The Dominant Model of Sannyās *and the Marginalization of Female Sadhus*

The scholarship on the varieties of female renunciation in contemporary South Asia has shown that female sadhus across religious and sectarian traditions variously struggle to legitimate their unusual religious worlds to others (Knight 2011; DeNapoli 2009b; Khandelwal, Hausner, and Gold 2006; Khandelwal 2004; Gutschow 2004; Vallely 2002; Bartholomeusz 1996; Ojha

1985).[15] Lisa I. Knight's (2011) book on Bauls discusses that female Bauls interrogate through their practices (e.g., their song performances) the dominant (and static) idea that "real Bauls live under trees" and enjoy unencumbered and carefree lives. The women with whom Knight worked suggested that "true" Bauls not only navigate multiple (and conflicting) societal expectations, but also, through those daily negotiations, adapt what being a Baul means in empowering ways. The sadhus' statements about who real sadhus are and what real *sannyās* is illustrate a specific manifestation of what the literature suggests constitutes a more global concern for legitimacy among sadhus—one which cuts across gendered and sectarian lines.

It is fair to say that sadhus, women *and* men, are concerned with constituting and maintaining perceptions of their authenticity to others (Knight 2011; Lamb 2002; Gross 2001; Khandelwal 1997; Narayan 1989).[16] But why do sadhus think about this particular issue? Why does this pattern exist for those who have presumably "thrown down" [17] worldly concerns? Several factors account for this shared renunciant anxiety. The first issue involves the permanent or inescapable nature of *sannyās* itself. As the sadhus whom this book describes say, and as the sadhus portrayed in other scholars' works attest, *sannyās* is a difficult path that demands emotional, spiritual, and physical fortitude from its practitioners (Khandelwal 2004, 14).[18] In Ganga Giri's words: "*Sannyās* is difficult. Not everyone can become a sadhu." The difficulty that sadhus attribute to *sannyās* is related to the intense religious commitment it requires. Khandelwal concurs in her observation that *sannyās* "ideally is a single-minded pursuit of spiritual liberation that demands a total . . . break from the ordinary household interests and activities of the Hindu laity" (24). Thus, the decision to renounce is permanent. It is "both a radical and irreversible move" (ibid.). When a person becomes a sadhu, she or he is expected to sever all ties to the social world; to abandon her or his former social identity as a householder; and to separate from the sticky web of connections that emplaced her or him as a householder in that world. Khandelwal explains that

> Household life is aimed at the moral and material prosperity of one's family, so householders are expected to be concerned with getting married, having children, earning money, offering hospitality to guests, performing ritual sacrifice, worshipping gods and ancestors, and generally following the rules of moral conduct (dharma) as defined according to social class, stage of life, and gender. . . . The goal of following one's dharma is to ensure prosperity in this life and the next. Renouncers, by contrast, are concerned not with a good rebirth but with liberation from the cycle of birth, death, and rebirth (Khandelwal 2004, 24).

Equally as important, though, *sannyās* is difficult because it demonstrates in theory and in practice a way of life positioned outside of the mainstream. Sadhus inhabit the margins of Indian society. Their lives exemplify the (intentional) breaking away from everything that society typically holds dear. A common renunciant trope is that sadhus live on the periphery of the world they have renounced (Dumont 1960; Heesterman 1985). This idea is well expressed by the ideal (and dominant) model featured in authoritative (Brahmanical) texts on *sannyās*, such as the *Upaniṣads*, the *Saṃnyāsa Upaniṣads Yatidharmasamuccaya*, and the *Yatidharmaprakāśa*. Here, *sannyās* represents a radical, negative, and anti-nomian way of life that expects sadhus to abandon everything (name, family, wealth, home, community, status) for the divine (Olivelle 2011; 1996; 1992; 1986; 1981; 1978; 1975). The classic values illustrative of *sannyās* in these Brahmanical texts, which buoy its dominant ideology of world denial, are detachment, itinerancy, individualism, and solitude. The construct of the ideal or real sadhu, then, constitutes a function of one's detachment from the world, an attitude from which the other corollary virtues are thought to stem. To that extent, *sannyās* images an extreme alternative to the cultural norms of householding, marriage, and family. In these texts, "giving up" everything implies renouncing not only things, places, and people, but also ideas, with respect to the normative sociocultural constructions that entrap people in what is understood to be an illusory and impermanent world.

For example, sadhus renounce the dominant societal notion that their social-cosmic duty (*dharm*) to their gods, ancestors, and gurus (known as the "three debts") consists in performing the requisite Vedic sacrificial rituals, marrying,[19] and continuing the patriline by having (male) children, who will perform their parents' last rites in order to promote their safe passage into the heavenly afterworld (Olivelle 1992; 1996). Such actions and the worldview they support, these texts argue, stem from an ignorance that obfuscates the true nature of the universe and keeps people stuck in *sansār*. The *Muṇḍaka Upaniṣad* offers its own strong words on this issue:

> These are indeed unsteady rafts, the eighteen sacrificial forms, which teach an inferior ritual (*karma*). The fools who hail it as superior (*śreyas*) sink repeatedly into old age and death.
>
> Living in the midst of ignorance, self-wise, and thinking themselves to be learned, the fools go about hurting themselves, like blind men led by one who is himself blind.
>
> Living endlessly in ignorance, the fools think "We have reached our goal!" Because of their passion, those who perform rites (*karmin*) do

> not understand. When their worlds are exhausted, therefore, they fall down wretched.
>
> Regarding sacrifices and good works at best, the fools know nothing better (*śreyas*). After enjoying the highest heaven of good acts (*sukṛta*), they enter again this or even a lower world (*Muṇḍaka Upaniṣad*, 1.2.7–10; Olivelle translation, 1992, 41).

Sannyās' radical worldview contains within it the seeds for its predominantly countercultural attitude (Olivelle 1995). Within this alternative ideological system, sadhus, dead to the world, live on its margins, wandering here and there, without a care in (or for) the world. In this sense, female sadhus, as with sadhus in general, stand outside of the social mainstream. But the "mainstream" signifies more than the normatives of householding and family, against which *sannyās* exemplifies radical alterity. It also concerns a particular kind of vision or discourse about asceticism as practiced. After all, there are Hindu canonical texts, such as *The Laws of Manu*, that enshrine *sannyās* as a life option, even as an expectation in the ideal sense; but in these contexts, too, it is restricted to high-caste men and reserved for the last life stage—after a man's debts have been paid—in the classical system.[20] In those instances where the texts craft *sannyās* as mainstream, *sannyās* describes an exclusive institution, and the mainstream speaks to an elite prerogative to which a minority population has access. The notion of the "mainstream," then, that this book spotlights has to do with what (most) classical texts say and what many people say (suspiciously) about asceticism as practiced, and not just as it is practiced by women. It characterizes an "external" view of *sannyās*. In either sense, female sadhus are positioned outside of the mainstream, because they are often seen as inhabiting the periphery of a mostly householding society—and, more significantly, because the mainstream imagination in its dual and interrelated forms constructs them as marginal to what is commonly conceived (and perceived) as the exclusively masculine and orthodox phenomenon that constitutes *sannyās*-as-lived. In their ideal depictions of sadhus, both texts and the popular imagination generate a dominant model of *sannyās* that makes it a tough act to follow, for men and especially for women. This model promotes a standard of legitimacy against which sadhus, sometimes even the sadhus discussed in this book, measure themselves and are measured by others. One of this book's objectives is to offer an "internal" view of asceticism as practiced, one that is shared and molded by the female sadhus I collaborated with, and that not only challenges but also reconfigures mainstream perspectives.

A third issue tied to sadhus' concerns with legitimacy is the lack of any centralized institutional authority in *sannyās* (Khandelwal 2004). Khandelwal explains that, "sannyasa operates on a free market model without any authoritative hierarchy. The current Dashanami monastic heads are not like Popes charged with the responsibility for determining the saintly authenticity of particular holy persons. There are little in the way of institutional constraints on who can call herself a sadhu or wear the ochre robes of sannyas" (45). While the decentralization of authority in this institution has promoted the heterogeneity of *sannyās* as a lived cultural phenomenon, which Khandelwal describes as, "the sociological indeterminacy of renunciation" (5), the fact that it is "loosely institutionalized" (8) nonetheless opens the door for less than noble characters to don the respected *bhagwā* robes and pose as sadhus simply to take advantage of others. *Sannyās* has an unflattering reputation for attracting the "criminal element" to its ranks, and stories of frauds, mostly men, abound in the oral and literary cultures of South Asia (Khandelwal 2004; Narayan 1989; R.K. Narayan 1958; Bloomfield 1924).

In my fieldwork experience, I observed a fascinating discursive tension in the dichotomous ways that the sadhus and the householders talked about this class of religious practitioners (cf. Brown 2001 for a similar discussion about mixed perceptions about the legitimacy of Thai Buddhist renouncers). On the one hand, in the context of a conversation about a specific sadhu (or sadhus), people often spoke glowingly about that sadhu, citing her or his practices or views as incontrovertible evidence of her or his spiritual loftiness. On the other hand, in the context of a conversation about a generalized sadhu population, people categorically called them frauds (*pākhaṇḍī*), "useless" (*bekār*), and predatory animals (*jānwar*). The particular example always seemed to serve as an exception to the general rule. "This is the *kali yug* [age of darkness]. You can't trust sadhus anymore," the Rajasthani sadhus (and householders) cautioned me. My Brahmin family refused to allow me to travel alone to interview male sadhus whom they did not personally know.[21] While popular perceptions of a "loose" sexual morality were woven in people's ideas of fraudulent sadhus, these discourses also had gendered implications. Generalized female sadhus were seen as promiscuous (i.e., they had multiple male partners with whom they were sexually involved), but generalized male sadhus were viewed as sexually aggressive (one sadhu said, "They only rape women"). The sadhus told me that the difficulty of their path was in large part due to the ominous presence of lecherous sadhus, who prey on the sexual vulnerability of women living alone and on their own.

Finally, what makes emphases on legitimacy a gendered issue for female sadhus has to do with the orthodox understanding that *sannyās*, as conceived in a number of Brahmanical texts (e.g., *Saṃnyāsa Upaniṣads; Mānava Dharmaśāstras*), represents a valid life for men, but not for women. Hence, in the dominant model of *sannyās*, women are marginalized. Knight (2011) similarly observes that the dominant discourse on Bauls as itinerant and carefree singers who wander the countryside reproduces a gendered masculine experience and role that consequently marginalizes Baul female practitioners. In the case of *sannyās*, because it was conceived with men in mind, the dominant model validates their role, while patently denying women one altogether (DeNapoli 2009b). *Sannyās*, as it is represented in these texts, is an elite, predominantly male, and high-caste orthodox institution in the Hindu traditions that frequently has refused to recognize women as legitimate practitioners (many women thus do not have institutional support for their renunciation), and has barred them from seeking initiation into its orders (Khandelwal, Hausner, and Gold 2006; Khandelwal 2004, 8; Teskey Denton 2004; Ojha 1981; 2011).[22] Thus, by denying them a role, Brahmanical *sannyās* denies women legitimacy. The orthodox Dashanami tradition exemplifies—in its institutional power structures, public and administrative roles, and hierarchy—the high-caste (and male) elitism inherent in this model of *sannyās*; indeed, only four of its ten branches initiate women into *sannyās* (see also Chapter 4).[23]

The predominant themes of detachment, separation from home, family, and community, perpetual wandering, and solitude highlighted in the dominant model illustrate gendered masculine experiences and interpretations of *sannyās*, as well as patriarchal concerns. The intentional exclusion of women in this model is evident in that it constructs *sannyās* in opposition to domesticity, householding, and life in the world in general, all of which are associated with misogynist ideas of the feminine (Khandelwal 2004; Wilson 1996). In orthodox (Hindu) constructions of gender, womanhood and domesticity are linked, fashioned as two sides of the same fundamental coin of femininity. In this framework, domesticity describes the gendered (and private)[24] feminine realm of women's everyday lives and worlds; womanhood characterizes the relational roles of motherhood, wifehood, and more globally, caregiver (Wilson 1996; Khandelwal and Hausner 2006). Female sexuality is seen in the Brahmanical (non-renunciant) texts as auspicious and beneficent (Gold and Raheja 1994), as it ensures the continuity of existence in the world (married Hindu women are considered as manifestations of the goddess Lakshmi).[25] By contrast, in many renunciant texts, female sexuality—an ever present (and dangerous) temptation in the minds of the texts' male authors—symbolizes a death sentence for sadhus. *Sansār*, which the Brahmanical texts equate with "the world," and, hence, with the cycle of birth, death, and rebirth, typically serves as a pejorative trope for the feminine, as it is through the womb that beings enter into *sansār*; that is, into the web of death (Wilson 1996). Similarly, home, family, and sexual activity connote the threatening idea of the feminine, the negative notion of worldly life. Therefore, in escaping the world, sadhus also escape the feminine and everything it signifies, as it is tantamount to entrapment, and to death and suffering (Wilson 1996).

Given that, according to Brahmanical representations of gender, women's gendered identities constitute a function of their relationships with men (fathers, husbands, brothers, sons), and, in the view of the *Laws of Manu*,[26] their dependence on men (to be a woman is to be dependent on men *in this text*), and their lives a function of their domestic roles, the idea of female renunciation is anathema to the dominant model of *sannyās* (Olivelle 1993; Khandelwal 2004). It leaves no room for the possibility of female sadhus (one text calls them "repugnant").[27] As Khandelwal observes, female renunciants constitute "categorical anomalies" (5) in Brahmanical *sannyās*. Men have the right to renounce because their lives (and roles) are not tied to the home in the ways women's are believed to be (Leslie 1991a; 1991b). As there are fewer social restraints on their freedom of movement in the society, more life options are available to men than to women. The freedom of movement that the orthodox institution of *sannyās* ideally provides sadhus signifies an extension of the freedom that *men* as a class of people already experience in Indian culture. Women, particularly high-caste women, are much more restricted in their everyday movements beyond the home than are men. They are expected to be in the home, fulfilling their domestic (dharmic) responsibilities by caring for their families (i.e., their husband's children and parents). Not doing so brings disrepute on them and their kin.

Thus, when women become sadhus, they are seen as transgressing normative gender roles (Khandelwal 2004). Khandelwal and Hausner (2006) explain: "In South Asia... the social expectation that women will marry and procreate is overwhelming, and choosing to live as a nun, *yogini*, or *sadhvi*—a female renouncer—is considered foolish, unwise, or downright defiant" (1). In opting out of the norm, female sadhus have chosen an uncommon life that, in its ideal construction, challenges the dominant (and popular) androcentric representations of femininity. Female sadhus are attempting to escape many of the constrictions that once defined them as persons (which is not to say that they are seeking to escape their femininity, as I discuss in Chapter 2, but rather that they resist the cultural restraints that keep them from realizing their full potential as women). Khandelwal and Hausner concur that, "being a woman means that cultural expectations are all the more confining, and the steps required to break away all the more challenging" (3).

Singing Mira's Bhajans *and Empowering Female Sadhus in* Sannyās-*as-Lived*

Although their prestigious position often draws admiration from the Hindus whom they meet and interact with, female sadhus are still seen as suspicious for sidestepping orthodox expectations of becoming dutiful wives and loving mothers (see Chapters 2, 3, and 6). The sadhus' rhetoric of renunciation is replete with songs and stories on this subject. Shiv Puri, a sadhu I worked with, performed a number of *bhajans* (and narratives) in a *satsang* that occurred at her ashram on July 18, 2005. The majority of those songs made explicit, in their texts and contexts, the dominant societal expectations of being "good" wives and mothers that inform and structure women's everyday lives and, thus, impinge on their options, especially as concerns taking *sannyās* (cf. Knight 2011 for a similar discussion of conflicting expectations of Bauls).

On that day, Shiv Puri's *satsang* consisted of a group of (married) village Rajput women (several of them said they were Shiv Puri's biological relatives), who represented themselves as her devotees. The context of that *satsang* suggested that Shiv Puri performed these songs as a communicative means of describing her idea of the nature of women's daily struggles on the renunciant path. These songs discussed the religious lives of extraordinary women like Rupa Rani, Karma Bai, and Mira Bai. The song I document here is attributed to the legendary Rajasthani *bhakti*-poet saint (*sant*) Mira Bai (circa sixteenth century). Singing this *bhajan*, Shiv Puri articulates the difficulties she faces as a female sadhu. In the discussion that follows, I analyze Shiv Puri's *bhajan* and its performance context, as they illustrate the central ideas, themes, and claims underlying this study of female renunciation. The points made in Shiv Puri's song show us that how *sannyās* seems from the inside—that is, from women's perspectives, Shiv Puri's and Mira's perspectives—does not follow the dominant, external model. What follows is the *bhajan* I recorded.

To give some context to the terms used in the *bhajan*, Mira Bai was born into a high-caste (and royal) community of warriors (Rajput), and the name of that community is Rathore. There are thirty-six clans of Rajputs and the Rathores ruled the Marwar (Jodhpur and Pali districts) region of Rajasthan (Harlan 1992). In this *bhajan*, Mira is referred to as "Princess of the Rathores." This title distinguishes her Rajput clan identity from other Rajput clans, such as Sisodiya—the community in which Mira's husband was born—Jhala, Chauhan, Chundavat, etc. Mira Bai was born in the town of Merta, and the *bhajan* also addresses her as "Mira of Merta." Chittorgarh decribes the name of the erstwhile capital of the Mewar (Udaipur district) region of Rajasthan, where the Sisodiyas, the clan into which Mira was married, established its sovereignty.

Oh Mira! You've set yourself towards Sri Krishna,
And have become lost in him.
Leave him, Oh Mira of Merta!
Oh Mira, Queen of Merta!
Mira, Princess of the Rathores,
Remain in Chittorgarh.
How does Krishna belong to you?
Mira, remain in Chittorgarh.
How does Krishna belong to you?

Mira, take the advice of Chittorgarh's king to heart.
You are the princess of the Rathores,
And I am the prince of the Sisodiyas.
Make him your husband,
And take him into your heart.

Mira says: My heart has settled on Giradhari [Krishna].
He is my truth.

Oh Mira of the Rathores,
You are living amongst those sadhus.
Leave behind being with them, Oh Mira, Queen of Merta,

Oh Mira, Princess of the Rathores.
Leave behind being with all those sadhus,
And live with the king.
Your Giradhari isn't yours.

Mira, live with the king,
Giradhari isn't yours.

Mira says: I like being with the sadhus.
This gathering (satsang) with the sadhus
Pleases my heart.
My Giradhari is the truth.
He's real, Oh King of Chittor,
Oh Prince of the Sisodiyas.

Oh Mira of Merta,
Take off the bhagmā [saffron] clothes.
Mira, take off those bhagmā clothes you're wearing.
Oh Queen of Merta,
Oh Princess of the Rathores.

Mira, put on your colorful and sparkly clothes.
For whom are you wearing these bhagmā clothes?
Giradhari isn't yours.
Mira, put on your colorful and sparkly clothes.
For whom are you wearing these bhagmā clothes?
Giradhari isn't yours.

Mira says: Wearing the bhagmā clothes pleases my heart.
Oh King of Chittor,
Oh Prince of the Sisodiyas.
Oh King, Giradhari dwells in my heart.
He is my truth.

Mira, the Tulasi mālā [rosary] you are wearing around your neck,
Take it off!
It doesn't make you beautiful.
Oh Queen of Merta,
Oh Princess of the Rathores.
Mira, take off the Tulasi mālā,
And wear, instead, a necklace of precious stones.
Giradhari isn't yours.

Mira says: I don't like wearing necklaces of precious stones.
Wearing the Tulasi mālā pleases my heart.
Oh King of Chittor,
Oh Prince of the Sisodiyas.
My Giradhari is real.

Mira, you are a princess.
Leave behind this sleeping on the ground.
Oh Queen of Meta,
Oh Princess of the Rathores.

Mira, sleep on this bed.
How is Giradhari yours?

Sleep on this bed.
How is Giradhari yours?
Mira says: Sleeping on the ground pleases my heart.
Oh King of Chittor,
Oh Prince of the Sisodiyas.
My Giradhari is real.

Shiv Puri's song weaves a telling tale about the common conflict between following one's own personal desires, and upholding the societal pressures that women like Mira Bai (i.e., female sadhus) struggle with;[28] how they are pulled in opposite directions in terms of doing what their "hearts" tell them to do, and what society expects them to do (see Chapter 6). Shiv Puri's use of Mira's life, as imagined in this *bhajan*, to speak about her own personal experiences as a renouncer is significant, as Mira has been a controversial figure in Rajasthan (cf. Pauwels 2011; Hawley 2005; Mukta 1997; Martin 2007; 2000b; 1997; Harlan 1992, 215 and 218). She shunned both society's and her family's expectations for her as a princess born into one of India's most privileged classes (Rajput), and followed her heart in loving Krishna as her all-in-all. Drawing on Mira's extreme example indicates how unusual and outside the mainstream imagination female sadhus like Shiv Puri are. For a high-caste Rajput woman like Shiv Puri to sing this song shows the negotiations she makes as a sadhu. Although Mira does not call herself a renouncer in this *bhajan*, her wearing of the *bhagmā* clothes (such as the ochre-colored clothing worn by renouncers) indicates her taking of *sannyās*. In this way, Shiv Puri's performance suggests that she views Mira Bai as a sadhu-renouncer like herself. Singing this *bhajan* makes it possible for Shiv Puri to ally herself with Mira Bai. Shiv Puri appropriates what she imagines to be Mira's struggles and innovations on the sadhu path as her very own. The commentary Shiv Puri provides afterwards, which I consider as part of that performance, clarifies Mira's renunciant role. She says, "She who was Mira Bai became a *sant*, she became a sadhu [she renounced the world]. Her husband told her to take off her *bhagmā* clothes and wear worldly clothes. He told her to take off her Tulasi *mālā* and wear nice shiny jewelry. He was telling her what to do. He was explaining the situation to her. But Mira was saying, 'My Lord Krishna is great.' This is what the story is about."

The "story" in this song illustrates the dominant cultural idea that women, especially a high-caste Rajput[29] princess such as Mira Bai, should remain in the protection of their homes, safeguarded by their male (and elder female) kin, and not wander—as renouncers are expected to do—here, there, everywhere singing *bhajans* with "all those sadhus." This is the "situation" that, as Shiv Puri signals, the future king tries to explain to the resistant Mira Bai. Wandering with sadhus, as the song suggests, casts a shadow of doubt on women's reputations as "good" and "obedient," which, in effect, tarnishes others' perceptions of their character as sexually chaste to their husbands (cf. Knight 2011). Note that the *bhajan* implies the common understanding that unfamiliar (male) sadhus cannot be trusted. This orthodox and primarily high-caste expectation is effectively voiced through the mouth of Mira's husband, the heir of the Sisodiya dynasty, Bhoj Raj (see Chapter 3). But his words fall flat on her ears. She instead poses several challenges to him and, by extension, to the dominant (and Brahmanical) patriarchal construction of gender norms. In this way, the *bhajan* brings into focus not only the dominant sociocultural perspective on gender roles, but also, through Mira's position, an illustrative counterpoint, and, to that extent, an alternative to that dominant view. By invoking Krishna as her "truth" (she says: "my Giradhari is real"), Mira questions the idea that she belongs to the prince and is *his* wife. The song indicates that Mira sees herself as Krishna's partner (the prince's statement that Giradhar does not belong to Mira indicates that she sees herself as married to Krishna), rather than as any mortal man's wife. Mira, therefore, creatively sidesteps the gendered societal expectation of having to fulfill the role of wife (and potentially mother) by singing *bhajans* to God (i.e., becoming a sadhu) and, through that practice, joining herself eternally in spiritual matrimony to her Lord Krishna. Similarly, moving between the two very different worlds of the palace and the sadhus depicts the everyday negotiations that Mira makes, until a threat on her life forces her to leave the palace for good.

Moreover, by refusing to live in the manner that the Sisodiya prince expects (as a privileged Rajput princess and as an obedient and high-caste Hindu wife), Mira challenges the dominant assumption that women's lives and identities are defined only (or specifically) in terms of their domestic roles. Her life of singing *bhajans* scripts an alternative role, albeit an unusual one, for women to the more dominant (and expected) roles of wife and mother (cf. Pauwels 2011; Harlan 1992; Martin 2007; Hawley 2005; Khandelwal 2004). The example provided by Mira's feminine gender in her actualizing of an alternative life of singing *bhajans* to *bhagwān* carves out a legitimate space for women to renounce the world and dedicate themselves to the divine. Her model makes possible for women what the dominant model represents as impossible for them.

The renunciant worldview implied in Shiv Puri's *bhajan* is expressed through the related symbols of Mira's wearing of the *bhagmā* clothing and her use of the Tulasi *mālā*[30] (for prayer), her participation in sadhu-*satsangs*, and her life of relative simplicity (sleeping on the floor instead of on a comfortable bed). In these ways, Mira's renunciation symbolically signals the dominant ideology of *sannyās* in terms of abandoning common creature comforts that prevent people from realizing God (note that she does not abandon home, community, or society). Mira's renunciation promotes the radical worldview of *sannyās* in the sense that the (conventional) institutions of marriage, family, and householding are seen as trapping people in *sansār*. Her resistance to the prince's expectations manifests her staunch refusal to be reborn in *sansār*. By renouncing the world, Mira intends to unite with her Giradhar in his heaven, and never return in that cycle. In actualizing this alternative, she enacts the oppositional (and controversial) view that becoming a sadhu is more rewarding than becoming a wife and mother, because she receives "real" immortality and an enduring love that those social roles could never provide her.

But notice that the renunciation implicit in Mira's behavior is explicitly recast in this *bhajan* as a radical form of *bhakti*. That is, Mira Bai sees her actions, fueled by detachment, as expressing an unyielding love for Krishna, a *bhakti* attitude par excellence. Hence, even as the *bhajan* performs a classic renunciant worldview, it refashions what *sannyās* is at the levels of theory and practice through the lens of Mira's uncommon *bhakti*. In this light, *sannyās carefully crafted as the bhakti of the sants*—what I describe as "devotional asceticism"—provides the female sadhus portrayed in this book with a creative alternative to the expected scripts of marriage, motherhood, and domesticity.[31] Mira's asceticism, as practiced, also supplies them with a female alternative for imagining and embodying *sannyās* in a way that moves far beyond its mainstream representations. Because Mira's singing as *sannyās* substantiates a religiosity that the sadhus identify with, they use her example to claim what "real" *sannyās* is about, from the inside.

Reconstituting *sannyās* as *bhakti* through their singing, storytelling, and sacred text practices, the female sadhus soften the perceived stigma of their unusual roles and the popular perception of their transgression of gender norms (but cf. Khandelwal 2004, which characterizes female *sannyās* as a transgressive act). *Bhakti* is often seen as a feminine mode of acting in the world (Ramanujan 1999c; Prentiss 1999). By constructing *sannyās* as *bhakti*, the sadhus express through their practices that renunciation represents an extension of women's everyday devotional worlds.[32] Using the idiom of singing to characterize *sannyās* presents a powerful way for the sadhus to foreground their individual gendered concerns and practices, and removes popular perceptions of their *sannyās* as threatening to the patriarchal order (see Chapter 2). Singing Mira's *bhajans* helps sadhus like Shiv Puri to articulate this perspective. While the scholarship on *bhakti* and *sannyās* tends to exist in two separate categories, studied under the rubric of South Asian studies on gender and religion, scholars still know little about the ways that sadhus in contemporary contexts think about the relationship between these categories.

Shiv Puri's *bhajan* performance suggests that Mira views her renunciation as singing *bhajans*—as a form of *sannyās* experienced and established in a devotional and, more precisely, a *sant* kind of way.[33] I emphasize here that Shiv Puri's performance reconfigures Mira's *bhakti* as *sannyās* (and that it is not only *bhakti*), and by doing so interrogates the standard parameters for what renunciation means in *sannyās*-as-lived.

To that extent, Shiv Puri's performance suggests that Mira Bai further displaces, this time, the orthodox Brahmanical notion of renunciation as central to how "real" sadhus, men and especially women, practice *sannyās*, by illustrating through her devotional asceticism that *sannyās* has multiple complementary or competing lived expressions, that it is practiced "on the ground" in a plethora of ways, and more specifically, that Brahmanical *sannyās* constitutes one of a variety of types of *sannyās* in contemporary South Asia. By singing with the sadhus, the *bhajan* suggests that Mira participates in a kind of *sannyās* that does not involve escaping the world (home, family, community). But this inside view of Mira as a renouncer, and of the asceticism she makes available, appears to apply only to the female sadhus with whom I worked. While many people[34] I talked to viewed Mira as a "great" *bhakt*, and a "true" example of righteous living,[35] they did not link her religiosity to *sannyās* per se. Unlike the female sadhus, none of them ever characterized Mira Bai as a "*sannyāsī*." Nevertheless, devotional asceticism as the female sadhus live and experience it, in various contexts, represents a radically different *sannyās* than the standard Brahmanical version, as well as a gendered alternative to it.

From this vantage point, Shiv Puri's performance effectively legitimates her own renunciation (and her right to take it) by positioning her sadhu religiosity outside of the dominant model (and institution) of Brahmanical *sannyās* and, thus, within an alternative tradition of female renunciation as exemplified by Mira (see Chapter 3). As a Dashanami renunciant, Shiv Puri's use of Mira *bhajans* to authenticate herself as a sadhu is not surprising. There is no institutionalized tradition of *sannyās* in Mira's name in Rajasthan (or elsewhere in India) as there are traditions in Kabir's or Dadu Dayal's names (two male medieval *bhakti*-poet saints in North India). Nevertheless, many female sadhus like Shiv Puri and Ganga Giri exist, regardless of the sect or tradition they took initiation in, or even if they were formally initiated at all (see, for example, Martin's 1997 study of modern Mira Bais in North India, many of whom never took initiation into any sect). These sadhus create their individual lived traditions of *sannyās* on their own and outside of established institutional structures by, as I suggest, singing *bhajans* to God.

Thus, while the model of singing *bhajans* as *sannyās* offers a new interpretive lens for conceptualizing renunciation-as-lived, I also believe that the female sadhus' use of *bhajans* (and other forms of religious expressive culture) to construct their worlds, as Mira's model attests, is not anything new in religion-as-lived in this part of the globe. And, while the dominant model of *sannyās* marginalizes women by denying them legitimacy, the model that the sadhus construct in their practices not only grants women legitimacy, but also shifts their peculiar position from the periphery to the center of *sannyās*. Female sadhus are atypical, and like their male counterparts, their unconventional lives position them outside of the mainstream—but not outside of society. Hence, they, too, inhabit the social margins, and more so than do male sadhus. But their being atypical is no reason to see them as marginal to or in *sannyās* itself. The dominant academic discourse on *sannyās* tends to assume that, because female sadhus in the Hindu traditions, in particular, are marginalized in the Brahmanical (text-based) model, they are similarly marginal in and to the lived practice of *sannyās*.[36] By shifting our focus from the standard model to that which sadhus create and live in their practices, scholars push back against the tendency to represent female sadhus as marginal and view them instead as central, creative, and dynamic figures in the broader phenomenon of *sannyās*-as-lived in South Asia.

Organization of the Book

This book has nine chapters organized in terms of the interwoven genres of story, song, and sacred text. Chapter 1, a background chapter, lays the foundation for the discussions that follow. It locates female sadhus' practices within a performance studies-centered model of religious expressive culture and discusses the concept of "vernacular asceticism" as a lens for thinking about *sannyas*-as-lived in contemporary North India. The chapter also includes a discussion of the field methods I used to collect and analyze my data, the *satsang* contexts in which female sadhus gather with others and sing to God, and Rajasthan's cultural context.

Chapter 2 analyzes the personal stories of female sadhus as a constructive act for exercising female agency and validating female religious authority in vernacular asceticism. It explores the themes that female sadhus underscore in constructing their views of *sannyās*, which, in turn, make it possible for them to authenticate alternative life scripts in empowering ways. The chapter describes female sadhus' use of an ideology of exceptionalism through emphasis on the competing motifs of destiny and action as a way to craft singing as *sannyās*. The chapter suggests that female sadhus' personal narrative constructions may help scholars of religion to understand the ways that female sadhus in South Asia more globally tell their own stories as a means to experience, interpret, and represent their unconventional worlds to their interlocutors.

Chapter 3 considers the vernacular religious narratives of female sadhus and their telling of local and regional hagiographical tales, particularly those concerned with mythic female *bhakti* saints, to legitimate their role and the authority it engenders. This chapter shines light on the multiple value systems inherent in female sadhus' narratives, and how sharing those stories with their devotees in *satsang* makes it possible for them to reinterpret the dominant Brahmanical values of suffering, sacrifice, and struggle in light of mixed (and competing) *bhakti* frameworks, gendered ideologies of female suffering and power, and martial (warrior) perspectives. The chapter further discusses female sadhus' use of narratives associated with Mira Bai to construct a gendered lineage and genealogy of their female sadhu tradition in Rajasthan.

Chapters 4, 5, and 6 constitute a tripartite series of chapters that investigates female sadhus' practices as they articulate an ethos of caste ambivalence in vernacular asceticism. These chapters depict a confluence of performance genres in the forms of song, story, and sacred text in the sadhus' rhetoric of renunciation and have a specific social element in mind: they illustrate how, and in what contexts, caste status matters to female sadhus and the role of regional princely traditions in their representations of caste. Chapter 4 describes the ways in which female sadhus' practices perform exclusionary interpretations of *sannyās* that not only distinguish sadhus on the basis of their birth groups (*jātī*), but also assign values of power and privilege to some sadhus and not to others because of those groups. The ambivalence that female sadhus communicate by pressing on, in particular, the heroic values of bravery, sacrifice, and protection as high-caste characteristics reinforces and reproduces controversial ideologies of upper-caste superiority and caste essentialism in this vernacular expression of *sannyās*. While Chapter 4 focuses on the practices of high-caste sadhus, Chapter 5 spotlights the life and work of a local tribal sadhu, and Chapter 6 looks at the practices of a sadhu from a (formerly) disadvantaged caste group. Both Chapters 5 and 6 seek to understand if the individual sadhus described in them support or challenge the dominant Mewari ethos of caste ambivalence.

Chapter 7 addresses female sadhus' sacred text practices. This chapter discusses "textual" performances centered on recitation of the *Rāmcaritmānas*. A vernacular-language text composed by the medieval poet-saint Tulsidas, and embedded within the broader *Rāmāyan* epic narrative tradition, the *Rāmcaritmānas* presents an important genre of performance in the sadhus' rhetoric of renunciation. The chapter also examines the strategies by which female sadhus construct themselves as "scriptural"—that is, how they perform a relationship with the literate textual tradition of Tulsidas' *Rāmcaritmānas*. It looks at their ideas of the text and their adaptations of that idea in performance, and just as significant, argues that the performing of "texts" confers power, authority, and legitimation for female sadhus in asceticism as practiced. The chapter further suggests that, in the performing of texts, female sadhus draw out and rework concepts that underscore a perspective of asceticism as relational and emplaced in community.

Chapter 8 analyzes female sadhus' *bhajan* performances. Since female sadhus use the provocative metaphor of "singing *bhajans*" to represent asceticism as practiced, the chapter explores what *bhajan* singing means to them through the lens of their songs and stories. It contends that the singing of *bhajans* helps female sadhus to perform a view of asceticism that models the celebratory and interpersonal religiosity of India's medieval *bhakti* poet-saints (*sants*), and to expand the boundaries of *sannyās* beyond its classical Brahmanical formulations in the creation of a legitimate female space in vernacular asceticism. The chapter is divided into four parts. The first part examines female sadhus' views of the efficacy of *bhajan* singing as articulated in their conversational narratives and the themes of singing *bhajans* as transformative ascetic practice, as a symbolic medium of exchange, and as *sevā* that are foregrounded in those narratives. The second part explores the interpretive frameworks behind female sadhus' views of singing as *sannyās*. It investigates their representations of *bhajan* as a medium of transformation through analysis of the concept of *tapas* ("heat"), and suggests that their views of *bhajan* as *tapas* imply a contrast between *bhajan* and *bhakti*. The emphasis that female sadhus place on *bhajan* singing as *tapas* suggests that they see *bhajan* as different from *bhakti* and becomes a way to distinguish between householder and sadhu types of *bhakti*. Part three looks at the relationship between *brahmacārya* (celibacy) and *bhakti* in sadhus' practices, and contends that the creation of devotion through singing is as significant to female sadhus as is the production of heat in the Brahmanical model. Part four explores sadhus' singing of *bhajans* to construct *sannyās* as consistent with the established *sant bhakti* tradition. The *bhajans* to which female sadhus attribute efficacy are those drawn from the *nirguṇī* poetry of the *sants*. This section discusses female sadhus' *nirguṇī bhajans* as resources for crafting *sannyās* as the asceticism of the *sants*.

Finally, the Conclusion outlines the differences between the sometimes competing, sometimes complementary, models of Brahmanical *sannyās* and female sadhus' asceticism. To this end, the chapter reviews the book's chief arguments and summarizes the concepts integral to female sadhus' religious worlds. It also discusses the themes of creativity, ambiguity, and power evident in this example of vernacular religion in Rajasthan. The chapter further considers the implications of devotional asceticism as a new model of *sannyās* and, in female sadhus' practices, as a gendered expression, for the broader study of *sannyās* in South Asia.

I

Performing Asceticism and Redefining Definitional Boundaries

If there is love, we'll meet again. This whole world is a carnival of meeting and parting.[1]

—GANGA GIRI MAHARAJ

THE LITERATURE ON *sannyās* recognizes the significance of sadhus' use of religious expressive culture to transmit their religious traditions. But scholars know less about how sadhus construct particular interpretations of *sannyās* and, through those practices, gendered worlds. This book addresses this lacuna in the current scholarship. Thus, in this performative ethnographic study on female renunciation in Rajasthan, I concentrate on those practices through which the sadhus perform singing *bhajans* as *sannyās* because they offer a resource—and a performance strategy—for refashioning the dominant definitional parameters of renunciation beyond its traditional association with the orthodox Brahmanical model. In their performances, the sadhus neither reproduce Brahmanical *sannyās*, nor constitute a gendered version of it. I find it necessary to distinguish between the sadhus' *sannyās* and Brahmanical *sannyās* for three chief reasons. The scholarship often presents the dominant model as the singular, authoritative ideal against which lived expressions are compared; those expressions are thus seen as individual (i.e., "unofficial") permutations of the textual model (but cf. Lamb 2002). Similarly, because *bhakti* is mostly peripheral to that model, *sannyās* crafted on *bhakti* ideologies is also viewed as an exception[2] to the imagined norm (Ojha 1983; Miller and Wertz 1996). Furthermore, in much of the established literature on the subject, *sannyās* is equivalent to the orthodox institution of Brahmanical *sannyās* (but cf. Khandelwal 2004). However, to see Brahmanical renunciation as a type of *sannyās* in the larger renunciant landscape unsettles its privileged position in the scholarship.

Since this book is framed as a performative study, let me explain what I mean by "performance." In my use of the concept, I draw on the overlapping theoretical frameworks of performance studies-centered and folkloristic studies (Bauman 1977; 1992; Briggs 1988), and practice-oriented studies (Bourdieu 1991; de Certeau 1984), to describe "aesthetically heightened" practices through which participants create their worlds in ways that "reproduce a social order... critique and undermine it, or something in between" (Raheja 2003, 5). Using performance-centered models to analyze female sadhus' practices seemed the best hermeneutical avenue to pursue, as it exemplifies a way of speaking that the sadhus I worked with privilege in conceptualizing their lives. They often answered my questions by performing a song or a story.[3]

Performance is thus seen as an emergent phenomenon (Sawin 2004; Bell 1997; 1998; Schieffelin 1985) that is "inherently constructive and strategic, producing specific types of meanings and values through particular strategies" (Pintchman 2007, 4). The idea of "strategy" implies the interpretive shifts that occur by means of performance (e.g., the sadhus' singing *bhajans* to construct Mira as a renouncer, rather than a *bhakt*[4]). Every performance context has its own key structural components (e.g., setting or event; sender and receiver; medium and code; text and message) and cues (aspects of the performance context that the participants themselves foreground) that further shape and contextualize the performances and their meanings for the participants.[5] *Satsang* functions as a performance context for the sadhus' constructions of *sannyās*. Hence, every *satsang* signifies a context of devotion for the participants and frames the performances that arise in those contexts as *bhakti* for those participants. Because of the shifting contexts in which performance occurs and the shifts that emerge with each occurrence (Flueckiger 2006, 25), performance provides a rhetorical strategy and a locus for the individual expression of complex agency (see Chapters 2 and 6), with which participants can "manipulate and negotiate with tradition to create meaning of their own circumstances" (Flueckiger, 25). My use of performance to frame the sadhus' practices positions this book within a larger field of studies that approaches religious expressive culture as constructive activity (Jassal 2012; Knight 2011; Flueckiger 2006; Kelting 2001; Gold and Raheja 1994).

Exploring the sadhus' everyday lives through the lens of performance-based models helps us to see how they create and imagine *sannyās* in practice to "resonate with their own preoccupations and interests" (Pintchman 2005, 3). We are also able to understand with increasing specificity that *sannyās* and its gendered constellations constitute emergent cultural performances that are continuously (re)constructed and (re)enacted by means of performative practices (Bell 1998). It is important, therefore, for scholars of religion to distinguish between sadhus' discursive and expressive practices in renunciant representations of *sannyās*. In its many manifestations, performance offers the sadhus a powerful cultural resource for communicating what they might not (or cannot) say directly. In the words of historian James Scott, "Oral traditions, due simply to their means of transmission, offer a kind of seclusion, control, and even anonymity that makes them ideal vehicles for cultural resistance" (1990, 160, cited in Narayan 1995, 258; cf. Jassal 2012). Similarly, as folklorist Roger Abrahams pointed out, performance serves as "an implement for argument, a tool for persuasion" (1968, 146, cited in Narayan 1995, 258). Hence, it behooves scholars to pay particular attention to what renouncers *do* with their words, and not just what they say with them; that is, to inquire into the ways in which performance constitutes an important interpretive context in which renouncers creatively construct and establish their views of what *sannyās* means to them, and the role of *bhakti* in those constructions.[6] The sadhus' *performances* of their rhetoric often articulate a counterpoint view to their discursive statements about *sannyās*. Their singing, storytelling, and sacred text practices contextualize their discourses and function as prescient commentaries of their "official" statements, and thus tell us a great deal more about these sadhus' experiences of *sannyās* than their words alone usually communicate.

In performing their rhetoric of renunciation, the sadhus establish a broad spectrum of meanings and interpretations for what they believe *sannyās* and being a sadhu mean in renunciation-as-lived. A number of scholars have noted that the varieties of *sannyās* in South Asia cannot be pinned down to any single category of experience or practice that comprehensively describes what that is for all its practitioners (cf. Lamb 2011; Khandelwal 2004; Gross 2001; Miller and Wertz 1996). There are as many ways to live *sannyās* as there are sadhus living it. Oddly enough, however, what has been overlooked is that renunciant expressive culture makes it possible for the plethora of meanings imagined as *sannyās* (and sadhu) to flourish on the ground. The performativity of the sadhus' rhetorical practices demonstrates that the idea of *sannyās* is always emergent, situated in those contexts in which it is conceived and enacted in everyday life. It is well-known that "sadhu" has a wide and fluid semantic range in the lives of those who use it to represent themselves and their spiritual commitments. "Sadhu" is not synonymous with "renouncer." And yet, the fact that the sadhus I met who have renounced the world draw on this term, and *sant*, to construct themselves and their way of life says something significant about their individual understandings of *sannyās*-as-lived. In our meetings the sadhus often identified a person (usually a woman) in their local communities as a renouncer-sadhu like themselves ("she sings *bhajans* like us"),[7] whom I did not associate with *sannyās* because, at the time,

I had grounded my idea of this concept within the more narrow focus set forth by the dominant model (see also the methods discussion below). Let me make clear that the sadhus themselves characterize their practices of singing, storytelling, and textual recitation as *sannyās* or *tapasyā*. The breadth of view performed by sadhu/*sannyās* in their *satsang* practices, especially their use of Mira's model, helps to legitimate their unusual (and public) positions as female renouncers. In most performance contexts, to these sadhus, being a sadhu involves living out *sannyās* in the manner characteristic of the *sants* of North India, such as Mira Bai, Tulsidas, and Kabir. In the sadhus' views, "real" sadhus practice a contemporary version of *sant sannyās*, even though the *sants* themselves were sometimes critical of *sannyās*.

By constructing *sannyās* through their performances, the sadhus engage in an interpretive process of "bricolage": a term coined by anthropologist Claude Lévi-Strauss (1966), it describes the eclectic blending together of multiple cultural resources in the crafting of religious worlds (see McGuire 2008 for a discussion on bricolage; and Bowman and Valk 2012).[8] More specifically, in the construction of *sannyās*, the sadhus creatively and purposefully draw on the dominant Brahmanical model of renunciation, classical and orthodox *bhakti* paradigms, *sant* and heterodox *bhakti* paradigms, gendered ideologies of female suffering and power, Brahmanical (high-caste) ideologies of caste, as well as local (Mewari) princely traditions of the martial Rajput, mixing and modulating these resources. Let us return to Shiv Puri's Mira *bhajan* as documented in the Introduction once more. Recall that the symbols of the *bhagmā* clothes and the Tulasi *mālā* that Mira proudly wears in crafting herself as a sadhu represent Shaiva and Vaishnava practices of *sannyās*, respectively. Mira's innovative blending of different elements in her individual practice of renunciation exemplifies the creativity with which the sadhus engender and embody their tradition of devotional asceticism. Their creative syncretism and hybridity shows at the levels of belief and action, and in *satsang* contexts, what I characterize as the phenomenon of "vernacular asceticism," that is, renunciation as it is lived in dynamic and fluid ways, and in local, everyday contexts (i.e., through use of local idioms, metaphors, and categories of religious experience).

As with the idiom of "singing *bhajans*" as *sannyās*, my use of vernacular asceticism as an analytical tool brings to the study of renunciation a new way of thinking about the flexibility of *sannyās*-as-lived in South Asia. It is drawn from Leonard Primiano's (1995) idea of "vernacular religion,"[9] and Joyce Flueckiger's (2006) concept of "vernacular Islam,"[10] which she characterizes as a level of practice and experience performed in the everyday healing practices of Amma, a *pirānimā*[11] with whom Flueckiger worked in South

India.[12] Vernacular asceticism expands the boundaries of "what counts"[13] as *sannyās* in religious studies scholarship, to include a form of practice and experience—namely, singing *bhajans* as devotional asceticism—that has been underrepresented in studies on renunciation. In addition, it draws attention to the complexities and nuances of the sadhus' lived practices, and the fact that they may be used both to empower and disempower them. In discussing the ambiguousness of lived practice, Sherry Ortner (1990) noticed that "the most interesting thing about any given case is precisely the multiplicity of logics operating, of discourses being spoken, of practices of prestige and power in play. Some of these are dominant—'hegemonic.' Some are explicitly counterhegemonic—subversive, challenging. Others are simply... present because they are products of imagination that did not seem to threaten any particular set of arrangements" (45, cited in Gold 2000b, 207).[14]

"Meeting and Parting in the Carnival of Life": Performing Asceticism as Relational

Thus, the study of vernacular asceticism *as* the study of the ways that sadhus selectively create themselves in their practices—in this case, through the prism of the Rajasthani sadhus' singing, storytelling, and textual performances—makes visible all those dynamic aspects of their lives that have been made invisible by the more common definitional parameters of renunciation. This book stresses singing *bhajans* as an orienting metaphor for these sadhus' *sannyās* because it foregrounds an innovative way to envision *sannyās* -as-lived by a nonelite (i.e., non-educated and nonliterate) and predominantly minority group of practitioners. In the context of this study, vernacular asceticism establishes a relationship between two domains of practice, namely, singing and *sannyās*, to emphasize a devotional—and female—approach of experiencing renunciation. Tweed (2006) says that an orienting metaphor "is a lens and a vehicle. It directs language users' attention to this and not that, and it transports them from one domain of language, experience, and practice to another. In my terms, it prompts new sightings and crossings" (46). Orienting metaphors "illuminate some features of the terrain while obscuring others" (ibid.). The foremost purpose of this book is to facilitate "new sightings and crossings" of *sannyās* beyond its dominant values and ideals of meditation, detachment, fierce psychosomatic penance (*tapas*), itinerancy, and solitude. From this vantage point, the study of vernacular asceticism challenges a number of operative dichotomies, such as the static "utopian"[15] representation of *sannyās* as typically "other-worldly" and, thus, as transcending the limiting conceptual boundaries of space, place, and time (but cf. Hausner 2007; Khandelwal 2004) by locating the expression analyzed here in particular contexts.[16] *Sannyās*-as-lived means that it is always situated in thought and activity. As we will see, the sadhus' practices perform *sannyās* as sometimes other-worldly and most of the time as this-worldly (see Chapter 7).

Moreover, the study of vernacular asceticism contests the notion that lived *sannyās* represents a "folk" or "popular" (i.e., Little) expression articulated against an "official" (i.e., Great) institutionalized version of *sannyās* (but cf. Khandelwal 2004, 27–29). This book, following the astute insights of Bowman and Valk (2012), avoids the tendency in religious studies scholarship to distinguish (and thus make implicit value judgments) between popular and official religion. While there are "bodies and agencies of normative prescriptive religion," like the orthodox Dashanami monastic centers which are established at the four corners of the Indian subcontinent,[17] I agree with Primiano that "there is no *objective existence* of practices which expresses 'official religion.' No one, no special religious elite or member of an institutional hierarchy…lives an 'officially' religious life in a pure unadulterated form…There is always some passive accommodation…some active creation, some dissenting impulse, some reflection on lived experience that influences how these individuals direct their religious lives" (1995, 46, emphasis mine). In their vernacular practices, the female sadhus combine normative and non-normative, orthodox and unorthodox, and Brahmanical and *bhakti* elements, and bring this synthesis into its new context of *sannyās*. Integrating singing and *sannyās* through performance, the sadhus bridge two seemingly disparate traditions of thought into an eclectic tapestry.

Furthermore, vernacular asceticism questions the idea that *sannyās* requires radical separation from family, home, community, and society. Relationships constitute a salient theme in the sadhus' *sannyās* (see Chapters 6 and 7). Their interpretations of *sannyās* as singing *bhajans* imply creating and sustaining loving connections with others, both disciples and devotees, which their practices help to create. In her *satsangs*, Ganga Giri prefaces her performances with the statement, "Love is what God is. This is *sannyās*." Although most of them, as the dominant model prescribes, have left their homes and families (e.g., husbands, children, and in-laws) and live on their own or, in several cases, with another sadhu—usually a guru or guru-brother—some of the sadhus have not (see Chapters 5 and 6). More significant, the majority of sadhus certainly have not abandoned their ties to family and community in the typical sense that "leaving behind everything" suggests in the mainstream view. These sadhus have not erased their loved ones from their hearts and minds, but rather have redefined those relationships, particularly the relationships with their biological children, in the context of guru and disciple. Shiv Puri, for example, lives with her son, his wife, and their three children in an ashram that Shiv Puri had built almost twenty years ago with donations from her devotees (see Chapter 2). Shankar, her son, looks after the ashram, and Sonam, his wife, performs the daily *pūjā* (worship ritual) in the seven goddess temples established on the property[18] when Shiv Puri travels to the neighboring states of Gujarat and Maharashtra to visit devotees and raise funds for her ashram.

Refashioning relationships with kin in spiritual terms enables sadhus like Shiv Puri to gain access to material and financial resources (e.g., to secure trusted people to manage their ashrams in their absence) while engendering perceptions of female respectability. Having relatives nearby, especially male kin, offers the sadhus protection against physical and sexual danger, because as women mostly living alone and on their own, they are vulnerable in their society. As other scholars have also noted, women who live alone in South Asia are unusual, and that can foster doubts about their reputations (Khandelwal and Hausner 2006). The sadhus, too, worry about others' perceptions of their reputations as "good" women, and frequently structure their lives in a manner that allows them to safeguard their reputations.

Maya Nath, for example, not only has her grandson, also named Shankar, visit her ashram daily, which is located on a main thoroughfare between Rajasthan and Delhi, but also employs a young man from the village as a nighttime temple guard (*caukidār*). These accommodations are the result of a traumatic incident that occurred some years back, in which thieves came on the property in the middle of the night and stole several of her shrines' *mūrtīs* (sacred images).[19] Thus, the reconfiguring of their relationships with others enacts the sadhus' maneuverings of conflicting expectations and illustrates the creativity with which they broaden (and challenge) the dominant definitional parameters of *sannyās* in a gendered way. The data documented here supports the observations of other scholars that female renouncers value their relationships with others (both kin and non-kin) and the community those networks create, but that they also adapt those relationships to accommodate their spiritual concerns (cf. Khandelwal 2004).[20]

Before I engage in a discussion of field methods, I want to leave my readers with one last metaphor that illuminates, in the practices of these sadhus, the vernacular idea of *sannyās* as relational, while obscuring the values of separation and detachment. Taking my cue from the sadhus themselves, I characterize this metaphor in the specific terms of vernacular asceticism as a carnival (*melā*) of meeting and parting in the movement of life. I document this experience of *sannyās* by presenting and analyzing a *bhajan* that Ganga Giri, Tulsi Giri, and Jnan Nath performed together at Ganga Giri's ashram, with a group of multi-caste householders present, on February 18, 2005. By juxtaposing the domains of the carnival and *sannyās* together, their performance reworks what *sannyās* means and how "real" sadhus practice it. Here is that song:

Take the name of God [alakh] daily;
Take the name of the Master [sahib] daily.

Chant God's name and remember its qualities.
Let's go together to God's country,

To the Master's country,
To the country of someone well-known.

Take the name of God [alakh] daily;
Take the name of the Master [sahib] daily.

Hey brother, those who chant God's name
They neither die nor are they reborn
Nor do they get old.
Put on the ochre robes and renounce the world!

Hey brother, those who chant God's name
They neither die nor are they reborn
Nor do they get old.

The mind is like a wild horse;
Tie a saddle on it and control that unruly horse
With a great desire in your heart.

Put on the ochre robes and renounce the world!
And let's go together to God's country,
To the Master's country,
To the country of someone well-known.

The servant Kabir says
The servant Kabir says

"You have treated us very well."
Hey, the servant Kabir says
The servant Kabir [says]
"You have treated us very well."

In this *satsang*, as in most of the *satsangs* in which she participates, Ganga Giri runs the performance. The *bhajan* the sadhus sing is attributed to Kabir (ca. fifteenth century), who is known for his probing insights. Prior to their singing session, Ganga Giri shares an illustrative commentary that frames the meaning of this song's performance for the audience. She says,

> Everyone's country [*deś*] is the same. This world [*duniyā*] we live in is a carnival [*melā*], where everyone meets [*milnā*] and parts [*bicaḍnā*]. This world is a *melā* of meeting and parting. [Tulsi Giri interjects: That's right!] But everyone's country is the same. We all came here from that country only. We came here to make a carnival. But we have to return [to our country]. Therefore, remember God. Then you will reach there. We all come from the same home [*ṭhikānā*]. But we also have to return to the same *ṭhikānā*. Everybody is the same. If you think everyone is different, this is ignorance. All of us come from there. We hardly come from here. Remember, this place is a *melā*. Behave well. Be like a diamond. Here, we're in a *melā*. If you won't recognize God's country, then it will always be far away. You'll stay here and get pushed around. Keep the name!

This statement relates that the sadhus imagine and experience *sannyās* as a relational path of "meeting" and "parting" with householders and other sadhus in the "carnival of life." Singing the *bhajan* grounds their view in an embodied practice and performs *sannyās* as an ongoing network of relationships of love and (spiritual) companionship. Their singing indexes the performance frame of "*sannyās* as love" through which Ganga Giri structures her practices. The image of worldly life that she constructs through her emphasis on the carnival motif is positive, celebratory, and interpersonal—people come into this world, meet others and live their lives, and then depart *together* (as sadhus) to God's country. "Let's go *together* to God's country . . . to the [place] of someone well-known" underscores that *sannyās* is not necessarily a solitary path, but that it also involves creating skeins of connections with people "in the world," which, as this song indicates, are necessary on the journey to God's "home." That image cues the audience to see *sannyās* in a specific way and reinforces the sadhus' views of *sannyās* as relational. It also contrasts with the bleak image of the world as a dark place of constant suffering and pain (*duhkh*), where the shunning of loving relationships becomes downright essential.

The sadhus' *bhajan* performance crafts a *sannyās* that privileges female concerns for meaningful (spiritual) relationships, which, in turn, help them to survive independently in the world as female renouncers. As we will see, the sadhus depend on the compassion, loyalty, friendship, and generosity of others—sadhus do not work or earn money like householders; any money they have comes from donations. Their survival is tied to and sustained by their networks of relationships with their devotees (including myself, the American ethnographer who sat at their feet and recorded their oral traditions). The idea of *sannyās* that these sadhus perform in this gathering is that singing *bhajans* embodies *sannyās* and creates the relationships that help to define and sustain *sannyās* as a way of life for them. Thus, the female sadhus' *melā* metaphor of *sannyās* as relational orients a view of vernacular asceticism that parallels historian of religion Robert Orsi's (2005) idea of lived religion—as a "network of relationships . . . between heaven and earth with the specific shapes that relationships take in particular times and places" (2).

In sum, the study of vernacular religion, as this book demonstrates, highlights a method of attending to the personal and the particular that reveals the ways in which people craft their lives with meaning, integrity, and dignity through everyday—and often mundane—practices (Jassal 2012; Knight 2011; Khandelwal 2004, 11–14; Pintchman 2007; Flueckiger 2006; Sered 1992). Orsi describes humanistic studies focused on the particular as committed to "examining the variety of human experiences . . . to make contact across boundaries—cultural psychological, spiritual, existential. It is a . . . disciplined attentiveness to the many different ways men, women, and children have lived with the gods and to the things, terrible and good, violent and peaceful, they have done with the gods to themselves and others" (2005, 203; cf. Tweed 2006).

Ethnographic Methods: Fieldwork Collaborators and Fieldwork Assistants—Conducting Research in Rajasthan

This book is based on three years of ethnographic research with thirty-nine sadhus of the Dashanami and Nath orders. I conducted fieldwork in three districts of Mewar: Udaipur, Rajsamand, and Banswara. In Udaipur district, I worked in the city of Udaipur, as well as in the towns of Gogunda, Mavli, Nathdwara, Kelwa, Oghna, Sarsuniya, Salumber, Kirat, Oden, and Ghora Ghati; and in the villages of Losingh Dilwaria, Shyalpura, Kavita, Maruvas, and Gadavara. In Rajsamand, I worked principally in Kumbhalgarh. In Banswara, I worked in the villages in which the temples of Bheneswar and Baliya Mata Ki Dhuni (lit., "fire pit of the sacrificial Goddess") are located. Because of its central location in Mewar and easy access to transit ways, I made Udaipur city my primary base of residence and lived with three different Hindu families over the course of ten years of research. While I predominantly collaborated with female sadhus, I also worked with fifteen male sadhus for comparative purposes. My meetings with the female sadhus often involved meeting male sadhus who were the gurus or the guru-brothers of female sadhus. Out of the twenty-four female sadhus I worked with, eight of them resided in the same ashram or temple as their male gurus or guru-brother(s). With one exception (see Chapter 6), the rest of the sadhus lived independently in ashrams they managed. The twenty-four sadhus who participated in my study represent a population sample of female Shaiva renouncers in Mewar.

Locating female sadhus in the beginning stages of my fieldwork in Mewar was tough (cf. Knight 2011; Khandelwal 2004). Many householder acquaintances and some Indian university professors told me that such women did not exist in Rajasthan (one professor patently denied the existence of female Hindu sadhus and said that I should work instead with Jain *sādhvīs*, which he considered a legitimate sociological category). They said that I would find "real" "lady" sadhus either living in coenobitic ashrams or alone in hermitages along the Ganges River in Haridwar and Rishikesh (Khandelwal talks about a similar experience in her fieldwork). People also said that while there were a few local women who "occupied" themselves with "religious matters" (in their words, "they chant '*rām-rām*' all day"), they were simply "widows," and not sadhus. I realize that these kinds of statements make explicit popular assumptions about what renunciation is, and singing *bhajans*, to these acquaintances, did not constitute legitimate sadhu behavior. They associated singing *bhajans* with common perceptions of female householder religiosity and distinguished *sannyās* as something more difficult than singing *bhajans* (which demonstrates why female sadhus' use of this idiom to craft themselves as ascetics is an apt model for voicing gendered concerns, despite the fact that people do not take them seriously). This assumption shows just how widespread the dominant model of *sannyās* is in the mainstream imagination, not to mention people's use of it to judge renunciant authenticity. It also depicts that male experiences of *sannyās* represent the standard against which female sadhus' practices are often measured.

To assist me in my research and data collection, I hired a field associate, Manvendra Singh Ashiya, a twenty-four-year-old Caran man.[21] He accompanied me on most of my fieldwork journeys and participated in my meetings with the sadhus in various ways. In addition to helping in translating some of my conversations with the sadhus, Manvendra assisted me in conducting interviews and in taping the sadhus' oral performances. My interactions with the sadhus always occurred in Hindi. I am trained to speak modern standard Hindi, which, as I learned, is the *lingua franca* of educated Indian intellectuals; however, it is the local "*bolcāl*" (everyday) Hindi that one hears spoken in the streets and bazaars, in the home, and more importantly, in ashrams. Many sadhus spoke one of several Rajasthani dialects (e.g., Marwari, Dhundari, or Mewari); some also spoke Gujarati, and some (Western) Hindi. The majority of the sadhus, though, spoke a colorful medley of Hindi, Mewari, and Bhojpuri. Born in eastern Rajasthan, Manvendra speaks Rajasthani, the standard Hindi that I speak, and several other Indian languages. Whenever the sadhus switched from speaking the Hindi that I could understand and converse in to speaking a dialect of Rajasthani, Manvendra helped to translate their Rajasthani into Hindi for me.

Usually, after several meetings with the sadhus, it became evident to me who was interested in participating in my study and who was not. Although I ended up working with a total of thirty-nine sadhus, the bedrock of my research is drawn from the observations, interactions, and conversations I conducted with fifteen female sadhus and five male sadhus. In her work with the female Muslim healer Amma, Flueckiger describes the issues involved for the fieldworker, who must decide with whom she will conduct research: "While the experience of every individual is worthy of documentation and study, not all individuals are equally articulate, observant, interpretive, or dramatic in relating their own or others' experiences" (2006, 22). The twenty sadhus whose lives and practices I describe and analyze in this book were clearly interested in my project. As the most articulate and communicative of my collaborators (i.e., they liked to sing songs and tell stories and they were seen as good singers and storytellers), these sadhus played an active role in shaping my research schedule and field methods. They taught me about the diversity and meanings of their renunciant traditions; they patiently and thoughtfully answered my questions about their lives and practices; and, in the case of four female sadhus (Ganga Giri, Tulsi Giri, Shiv Puri, and Sad Giri), they reviewed a number of my translations and transcriptions of their performances and some of the interviews I conducted with them.[22] Not only that, a few of the sadhus sponsored public feastings (*bhaṇḍāras*) on my behalf, which other sadhus from various sadhu traditions and lineages were invited to participate in as well. Such opportunities gave me access to a larger local community (*samāj*) of sadhus and sensitized me to the social culture of *sannyās* in Mewar, particularly in terms of the negotiated hierarchies among different orders and even among members of the same order. Thus, while I chose to work closely with twenty sadhus, it is also accurate to say that they, too, chose me and my project.

Renunciation, Relationships, and Reciprocity: Becoming an Ethnographer-Disciple

The process of conducting ethnographic fieldwork, as a number of anthropologists, ethnographers, and scholars of religion have discussed, is inextricably linked to developing personal relationships with our collaborators beyond the static and Cartesian researcher/informant binary.[23] My interactions with the female sadhus constituted a function of the relationships of reciprocity we created together "in the field." These connections developed on account of the time I spent working with these sadhus, and, whether at their requests or of my own volition, sharing personal details about my life with them. While I was not able to meet with all fifteen of the female sadhus every day (both the distances between their ashrams and the sheer number of female sadhus with whom I had established friendships would have made this goal unwieldy), I visited six of the fifteen sadhus—those who lived in Udaipur city or district—four to five times a week, and interacted with each of the fifteen sadhus at least once every three weeks.[24]

As my relationships with the sadhus became more personal, my status changed from ethnographer-fieldworker to ethnographer-disciple. The sadhus marked my new status by calling me their disciple (*celī*). There was no official initiation ritual to mark this alteration. The sadhus simply said, "You belong to me now," or "You are my disciple."[25] It goes without saying that to become the disciple of not one but fifteen sadhus is no easy task to accomplish for any person; it is a responsibility not to be taken lightly by the student and may have serious ramifications for those who underestimate, abuse, or exploit that relationship. My host families and Manvendra Singh often discussed the seriousness of the guru-disciple relationship. In these contexts, someone always invoked a well-known idiom about gurus, which I will paraphrase as follows: "If you upset God, God will forgive you. But if you upset the guru, even God can't help you." Sohan Lal Chechani, whom I called "Dadaji" (grandfather), a householder who introduced me to many female sadhus, said, "Look, these sadhus will expect something from you. If you become their disciple you cannot refuse them. You will have to give them whatever they ask [for]."

I emphasize here that I never told the sadhus that I considered myself as their disciple. To do so, in my view, would have been duplicitous, especially since all of the sadhus knew that I was working with other sadhus. I knew that if I agreed to become one sadhu's disciple, not only was word bound to get out in the local sadhu *samāj*, but also that my initiation as a particular sadhu's *celī* would inevitably change my relationship with the other sadhus in my field study. How initiation would change my relationship with other sadhus I was not exactly sure. I only knew that it would, and thus decided not to pursue initiation from any sadhu. I negotiated my position with the sadhus by carefully sidestepping the initiation issue as best as I could.

For example, whenever a female sadhu asked me directly to become her disciple, I gingerly said that I would wait for *bhagwān* to guide me in my decision. Those sadhus who approached me with such a request accepted my response.[26] No one ever forced the issue afterwards (though, sometimes, some of the sadhus' devotees would remind me of the invitation). These instances aside, however, most of the sadhus did not ask me to become their disciple. Rather, they acted as if I already were their disciple. I neither accepted nor denied their statements, but allowed them to determine the nature and terms of our relationships. The sadhus themselves constructed my identity as their "*pardesi celī* [foreign disciple],"[27] and publicly promoted this identity to others. Sad Giri, for instance, called me Gori Giri ("white Giri" [lit., "mountain," a branch name in the Dashanami Order]) and told other sadhus that I was her disciple. That is, Sad Giri called me her disciple, but the other sadhus did not hear this as an official statement that she had formally initiated me as her disciple. While I had concerns that being an "informal" disciple of the female sadhus would create obstacles in my being able to conduct research that required a formality which belies the intimacy shared between sadhu and *celī*, I learned that the sadhus actually wanted to share more about their lives and traditions with me than they probably would have had they perceived me only as a foreign ethnographer.

Although the sadhus emphasized the disciple aspect of my identity, they never lost sight of the ethnographer side of my identity. They seemed to understand what anthropologist Lila Abu-Lughod (1993) has suggested about the construction of identity in the ethnographic encounter: namely, that identities are situated in particular historical, social, political, and ethnographic contexts. As the contexts of our encounters with collaborators shift, our identities, too, change and transform. Despite this ever-present fact of my researcher identity (after all, I was in India to collect and document their traditions), it did not seem to matter to the sadhus with whom I established personal relationships that I was a researcher or that I was meeting with other (male and female) sadhus in and beyond Rajasthan. What mattered instead was that I was *their* disciple; that I was sincere in my desire to learn, understand, and share their teachings and practices with others "in [my] country"; and importantly, that I came back to the sadhus again and again.

Renouncing Assumptions, Embodying Knowledge: The Fieldwork Practices of an Ethnographer-Disciple

Even as an informal disciple, the sadhus had certain expectations of me. One of those expectations was that I would behave in a manner that would not bring disrepute on me or my host families.[28] That is, as a single woman, I was expected to abstain from having sexual relationships with men, both Indian and foreign. Because I had divulged the details of my personal life, and therefore, my single *and* celibate status, there was the implicit expectation in my interactions with the sadhus that I would remain celibate throughout the research process (which I did!).[29] There was one event that made quite clear to me where the sadhus stood on the sensitive issue of my sexual practices. In July 2003, I went to visit Tulsi Giri who, at the time, had been residing with her guru in Udaipur city, near Dudh Talai. When I approached her she was noticeably upset. "How could you, Anita?"[30] she bemoaned. "How could I what?" I asked, growing increasingly concerned with the sound of her voice. "We know that you like to work with sadhus but did you have to marry one?" I thought that I had heard Tulsi Giri incorrectly, so I quickly called Dadaji over to the scene. As they spoke, I put the pieces together: approximately a week earlier there had been a young foreign woman from Austria who had married a sadhu at the Mahakaleshwar (Shiva) Temple, behind which sadhus like Ganga Giri, Devi Nath, and Jnan Nath resided independently in their own ashrams and temples (see the newspaper clipping of this published incident, which is titled, "Foreign Woman Falls for Indian Baba," below).

Tulsi Giri is nonliterate, so when I asked how she had heard about the incident, she told me that Ganga Giri, who told her the story just two days before, had heard from some devotees that "that foreign girl who comes to you every day has married a sadhu right here at Mahakaleshwar." The news spread among the sadhus like wildfire. In my panic-stricken state, and with Dadaji's assistance (he laughed the whole time, but this was no laughing matter to me), I explained to Tulsi Giri that the woman in the newspaper was not me. She was from Austria and I was from America (to which Tulsi Giri innocently said, "What's the difference?"); and that woman's name was Sandra, and my name is Anita. Tulsi Giri seemed to understand that there had been a grave miscommunication and said, "I knew our Anita wouldn't do that. I told [the others] it wasn't you [in the newspaper]. But who listens to Tulsi Giri?" I spent the next month explaining to every sadhu I visited in that time frame that I was not the woman in the newspaper.[31] When I got around to reading

राजस्थान पत्रिका उदयपुर, मंगलवार, 8 जुलाई, 2003

गोरी मेम को भा गया बाबा!

उदयपुर, 7 जुलाई।

दो बच्चों और पत्नी को छोड़ कर सन्यास ले चुका उदयपुर का राकेश अहीर उर्फ शंकर बाबा को आस्ट्रिया की करीब तीस वर्षीय सान्द्रा को भा गया। दोनों ने सोमवार को यहां महाकालेश्वर मंदिर में भगवान को साक्षी मानकर विवाह कर लिया। सांद्रा राकेश को गॉडगिफ्ट मानती है।

पेशे से प्राइवेट स्कूल में फिलोसॉफी विषय की अध्यापिका बताने वाली सान्द्रा गत वर्ष भारत भ्रमण पर निकली और गत मार्च में वह पुष्कर [अजमेर] पहुंची। तेईस मार्च को उसका 31वां जन्मदिन था। कोई परिवार का सदस्य, साथी-मित्र नहीं होने के कारण उसने अकेले ही अपना जन्मदिन मनाया। वह ऐसे मौके पर अपने आपको काफी अकेला महसूस कर रही थी।

सान्द्रा बताती है कि उस रात उसने जैसे तैसे बिताई और अगली सुबह उठने के बाद उसने सबसे पहले वहां घूम रहे राकेश अहीर को देखा, जो पहली नजर में उसे भा गया। सान्द्रा ने बताया कि पुष्कर में दोस्ती होने के बाद उन दोनों ने भारत भ्रमण किया। वे नेपाल भी गए। वहां से करीब दो माह पूर्व वे उदयपुर पहुंचे। वह कहती है कि उसने कभी शादी के बारे में नहीं सोचा था दोस्त तो उसके कई हैं। लेकिन राकेश को पाकर वह उसे अपनाने से स्वयं को रोक नहीं पाई। राकेश को वह गॉडगिफ्ट मानती है। वह उसे अपने आस्ट्रिया ले जाना चाहती है। लेकिन बिना पासपोर्ट के राकेश को अपने साथ ले जा पाना संभव नहीं है।

इसके लिए वह राकेश को साथ लेकर विभिन्न सरकारी कार्यालयों का चक्कर लगा रही है। पासपोर्ट बनवाने

उदयपुर के महाकालेश्वर मंदिर में सोमवार को भगवान को साक्षी मानकर एक दूसरे को माला पहना कर विवाह बंधन में बंधे सान्द्रा व राकेश। - पत्रिका फोटो

प्रक्रिया को लेकर सान्द्रा ने स्थानीय प्रशासन के प्रति आक्रोश जाहिर किया। स्वयं को करीब पचास करोड़ रुपए की मालकिन ... कहती है कि आस्ट्रिया में स्कूल में उसका दो लाख रुपए मासिक वेतन है, जिसमें से कटकटा कर उसे एक लाख रुपए मिल जाते हैं। बड़ा आलिशान मकान है, जिसे किराए दे रखा और उसके किराए से वह विश्व भ्रमण पर निकली हुई है। सान्द्रा और राकेश अहीर ने सोमवार दोपहर महाकालेश्वर मंदिर में भगवान को साक्षी मानकर एक दूसरे के गले में माला पहनाई और वे विवाह बंधन में बंध गए। कभी देहलीगेट पर तांगा चलाने और लंगड़ाते घोड़ों की नाल लगाने वाला करीब चालीस वर्षीय राकेश अहीर अब अपने आपको को भोले बाबा का भक्त बताता है। उसके गुरु ने ही उसे शंकर गिरी बाबा नाम दिया है।

वह कहता है कि दो वर्ष पूर्व उसने घर-परिवार त्याग कर सन्यासी जीवन अपना लिया था। लेकिन पुष्कर में सान्द्रा से मुलाकात के बाद वह भी उसी का होकर रह गया। वह सान्द्रा के साथ आस्ट्रिया जाना चाहता है। लेकिन स्थानीय प्रशासन उसके पासपोर्ट में बाधक बना हुआ है।

उधर, स्थानीय पुलिस प्रशासन का कहना है कि भूपालपुरा स्थित कृष्णपुरा निवासी राकेश अहीर शादीशुदा होकर दो बच्चों का पिता है। उसके खिलाफ शहर के भूपालपुरा थाने में विभिन्न प्रकृति के आपराधिक प्रकरण दर्ज रहे हैं। इनमें जानलेवा हमला, अवैध रूप से हथियार रखने, मारपीट जैसे मामले दर्ज थे। इसके अलावा उसकी पत्नी ने भी दहेज प्रताड़ना का एक मामला दर्ज कराया था।

हालांकि इन मामलों का अदालत से निस्तारण हो चुका है। पासपोर्ट प्रक्रिया पूरी होने में विलम्ब के बारे में पुलिस प्रशासन का कहना है कि राकेश न्यायालय में निस्तारित मामलों की प्रतियां उपलब्ध करा दे तो उनकी तरफ से कोई देरी नहीं है। अदालती निर्णयों की प्रति तो उसे ही उपलब्ध करानी होगी। [कास]

FIGURE 1.1 Newspaper clipping of foreign woman who marries Indian sadhu. Image photocopied from the Rajasthan Patrika Newspaper (July 8, 2003).

about this incident—Dadaji's neighbor, who was convinced that the woman in the newspaper was me, shared his copy with me upon my request—and looked at a picture of Sandra along with her new husband, Rakesh Baba, I was instantly struck by the physical similarities between us (see Figure 1.1). The whole experience taught me that my behavior *as an unmarried woman* in the local sadhu community affects the sadhus' (and their devotees') perceptions of me, which affects not only my being able to conduct research with them, but also the kinds of relationships I am able to have with them, and thus, the kind of data I receive.

Another expectation that the sadhus repeatedly verbalized in our interactions was that I learn their traditions "from my heart," meaning that I internalize them. Needless to say, participant observation with the sadhus went beyond observing their performances and asking them questions about their lives and practices. In *satsang*, the sadhus repeatedly insisted that I sing *bhajans* or recite chapters of the Tulsi *Rāmāyan* or *Bhagavad Gītā* with them. In doing so, the sadhus themselves implied that "real" ethnographer-disciples, like "real" sadhus, sing to *bhagwān*. So, after I had transcribed a song, I made sure to memorize its lyrics and the melody in which the sadhus had performed it. When I learned a song well enough, I was not only singing it in *satsang* with the sadhus (which they considered an impressive display of my own knowledge), but also on my own (and with my host families). This practice of singing some of the same songs that the sadhus sang enabled me to create my own status and authority among them. Before I developed my modest performance repertoire of *bhajans*, the sadhus characterized me as "*bholī-bhālī*"—that is, as innocent and, more precisely, naïve about their way of life (and about living in India). One time, early in 2005, Tulsi Giri asked me to sing a *bhajan*, to which Ganga Giri said, "What can she sing? She has no knowledge of *bhajans*. What does she know?" Her comment pierced my ego like a razor blade. I never forgot it. But the experience taught me that my role as an ethnographer-disciple pivoted on my ability to perform both with *and* for the sadhus. After I had learned a few songs I had recorded from them (a skill I developed with the help of my Brahmin family, who encouraged me to learn *bhajans*), I began to sing for the sadhus. By doing so, they, including Ganga Giri, started to characterize me as "a knower." My own singing of songs, in fact, prompted the sadhus to sing and comment on their *bhajans*.

At the same time, this practice allowed me to experience a different type of relationship to the data I was collecting than I would have had had I only recorded and translated them. That is, I began to embody the sadhus' performances as verbal forms of knowledge and power that informed my own understanding of devotion, and by extension, of *sannyās*. To this extent, I experienced their songs, stories, and sacred texts in the ways that the sadhus themselves had described: as living entities whose knowledge and power become embedded in the fiber of the singer's being with every single performance, transforming her from within. Furthermore, I began to understand the nature and complexity of the sadhus' embodied relationships to their vernacular practices, and that their individual experiences of *sannyās* were directly linked to the knowledge that was created by means of their performances of song, story, and sacred text.

Yet, to understand asceticism as practiced by the sadhus, I had to do more than learn to sing *bhajans* and recite texts "from the heart." I also had to learn *how* to listen carefully for the concepts, categories, idioms, and frameworks through which these sadhus experienced and interpreted their lives. Folklorist Elaine Lawless (1993) has said that "learning how to be a good scholar means learning how to listen." This insight has clearly been the case for my own development as a scholar and fieldworker in India. Learning how to conduct research with sadhus, both men and women, who have, at least ideologically speaking, "died to the world," has been a process of discovering, and as such, of renouncing my own presuppositions about *sannyās*.

When I began conducting field research, I told my collaborators, renunciants and householders alike, that I came to learn the Hindi language and study Hindu religion, though I made explicit that I was especially interested in learning sadhu-*dharm*, or the religion of sadhus. This presentation of my research motivations, however, was much too broad a category, and the ways that the female sadhus, in particular, answered this question revealed, on the one hand, my own "context-free" presuppositions about renunciation and, yet, on the other, the "context-sensitivity" of conceptual categories, like *sannyās*, in the field. Hearing my questions about sadhu-*dharm*, the female sadhus offered the generic (and predictable) response: "Speak the truth; do good work; and serve others with love." Whereas I had interpreted sadhu-*dharm* to exemplify a particular (and dominant) set of attitudes, behaviors, and presuppositions that demonstrate renunciation-as-lived, such as detachment, isolation, wandering, and meditation, the sadhus' responses indicated an elastic view of the term. For the sadhus I knew, sadhu-*dharm* implied, in part, that their duty (*kartavya*) as renunciants was to teach others about the path of (righteous) action, devotion, and knowledge through means of their expressive practices. With my own assumptions of renunciation in mind, I pressed the sadhus to discuss the values and virtues that were more central to the mainstream imagination than to their own gendered experiences. No wonder, then, many of them said something like, "Look, I am uneducated (*anpaḍh*). You should go to [such and such male sadhu] who can tell you what you want to know. I am only first-class [or first grade] passed. What can a first-class passed person know?"

But the sadhus *do* know renunciation—not as an abstract construct or androcentric model, but rather as a situated "lived practice" experienced through their songs, stories, and sacred texts (Narayanan 2003; Smith 1963). W. C. Smith's statement that "The participant is concerned with God; the observer [is] concerned with 'religion,'" or, in this context, "renunciation," was certainly the case with the sadhus, and with me, the ethnographer-disciple (Smith 1963, 131). Thus, when I *heard* the significance these sadhus attribute to their everyday vernacular performances, I understood that such situated practices function as interpretive strategies through which they conceptualize and construct *sannyās* as relational and celebratory—as a female way of being a sadhu. Hence, I began actively soliciting their performances (see also Jassal 2012; that author used a similar method in her fieldwork with multi-caste women singers in North India). I refrained from asking general questions such as, "what is renunciation?" Instead, I asked, "Why does Mira Bai leave her palace to sing with sadhus?" "Is Mira's singing of *bhajans sannyās*?" or "How do devotees (*bhakts*) 'cross over' the ocean of existence, and what does the ocean of existence mean to you?" That is, I drew on the content of the songs, stories, and sacred texts that the sadhus performed in specific *satsang* contexts to ask particular (and more relevant) questions about *sannyās* as practiced in North India. Furthermore, I framed my meetings with the female sadhus by telling them, "I have come to hear your *bhajans*. Will you sing for me today?" Reframing my project and my questions produced a marked difference in their perceptions of me and my project, and this change shaped the data I received. It also created *satsangs* on the spot with the female sadhus and any guests who happened to be at their ashrams. Seeing my desire to learn their practices—whether it was memorizing the lines of a *bhajan* or learning how to make a proper *capātī* (unleavened wheat bread)—the sadhus generously shared their traditions (and their meanings) with me. Santosh Puri said, "I have so many *bhajans* to fill your tapes with."

Setting the Stage: Satsang *as a Context for Vernacular Asceticism*

Satsang functions as a vibrant context for meeting and parting in the sadhus' *sannyās*, for creating and sustaining connections with others in the *melā* of life. Here, the participants (*satsangīs*) gather together for a period of time, engage in the practices of singing *bhajans* (by which they remember and worship the divine), and then depart from *satsang* and return to their work-a-day lives. While the time that the *satsangīs* spend together is temporary, *satsang*, because of the practices emplaced there, creates community (i.e., a community of truth) among them, and the bonds they build together are strong enough that they keep returning to *satsang* in order to sing and remember God. *Satsang*, as the *melā* metaphor in the sadhus' practices implies, is enjoyable for the participants, and the performances that emerge in those contexts are often seen as entertainment, where people leisurely reflect on God's sacred mysteries. For many of the householders who attend them, *satsang* offers a welcomed respite from their worldly activities. *Satsang* vividly illustrates that human religiosity can be, and often is, a celebratory rather than a solemn activity. *Satsang* is not by definition a singularly renunciant practice, though most renouncers engage in it. The sadhus I met, however, consider *satsang* as a defining element of their vernacular asceticism. In general, the idea and practice of *satsang* is historically associated with Vaishnava Hinduism, the classical devotional movements of the Alvars and Nayanars[32] of South India, and the medieval *sant bhakti* traditions (Hawley 2005; Prentiss 1999; Schomer and Mcleod 1986; Hawley and Juergensmeyer 1988). *Satsang* appears to have been a predominantly Vaishnava practice, and the *sants*, according to some historians of *bhakti*, adopted and adapted it from the Vaishnavas. Every *satsang* is unique, as the people who attend it, the locations where it is held, the times in which it happens, the explicit and implicit motivations underlying its occurrences, and the practices foregrounded in it, change and shift. Nonetheless, general patterns undercut the specificities of individual *satsangs* that distinguish them as sites of vernacular asceticism. I will discuss those here as I observed them in the practices of the sadhus.

Satsang can happen anywhere, wherever the sadhus desire to connect to God. In my experience, it has occurred at the sadhus' ashrams, temples, or shrines; in their devotees' homes; in several cases, in the home of my Brahmin host family[33]; and, in the cars, buses, and trains in which I traveled with the sadhus. *Satsangs* can be organized as a large multi-day event for the display of cultural performances (where three meals are usually served to participants), or as an intimate gathering, consisting of a handful of people, that stretches over a twenty-four-hour period, or half a day. In the *satsangs* in which I participated, the former mostly characterizes *satsangs* that happened in the context of a *bhaṇḍāra* sponsored by a sadhu to commemorate her guru's *mahāsamādhi*,[34] while the latter describes *satsangs* where there were no less than two people (me and a sadhu) and no more than ten people (usually a group of three or four sadhus and five or six householders gathered together). In the context of these small gatherings, the sadhus prepare, with the help of their devotees and me, chai and food (e.g., lentil soup, *capātī* and a vegetable) for everyone. "This," as Ganga Giri says, "is what *sannyās* means."

Wherever they happen, *satsangs* are always public (and popular) events, meaning that anyone can attend them, regardless of gender, caste, class, or religious identity (but see Chapter 6). The public nature of *satsangs* is related to the public position of sadhus. As public religious figures, sadhus are ideally available to people all the time. The popularity of *satsangs* in *sannyās*-as-lived, and in the vernacular asceticism of the sadhus, has to do with the primarily heterodox (and egalitarian) *sant bhakti* attitude informing them that an individual's caste, color, gender, class, and religion have no significance whatsoever in the eyes of the divine (Lorenzen 1996; see Chapters 6 and 8). In these contexts, a person's status is tied neither to caste (or educational) status nor to gender, but rather to the intensity of his or her devotion for the divine, however it is conceived. In this framework, *satsang* signifies a context where religious and social differences, and gendered and caste status hierarchies, are ignored (but not erased), in the creation of a community in which *satsangīs* stand together, and before God, as spiritually equal participants. The sadhus enthusiastically welcome anyone who comes to their ashrams or temples to sing *bhajans* with them. In my own case, the sadhus believe that my wanting to sing *bhajans* with them, though unusual for foreigners, is related to the ripening of the good karmic impressions (*sanskār*) of my previous lives (cf. Khandelwal 2004 for a similar experience in her work with female renouncers).[35] Similarly, while the *satsangs* in which the sadhus participate consist of a mixed-caste gathering of participants, most of the sadhus who lead the *satsangs* at their ashrams are primarily from high-caste Brahmin or Rajput backgrounds.

Satsangs can take place at any time of the day, and they have no formal structure as to how they are ordered. The daily visits of people, other sadhus and householders, at the sadhus' ashrams or temples provide an occasion for them to engage in *satsang*. The sadhus are always excited at the opportunity to sing, tell stories, and recite sacred texts with or for others, whether these occasions are planned ahead (e.g., a visit from me) or impromptu (which most of them are). No sadhu I worked with turns people away from their ashrams or temples in order to sing *bhajans* by themselves. "Sadhus should remember God," Ganga Giri says in her *satsangs*. What her practices and those of the other sadhus suggest is that singing with others helps sadhus to achieve that goal. Thus, the enthusiasm with which the sadhus approach and participate in *satsang* is linked to their being able to access and experience the divine *in the company of others*. Recall the words of Ganga Giri's *bhajan*: "Let's go to God's country together, to the country of someone well-known." Therefore, while *sannyās* is often seen as a solitary path, the sadhus' *satsang* practices depict that vernacular asceticism also constitutes a fundamentally social way of life. To them, singing *bhajans* with others is as, if not more, significant as singing or meditating alone.

Many of the sadhus' *satsangs* are loosely structured, organized on the basis of the vast oral traditions that the *satsangīs* themselves want to sing and or listen to, or what the sadhus themselves feel like performing on that day, for others (cf. Narayan 1989). Often *satsangīs* will solicit a specific song or story they like from a sadhu (because she sings the song or tells the story in a manner which that person enjoys), and she will sing that *bhajan*, or tell that story. Every time Manvendra and I visit Shiv Puri, she performs a particular Mahadev (Shiva) *bhajan* because she knows that Manvendra and I like hearing her perform it. During fieldwork, I became fascinated by the life of Kabir (he is, after all, thought to be one of the most direct and acerbic poet-saints in the medieval *bhakti* movements) and asked the sadhus to perform *bhajans* attributed to him from their repertoires. Requesting sadhus to perform a particular song, story, or sacred text, in turn, sensitized me to the depth and breadth of their individual knowledge of regional and pan-Indian oral traditions. Similarly, when the sadhus realized my interest in learning about the lives of female saints like Mira Bai or Karma Bai, for instance (see Chapter 3), their *satsangs* centered around performances of songs and stories attributed to and associated with those saints. "Did I sing the *bhajan* in which Mira Bai sells Govind?" Tulsi Giri asked me, which evoked a Mira *bhajan satsang*. Sometimes a sadhu will mention a specific *bhakti* figure like Narsi Mehta (e.g., "Narsi Mehta songs are sung in Gujarat"), and simply my asking "who was Narsi Mehta?" evokes a series of song and story performances about him.

Furthermore, the sadhus perform their traditions in order to make a point about an issue in the topic of conversation. Although *satsangs* are, foremost, performance contexts for group worship of the divine (but not for formal worship in the more standard sense of ritual), they also serve as (informal) conversational contexts, and the sadhus' performances of song, story, and sacred text frequently arise from conversations emplaced in those contexts. To take an example, the gold jewelry (e.g., earrings and bangles) worn by the female householders attending a *satsang* one afternoon in February 2005 at Ganga Giri's hermitage prompted her to narrate a story about the ill effects of the *kali yug*, in which, in her view, degenerate activities like alcohol consumption, wearing gold, lying and cheating, prostitution, and—perhaps worst of all—not feeding sadhus who beg at one's door, describe the dismal state of the cosmos. This story evoked another story performance from Ganga Giri, this time about King Karan, a character from the *Mahābhārat*[36] epic, who, because he did not feed the begging sadhus who appeared at the doorstep of his palace, but rather "gave them gold coins," was reborn in a heaven where, though he lived in a palace much like his earthly one, he starved every day. Ganga Giri's stories performed for her audience the more global message of the importance of "catching hold of God in one's heart." At the same time, though, her performances indicated the values that she views as illustrative of her vernacular asceticism—that sadhus do not wear gold,[37] and thus *satsangīs* should consider removing their jewelry before they come for *satsangs* at her place, and that sadhus depend on their relationships with others to sustain themselves physically in the world.[38]

In conclusion, *satsang* constitutes a dynamic context in which many different types of exchanges—both spiritual and material—take place at various times and in various locations between various types of sadhu and lay personalities, and where, most importantly, participants can direct their energies to creating relationships of love with each other and with the divine. By writing ethnographically about the sadhus' practices as they arise, develop, and change in *satsang*, I, too, direct my readers' attention to a less known form (and gendered experience) of *sannyās* in South Asian and religious studies that is created and lived in such contexts (but is not tied to those contexts). I suspect that *satsang* as a context for not only *sannyās*-as-lived, but also gendered constructions of *sannyās* as it is lived, has been overlooked in the scholarship on renunciation because it represents a quotidian experience in the practices of many renouncers, men and women. The sadhus whom I describe in the following pages are thoughtful, wise, and compassionate people, who are transforming, in subtle and yet significant ways, the lives of those whom they teach, and to whom they are passing on their oral traditions. It is my hope that this study of Rajasthani female sadhus will shift the direction of future studies on asceticism as practiced and that more studies on sadhus' vernacular practices in South Asia will continue to emerge and push back against dominant definitional boundaries for what "counts" as *sannyās*.

The Rajasthani Cultural Context

Rajasthan as a cultural region matters to the sadhus, and their constructions of *sannyās* is related to their common perceptions of Rajasthan, specifically Mewar, as "the land of the brave [*vīr*]" (see Chapter 4). The North Indian state of Rajasthan is hardly a homogenous sociopolitical and cultural entity, but rather consists of a plethora of ethnicities, cultures, languages, and religious and social groups (Lodrick 2001; Schomer et al. 2001). The dominant religion is Hinduism, followed by Jainism, Islam, Sikhism, and Christianity. The region's climate is arid or semiarid, and its landscape is signaled by the presence of the great Thar Desert in the northwest and the stunning Aravalli mountain range in the southwestern part of the state. The principal district in which I conducted fieldwork, Udaipur, is located in southwest Rajasthan, and represents the former capital of the erstwhile princely state of Mewar.

The rather small size of Udaipur, which is characterized in the tourist literature I purchased from the local bazaars as the "Venice of the East," belies the relatively large population of people residing in this district. When I first arrived in Udaipur in 2001, the district's population was approximately 390,000. In the last ten years, however, the population has increased threefold, to over 900,000 residents. Today the bustling Udaipur city contains over a dozen or so Internet cafes;[39] popular coffee houses such as Café Coffee Day,[40] which is similar to Starbucks; a DHL domestic/international postal service; and there was talk in 2006 among local bazaar owners of the popular fast-food chain McDonalds coming into the city.[41] As Lindsey Harlan has described (1992), Udaipur exemplifies "the juxtaposition of tradition and innovation" (4). Here, as elsewhere in India, one finds ancient temples and royal palaces situated amid modern buildings and convenience shops, and auto rickshaws vying for precious road space not only with pedestrians and animals, but also with the latest models of cars and sport utility vehicles.

Situated atop a hillock, Udaipur city has two major lakes: Lake Picchola and Lake Fateh Sagar. On the city's west side lies Picchola Lake. It is surrounded by ancient temple buildings (many of which are in a dilapidated state),[42] bathing ghats, many restaurants, bazaars (shops), and two- or three-storied private residences painted in bright colors—a scenery that imbues the area surrounding Lake Picchola (i.e., the "Old City") with its lively, and at times chaotic, ambience. To the north of Lake Picchola is Fateh Sagar Lake, an artificial body of water that was reconstructed in the early nineteenth century under the auspices of the Udaipur *mahārāṇā* (great king) Fateh Singh (ca. 1884–1930). The city also has three major temple complexes that patronize one of the three great deities Shiva, Vishnu, and the Goddess: Mahakaleshwar Temple, Jagdish (Vishnu) Temple, and Neemach Mata (Durga Mata). Besides these popular temples are the lesser-known temples, shrines, and ashrams, including those of the sadhus with whom I worked. Two of these sadhus live near the vicinity of Lake Fateh Sagar, one near Lake Picchola, and three others directly behind the Mahakaleshwar Temple. The rest of the sadhus, however, reside outside of Udaipur city, in temples and hermitages situated in small villages and towns.

A distinct Mewari ethos is evident in the practices of the female sadhus. This ethos is signaled by the presence of royal martial themes, which many of these sadhus emphasize, like bravery (*bahādurī; dikhavā*), courage (*himmat*), and sacrifice (*balidān; kurbān*). The majority of the female sadhus, and a few of the male sadhus, identify with these preeminent warrior ideals, considering them to be, along with *bhakti*, qualities of authentic sadhus. Most of the female sadhus characterize *sannyās* as a "difficult [*kaṭhin*]" path for "the brave of heart," likening sadhus to warrior-heroes.[43] Additionally, their rhetoric of renunciation consists of religious stories and *bhajans* about legendary sadhus, such as Baba Ram Dev (Chapter 6), Gopi Chand (Chapter 4), and Mira Bai (Chapter 3), who, as the female sadhus describe, not only possessed the warrior virtues of bravery, courage, and sacrifice, but also themselves came from (royal) warrior clans or castes.[44] The representation of warrior ideals by the sadhus as renunciant virtues reveals the ways in which the popular local perceptions of Rajasthan's martial history have captivated the minds and memories of its local inhabitants, including its female ascetics.

Rajasthan, the land of Rajputs,[45] has been described in both the scholarly and popular literature as "the land of kings." The formation of Rajasthan as an independent state occurred approximately two years following India's independence from British sovereignty in 1949 (Erdman 2001, 45). Prior to that time, Rajasthan consisted of a collection of separate provinces (or kingdoms) that were governed by individual Rajput rulers in cooperation with local British officials (Lodrick, 2001, 1–44). One of these provinces was Mewar, in southwest Rajasthan, and the representation of Mewar's martial history in classic British accounts (e.g., Colonel Tod's *Annals and Antiquities of Rajasthan* [1920]) highlights a string of semilegendary rulers (*mahārāṇās*) known for their valor, chivalry, and honor (cf. Harlan 1992; Schomer et. al 2001).[46] In the view of popular lore as cited in Ashok Singhpal's book, *Udaipur: The City of Lakes*, Udai Singh, a member of the Sisodiya dynasty of Rajputs, founded the city.[47] More important, the *mahārāṇā* established Udaipur on account of the advice (and blessings) that he received from a sadhu.[48] An account of this legend, as told by Singhal, follows:

> One ... day, while chasing a rabbit Maharana Udai Singh reached near Picchola, where, on a nearby hill he saw a meditating sadhu. Maharana went near him and touched his feet. Sadhu blessed Maharana and said, "If you will establish a city on this land then that city will never be conquered by your enemies." Maharana, acting on this advice of sadhu built a palace there ... (Singhal, no publication date is given).[49]

Well before British occupation of the region, Mewar's history, as well as Rajasthan's history more broadly, is marked by Rajput rulers' cooperation with as well as opposition to foreign rule by Islamic leaders (Lodrick 2001, 8). Beginning with the Turks, then the Afghans, and finally the Mughals, a time period spanning approximately three centuries (ca. the thirteenth through the sixteenth centuries), Rajput rulers not only resisted, but even accommodated, the various Muslim powers. Of the Rajput kingdoms, however, Mewar has gained the distinction for being the most resistant to (and defiant of) Muslim domination (Harlan 1992, 2; 2003). This distinction, according to the various accounts of Mewari history, derives from the fact that, unlike the other kingdoms, Mewar refused to form any political alliance with the Mughal Muslim Empire, most notably under the rule of Akbar (ca. sixteenth century). The conflict between the two powers resulted in the bloody battle at Haldigathi, Mewar, in which Mewar's *mahārāṇā*, Rana Pratap Singh (son of Rana Udai Singh), led thousands of soldiers, including ascetics,[50] into battle against Akbar's army, which included prominent Rajput chiefs (Lodrick 2001, 8). With the support of various Rajput kingdoms, Akbar was able to defeat Rana Pratap at Haldigathi in 1576 (ibid., 8). A life-size metal image of Rana Pratap Singh, along with his beloved horse who led him into battle, Chetak, located in the tourist center of Motri Magri (Pearl Hill) in Udaipur city, commemorates the battle at Haldigathi as a definitive moment in Mewar's martial history. Although Mewar was defeated by Akbar's imperial forces, tales of the bravery, courage, and sacrifice of rulers like Rana Pratap Singh, and later on, of *mahārāṇā* Karan Singh (ca. seventeenth century), *mahārāṇā* Jai Singh (ca. seventeenth century), and *mahārāṇā* Fateh Singh (nineteenth and twentieth centuries), continue to be told by Mewaris (both householders and sadhus), which enables them to construct not only a particular interpretation of Mewari history, but also a distinctive Mewari identity. Lodrick concurs:

> [I]t was the "Mewar" tradition of opposition to the Mughals that came to be accepted as standard Rajput history, a perspective on the past encouraged by nationalists during their struggle for independence from yet another alien central power during the 19th and 20th centuries. Centuries of Rajput rule and traditions of Rajput culture have thus set their imprint firmly on the minds of Rajasthanis, non-Rajputs as well as Rajputs, representing what has been called the Nostalgic-Romantic tradition in modern Rajasthani culture. (Lodrick 2001, 30)

Thus, the female sadhus' constructions of *sannyās* are intimately informed by an underlying Rajasthani (or Mewari) Rajput ethos of bravery, valor, and sacrifice, and by common local perceptions of Mewar as a land of heroic warriors who have sacrificed themselves in battle. Undoubtedly, these perceptions of Mewari (and, by implication, Rajput) identity have played an influential role in the female sadhus' characterizations of *sannyās* as, to use Ganga Giri's poignant words, "a battlefield of *bhakti*" (see Chapter 4). Moreover, their rhetoric consists of Mewari oral legends about the relationships fostered between sadhus and Rajasthani Rajput rulers, tales through which the female sadhus establish singing *bhajans* as a royal path of spiritual power (see Chapter 8). One of the reasons I pursued field research in Rajasthan, and in Mewar, is that I wanted to work with female sadhus living in a region of India that remains understudied in the scholarship on *sannyās* (but cf. Vallely 2002; 2006), and to learn whether or not, and to what extent, female sadhus draw on and reconfigure regional traditions in their practice of asceticism. While the heroic virtues of bravery, courage, and sacrifice accentuated in their vernacular performances are not uniquely Rajasthani, the sadhus' associating "singing *bhajans*" with the devotional asceticism of exceptional regional saints is what gives their female sadhu tradition its distinctly Rajasthani character. The next chapter looks at the ways in which the sadhus perform their personal narratives as a means to craft singing as *sannyās* and, in doing so, link their uncommon religiosity to that associated with the local *bhakti* poet-saint Mira Bai.

2

"By the Sweetness of the Tongue"

PERFORMING FEMALE AGENCY IN PERSONAL NARRATIVE

Because of destiny, people get everything—food, bread, the guru. Everything in life is a matter of fate.

—GANGA GIRI MAHARAJ

NARRATION OF PERSONAL stories performs a powerful way for the female sadhus to construct themselves as "real" renouncers. One February afternoon in 2005, while sitting in the courtyard of her ashram located behind Mahakaleshwar Temple, Ganga Giri described an occasion when she got on a public (government-run) bus and no seat was available. "This happened early on in [my] *sannyās*," she said. According to her account, weary from a day's traveling for the *Kumbh Melā* festival,[1] and barely enduring the weight of a heavy bag of cloth tucked under one arm, Ganga Giri found a way to change her difficult situation. She explained,

> I couldn't keep standing like that. I had to sit [down]... Nearby sat two policemen. Slowly, I approached them and said, "You may wear the uniform [*vardī*] of the government, but I wear the uniform of God. Keep this in mind." One of those poor fellows got up and said, "*Dattā* [a term of endearment for sadhus], please, you sit." I couldn't just say, "Hey, you stand up and I'll sit."... Like this, I have completed my life—by the sweetness of my tongue.

This brief vignette narrates a sadhu's status, power, and authority, as carried by the ochre-colored garb (*bhagwā*). The emphasis on vernacular speech practices described in this book requires shifting our focus from what Ganga Giri actually said to the policemen, or what she wished she had said to them, to her self-representation as a female renouncer. Key to this narrative construction is Ganga Giri's use of specific symbols like the ochre cloth to get what she wants: a seat on an overcrowded bus. In this way, the story indexes an underlying cultural value that Ganga Giri assumes sadhus, policemen, and others in Indian society share.

Moreover, the story constructs Ganga Giri as clever. The irony is that while Ganga Giri tells this story to emphasize her "sweetness," it instead shows her (and her words) being as sharp as a whip. She has an astute capacity for observation. Using her elite position to imply a set of cultural meanings and hierarchies (i.e., Ganga Giri's religious authority surpasses the policeman's secular authority), Ganga Giri puts the fear of God in the heart of that "poor fellow" and convinces him to relinquish his seat. The story presents her as having the "street-smarts" to live as a female sadhu and endure the difficult path of *sannyās*, which includes journeying alone as a woman in order to attend the sacred festivals and make the pilgrimages expected of sadhus. Shortly after telling this story, Ganga Giri shared another one about her travels with her late younger brother Prithvi Puri and his wife, whom Ganga Giri calls "Bhabhiji" (brother's wife). She said,

> When my brother and Bhabhi were alive, we went to the *Kumbh Melā*. There were so many men and women in that *Kumbh Melā*. But I never take tickets [to travel on trains and buses]. I never take tickets. I've travelled 50,000 rupees [approx. $1000 USD] worth without taking tickets. But my brother said, "No. You have to take a ticket. Otherwise the ticket taker will yell at us. You have to take a ticket." Okay. We took tickets for the Bhabhi and me. So the train came... There was the women's compartments where women sit and where men don't sit. There were two men sitting at that place. I could read the number and I said, "Look behind you. What is written? See to it. What is written?" Both of those men got up and went. I asked my Bhabhi to sit there. My Bhabhi said, "You are very smart." That's why I can travel. Do you understand? [Antoinette says "yes."] We were sitting in the women's compartments. We didn't have any place to sit. My brother was standing. I said let the Bhabhi sit because she was so fat. Behind it was written that it's the women's seats. I said, "Look behind you. What is written?" Both men got up. Bhabhi and I both sat [down]. Bhabhi said, "You are so smart. You are so smart." If you're not smart, then you will keep standing. Nobody will say, "Please sit." You have to fight for your rights.
>
> I have lived alone with the sound of snakes. Now I have become cool [*ṭaṇḍā*]. My nature has become calm. Now, age has come to me. I don't have to go anywhere anymore. I only have to stay in my hut.

> It's peaceful here. But when I will go out, I will live with the sound of snakes again. My nature has changed a lot. If I talk to somebody, I don't get angry... This is my way of speaking... I've had this habit [*ādat*] from the beginning. Even if it seems bad to someone, I will speak loudly. It is my habit from the beginning. I have lived alone. I have wandered alone... But now I have become cool and patient. But when I go out, I have the same habit. I keep the same habit when I go out. If I go out, I have to keep my habit the same. You have to keep your sharpness [*tej*] when you go out. Not everybody will like it. But why should have any fear of the world? There isn't any fear of the world anymore. Why should I live under the fear of the world?

As with the previous story, this one similarly brings to light Ganga Giri's gift of cleverness. She never directly characterizes herself as clever in either of her narratives. In the first account, the policeman's offering of his seat to her indicates her possession of this trait; in the second account, the Bhabhi herself attributes the characteristics of shrewd intelligence to Ganga Giri. "You are so smart," the Bhabhi says. This phrase appears three times in Ganga Giri's story.

The attribution of cleverness to Ganga Giri by others functions to legitimate her unusual religious role in the story. According to the sadhus, being a renouncer requires above-average intelligence.[2] "Sadhus should be smart; they should know things," Ganga Giri says. Her being seen as very "sharp" thus distinguishes her as a person, a woman, and a sadhu. Whereas her brother prefers to play by the rules (he implores Ganga Giri to take tickets for their seats on the train), Ganga Giri prefers to bend them. "I've traveled 50,000 rupees worth without taking tickets." And, unlike her brother and sister-in-law, Ganga Giri knows how to "fight for [her] rights." She interrogates what she perceives as ethical violations, like men sitting in the women's compartments. "Look behind you... See to it. What is written?" she says to the two perpetrators. "That's why I can travel," she emphasizes. Her strong words indicate that her cleverness and courage help Ganga Giri to navigate the difficult road of *sannyās* as a woman. "There isn't any fear of the world," she observes. A woman who can live "alone with the sound of snakes," meaning on her own and in strange places, has to be brave. The story supports the notion voiced by the sadhus that *sannyās* is difficult because of the uncommon traits it requires of practitioners.

By the same token, the narrative constructs Ganga Giri as special. Her cleverness, her courage, and the authority with which she relates her experiences give the sense that Ganga Giri is extraordinary. Just as her story guides its listeners (and readers) to interpret her uniqueness as illustrative of human effort, it also pushes another reading of the origin of her unique attributes—that they are the meritorious fruits of destiny. Has a particular fate endowed Ganga Giri with those characteristics that make her an ideal sadhu? To answer this question, I document the personal experiences of Shiv Puri, as she told them to me at her ashram, Munchaleshwar Mahadev,[3] on May 30, 2005. Her story offers a lens through which the sadhus' views on the relationship between human aspiration and destiny is clarified. Here is that story:

> My mother [Indra Kunwar] could predict the future. I said to her, "If you know all the things that will happen in the future, then you have to tell me about my future. What will happen to me? What difficulties [*taklīf*] will I have to endure? Ma, I took birth in this life, and what will happen to me? You know everything, so tell me?" I asked my mother this when she was sitting alone. When I asked her this question, my mother began to stare at me for fifteen minutes. She kept looking at me for fifteen minutes. She hit her hand on the earth so hard that a sound came. She slapped the earth so hard three times as if her hand would break. Afterwards, she told me that, "You will become a *mahārāj* [lit., "great king"; a respectful form of address for sadhus] and you will sit on the throne of a king and rule. People from all over will come to make your *darśan* [viewing]. People from every corner [of the world] will come to for your *darśan*." My mother saw that I would become a sadhu. I forgot what she had told me. I didn't remember what my mother had said. But from that day she began calling me "ap."[4] She used to call me "*tū*."[5] Afterwards she called me "ap." She said, "You will rule on the throne of a *mahārāj*." But I started to laugh. So, laughing, I asked my mother, "Ma, will I rule on the throne in this life or in the next life?" My mother gave the earth two more slaps and said, "You will become a *mahārāj* in this life." This has become true. What my mother said has happened. My mother said this and it slowly came into my mind. Two years later I became a sadhu.

Shiv Puri is destined to be a sadhu. Her mother predicts her unusual fate: that she will become a "great king" (i.e., she will become a sadhu) and "people from every corner will make her *darśan*." Her mother's prediction also allows for the possibility that Shiv Puri will have non-Indian disciples (such as me) as part of her constituency. In fact, Shiv Puri sees my being in her life and the relationship we have built together in the last decade as the ripening of destiny. Thus, Shiv Puri, like many of the sadhus, casts our work together in the aura of fate ("destiny has brought you into my life," she says). A destined sadhu, her mother's words nonetheless appear to influence Shiv Puri's life choices. In portending her fate as a sadhu, Shiv Puri's mother presents Shiv Puri with an alternative to householding (she was a wife and mother with three young children at the time that Shiv Puri's mother made this prediction). And, while she says she forgot what her mother told her on that fateful day, Shiv Puri manifests, through her actions, the extraordinary destiny that her mother has predicted for her. "My mother said this and it slowly came into my mind. Two years later I became a sadhu." Her efforts have created her destiny.

The structure of Shiv Puri's story inverts the emphasis on destiny and fate from that which is featured in Ganga Giri's story (i.e., Shiv Puri's story begins with an emphasis on fate and later shifts its emphasis to human effort, whereas Ganga Giri's starts with effort and moves to accentuating fate). Taken together, though, both stories highlight that these sadhus are exceptional. That is, they are unusual as sadhus (as noted earlier, less than 10% of the Hindu renouncer population consists of female sadhus) and they are unusual as women. Most of the sadhus and the female householders I talked to pressed on the point that a woman has to be fierce like a lion just to be able to live on her own in the world, especially as a female sadhu. Embedded in the sadhus' narratives is an ideology of exceptionalism—the view that God has chosen them to become sadhus in this life. An ideology of exceptionalism makes it possible for the sadhus to situate themselves in a framework that justifies their uncommon religious worlds and identities.

If, as several scholars have argued,[6] oral narratives relate "a shared understanding of the world" (Lawless 1988, 67) and represent "a primary linguistic vehicle" by which individuals make their worlds meaningful (Yamane 2000, 183), it behooves scholars to ask what themes the sadhus bring to light by talking about their personal experiences. I share anthropologist Laurel Kendall's concerns that scholars must "consider the manner in which living men and women experience and articulate, sometimes idiosyncratically, the symbolic constructs and ritual systems we present as ethnographic generalizations" (1988, 4). My inquiry stems from the observation that by virtue of their unconventional position as renouncers—a traditionally male ritual role—female sadhus have an ambiguous social status. Meena Khandelwal (2004) concurs that in Indian society *sannyās* and womanhood signify mutually exclusive categories. She explains: "[renunciation]...was created by and for elite [Brahmin] men" (5). Consequently, women who pursue *sannyās* as an alternative path, regardless of their age, caste status, and class position, are perceived as "anomalies." And although, as Khandelwal further elucidates, these categories of women "are respected by ordinary and even conservative people as sources of both spiritual power and everyday morality" (6), female sadhus are more often suspect for their perceived transgression of gender norms than are male sadhus. In this vein, Khandelwal suggests that female sadhus "transgress social norms . . . but construct themselves as exceptions" (21).

The precious few works available on asceticism as practiced in South Asia have shown the complexities of male sadhus' and female sadhus' everyday worlds by describing the contents of their life stories.[7] This scholarship, however, does not consider the telling of the life story as what folklorist Elaine Lawless calls an "alternative narrative strateg[y]" in individual self-constructions of personal experience and identity (1988; cf. Narayan 1989). Rarely do scholars ask how sadhus craft their personal stories in gendered ways and how their narrative performances bring into view gendered "narrative strategies" in their negotiating of power, authority, and agency (Lawless 1988; cf. Flueckiger 2006; Prasad 2004, 170; Sawin 2004).

Telling life stories offers an occasion for the sadhus to speak about the many ways that divinity acts in their lives and guides them in their daily decision-making. It also helps them to think about the relationship between human aspiration and divine will. These seemingly disparate streams of thought—a conspicuous feature of Indian narrative traditions in general, including epic and hagiographical genres[8]—permeate the sadhus' personal narratives and present competing ideologies at the level of everyday thought and practice. Wrestling with these concepts in the construction of their experiences and identities draws into focus the sadhus' understandings of agency—meaning, simply stated, the capacity to act and affect others' actions toward a desired outcome—which, in turn, interrogate predominantly western neoliberal models of agency as subversive (Mahmood 2005; Jassal 2012; Knight 2011; Patton 2004; Kratz 2000).

To take an example, before performing her rhetoric of renunciation, Ganga Giri likes to say, "Shivji rests in the throat, and Saraswati rests on the tongue. In the throat is Mahadev Shankar *bhagwān*. And Saraswati is on the tongue. You cannot sing just like that. You can only sing when the gods come. The songs don't just come [into the mind] like that. They're not lying on the road." Ganga Giri makes a specific argument about agency here. Her capacity to act, and influence others' actions, depends on divine forces beyond her immediate control. She sings only when the gods come and cause her to sing. To that extent, Ganga Giri sees herself as an *instrument* of divine agency. Ganga Giri's view of agency compares to recent analytic models that represent (female) agency (and subjectivity) as an emergent phenomenon, i.e., as imagined and constituted by means of practice (Mahmood 2005; cf. Knight 2011; Keller 2002).

In her work on the women's Islamic piety movement in Cairo, Egypt, anthropologist Saba Mahmood argues, on the basis of her research, that agency is not experienced in the radical reenvisioning of patriarchal norms. Rather, it arises in the performative (re)interpretations of those norms (e.g., female modesty). Mahmood explains, "the most interesting features of this debate lie not so much in whether the norm of modesty is subverted or enacted, but in the radically different ways in which the norm is supposed to be lived and inhabited" (2005, 23–24). The personal narratives of the sadhus similarly indicate that their agency as female renouncers is exercised by means of the practices described in this book, and not through the subversion of normative patriarchal structures and institutions. Constructing singing *bhajans* as *sannyās* performs their agency. Another way, signaled earlier, involves what the sadhus say they do as they sing—they place their individual intentions at God's feet. The disclaiming of agency, therefore, also performs female agency in vernacular asceticism. The legitimacy that the sadhus attribute to their asceticism and the "fruits" that they say they acquire from singing *bhajans* result from their ability to surrender to a power greater than themselves.

Apart from shining new light on female agency in *sannyās*, personal storytelling opens up a discursive space for the sadhus to remember and praise God by discussing their individual experiences of God's immanent power and presence in their lives. The sadhus' performing of the rhetoric of renunciation, including the sharing of personal narratives, functions rhetorically as a testimonial to the mysterious workings of divine providence in the universe. After singing a song, narrating a story, or reciting a sacred text, Ganga Giri says, "God has come here [in *satsang*] and that's why we're remembering him. It's not that we remember God and then God comes. When God is close, the devotee remembers [him]." From this angle, the personal narratives analyzed in the following discussion represent, as Lawless has characterized for the female Pentecostal preachers with whom she worked, "spiritual" life stories (1988, 60). These stories, as with the vernacular stories featured in the next chapter, and their songs and sacred texts discussed in this book arose in *satsang* contexts—whatever facilitates an occasion to remember God is seen as *satsang* to the sadhus. But I approached their personal storytelling sessions as opportunities to ask the sadhus more direct questions about their lives. In that way, my queries encouraged them to tell their stories in a linear fashion. However, what should become clear to the reader, as she or he moves through the book, is the fluidity of these rhetorical genres in the sadhus' practices.

Thus, this chapter suggests that telling personal narratives provides a way for the sadhus to construct themselves not only as exceptions to gender norms, but also as sadhus who experience agency, power, and authority in a gendered way. Interwoven in their constructions are the three themes of duty (*kartavya*), destiny (*bhāgya*), and devotion (*bhakti*), which compose the core of the ideology of exceptionalism performed in their stories. Foregrounding these themes, the sadhus make explicit a gendered discourse on agency as instrumental, that is, as the result of divine will, in *sannyās*. Along with that, the sadhus promote a perception of difference, neutralize widespread societal views of their asceticism as transgressive (i.e., in taking *sannyās* they are only doing what God tells them to do), and sanction their identities as divine servants. While the sadhus invoke duty, destiny, and devotion to resist the notion of agency in their becoming sadhus (i.e., to deny that they have *chosen* to become sadhus), these concepts function as "disclaimers of intent" (Lawless 1988) with which they exercise female agency and establish their female sadhu tradition as an alternative to the mainstream representations. By analyzing the themes, we may understand the ways in which female sadhus in North India create and negotiate their authority, power, and legitimacy in an institution in which they are often seen as marginal.[9]

"Doing God's Work": *Duty*

In their personal narratives, *kartavya* appeared consistently and provided a conceptual frame out of which the sadhus stitched the content and structure of their stories. Almost all of the sadhus understood *kartavya* to mean their duty and responsibility to God or the Goddess, with whom they had developed an intense relationship or "connection [*dorī*]" since childhood. Their perceived connection with the divine was not only the most significant relationship in these sadhu women's lives; it also singularly determined how they lived as female renouncers.

As an illustration, Shiv Puri carefully described her intimate relationship with God and with the Goddess and their direct influence over her life, from the everyday "business" decisions she makes about running the ashram, to the spiritual decisions she makes about her religious practices. A sadhu in her early sixties (in 2005), Shiv Puri heads a sprawling ashram that is nestled between two mountains in a small town approximately fifty-six miles north of Udaipur city. For six months out of the year, she stays at her ashram, and the rest of the time she travels to Mumbai, visiting devotees and collecting donations for her growing temple complex. Her son Shankar, his wife, and their three children also reside at the ashram full-time. Shiv Puri's relationship with Shankar and his family is, as she explained, that of a guru and her disciples, implying it is not a biological one of mother and son. As the resident *pujārī* and *pujāriṇī*, Shankar and his wife perform the rituals to the different deities in the temple, including those to the goddess Kali Ma, and manage the temple grounds in

Shiv Puri's absence. In May 2005, right before the monsoon season, Shiv Puri and Shankar were overseeing the construction of another, larger ashram on her property, the purpose of which was to accommodate more guests at the site. One afternoon that summer, while holding her youngest "disciple," or granddaughter, in her lap, Shiv Puri discussed her relationship with God and the Goddess as one of duty. On his breaks from construction work, Shankar would stop by and listen to his guru's telling of her life story.

A [ANTOINETTE]: There's a lot going on here [at the ashram]. You're very busy, right?
SP [SHIV PURI]: How?
A: In maintaining the ashram.
SP: Actually, it's like this: Bholenath [lit., "innocent Lord"; a regional form of the god Shiva that is popular in Rajasthan] and Durga Mai [a name for the Goddess] talk to me through my soul [*ātmā*]. Now, when God tells me, "You have to do this" and "it's imperative that you do this," to me this means that I have to do whatever God tells me to do... Before I was a sadhu, I lived as a householder. I used to see so many *sants* [lit., "good people"] and sadhus that whenever they would visit [my home] I thought [that] I am seeing God [in seeing their form]. When I became a sadhu, I also traveled a lot in India; I traveled a lot with sadhus, but I didn't see God anymore [in their form]... I neither have the interest [*ruci*] to live amongst other sadhus, nor do I have any interest to live as a householder. God has directly released me from this ocean of existence [*sāgar se*] and made me happier [*sukhāntar karnā*] [because of it]. So, I have to do His work... Therefore, my only interest is to do God's work, and [God] will do the rest.

This passage implicitly relates the notion of *kartavya* as a determinative force in Shiv Puri's life through her use of the compulsory form of the Hindi verb "*karnā*," meaning "to have to do" (*karnā hai*). As a noun, *kartavya* means not only "duty," but also "what is to be done," and connotes the idea of responsibility and obligation.[10] Shiv Puri herself alludes to *kartavya* as her duty and obligation in her explanation at four different points in her story in the context of her statement, "I have to do God's work." This conversation on her life emerged from my observation about the construction work being done at her ashram. Shiv Puri responds to my statement by emphasizing that the work at the temple is not of her doing, but rather it is what Bholenath and the Durga Mai order her to do as their devotee. By framing her response in this way, Shiv Puri suggests the lack of personal agency on her part in determining the course of her life, carefully constructing her religious and social actions as an obligatory part of what she perceives to be a mutually dependent (*āpas men; paraspar*) relationship with God and the Goddess. In this framework, Shiv Puri's every action and every decision is singularly determined and guided by what God (*bhagwān* or Bholenath) tells her to do. As she makes explicit in this passage, Shiv Puri must obey God's word; it is her duty as God's devotee.

Although she does not use the word *kartavya* in this conversation, Shiv Puri has used it in many other conversations about her life and work. Like Shiv Puri, most of the sadhus referred directly to *kartavya* in descriptions of themselves as the "beggars [*bhikārī*]," or "peons [*caparāsī*]" of God, and of their life work as "a duty to serve." Incorporating both valences of the term, Tulsi Giri told me while we sat in the spacious ashram of her guru, Mahaprayag Giri, whom she was visiting for the upcoming holiday of *Guru Pūrṇimā*,[11] that "we sadhus are the beggars of God [*bhagwān ke bhikārī*)], and our duty is to serve you as a form of God." For the sadhus, serving humanity occurs through various means, such as sharing their teachings, offering counsel, singing songs and prayers, telling stories, reciting texts, and feeding others "with love." As Ganga Giri, the informal, "dada-guru" of Tulsi Giri, said: "Love is what God is [*prem hai jo bhagwān hai*]." These interrelated practices "perform" the sadhus' duty par excellence and depict different ways of doing "God's work," who, as they said, exists in everything and everyone.

Perhaps most significant to this analysis of *kartavya* is that the sadhus' duty to God stems from their being God's *bhakts* as well as from their being called by God to become sadhus in this birth, for the sole purpose of serving God or the Goddess in that capacity. In her study of Pentecostal women preachers of Missouri, Lawless has observed that these women's spiritual life stories consistently related the theme of their being called by God to "preach from the pulpit," in light of which they were able to legitimize their individual claims to spiritual power (1988, 76–80). In the sadhus' personal narratives we find use of a similar narrative idiom of "the call." Shiv Puri's statement that "God has directly released me from this ocean of existence and made me happier. So, I have to do his work," indicates her perception that her life represents God's decision, and not her own, with which she is clearly, as she says, "happier" as a result. Shiv Puri also suggests that, though chosen by God, she, too, has to make a disciplined effort to live the kind of life that God has decided for her. That is, God may have decided her fate, but, in the end, Shiv Puri has to act in a manner that demonstrates and brings about God's plan for her life.

Thus, to the sadhus, *sannyās* represents the actualization of a divine directive. And, not unlike the meanings that the Pentecostal women preachers whom Lawless describes attributed to their uncommon positions of authority, the extent to which the sadhus succeed in their path itself serves as ever present proof of God's power over their lives (1988, 76). The sadhus, therefore, exercise agency by taking control of their lives (after all, they decide whether or not to follow the plan that God has for them). Yet, mindful that direct claims to the status and authority conveyed by their position could, in fact, delegitimize them as "good women" in the eyes of their society, the sadhus' agency is carefully couched in terms of being the result of God's will. The sadhus' life stories suggest, then, that they experience agency in an "instrumental" way (Keller 2002).

In her cross-cultural analysis of spirit possession, historian of religion Mary Keller formulates the hermeneutic of instrumental agency and suggests that it challenges widespread academic (and Western) views of agency as individualistic and voluntaristic (2002, 73–102). She says, "Reflecting on these terms, the most fundamental analysis of the agency of the possessed body is that it is instrumental in the possession. Consciousness is overcome, and the body is used like a hammer or played like a flute... so that the possessed body is an *instrumental agency* in the possession" (Keller 2002, 74; emphasis in original). Though Keller's analytic applies to the experiences of possessed women, it can also be used to explain the sadhus' experiences of renunciation. Like the possessed women whom Keller describes, the sadhus, too, see themselves as instruments "played" by God. They believe that their individual actions align with and manifest divine intentionality. At the same time, the sadhus' instrumental agency signals the corollary notion that they perceive themselves as "receptive" (Keller 2002), rather than as passive to the possibility of divine motivations acting on and pushing them in new or unexpected directions. Seeing their lives and their actions through the gendered lens of receptive agency, the sadhus navigate societal expectations and their individual desires, as only a fool would question God's ultimate authority, by virtue of whom they are able to script alternative lives. To that extent, the sadhus' emphasis on duty disclaims intention in their becoming sadhus.[12] By disclaiming intention, they are able to exercise instrumental agency as female sadhus and work within normative androcentric constructions of femininity. But how did the sadhus know they were chosen by God? What were the signs that led them to such an interpretation of their lives?

"Everything Happens Because of Fate": *Destiny*

To answer this question, we need to consider the next narrative theme of destiny, or fate. Almost every sadhu I talked to interpreted not only her asceticism, but also, more generally, all the momentous life events (such as the life cycle, or life-altering experiences of marriage, childbirth, widowhood, death, meeting the guru, and initiation into *sannyās*) as the result of destiny. What is more, the social realities of existence (such as caste and class status, education levels, disease or health, the food eaten on a specific day, the conversations in which they engaged, and so forth) illustrated to the sadhus the ripening of their *bhāgya*. Included in this framework was my relationship with the sadhus, who called me their sister, friend, or disciple, and told me that my meeting sadhus in India happened "because it was written in my destiny."

An example of the way that the sadhus viewed their asceticism as the result of destiny is the personal narrative of Ganga Giri, who shared many stories about her experiences of meeting her guru, Gauri Giriji, in Kashi.[13] On the day that Ganga Giri narrated the story of how she first met her guru, Manvendra Singh was also present. In her words:

GANGA GIRI [GG]: My guru was at the Sri Mahant Akhara [place of assembly for Dashanami sadhus] in Kashi. He gave me *dīkṣā* [initiation] when he was eighty-five years old... He was eighty-five years old, but his body was like an elephant's, big and fat. My guru was old. He was the Mahant [director] of the *akhāḍhā* [ascetic order] forty years.

MANVENDRA SINGH [MS]: He gave you *dīkṣā* [initiation]?

GG: Yes, he gave me *dīkṣā*... This was my fate [*kismet*]... I didn't know that I'd go to Kashi without a penny or that I'd come to wear the ochre robes [*bhagmā pahanā*]... [My guru's] name was Sri Mahant Gauri Giri.

MS: Gauri Giriji?

ANTOINETTE [A]: O.k., Gauri Giriji was your guru.

GG: He lived in Kashi... But, originally, he lived here in Udaipur, in the village of Savina. He stayed in Chittor at the Kali Mata temple [a Kali temple located within the Chittorgarh fort]. Then he stayed at another [unnamed] Goddess temple near Ayar [name of a colony in Udaipur] and lived there for nineteen years. He lived during the royal court [*darbār*] of Fateh Singh [ca. 1884-1930; the great grandfather of Udaipur's current Maharana, Arvind Singh]... It's been many years.

MS: How many years have passed since then? Sixty, seventy?

GG: Yes. It was during the time of Fateh Singh. He stayed [at the Kali Mata temple] for twenty years, and then left [for Kashi]. He knew the language of this place [i.e., Rajasthan].

MS: The Mewari language?

GG: Yes. He noticed the way I lived and started to speak [Mewari] to me. He asked me, "Bai [sister], where do you live?" But people don't speak like this in Kashi.

MS: No one will speak Mewari there.

GG: Yes, they don't speak like this [in Kashi]. I looked around for this voice and didn't see anyone. I was sitting outside of the door [of a temple, the name of which is unspecified here]. It was shut. There was no one outside talking. I looked and saw the door was shut, but the window was open. He asked, "Which village do you live in? I am from Sarara village. What is your *gotra* [i.e., an exogamous subdivision of a caste group]? Are you a Goswami [which is, actually, Ganga Giri's *gotra*]? Did you make the *darśan* [i.e., a sacred viewing] of Lord Vishvanath? Are you hungry? Do you have to eat?"

I didn't speak to him. But I had to eat. I was hungry.

He had this gold tiffin[14] with three parts. Each part could fit a kilo [of food]. It was so big that tiffin. He took it and went to Shankartaya [the name of her guru's *akhāḍhā*] to bring bread... It's a small place, our *akhāḍhā*. My guru Maharaj used to sit and do *sādhanā* [spiritual practice]. He did this for forty years. Afterwards, he became old. Later, someone else sat on the seat [i.e., took over the *akhāḍhā*]. He used to care for that small place; he used to come to the *akhāḍhā* to take *rotīs* [breads]. He said, "Child [*betā*, unisex term of endearment for children], I am going to take *rotīs*. Don't go." He told me, "Come on, child. Let's go. When did you eat *rotī*? Let's go. I am your father and you are my daughter." There wasn't any wrath in his words. But I didn't have any faith. I thought, "Where will he take me?" I had never seen him before. They [i.e., some sadhus she had seen at the temple where she originally heard her guru's voice] told me, "He's our very old *mahant* [i.e., institutional head of the ashram]. Go with him [to the *akhāḍhā*]."... I thought if he walks ahead of me, I'll go in another gulley and leave. But he made me walk first. He said, "You go first." I asked myself, "Is this destiny? What's happening to me?"

MS: It was your destiny...

GG: Because of destiny, people get everything: food, bread, the guru. Everything in life is a matter of fate.

Even before she had narrated this story about Gauri Giriji, Ganga Giri had mentioned a number of times in our meetings that she had "found" her guru in Kashi "because of destiny." Her phrasing of the sentence relates this idea: "*mujh ko guru mile.*" To express the notion of meeting someone in Hindi requires use of the indirect construction of the verb *milnā*, meaning "to meet." Depending on how one phrases the construction, the sentence can convey either the idea of direct agency, as in the speaker intended to meet someone, or it can convey potentiality, that the encounter happened "by accident" or "by chance." In this case, an accurate translation for *milnā* would also be "to find," as in "to come upon by chance."[15] Ganga Giri's wording of the sentence communicates the latter (and, as I suggest, receptive) sense of the term—her encounter with the guru was "by chance," an encounter she had not intentionally planned or expected. In her story, too, she specifically interprets her experience of meeting Gauri Giriji as one of chance, emphasizing destiny at three different points and telling her audience that "this was my fate."

While it is commonly said in India that individuals seeking to renounce the world go to Kashi (or Haridwar) with only that intention in mind, Ganga Giri's interpretation provides a counterpoint to this assumption. Not only did she not know that she would find her guru in Kashi, but she also did not know that she would "come to wear the ochre robes" by travelling to Kashi. Everything that happened to her there was unplanned and unexpected. Once she arrived in Kashi, Gauri Giriji, as Ganga Giri performs the story, seemed to know from the moment of their initial encounter that Ganga Giri would become his disciple, and he actively pursued her. But Ganga Giri resisted his attempts. Both her explicit resistance to Gauri Giriji and her implicit fear of him similarly support her view that destiny, and not her own personal choices, played a role in her becoming a sadhu. In the end, however, Ganga Giri became Gauri Giri's disciple and renounced the world, because it was her fate. She accentuates this at the end of her story: "[b]ecause of destiny, people get everything: food, bread, the guru. Everything in life is a matter of fate."

Not only is "everything in life," as Ganga Giri highlights, "a matter of fate," it is, more significantly, "written" by God or, as some of the sadhus told me, by God's attendant, the goddess Vidhata Mata, in a book that is kept, as the sadhus say, "in God's office [*daftar*]." According to the sadhus, at the time of our death, God "reads [*bāncnā*]" what has been written in the book and therewith pronounces our fate, which cannot be changed. Of course, in their descriptions of *bhāgya*, the sadhus emphasize that it signifies the cumulative effect of all our actions from a previous birth (*pūrva janam*) and manifests in the present birth at the appropriate moment. In this light, while God writes our every word, thought, and deed in God's book, we—or more precisely, our actions—(*karm*) affect and, thus, plot the course of our future births.

Another sadhu, Maya Nath, who manages a popular Bholenath temple with an adjoining ashram approximately fifteen miles outside of Udaipur city in Gogunda, similarly recited a local idiom that effectively highlights the impact of both *bhāgya* and *karm*, destiny and action, in determining the course and shape of a person's life: "You act [as if] no one is watching, but I [Vidhata Mata] write [your deeds] page-by-page." Ganga Giri gave me an elaborate explanation of how she perceives the interface between *bhāgya* and *karm*. She said,

> Whatever we say, whatever we think, automatically becomes written in [God's] book. It gets written in our future [*bhāg*]. This is our destiny. Our actions [*karm*] turn into letters [*akṣar*]... Every thought will turn into a letter.... If you curse [*gālī denā*] someone, that, too, will be written in your destiny... Like, you are writing [my words] here [in your notebook]... In that way [our destiny] is being written there [in God's book].

Thus, by invoking the dual narrative themes of destiny and *karm*, the sadhus related "opposed and complementary" notions of agency in their taking of renunciation (Babb 1983, 173; cf. Mahmood 2005 for a discussion of modes of agency). Citing the research of Sheryl B. Daniel and E. Valentine Daniel, who discuss the availability of two alternative theories of fate, namely "headwriting" and *karm* in Tamil Nadu, Lawrence Babb has suggested that,

> [T]o refer to headwriting is to establish a frame of reference in which the individual ultimately has no control over his actions and is thus not finally responsible for his destiny. Conversely, to stress karma is to lay emphasis on willful action, and thus to imply genuine moral responsibility. Which of these frames of reference is chosen depends on the interests and intentions of the chooser. If he wishes to elude blame for some misdeed, or to console himself with the thought of the inevitability of some misfortune, then the fatalistic interpretation will have an obvious appeal. But if he wishes to stress the culpability of the performer of some misdeed, or to encourage himself in the belief that the course of his destiny can be altered for the better, then the karmic frame of reference is the most suitable recourse. (Babb 1983, 173)

Babb's thesis is helpful in analyzing the sadhus' emphasis on *bhāgya* and *karm* with which they negotiate their ambiguous positions as female renouncers. Interpreting their lives through the framework of destiny, the sadhus not only invoke a higher moral order (which no one can judge) to sanction their asceticism, but also exercise their agency as female sadhus in a chiefly patriarchal society and religious institution that often marginalizes them because they are women. By emphasizing destiny as the original source of their *sannyās*, the sadhus suggest that they have little or no control over becoming renouncers in this birth. In their perspectives, destiny will happen when it is meant to happen, and when it does, they cannot be stopped by anyone from manifesting their destiny of becoming sadhus (as Ganga Giri said, "Who could stop me [from becoming a sadhu]?"). Much like the concept of duty, the sadhus' emphasis on destiny in representing their asceticism serves as a disclaimer for performing female agency as receptive (and not intentional) in *sannyās*, rather than an excuse for passivity.[16] Perceiving their lives through this popular cultural lens enables the sadhus to take control of their lives and, by extension, their destinies.[17] The idea of destiny promotes the instrumental agency of the sadhus, motivating them to act and manifest the life that they say God has chosen for them in the current birth. Evidence that destiny creates agency in renunciation is underscored by the fact that most of the sadhus juxtapose the notions of destiny and *karm*, implying that individual action works in close conjunction with destiny. Thus, while destiny operates as a shared cultural framework for many Indians—Hindu, Muslim, or Christian—the sadhus refer to this concept in their interpretations and constructions of asceticism as a way to legitimate their unusual lives.

The integration of the combined narrative themes of *bhāgya* and *karm* provides an idiom with which the sadhus suggest that their renunciation represents neither a personal choice to break away from society's constructed normative gender roles, nor an escape from domestic hardship, as their society often erroneously assumes. Instead, though asceticism is a divinely prescribed path of action, it is first and foremost considered to be a destined path of devotional and dutiful action to the sadhus. And while destiny may put them on that path, the sadhus understand that they still have to make "good" and disciplined efforts to manifest what they believe is their legitimate destiny. As Sharda Puri, a sadhu from Losingh village in Udaipur district, explained: "Just as the lines of destiny can be increased by good works, so can they can be erased, too, by bad works." In their views, *bhāgya* and *karm* mysteriously interface and intertwine in the actualization of what they perceive as a divine directive, which the sadhus feel in their souls (*ātmā*)—that inner, secret place where God and the Goddess speak to them.

Since it is impossible to prove, empirically at least, that one's religious life represents the fated fruit (*phal*) of the good works (*karm*) from a past life, the sadhus understand their lives more globally as the product of "God's will [*bhagwān kī iccā*]," even as they affirm the importance of *karm* as source of destiny. And, in India, people can easily inquire about their destiny by visiting either the family astrologer (*jyotiṣī*) or the family guru, who, based on details such as the time, day, and place of birth, reads the supplicant's horoscope by consulting several astrological texts. Other avenues for determining destiny include, but are not limited to, the prophecy of holy people and visions (*darśan*) of divine beings (or even family members with prescient abilities).

All of these cultural mediums for predicting destiny are indicative of God's will. As such, it is not unusual to find them as salient motifs in the sadhus' personal narratives.

For instance, parts of Shiv Puri's life story underscored each of these motifs in order to support her interpretation of her asceticism as the manifestation of her destiny. As her namesake suggests, Shiv Puri was born on the Hindu holy day of *Shiva Rātri*, a festival honoring the god Shiva; due to the auspicious day of her birth, Shiv Puri's parents named her Shiva. Three days after her birth, however, her mother went mad (*pāgal*) for eighty days. After relating these events to the family astrologer, Shiv Puri's father learned that his daughter would become a sadhu by the age of thirty-two. As she told me, "that astrologer explained all the details of my birth to my father and said, 'when this girl of yours is thirty-two, she'll surely become a sadhu. It's final, fixed.' This happened when I was only three." Two more events revealed to Shiv Puri her alternative life path: a vision or appearance (*dṛṣṭānt darśan*) of the deities Bholenath and Durga Mai, who told her that she would become a sadhu exactly two years after the birth of her third child, a son; and a powerful prophecy made by her mother, Indra Kunwar, that she would "sit on the throne of a sadhu, and people would come from all over India to pay her their respects."

In response to my question, "How did you know that you would become a sadhu in this life?" Shiv Puri vividly recounted her experience of having received the *darśan* of Bholenath and Durga Mai, suggesting that this vision provided proof of her destiny. With her "disciple," Shankar, sitting by her side, this is how Shiv Puri told me and others present that story.

SP: I was telling you [before] that I had Chanda [my eldest daughter] and one more girl. Then my soul made a request to God: "Bholenath, I am about to leave [my family]." This happened. So, [after a while], Bholenath told me, "A son has been born [to you]." Bholenath spoke to me as if I already had a son; but I didn't have a son. Twelve months before [Shankar was born], God told me this. He said, "Now don't leave [to become a sadhu] for two more years." [In the vision] I could see myself with a young son, and I had placed him on my shoulders.

[MALE AUDIENCE MEMBER]: This was a dream?

A: This happened to you in a dream?

SP: (emphasizes) This [experience] was nothing like a dream. I had a vision [uses the Hindi word "*dṛṣṭānt*" to describe her experience]. [Shiv Puri returns to recounting this visionary experience] With the child on my shoulders, I climbed a step; there was water coming from somewhere.

I climbed another step. I kept climbing like this, until I reached the top of a mountain. There was a Shivji temple over there.

A: O.k.

SP: It was a Shivji temple, but inside I couldn't find Shivji. I only saw the sparkling of diamonds. None of the gods and goddesses were present [in the temple]. So, a grandmother-like figure appeared [to me]. I said [to her], "Maharaj [a respectful way of addressing the caretaker of a temple], whose temple is this?"

She said to me, "This is the temple of three-hundred and sixty million gods and goddesses." She spoke like this. I went inside and saw that there wasn't a single god. So, I told her, "There isn't a single god in here!" [But then she responded]

"Your personal god is just coming." Nandi [the cow who appears with Shiva] was seated [in the temple]... My son grabbed his feet, and then Shivji appeared. Shivji appeared in this form [points to the poster on a nearby wall that depicts an ash-covered Shiva as an ascetic].

A: He appeared [to you] in that form?

SP: With this form. He gave me *darśan* four times.

A: In that form, right?

SP: Yes, in that form.

A: O.k., in the form of an ascetic... And when Shivji appeared before you [Shiv Puri finishes the thought]

SP: It was only this form of Shiva [who appeared].

A: Right, but this form came in a dream?

SP: No, not a dream.

[MALE AUDIENCE MEMBER/VISITOR AT SHIV PURI'S ASHRAM]: She said "*dṛṣṭānt*" it means a feeling, a sight [of the deity] came to her.

SP: [repeats the word] *Dṛṣṭānt*... It happened in an awakened [*jāgṛt*] state.

[MALE AUDIENCE MEMBER]: Meaning, when God gives *darśan*, he himself comes directly to you.

A: O.k.

SP: [In this state] My eyes were opened, and then the sight [*nazar*] [of Shiva] came. Then, the light [*prakāś*] was falling [from Shiva's palm that was facing her]. From [Shiva's] hands, the light was falling. He was giving [me] blessings [*aśirvād*].

A: O.k.

SP: The light was so strong that my eyes closed suddenly. Then God spoke the *guru mantra* [i.e., the sacred poetic verses the guru whispers into the disciple's ear at the time of initiation] from his very mouth [*mukhāvind*]. I learned it.

A: [Shivji] gave you the *guru mantra*?

SP: I studied that *mantra*. Shivji gave the *guru mantra*, right? Then Mother [referring to Durga Mai] was standing nearby him [to Shivji]. I said, "Mother, you, too, give me blessings." She said, "Make a request; make a request. What do you need?" I said, "I need to see everything in this world in the form of the mother."

A: [You wanted to see] Everything in the form of the Mother.

SP: Yes. [I said] "I need to see everything in the form of the Mother; not anything bad." The mother said, "So be it" [*tathāstu*]. Shivji gave me *darśan*. A year later, he was born [pointing to Shankar who is seated by her side].

In this segment of her story, Shiv Puri's telling reinforces her perception of the personal relationship she has with Bholenath and Durga Mai. Just as these deities ordered her to build a bigger ashram for the growing number of devotees who visit the site, in the same way they, or at least Bholenath (whose name she interchanges with Shiva's throughout the story), told Shiv Puri to remain a householder for two more years after the birth of her third child, Shankar. The deities communicate with Shiv Puri through means of her divine visions, which she refers to as *dṛṣṭānt*, and which happen to her while she remains in "an awakened state." More significantly, to justify her view that destiny played a role in her becoming a sadhu in this birth, Shiv Puri's narrative construction of her visionary experience pivots on her receiving the *guru mantra* from Shiva—those sacred syllables the guru whispers into the disciple's ear at the time of initiation (*dīkṣā*) into renunciation. The ascetic form in which Shiva appears to Shiv Puri in her vision is also especially significant, as it symbolically portends her fate to become a sadhu.

Through her telling Shiv Puri not only constructs herself as the disciple of Shiva and Durga Mai, but also performs her perception that God initiated her as a sadhu. The vision itself constitutes a form of initiation into the tradition of renunciation while Shiv Puri is still a householder. Her being a householder at the time of her initiation seems to have posed no obstacle for Shiv Puri because, as she emphasized in an earlier conversation, since her childhood she had considered herself as a sadhu, not as a householder. Her narrative reconstruction of the vision in which she sees herself carrying a boy child on her shoulders also implies that the deities sanctioned her householder status, at least for a little while. Her being a householder might even signify to Shiv Puri a form of *kartavya* to the gods, on account of which Shiva and Durga Mai send to her womb a disciple who will help her to run her ashram so that she can serve the gods as a sadhu later on in her life. That is, from the narrative's point of view, that the child in the Shiv Puri's vision is the same person who helps her to manage her expanding ashram today is hardly coincidental—Bholenath and Durga Mai know what is best for Shiv Puri, even if it means that she must remain a householder, albeit temporarily, in order to fulfill her duty to them as a sadhu.

In other conversations, I learned that Shiv Puri does, in fact, have a mortal guru; however, she only recognizes Shiva and Durga Mai as her formal teachers. On the same day she told me this story, Shiv Puri also said, "I didn't learn from a guru; I didn't learn from anyone. I made a guru; but I didn't learn from anyone. Shivji gave me the *guru mantra* directly." To be sure, by attributing her initiation into *sannyās* to Shiva and Durga Mai, Shiv Puri legitimates her spiritual position as a female sadhu in what is often viewed as a male-dominated tradition of renunciation. At the same time, though, Shiv Puri suggests that her relationship with the divine and its duties supersede all other types of relationships—not only the spiritual relationship she has with her mortal guru, but even the worldly relationships she once had with her children and family as a householder. Although essential to an interpretation of Shiv Puri's life, similar external portents of destiny appear as motifs in only some of the sadhus' stories. Lacking these signs, how did the sadhus know that destiny played a crucial role in the unfolding of their lives?

"I Found Truth in…Singing Bhajans to God": *Devotion*

Like duty and destiny, devotion also appeared as a defining narrative theme in the sadhus' life stories. Their descriptions of *bhakti* strengthened their claims of having an intimate relationship with the divine (imagined as both with and without characteristics) and refracted the larger frame of duty in which their story constructions emerged and took shape. They conceptualized *bhakti* as an intense feeling of love, respect, and devotion to God and expressed it in their daily lives through private or communal devotional singing (*bhajan satsang*), prayer and meditation, scriptural recitation, and deity worship in temples or other sacred places.

In all of the stories of the sadhus interviewed, devotion arose "automatically" in their childhood. The immediate and unexplained arising of devotion at a time in their lives when they should have been "jumping and playing" like other children their age signaled to the sadhus the ripening of their destiny and the beginning of a life of singing *bhajans*. Ganga Giri explained:

> When I was young, my father was a *satsangī* [one who held devotional meetings or *satsangs*]. He used to sing *bhajans*. My grandfather, the

> old man, used to sit in the front [of the *satsang*] and sing *bhajans*, too. His disciple was also an old man who also sang *bhajans*. I started singing *bhajans*, too. I was crazy [*bāvlī*] then, I just kept singing to God and [did] nothing else. I still remember that time. I must have learned three-hundred and fifty *bhajans* by the time I was five or six years old, just while playing and jumping in my childhood.

As with Shiv Puri's implicit use of *kartavya* in the telling of her life story, in this passage, too, Ganga Giri does not explicitly use the word *bhakti* to represent what might strike the reader as an exceptional childhood religiosity. However, threaded throughout her story is the view that singing *bhajans* is equivalent to an experience of the arising of the kind of *bhakti* that ultimately leads to *sannyās*. The phrase "singing *bhajans*" not only foregrounds the notion of uncommon devotion to God—uncommon because it starts at an early age and consumes the mental landscape of the practitioner—but also functions as a vernacular narrative trope that signifies Ganga Giri's singing experiences as *sannyās*. In my conversations with the sadhus I realized that their repeated use of "singing *bhajans* to *bhagwān*" acted like a shared gendered code, or symbolic language, alluding to the spontaneous and all-consuming devotional experience of the divine.

During extended interviews, when asked to define *sannyās*,[18] the sadhus always talked about the concept by drawing on the metaphor of "singing *bhajans*." As Ganga Giri said, "renunciation means to sing to God." Making the association that singing *bhajans* signified the practice of *bhakti*, I queried the sadhus further to learn whether they, too, saw *sannyās* as a type of *bhakti*. Without exception, they replied that *sannyās* and *bhakti* represent "the same thing [*ek hī bāt hai*]." Ganga Giri, for instance, explained that "renunciation is simply *bhakti*; there is no difference between them." In this light, whether explicit or implicit in the sadhus' narratives, the theme of *bhakti* is polyvalent and must be understood in terms of a broader context of meaning, in which "singing *bhajans*" simultaneously identifies a metaphor for renunciant *bhakti* and for *sannyās*. To the sadhus, singing performs their idea of *sannyās* par excellence, as it allows them to dedicate themselves to God, and in doing so, fulfill the destinies for which they were born.

Concomitant with their experiences of the spontaneous emerging of *bhakti* were also feelings of detachment (*vairāg*) from family members, school, and household responsibilities, and especially from the pressing societal expectations of marriage and domesticity. Tulsi Giri told me that, "from the beginning of my life, I found truth [*satya*] by singing *bhajans* to *bhagwān*." Absorbed in the intensity of her renunciant devotion, Tulsi Giri became detached from constricting societal concerns, because of which she vehemently resisted her parents' repeated attempts to arrange her marriage. She explained, "I didn't want to marry... I took the wedding jewelry that came from my in-laws and threw it [away]." Devotion to God, therefore, not only facilitated the sadhus' detachment; it also made them brave.[19] A common pattern in their stories was rebellion against parental (or anyone else's) attempts to thwart their devotional, and by extension, their blossoming asceticism. A vignette from Ganga Giri's story relates this idea:

> My father used to say, "Don't sing *bhajans*." I said, "you keep singing *bhajans*, so why can't I sing?" He said, "we can sing, but you don't sing!" I asked why, and he said, "because then you'll become *abhisānī*." I said, "What is *abhisānī*?" He said, "it means you'll become a sadhu." I used to say [to him], "I will sing *bhajans* and become a sadhu." I must have said this ten times, at least.

Here, Ganga Giri suggests that becoming a sadhu in adulthood seems to be "continuous" with her childhood experiences of singing *bhajans* to God and, along with that, of detachment from the world (cf. Bynum 1992; see also Khandelwal 2004, 181–84; Vallely 2002). While the ceremony of taking initiation into renunciation may formalize (legally and socially) the women's renunciant identities, the ritual itself does not signify a cognitive rupture from the perception that they have always maintained of themselves in their childhood and adulthood—that of singing as *sannyās*. A. K. Ramanujan (1999a, b, c), Caroline Walker Bynum (1987), Tessa Bartholomeusz (1996), Meena Khandelwal (2004), and more recently, Lisa Knight (2011) have argued that women's renunciation and, more precisely, the symbols, idioms, and categories that women use to represent their experiences of it, signify "continuity"—rather than liminality—with their biological and social roles as mothers, nurturers, and caretakers, in contrast to male experiences of rupture from their everyday roles (cf. Gold 1994, 151). As Bynum has explained,

> [W]omen's sense of religious self seems more continuous with their sense of social and biological self; women's images are most profoundly deepenings, not inversions of what 'woman' is; women's symbols express less contradiction and opposition than synthesis and paradox. (Bynum 1987, 289)

In the sadhus' cases, the theme of singing *bhajans* effectively links the religiosity or religious tendencies of their childhood with their renunciation of the world in adulthood, and hence, validates their *sannyās* and renunciant identities. Moreover, as with duty and destiny, the sadhus' emphasis on (radical) devotion points to a gendered disclaimer of intention with which they exercise instrumental agency as female sadhus in *sannyās*. The motifs of duty, destiny, and devotion, however, more than justify the sadhus' *sannyās* and affirm their agency; they also situate the sadhus in a pan-Indian framework of extraordinary female devotional religiosity.

Accentuating duty, destiny, and devotion, the sadhus construct their lives in ways that reflect themes similar to those found in classical and vernacular-language narratives about the religious lives of India's legendary (and controversial) female *bhakti* saints, such as the earliest poet-saint, the Tamil Nayanar Karaikkal Ammaiyar (cf. Pechilis 2011),[20] the Kannada saint Mahadeviyakka, the Tamil Alvar Antal, Bahinabai of Maharashtra, Mira Bai of Rajasthan, and Lalleshwari of Kashmir (Ramanujan 1999b). In fact, the sadhus' telling of their life stories parallels their telling of vernacular narratives about the Mira Bai's life, in which duty, destiny, and devotion, as well as rebellion against authority, appear as salient themes.[21] In his study of the unconventional lives of female *bhakti* saints, A. K. Ramanujan has isolated five key patterns: early dedication to God; denial of marriage; defying societal norms; initiation; and marrying the Lord (1999b, 270–278). With the exception of marrying the Lord, the sadhus' narratives feature all of these themes. Such correspondences, first of all, strongly suggest these sadhus' familiarity with the structure and content of the narratives of famous female *bhakts*, particularly, in this case, those associated with the local Rajasthani saint Mira Bai—and their use of such narratives as possible models of gender for constructing and interpreting *post facto* singing as *sannyās*.

Second, the sadhus' emphasis on duty, destiny, and devotion suggests that they draw on vernacular models of gender to craft a female sadhu tradition—what I have characterized as devotional asceticism—as an alternative to the dominant (and gendered masculine) tradition of Brahmanical *sannyās*. These narrative patterns, along with defiance of social norms, bespeak the gendered religious experiences of women, illustrating, as Bynum and Lawless have discussed, the significance of gender in the selection of themes and in the attribution of meaning to those themes. But what are the larger implications of duty, destiny, and devotion for the sadhus?

Conclusions: Performing Ideologies of Difference in Female Sadhus' Stories

It is immediately evident that foregrounding duty, destiny, and devotion serves to create the sadhus' "perception of difference"[22] vis-à-vis three distinct groups of persons: all householders, women in general, and most male sadhus who have been initiated in the Dashanami or the Nath orders. A perception of difference links into and cues the embedded ideology of exceptionalism performed in their stories. More specifically, their destiny to become sadhus makes them, as people, different from all householders, because, in their worldview, we are what our fate would have us be. Destiny not only assigns group membership, it also draws boundaries of difference between groups—in this case, between householders and sadhus. But even this proposition has to be nuanced, because for the sadhus difference exists not just among people of the same gender, but among people of the same group (householders or sadhus). Apart from the notion of destiny, what else informs the sadhus' perception of difference from women in general?

A consistent subtheme in the sadhus' stories involves the characteristic of fearlessness, whether dealing with family, strangers, divine or demonic beings, wild animals, or with the realities of traveling alone as a female sadhu in cities, towns, and jungles. For example, Shiv Puri enjoyed going alone to the jungle and did so regularly throughout her childhood and early adulthood (a practice her natal family found troublesome). On one of her excursions Shiv Puri encountered a tiger. What she saw, however, was not a tiger. She explained:

> I heard people screaming in the background, "Tiger! Tiger!" and, all of a sudden, the beast jumped out in front of me... Running toward me it moved like a motorcycle. But what did I see? I swear to you I saw a donkey, not a tiger; at the same time, I thought, "he sure moves fast for a donkey!" The whole situation struck me as odd, but I wasn't afraid...I wasn't afraid as a child and I'm not afraid now. I stopped fearing a long time ago.

Narrating a story about traveling on a train, Ganga Giri also described a fearless attitude when she was approached by the ticket-taker. She said: "I traveled alone on trains, without a ticket. When the ticket taker came, I showed him my eyes...All this was the power of my *bhajans*."

Both narratives construct the sadhus as fearless. But Ganga Giri's story makes explicit the idea that this characteristic is not a "natural" component of her gender. Rather, it derives from the "power of [her] *bhajans*" (but see the next chapter for a discussion of the sadhus' views that their feminine gender equips them to be better sadhus than men). The sadhus' fearless attitude comes from the power evoked by the vernacular practices that encompass their idea of "singing *bhajans*." Recall Ganga Giri's description of herself in the context of her story about traveling with her brother and Bhabhi on the train: "I have lived alone with the sound of snakes... why should have any fear of the world? There isn't any fear of the world anymore. Why should I live under the fear of the world?" To the sadhus, the power of courage created by singing *bhajans* distinguishes them from women in general, who, in the view of dominant patriarchal constructions of femininity, are represented as passive, weak, and dependent (Doniger and Smith 1991, 197–198). Let me clarify that many householder women would not represent themselves as weak, passive, or dependent. As several scholars have shown, throughout South Asia women's oral traditions laud the inner powers (and prescience) of women, which are linked to their religious practices, and which provide alternative images of the feminine to dominant classical Brahmanical understandings (Gold and Raheja 1994; Narayan 1997; Raheja 2003; Gold 2003; Lamb 2003). By constructing themselves as brave by reason of the power that singing *bhajans* gives them, the sadhus interrogate mainstream notions of femininity and legitimate their asceticism by situating it in the broader framework of what is typically seen as female religiosity.

For the sadhus to resist dominant representations of femininity through emphasis on their bravery is not a denial of their womanhood. On the contrary, they identify as women in their personal narratives, but view themselves through an alternative lens of femininity, one that includes implicit understandings of gender androgyny, rather than static male/female polarities.[23] Shiv Puri's story of her vision above, in which she received blessings from Shiva and Durga Mai, may express an underlying perception of gender androgyny in her embodiment of the power of God and the Goddess. From a comparative perspective, the sadhus' perceptions of themselves as brave on account of their uncommon *bhakti* to God parallels the self-understanding of Amma, a female Muslim healer living in Hyderabad, whose life, rhetoric, and practices are the focus of Flueckiger's ethnography on gender and vernacular Islam in South India (2006; 2003). As Flueckiger observes, based on her examination of Amma's statements, life narratives, and testimonials, Amma attributes her healing power to her inner courage, which she says arises from her devotion to Allah (Flueckiger 2003, 94), and which she says makes her different from other women in general. Like the sadhus, then, Amma "on many levels... identifies" with her "caste" as a woman but, unlike the sadhus, she sees her life and work as a healer "to be outside the bounds and possibilities of her gender" (Flueckiger 2003, 78).

While their role accords them status, the sadhus believe that singing *bhajans* endows them with the power and authority to practice asceticism, as they act on behalf of the divine. However, only by disclaiming agency can the sadhus exercise instrumental agency, and thus, establish female status, power, and authority in vernacular asceticism. To put it in Lawless's terms, as "disclaimers of intent (1988, 76)," duty, destiny, and devotion make it possible for the sadhus to neutralize societal perceptions of their asceticism as intentional and transgressive and represent themselves via the metaphor of singing *bhajans* as respectable women who live to serve God. By the same token, foregrounding these paradigmatic concepts, the sadhus challenge normative patriarchal formulations of womanhood and, by taking *sannyās*, script an alternative (and valid) way of life. Importantly, the use of such disclaimers distinguishes the female sadhus from the male sadhus with whom I worked. So, can we conclude that the themes that the female sadhus accent in the telling of their personal narratives are intrinsic to women's life stories?

It is important to state that the female sadhus' personal narratives perform gendered constructions in comparison to those of the male sadhus, who belong to the same orders as the female sadhus. More specifically, in contrast to what the female sadhus say about asceticism, the male sadhus say that it represents the intended result of their own "hard work" and "disciplined efforts." Illustrating this point are the words of a well-respected male sadhu from Kumbhalgarh district, Devendra Digambara Saraswati Maharaj: "Our own two hands create our destiny."

Thus, the male sadhus' stories bring to light the themes of action (*karm*), effort (*prayās*), and practice (*abhyās*). In doing so, the male sadhus construct agency as active and intentional, rather than as receptive and instrumental. Be that as it may, duty, destiny, and devotion, while central to the female sadhus' stories, illustrate themes found in *bhakti* traditions globally, rather than only in the lives, writings, and practices of female *bhakti* saints. These concepts are especially pronounced in the hagiographies of the (mostly) male Vaishnava devotional saints featured in Nabhadasa's *Bhaktamāl*. Here, we find destiny and devotion, in particular, invoked as interpretive scaffoldings through which *bhakts* construct meaning of their circumstances. The next chapter discusses what the female sadhus say about the differences between the *bhakti* of female saints and that of male saints. For now, I suggest that in addition to regional and pan-Indian models of female devotionalism, the sadhus draw on a more generalized *bhakti* discourse, in which the themes analyzed in this chapter surface as key elements, to distinguish their sadhu tradition from the mainstream imagination of *sannyās* and legitimize devotional asceticism by linking it to an established *bhakti* tradition.[24] Perhaps the "sweetness" that Ganga Giri attributes to her rhetoric of renunciation performs a view shared by the female sadhus: that *bhakti*, in general, offers a "sweeter" model of *sannyās* than the Brahmanical one. The connection that the female sadhus make between their lives and those of exceptional *bhakti* saints, including Mira Bai, allows them to cross beyond the threshold of the dominant model and construct *sannyās* through categories and experiences that make sense to them as women, like that of singing *bhajans*.

By carefully walking the difficult road that leads to union with God, the sadhus, much like the Baul women in India and Bangladesh whom Lisa I. Knight describes, navigate, through performance of their personal narratives, their unusual religious role and normative gender expectations (cf. Knight 2011). They further acquire—through their humility, cleverness, and emotional strength—the status, power, and authority conveyed by their spiritual position. Ganga Giri's story about her encounter with the two policemen described at the beginning of this chapter performs this view. Not only does this story illustrate the nature of female sadhus' everyday negotiations of power, but it also acutely comments on how the negotiating of agency, too, is (and, perhaps, will remain) a gendered issue for female sadhus. Most significantly, even in its rejection of agency, the story vividly offers its listeners (and readers) a way to imagine and enact female agency in a patriarchal society and *sannyās*. Thus, despite the many obstacles involved, the worlds of female sadhus are possible and flourish "by the sweetness of [their] tongue[s]."

3

"Forget Happiness! Give Me Suffering Instead"

NEGOTIATING GENDER AND ASCETICISM IN VERNACULAR NARRATIVE

Women in India have to endure many restrictions and follow many difficult customs. But they have developed so much śakti because of it.

—SHIV PURI MAHARAJ

THE SADHUS' MOST tellable stories are those drawn from both the more and less well-known Indian mythological and hagiographical oral narrative traditions. These are the stories the sadhus want to tell; the stories they are not self-conscious about telling; and the stories their supplicants ask them to tell. I have seen the sadhus' devotees beseech them for a specific story not only because of the expertise with which they perform it, but also because the audience enjoys hearing that story and the message it imparts again and again. Many of these stories are what the sadhus heard their own parents and grandparents tell them in their childhood. Thus, these stories, in particular, have become part of a received tradition of exemplary narratives whose significance lies in the nature of their moral import. In this chapter, we shift our focus from the sadhus' personal narratives to their vernacular narratives, which they characterize as *kahāniyān* and which, like their personal stories, songs, and sacred texts, constitute the rhetoric of renunciation performed in *satsang*. By "vernacular narrative," I mean the local or regionally based religious stories that the sadhus perform in the *bolcāl* (everyday)—North Indian languages of Hindi, Rajasthani, and Gujarati to construct singing *bhajans* as *sannyās*. This genre includes tear-jerking tales of *bhakts* who endure horrible suffering (*duhkh*) in order to "meet God." Of all the vernacular tales in their repertoires, the stories about the troubles (*pareśānī*) of *bhakts* are the ones that the sadhus tell the most, and with which they most strongly identify as female renouncers. In their view, suffering on the difficult road to God confers power on *bhakts* and, by implication, on sadhus. What is more, because troubles arise when the *bhakts* prioritize singing *bhajans* to God above everything else, suffering displays the virtuosity of the sadhus' devotional asceticism.

Narrative Frameworks and Female Sadhus' Construction of Sannyās

As an illustration, one of Ganga Giri's favorite stories is drawn from the *Mahābhārat* epic, and is about Kunti, the virtuous queen mother of the Pandava brothers. In telling this story, Ganga Giri draws attention to the episode in which the bloody battle for the throne between the Pandavas and the Kauravas has come to an end, and the leadership of the kingdom has become, once again, established in the hands of the Pandavas. Describing this event, Ganga Giri says,

> At the time when the Kauravas were killed, Shri Krishna said to Kunti, who was his aunty, "We have killed our enemies, [because of which] you have received peace [*śānti*]. Now ask, what [else] do you want?" Shri Krishna spoke like this [to Kunti]. Kunti, the mother of the Pandavas, said, "I need suffering [*duhkh*]." [Shri Krishna] said, "But you have suffered your whole life. You have the throne back now, so why are you asking for more suffering?" Then mother Kunti said, "To hell with happiness [*sukhe ke māthe par sule paḍhe*]! You forget God when you're happy [Ganga Giri substitutes "Ram" for God here]. Give me suffering so great that it will make [me] chant the name of God [*prabhu*]." [Krishna] told her, "Thank you, aunty. Thank you." When there's happiness, people forget [God's] name, but [during times of] suffering, they remember. You have to sacrifice happiness [*balihārī karnā*]. Suffering is good. Suffering is good.

Ganga Giri tells this story to audiences of multi-caste Hindu (and occasionally Jain) householders, who visit her ashram daily in order to pay their respects and discuss their life troubles. Over steaming cups of sweet tea (*chai*) and, if available, cookies Ganga Giri gently encourages these concerned men and women, who sit at her feet on tattered burlap sacks, sometimes on the brink of tears, to have faith and remember God through their difficulties. And, after a momentary pause, she shares the Kunti narrative to relate these teachings. Through performance of the Kunti story, Ganga Giri counsels her visitors to value suffering—which she thinks householders often avoid out of fear and ignorance—and to turn life's unexpected tragedies into powerful experiences of personal transformation. In these contexts, Ganga Giri performs the Kunti story to express what she considers the important religious and moral values by which householders empower themselves in their everyday lives.

But whether or not she is teaching householders, Ganga Giri performs this story from her extensive narrative repertoire because it also portrays the virtues she values as a sadhu. Sadhus, too, constitute regular members of Ganga Giri's audience. Sometimes they (and I) are the only participants in a *satsang*. Ganga Giri's telling her stories to sadhus, whether they are her disciples or not (and most of them are not her disciples), performs for them her idea of what *sannyās* is. Their being a part of the audience shapes Ganga Giri's telling of her tales as much as the householders in attendance affect it. Tulsi Giri, whom we met in Chapter 2, often visits Ganga Giri at her ashram and listens to her stories, commenting on their meanings, and sharing stories of her own. Despite having been initiated by another sadhu, Tulsi Giri calls Ganga Giri her guru. Ganga Giri's stories, like the Kunti story, have influenced Tulsi Giri's view of *sannyās*.

In this Kunti story (and in the other versions she tells), Ganga Giri emphasizes the virtues of suffering (*duhkh*) and sacrifice (*balihārī*). She indexes two concepts that define the dominant representations of Brahmanical *sannyās*, and which direct her own understanding of the meaning of *sannyās*-as-lived.[1] Analytically speaking, what I find significant has to do with the similarity between Ganga Giri's conception of suffering as "good" and the Brahmanical, textually articulated, renunciant practice of *tapas* (Hindi, *tap*). This term literally means "heat," but more generally refers to austere practices of penance and self-denial that sadhus voluntarily and intentionally undertake for spiritual development and transformation (Klostermaier 1996; Pearson 1996, 55; Olivelle 1992; 1995; 2004; Gross 2001, 326; Stoler Miller 1998). Robert Gross has said that "In general, *tapas* is . . . equivalent to asceticism and world renunciation" and, thus, connotes experiences of suffering and sacrifice (2001, 326–327). Klostermaier has also discussed the specialized ways that sadhus are thought to practice *tapas* as voluntary suffering:

> *Tapas* may mean anything, from real self-torture and record-breaking austerities to the recitation of sacred syllables and the chanting of melodies. Fasting, *prānayama* (breath control), *japa* (repetition of a name of God or a short mantra), and study of scriptures are among the most common practices. At the *melās* [large festivals in which sadhus gather together for the purpose of religious teaching and practice] one can observe other varieties of *tapas*: lying on a bed of thorns or nails,

> prolonged standing on one leg, lifting one arm for years till it is withered, looking straight into the sun for long hours, and spiritual sportive feats. Many ascetics keep silence for years... Although perhaps under Christian influence the practices associated with *sādhanā* are often associated with theistic ideas not very different from the ideas of the value of voluntary suffering and self-mortification, originally they had nothing to do with either ethical perfection or pleasing God. *Tapas* used to be seen as psychophysical energy, the accumulation of which determined one's position in the universe. The aim, therefore, was to reach a higher position with greater power through *tapas*. (1994, 56)

As Klostermaier observes, *tapas* provides a pertinent religious framework within which sadhus imagine and understand voluntary physical and mental experiences of suffering as a type of *sādhanā* (spiritual discipline) practiced for the purpose of creating and developing inner power. Gross concurs, "Without *tapas* and without the sense of self-sacrifice that it suggests, spiritual realization and salvation are not possible" (2001, 327). In Brahmanical *sannyās* suffering construed as *tapas* is viewed as good by virtue of what it creates for sadhus. Klostermaier intimates that the value placed on suffering cuts across gender and sectarian divisions in asceticism as practiced. I have found, however, that the female sadhus spend more time talking about the religious and moral efficacy of suffering for *sannyās* than the male sadhus do. Although Ganga Giri does not explicitly associate *tapas* with suffering in the excerpted story, her performance not only constructs Kunti's suffering as *tapas*, but also *tapas* as voluntary suffering, which Kunti desires because of the power she expects to gain from it. Suffering pushes Kunti to keep God in her heart and to be united with God always. Ganga Giri's telling represents suffering as a conduit of divine encounter and establishes its value for *sannyās*.

Apart from suffering, Ganga Giri's emphasis on sacrifice, which similarly implies overlapping notions of penance, austerity, and self-denial, equally indexes an orthodox model of Brahmanical *sannyās*. As a term, renunciation traditionally denotes "to throw down," "to give up," or "to sacrifice" worldly desires and attachments (Olivelle 1975; 1981; 1992; 1996). In his analysis of the theology of renunciation expressed in the *Saṃnyāsa Upaniṣads* (authoritative texts on the radical lifestyle of leaving everything behind), Olivelle has discussed that *sannyās* literally means "discarding" or "abandonment" (1992, 59), and that a renouncer "is defined by what he has given up rather than by what he does" (1992, 67). The female sadhus voice related understandings of renunciation in the context of the telling of their personal narratives. From their perspectives, *sannyās* broadly designates a life of penance, poverty, and detachment, a life of sacrifice and suffering, in which sadhus (ideally) "give up" material items and objects, and, more precisely, those mental attachments that ensnare vulnerable humans in an illusory and impermanent worldly existence and prevent them from realizing their full spiritual potential.

But the relevance of the Kunti story to Ganga Giri extends beyond its promotion of the Brahmanical concepts of sacrifice and suffering characteristic of classical notions of *sannyās*. The religiosity enacted by Kunti's devotion to Krishna signifies a significantly different experience than most representations of *sannyās* featured in the orthodox renunciant texts. In his description of *tapas* quoted above, Klostermaier describes that the purpose of *tapas* was not for sadhus to experience a theistic conception of deity, but rather, as he stresses, either to become greater than deity, through the accumulation of inner power, or, as developed in classic yogic traditions, to become deity itself (cf. Sherma 2004; Olivelle 1992; 1996; Stoler Miller 1998).

In Ganga Giri's telling, while Kunti's religiosity enacts and embodies what the Brahmanical idea of *sannyās* is all about—despite her being a householder and not a sadhu—her devotion to Krishna indicates that an underlying *bhakti* framework is at work in Ganga Giri's performance. We might say that in her view of suffering as "good," Ganga Giri invokes both Brahmanical and *bhakti* views to interpret her story. Describing Indian perspectives on suffering, Karl Potter explains that the *bhakti* traditions have their own compelling version of the concept:

> Now [the] lower-class values [of *bhakti*] are uppermost; there is glory in servitude, even servility, as in the prapatti doctrine of Srivaisnavism. Now moods (*rasas*) come to be of central interest to philosophers. Instead of turning one's back on vicissitudes and seeking a cure, one immerses oneself in those vicissitudes... Now there is suffering: Radha suffers as she longs for Krishna, and the *bhakti* advice is worlds apart from the classical Indian philosophical position—she should lose herself in Krishna, not as the *jīva* loses itself in Brahman, but as the devoted long-suffering servant loses himself in his master, or the lover in his or her beloved. (1986, 5)

Whether the concept of devotion is overtly expressed in the sadhus' performances of their vernacular stories or not (and, in the stories examined below, *sannyās* recast as singing *bhajans* is the cardinal theme), we need to understand that multifaceted *bhakti* frameworks are embedded features of the performance contexts in which they and I participated, and in which the female sadhus put their worlds together. Their ideas of *satsang* as illustrative of *bhakti* indicate that their rhetorical practices arise in *bhakti* contexts that orient their experiences of *sannyās* as singing *bhajans*. In *satsang*, the sadhus reconfigure classical and mainstream Brahmanical virtues in the new (and female-oriented) context of *bhakti*, widening the definitional parameters of *sannyās*.

But an important question arises: What if Ganga Giri had performed the story of the sage Mandavya from the *Mahābhārat* instead of her favorite Kunti narrative? His is also a tragic tale of physical and mental suffering and sacrifice, which Mandavya endures by being cruelly impaled on a stake by soldiers on the orders of a king, who think he is a robber disguised as a sage in the forest (Rajagopalachari 1994, 38–40). Would Ganga Giri perceive his suffering and sacrifice, his *bhakti*, to be any less meaningful because of his gender? Would she even reconfigure these renunciant concepts through means of *bhakti* frameworks in interpreting his *sannyās*?[2] We need to ask what role, if any, does the gender of the devotees featured in the sadhus' vernacular religious narratives play in their constructions of devotional asceticism?

Although I never heard Ganga Giri speak about Mandavya in our conversations (which is not to say that she is not familiar with this tale), she performs narratives of other renowned male *bhakts*, such as Dhanna Bhagat, Suganmal, Jad Bharat, Prahlad, Kabir, and Narsi Mehta, who also represent paragons of the sadhus' view of singing *bhajans* as *sannyās*. In commenting on these stories, Ganga Giri selects the virtues of suffering and sacrifice exhibited variously by the male *bhakts* as characteristic of renunciant *bhakti*. "To believe in God," she says prior to telling these stories, "you have to sacrifice everything to God." These performances, like those in connection with female *bhakts*, implicitly hinge on an understanding shared between Ganga Giri and her audience of the context as *satsang*. Moreover, the underlying function of her performances lies in teaching the importance of devotion to God. Ganga Giri's emphasis on sacrifice, while linked to the Brahmanical notion of "giving up" worldly desires and attachments for personal spiritual advancement, more precisely alludes to a common *bhakti* vision found in both the vernacular-language and Sanskritic *bhakti* traditions of "leaving behind everything" in order to dedicate oneself to God. In Ganga Giri's view—which represents the majority perspective among the sadhus who told similar *bhakti* tales—male *bhakts*' struggles depict their fierce love of God, which the sadhus equate with renunciant *bhakti*. To them, without suffering, *bhakti* would not constitute *sannyās*. And yet, as vernacular asceticism more globally illustrates, gender makes a substantial difference in the ways in which *bhakti* is lived and experienced in the interlocking worlds of story and everyday life. Despite the fact that male *bhakts* undergo traumatic hardships in the proud name of *bhakti* to God—shocking ordeals that distinguish them from scoundrels in God's eyes (and to the sadhus)—they never suffer *because they are men.* The nature of their suffering as *bhakti,* and the behaviors demonstrative of that *bhakti,* are different from those of female *bhakts.*

Gendered Ideologies of Suffering

More specifically, in the sadhus' performances we discover an embedded gendered discourse on suffering, one with personal and social implications for the ways that the sadhus construct and experience *sannyās* in vernacular contexts. Their views on the significance of gender to *sannyās,* which their performances enable them to create, contrast with and challenge the dominant view of the Brahmanical model, in which gender is seen as irrelevant (Khandelwal 2004).[3] The sadhus' tellings suggest that the suffering experienced by female *bhakts* signifies not just a beneficial religious result of voluntary penance and self-denial (an important theme found in the stories about male *bhakts*), but more significantly, a social fact of their subordinate gender status in a patriarchal Indian society. In their interpretations of gender-related troubles, the sadhus weave a local version of what appears to be a universal religious ideology in their performances, according to which female power (*śakti*) arises from the suffering that women, and especially those on the *bhakti* path, experience because of their perceived lesser gender status. To the sadhus, women's *śakti* is engendered from several sources, like *bhakti* and *tapas,* as well as gender-related troubles. But just as important, their stories perform the shared understanding that gender-related struggles develop women's *śakti* and increase the spiritual capital of their *bhakti.*

The gendered "ideology of *sakti* [power] gained through suffering" (Egnor 1991, 15) that the sadhus weave into their performances does not articulate an exclusively female renunciant viewpoint. As several scholars have shown, householder women similarly imagine their lives, identities, and roles through use of the lens of a paradigm of suffering as empowering for women (see Wadley's edited volume 1991; Feldhaus 1982; Pearson 1996). The works of Margaret Egnor (1991), Holly Baker Reynolds (1991), Sheryl B. Daniel (1991), and Kenneth David (1991), for example, have shown that Tamil female householders conceptualize their daily sufferings as efficacious and meaningful sources of individual spiritual empowerment and religious transformation. Moreover, the Tamil householders whom they describe see female *śakti* in terms of the suffering created by their subordinate gender status. Egnor has stated that,

> none of these women saw a contradiction between her possession of *sakti* and her subordinate role as female. Nor did any of them see her

> subordination as the restriction of power which might otherwise have grown beyond control. On the contrary, for each woman the possession of extraordinary *sakti* came as a consequence of her subordinate status, or more accurately, as a consequence of the suffering that that subordination entailed. (Egnor 1991, 14)

Not only Tamil householders, but also Benarsi householders associate female moral, spiritual, and devotional power with the suffering experienced (either in the family, or more broadly, in the society) as a result of their (perceived) low gender status. In her study of householder women's *vrat* (votive) practices in Benares, Anne Pearson (1996) has discussed that the householders whom she worked with not only considered *vrats* to be a potent avenue for the accumulation of *śakti*, but also explained that suffering, whether it stems from women being "lower than men" in the social hierarchy or from their practices of intense self-control, "brings *shakti*" (1996, 216; Pintchman 2005). In an interview, one of Pearson's collaborators maintained,

> Everyone has some *shakti*, but women have more of it because they do more rituals and fasts. Women also gain *shakti* because of their place in the family. Husbands and fathers control women's wills. We must always be lower than men. You must control your own desires, too. You must have perfect fidelity to your husband even in thought. When women have children, they bear pain and suppress their own desires for their children. That brings *shakti*, too. (1996, 216)

And, finally, the famous female Maharastrian householder saint, Bahina Bai, comparably affirms a gendered ideology of suffering as empowering for women in her poetry and songs (Feldhaus 1982; Vanita 1989; Abbot 1985). One of the few female *bhakti* saints, as Anne Feldhaus has observed, to have reconciled duty to husband with devotion to God, Bahina Bai's autobiographical poems reflect a keen awareness of the ways dominant religious structures and institutions prohibit women from attaining the "highest goal" of divine union simply on the basis of their gender (Feldhaus 1982, 594; Vanita 1989, 59). Most of Bahina's struggles arise from her tumultuous relationship with her jealous and unsympathetic husband, a learned Brahmin priest who—at least until the time that he, too, converts to *bhakti* teachings—prevents Bahina Bai from divine worship and meeting with her guru, Tukaram, using threats and, in several instances, physical violence (Feldhaus 1982, 595–598; Vanita 1989, 58). During this difficult period, Bahina Bai expresses in one poem that her "daily life was full of troubles" (Vanita 1989, 58). And yet, Bahina values her suffering; she believes it serves as a conduit for inner strength, religious understanding, and devotional power. In one poem she suggests this idea:

> *(1) My body is responsible for my joys and woes. It is necessary that I suffer them.*
> *(2) But if this suffering means the putting far away of sin, I count it as a welcome good.*
> *(3) I wish the longing of my heart to express itself in singing God's praise, even while my body is suffering torture.*
> *(4) Says Bahini, "I suffer what is in my Fate."*
> *(Abbot 1985, 42)*

Bahina Bai believes that her suffering helps her to achieve inner purification of the soul and acquire *śakti*. More than just a vehicle for female empowerment, Bahina Bai further sees gender-specific suffering to be a way for females especially to unite with the divine. In another poem Bahina intimates this sentiment: "Fate's cord around me has at last been broken. My soul has become purified. God has shown me his mercy [meaning she had a divine vision of God]" (Abbot 1985, 42). Thus, the religious discourse attributed to the *bhakti* saint Bahina Bai, and the discourses on female *śakti* that female householders from various regions of India construct, collectively illuminate a conceptual framework that associates female spiritual power and moral authority with suffering created, in part, by a subordinate feminine gender status.

The reason for this brief excursion is to place the sadhus' use of a gendered religious framework of suffering into a broader analytic perspective. More significantly, I want to draw attention to the fact that not only female householders, but female sadhus in Rajasthan, too, make use of this ideology (or a localized version of it) in their practices to interpret and explain their narratives. This phenomenon might indicate more generally—however oblique or however direct—female sadhus' identification with householders, perhaps with all women, who suffer troubles on account of their female "caste," regardless of their spiritual power, marital status, age, and religious identity (Flueckiger 2006; Khandelwal 2004; Knight 2011; Jassal 2012).

This chapter argues that the sadhus' vernacular narrative performances draw on multiple religious paradigms with which they craft their female sadhu tradition as devotional asceticism. The telling of stories about exceptional regional and local female *bhakti* saints, whose singing to God exemplifies a gendered ideology of suffering that encompasses the virtues of sacrifice, struggle, and love, becomes a way for the sadhus to construct singing *bhajans* as *sannyās*. The chapter also contends that the sadhus' narratives perform what folklorist Patricia Sawin calls "coded protests" (2004, 98–134) against gender inequality and injustice, and, against what Shiv Puri herself describes as, "[the] many . . . restrictions that women have to follow" because of their subordinate gender status. Let me stress that in the contexts of the narratives analyzed below, the concept of coded protest does not, to my mind, designate the idea of resistance and subversion that scholars tend to read into female behavior that pushes back at or reinterprets normative patriarchal constructions of womanhood (for similar discussions see Jassal 2012; Knight 2011; Pintchman 2005, 179–194; Khandelwal 2004; Sawin 2004; Erndl 1997; Gold and Raheja 1994). With maybe one exception, none of the protagonists featured in the sadhus' stories intentionally or actively resist the dominant institutions and power structures that intentionally and actively subordinate them. Not only that, even when a *bhakt*'s actions parallel resistance, the sadhus do not see her behavior in that way. On the contrary, they describe her actions using the language of "the power of *bhakti*," which emboldens the *bhakt* to be able to worship God on her own terms and despite her maltreatment. The sadhus' performances globally affirm that singing *bhajans* performs a superior and feminine moral religiosity that makes it possible for women to be able to dedicate their lives to God. Their *bhakti* empowers them to critique peripherally, rather than challenge directly, hegemonic structures of injustice. In all of the stories, singing *bhajans* acts as the explicit instrument of societal change (if it happens at all); the women themselves simply want to exercise their right to worship God without fear of punishment. The stories further show that the power that singing *bhajans* creates allows women to pursue fiercely their religious goals—but it does not liberate them from oppression. To the sadhus, the power of one's *bhakti* is the only "real" power in the world. Other kinds of power, they say, distract *bhakts* from "meeting God."

While the sadhus' narratives do not explicitly challenge and analyze oppressive gender hegemonies, neither do they strengthen them either. Rather, their stories envision and offer singing *bhajans* as a real-life religious solution to the everyday conflicts women experience either because of their gender or their religiosity, or both (cf. Gold and Raheja 1994). The sadhus' vernacular performances underscore that women are not at all powerless victims against abuse and oppression. Rather their oppression contains the seeds for their empowerment and the development of their *śakti*. In the same vein, the sadhus' performances bring to light that singing *bhajans* rights the wrongs against female *bhakts* to the extent that, in at least one of the stories we will consider, the male perpetrators fall to their knees and beg the wronged woman to forgive their stupidity. Thus, in these ways, the sadhus' narratives perform a cautionary warning against the mistreating of women whose singing to God scripts an alternative role to those of wife, mother, and widow. Let us turn now to the stories of three female *bhakti* saints to discover how the sadhus construct singing *bhajans* as *sannyās* through their tellings. The stories of female devotional asceticism that we will explore are those of Mira Bai, Rupa Rani, and Karma Bai.

Three Narrative Portraits of Female Devotional Asceticism

"*Sacrificing all Happiness to God*": The Mira Bai Paradigm

Ganga Giri shared the following paradigmatic Mira Bai story after she told the Kunti tale. Because this Mira Bai telling immediately followed the Kunti telling, their contiguity suggests that these two narratives are connected in Ganga Giri's mind. While the Mira story highlights the theme of sacrifice, Ganga Giri's performance of it reconfigures this idea in the *bhakti* terms of singing *bhajans*. In framing her telling, Ganga Giri said, "Mira used to say this to the Rana [you have to sacrifice all happiness]," after which she told me and a group of householders this story:

GANGA GIRI [GG]: [The] Rana was [Mira Bai's] brother-in-law [*devar*], not her husband, [but] her brother-in-law. She used to invite sadhus and *sants* [to the palace]. She made them sing *bhajans*; she made them share knowledge. She used to feed them. The brother-in-law didn't like it, OK. He said, "We are from a big house [that is, we are royal Rajputs], but those sadhus are from every community [they come from high and low castes]. They sing *bhajans* here; they do *satsang* [communal religious gathering] here. And you make food and feed them. I don't like it." He didn't like it.

ANTOINETTE [A]: He didn't like it?

[GG]: The brother-in-law, he didn't like it. Mira's husband had died. She was married to Bhoj Raj. The husband's name was Bhoj Raj. Her brother-in-law prohibited her [from *satsang*, i.e., from worshiping God]. But she used to do *satsang* anyway; she used to compose *bhajans* herself and sing them with [the sadhus]. She used to feed them. But the Rana didn't like it. He used to say, "No!" So, what did he do? He sent her a bowl of poison, but it turned into nectar. The Rana sent a bowl of poison [disguised as milk] through a servant [girl] to Mira Bai [to kill her]. She was doing the *sevā* of God [meaning, she was worshipping God] at the time. "O.k., take this cup [of milk]," [the servant girl said]. She drank it, but God [*bhagwān*] turned [that poison] into immortal nectar [*amṛt*]. Nothing happened to Mira. Absolutely nothing. Why? God was there with her. God was walking along with her. You have to believe in [God] like Mira, and then you have to sacrifice [*arpan karnā*] all happiness to him.

This story accords with the earliest hagiographical representations of Mira's life featured in the sixteenth century text written by Nabhadas, the *Bhaktamāl* (lit., "Garland of Devotees"), and the eighteenth century text composed by Priyadas, the *Bhaktirasabodhini* (Martin 1999; 1996; Shukla-Bhatt 2007; Hawley 2005; 1988; 1987; Mukta 1997). In these frame stories, Mira Bai is born a Rajput princess from the royal clan of Mertiya at the end of the fifteenth century (ca. 1498); she enters into the reigning Sisodiya family by marrying a prince of Chittor, the former capital of Mewar. In her narrative, Ganga Giri identifies Mira Bai's husband as Bhoj Raj, who is widely thought to have died shortly after their marriage. Several scholars have speculated on the ambiguous identity of the Rana in the poems, songs, and stories attributed to and about Mira Bai, suggesting this figure may have been her husband, brother-in-law, or father-in-law (Hawley 2005; Martin 2000a; 2000b; Mukta 1997; Harlan 1992). Ganga Giri is certain, however, that the Rana appellation stands for Mira's brother-in-law, whom she identifies in other contexts as the Rana Kumbha.

In Ganga Giri's telling, the Rana is a vicious and calculating man. Of course, she makes this claim in all of her Mira performances that I have observed, exclaiming: "The Rana was a wicked man. He had no knowledge. He didn't know God." As the above telling shows, the Rana prohibits Mira Bai from worshipping God. Her devotional asceticism involves publicly meeting with *sants* and sadhus "of every caste," whom she feeds, and with whom she sings *bhajans*. However, "the Rana," as Ganga Giri stresses, "didn't like it." Nevertheless, Mira Bai continues to compose and sing *bhajans* publicly in God's name and to meet with strange, presumably male, sadhus. This story, particularly in its representation of Mira's determination to sing *bhajans* despite the consequences, captures the subversive and oppositional elements of female devotional asceticism. In most of the written and oral representations of her life, including Ganga Giri's, Mira Bai challenges orthodox notions of the *pativratā* ideal, according to which wives must worship their husbands as God; both some of the authors of these Mira sources, and the scholars who have analyzed the rhetoric associated with her name, have almost exclusively focused on Mira's acts of resistance as the defining qualities of her *bhakti*

(Shukla-Bhatt 2007; Hawley 2005; Jain and Sharma 2004; Martin 1999; 1997; Mukta 1997; Harlan 1992).

A case in point: in her insightful discussion of Mira Bai's life from the particular viewpoint of noble Rajput women, Lindsey Harlan has suggested that Mira exemplifies what Harlan refers to as the "*bhakt* paradigm," that is, a moral vision of "limitless" devotion to God in his Krishna form (Harlan 1992, 205–222). According to Harlan, because of what Rajput women themselves emphasize in their interpretations of Mira's life, underlying the *bhakt* paradigm that Mira illustrates is the not-so-subtle message of subversion and resistance to the *pativratā* ideal—a value that is cherished and emulated by female Rajput householders who seek to promote an "ethic of protection" in the expression of Rajput gender roles and duties. Harlan elucidates,

> If, as Rajput women say, Mira is the quintessential unbound *bhakt*, then we can appreciate how subversive unlimited *bhakti* really is. To commit oneself to God requires leaving home for the road and the forest. Nevertheless, *bhakti* is not something performed by saints alone. All women agree that one should be devoted to God but feel that this devotion must serve rather than interfere with devotion to a husband. Practiced in the home and for the benefit of the household, devotion to God enables women to become better *pativratas*... Encompassed by domestic concerns, *bhakti* reinforces the *pativrata* ideal. (1992, 222–223)

Similarly, in his examination of the lives of three *bhakti* saints of North India, John S. Hawley interprets the *Bhaktamāl*'s portrayal of Mira's life to be illustrative of the specific virtue of fearlessness (Hawley 1987, 52–72; Martin 1999).[4] In recognition of those qualities of Mira's religious character that Nabhaji, the *Bhaktamāl*'s author, highlights, Hawley further explains,

> Mention is... made [in Nabhaji's poem on Mira's life] of the fearless, shameless quality of Mira's personality, which is presented as if it emerged from her singing. The poem then cites the great example of Mira's fearlessness: the episode in which she gladly drank the poison her husband or in-laws served up to her. As if in consequence of her fearlessness, she had no reason to fear, for the poison turned to ambrosia in her throat. (1987, 56)

In his analyses of other "Mira" manuscripts, Hawley contends that "Mira is so successful as an embodiment of one Rajput ideal—brave independence of action," and therewith characterizes her as a "paragon of courage," an example of "fearlessness" (Hawley 2005, 117–137). In Hawley's view, which is based on multiple representations of Mira Bai in numerous sources, she stands for "a radical image of *bhakti* womanhood" (Hawley 2005, 130). Linked in their interpretations of Mira's devotional life to this "radical" theme of *bhakti* womanhood, scholars Neelima Shukla-Bhatt (2007) and Parita Mukta (1997; 1987), who study the Mira tradition in the region of Gujarat and neighboring Saurashtra, also understand the *bhajans* attributed to Mira to be indicative of her "resistance to oppression" (Shukla-Bhatt 2007, 282). Shukla-Bhatt maintains, "[t]he outspoken rejection of oppressive norms on the strength of intense love for Krsna... has come to be recognized as a hallmark of Mira's sensitivity and... has had an appeal across caste/class boundaries in Gujarat" (2007, 283). Mukta also concurs that

> Mira stands up in the bhajans, sharply and unambiguously, for personal liberties. Her resistance to social norms and obligations, and her assertion of liberties based on the dictates of her heart, form a major theme of a large body of bhajans in Rajasthan as well as Saurasthra. (Mukta 1997, 127)

Hence, on the basis of her disenfranchised collaborators' understandings, from Mukta's perspective, Mira represents "the voice of the oppressed people, just as the *bhakts* become Mira through their singing" (1997, 87; cf. Martin 1999). For the low-caste communities in which Mukta worked, Mira's image and life symbolize the exposure of, and more precisely, the possibility of an end to "a common suffering and a common humiliation" (Mukta 1997, 104).

My research with female sadhus in Rajasthan contributes an alternative to the current (and dominant) scholarly view on Mira Bai. To the sadhus, Mira Bai exemplifies not so much the *bhakt* paradigm, as Harlan has characterized, but rather a gendered feminine paradigm of singing to God as *sannyās*. Ganga Giri also indicates that Mira does not represent solely the virtue of fearlessness or the idea of resistance to oppression and orthodox social norms, though these themes are evident in her narrative. On the contrary, Ganga Giri accentuates the virtue of sacrifice when interpreting Mira's life. "You have to believe in God, and then you have to sacrifice all happiness to him [*arpan karnā*]," she explains at the end of her performance. But Ganga Giri's emphasis on sacrifice hardly distinguishes this Mira narrative from the other narratives of male devotional asceticism that she also performs. Remember, male *bhakts'* stories, too, bring out this valued renunciant virtue. A *bhakti*-constituted *sannyās* in the sadhus' practices is selectively founded on sacrifice as its distinctive virtue. Ganga Giri's *commentaries* on the Mira and the male *bhakt* narratives are, to the word, strikingly the same. However, her *performances* of these stories are different. Those performative shifts suggest that *bhakti* has different valences for female *bhakts* and male *bhakts*. So what distinguishes Ganga Giri's Mira telling from the other tales she tells?

Our answer rests in the content and structure of the narrative. In the first respect, highlighted in Ganga Giri's story is the understanding that Mira repeatedly suffered at the hands of the Rana (and, perhaps, at the hands of her in-laws). Although Ganga Giri does not mention in this story that Mira suffered, she does not have to make this point explicit, because the audience already assumes this implied detail to be common knowledge of the particular performance context. With the exception of perhaps a few minor details, all of the Mira Bai stories I recorded from Ganga Giri are related versions of a single tale—that of female suffering on the path of God.

Also implicit in the performance context is Ganga Giri's understanding that Mira's repeated sufferings stem precisely from cultural perceptions of her subordinate female gender status. In the eyes of the Rana, Mira's devotional asceticism (singing *bhajans*), a context where she experiences perhaps too much freedom, poses a serious problem to the norms of Rajput female behavior. Hawley concurs, "the milieu in which [Mira] belongs, that of a traditional Rajasthani princess, has definite almost inflexible expectations for women" (1987, 59; cf. Pauwels 2011). As several scholars have noted, Rajput gender norms require females to remain hidden in certain parts of the home, and to conceal themselves in public from the ever-present (and potentially harmful) male gaze (Schomer et al. 2001; Mukta 1997; Gold and Raheja 1994; Harlan 1992).[5] One method of concealment that Rajput and other high-caste women use in domestic spaces or public spaces is the veil (*pardā*) with which, it is thought, they safeguard their honor (*izzat*) and modesty (*śarm*), and by implication, the honor of the larger Rajput community from potential social ruin. To protect caste honor, Rajput women should avoid socializing with certain categories of men, like those who come from low castes. Mira, however, by placing herself in public male spaces and among sadhus from low-castes when she sings *bhajans* to God, disrupts Rajput requisites of normative female behavior and suffers as a result.

In the case of its structure, Ganga Giri's narrative focuses predominantly on Mira's suffering. This was the element of Mira's life most discussed by the sadhus who have told me and others her story. I was always struck by the fact that, of the twelve or so Mira narratives I received and recorded from the sadhus, only two describe in any detail her birth and childhood, and only one discusses her experience of "dissolving" into the *mūrtī* of God at the end of her life. The rest of the stories focus on Mira's trials of suffering within the Sisodiya palace. For instance, one of the first events that Shiv Puri vividly related in her narration of Mira's life story was the poison scene. She said: "They [the in-laws] tried to poison her. How they tortured [*satāyā*] Mira! But God turned that poison into nectar. Those people [the in-laws] really ate her head [a Hindi idiom that means to annoy someone or, in this case, to make her/him suffer]."

Thus, in selecting the virtue of sacrifice to perform Mira Bai's singing *bhajans* as *sannyās*, Ganga Giri synthesizes a key idea from the classical model with a gendered feminine ideology of suffering as a way to construct an inside (and female) view of what asceticism as practiced is about. To the sadhus, singing *bhajans* performs a superlative form of sacrifice, because it unapologetically puts God first and entails suffering with special respect to the gendered nature of the troubles which women who make God their all-in-all experience. But can the sacrifice that Mira decisively makes for God, by prioritizing above all else the singing of *bhajans* in the company of like-minded *bhakts*, accurately be defined as "defiance"? Does Mira's singing *bhajans* cause her to "transgress" the dominant cultural maps that orient (primarily) high-caste women's lives? From the outside, the answer seems clear: Yes. Mira's sacrifice of "all happiness" appears to stand for her defying of gender and caste norms. Singing to God in the manner that her unusual religiosity performs (i.e., in public and with non-kin men from all castes) makes it possible for Mira to follow what her heart says, and to "defy" those patriarchal prescriptions that attempt to fix definite parameters of legitimate female religiosity. From the inside, however, as voiced by the sadhus themselves—the view that the scholarly and popular literature has eclipsed, and which this book spotlights—the answer is: Not at all. Mira's sacrifice hardly speaks defiance. The sadhus view singing *bhajans* in Mira's way to be within the bounds of their gender, because sacrifice, whether it is done on behalf of one's family or one's deity, is seen as something women know all too well how to make. From the sadhus' perspectives, therefore, Mira's sacrifice enacts the duty (*kartavya*) of sadhus, which women are thought to be the most qualified at manifesting (see also Chapter 2 for a discussion of the sadhus' emphasis on duty in their life stories, to challenge perceptions of their asceticism as transgressing the bounds of their gender). Hence, the sacrifice that singing *bhajans* fuels embodies divine duty. That is, insofar as singing *bhajans* creates detachment by requiring *bhakts* to abandon all worldly "thirsts, lusts, and imaginations [*kapol-kalpit*]" at God's feet, it also creates attachment to God. Singing à la Mira's fine example defines the duty of renouncers. What is more, Ganga Giri's emphasis on the gendered dimensions of sacrifice and suffering through use of Mira's model establishes singing *bhajans* as a female form of renunciation. In this telling of Mira's life, Ganga Giri uses *bhakti* views of *radical* (female) *devotion as a form of divine duty* to perform Mira's singing *bhajans* as renunciant sacrifice.

The *bhakti* frameworks on which Ganga Giri draws are rooted in the paradigms of devotion illustrated in sources like the *Bhagavad Gītā* and the poetry and songs of the *bhakti* saints of medieval Indian history, such as Kabir, Narsi Mehta, and Dadu Dayal (see Stoler Miller 1986; Hess 2002; 1987a; 1987b; Schomer & McLeod 1987; Kishwar and Vanita 1989; Lorenzen 1996; Hawley 1988; 2005). Although no explicit mention is made in this Mira narrative of the *Bhagavad Gītā*, Ganga Giri recites this text every day, after she performs *pūjā* to the deities and the *dhūni* (fire pit). She also reads the text silently in the afternoons, when she has no visitors and can concentrate solely on the text. Its religious and ethical views provide an underlying framework with which Ganga Giri interprets sacrifice in her narrative performances of devotional asceticism as singing *bhajans*. In the *Gītā*, Lord Krishna instructs Arjuna, dejected by the thought of killing honorable men like his teachers and mentors in war, to fulfill his duty (*dharm*) as a warrior (*kṣatriya*) and fight on the battlefield of Kurukshetra against the Kauravas. He explains that Arjuna must perceive his actions on the battlefield not just in terms of satisfying his caste duty, but more importantly, as the manifestation of his religious duty to God; otherwise, he shall suffer the consequences of rebirth in the endless cycle of existence (Stoler Miller 1986, 29–39). In this light, dutiful action becomes represented in the text as a form of sacrifice that Arjuna must offer to Krishna: "Actions imprison the world unless it is done as sacrifice; freed from attachment, Arjuna, perform action as sacrifice!" Krishna teaches (*BG* 3.9, Stoler Miller 1986, 42). Actions performed as a sacrifice, in Krishna's view, also constitute a form of "surrender" (*BG* 3.30), or devotion, to the divine by which means devotees "worship me with true faith, entrusting their minds to me" (BG 12.2). As we can see from this example, the *Gītā*'s ideas of sacrifice as constitutive of duty and devotion inform Ganga Giri's views of these concepts in her performing of Mira's singing *bhajans* as dutiful sacrifice to the divine.

The *bhakti* frameworks illustrated in the rhetoric of the medieval poet-saints have also influenced Ganga Giri's interpretations of singing *bhajans* as *sannyās*. Medieval *bhakti*-saint views often construct notions of *bhakti* by invoking prescient metaphors of money or precious gems, such as diamonds and pearls (Hess 2002). In this framework, *bhakti* represents a form of spiritual currency that *bhakts* offer to God by singing *bhajans* in exchange for God's salvific vision, or union (see also Chapter 8 for a detailed discussion of this idea). Linda Hess has discussed the dramatic and elusive ways that Kabir draws on metaphors of money in the "upside-down" language of his poetry to communicate the significance of *bhakti* as singing *bhajans* to an impersonal God (Hess 2002; 1987a; 1987b; Schomer & Macleod 1987; Henry 1995; Hawley and Juergensmeyer 1988). Similar notions of *bhakti* are featured in the performances of the female sadhus. In the *satsangs* that she runs, Ganga Giri foregrounds the importance of *bhakti* by using the aforementioned metaphors of money or precious gems. A typical comment of hers in our meetings is "*bhakti* is expensive" or "a *bhakt* is like a diamond," i.e., *bhakti* represents a superior moral path. Even the statement "God is expensive," indicates Ganga Giri's use of a *bhakti*-saint framework to construct singing *bhajans* as *sannyās*. Compare Ganga Giri's portrayal of *bhakti* as "expensive" to Bahina Bai's: "You cannot buy *bhakti* in the marketplace. You cannot find it in the forest. In exchange for *bhakti* you have to give your heart" (Vanita 1989, 60; cf. Hess 2002).

Thus, the multiple *bhakti* frameworks embedded in the performance context of the Mira Bai narrative play a pivotal role in Ganga Giri's interpretation of sacrifice as singing to God; and thus singing *bhajans* as *sannyās*. To Ganga Giri, Mira Bai models sacrifice because she voluntarily "leaves everything"—despite the horrific gender-related sufferings she experiences at the hands of the "wicked" Rana Kumbha—in order to dedicate herself to the worship and remembrance of God. But a life of sacrifice and, by implication, suffering represents the precious "price" Mira Bai has to pay as God's female *bhakt*. That is, through her spiritual and physical sacrifices, which she performs by singing, Mira enacts duty and devotion to God. Mira's duty to God (what Hawley refers to as an example of *bhakti dharma*[6] in the lives of the *bhakti* saints [1987, 53]), as several scholars have observed, takes precedence over and, finally, supersedes (secular) duty to family, while also broadening orthodox notions of *stridharm*, or women's duty to their husbands and families, as Mira's duty to God in the form of Krishna constitutes a *bhakti* version of *stridharm* (Hawley 1987; 2005; Harlan 1992; Martin 1999; Jain and Sharma 2004).

More than duty and devotion, though, Mira's sacrifice of "all happiness" further suggests to Ganga Giri the quality of fierce love for God. As with sacrifice, the virtue of love, which is typically seen as feminine in *bhakti* traditions, appears as a pronounced theme in Ganga Giri's Mira stories. Though not stated in this Mira telling, in other tellings Ganga Giri affirms love as the defining feature of Mira's singing *bhajans*. This virtue, in fact, creates Mira as a sadhu par excellence in the views of the female sadhus. "Nobody loved God the way Mira did," Ganga Giri says at the end of one of her Mira *bhajan* singings, to which Tulsi Giri concurs, "That's right, sister! Mira really loved God." In this respect, the sadhus' view of Mira's singing *bhajans* as exemplary of the (feminine) *bhakti* value of love compares to and supports Hawley's observation that Mira's *bhakti dharm* reveals "an ethics of character that focuses on love" (1987, 53). More significantly, it suggests that the sadhus see singing *bhajans* as a female way of being a sadhu in asceticism as practiced. From their perspectives, Mira Bai "really" models the virtue of love by singing *bhajans* to God, and by feeding the sadhus and *sants*, who also participated in her *bhajan satsangs* to worship and experience God. To the sadhus, Mira Bai's singing practices perform religious charity (*dān*) and service (*sevā*), by which she makes explicit her fierce love for God.

"*Becoming Powerful through Struggle*": The Rupa Rani Paradigm

Our next narrative, of the life of the *bhakt* Rupa Rani, captures another exemplary theme of the sadhus' narratives of devotional asceticism: struggle (*kaṣṭ*). This renunciant idea becomes similarly reconstituted in performance by means of its explicit association with the *bhakti* notion of devotion to the guru, the story's leitmotif. In this performance, Shiv Puri, the performer, highlights and fuses ideals and concepts illustrative of multiple religious frameworks, including gender-related and caste-specific ones, to craft singing *bhajans* as *sannyās*. While Shiv Puri is younger than Ganga Giri by three decades, she, too, identifies female troubles and its forms as constitutive of singing *bhajans*. On the day that I visited Shiv Puri at her ashram in the middle of a sweltering July summer in 2005, I met five female Rajput householder devotees, two of them relatives of Shiv Puri, between the ages of twenty and fifty, who had arrived from a nearby village to pay their respects to her, their guru. Some of the women indicated in their comments to me that visiting Shiv Puri gave them respite from their daily householding duties. My visit encouraged Shiv Puri to call together an informal *bhajan satsang* session, consisting of her, her devotees, and her eighteen-month-old granddaughter, whom Shiv Puri held on her lap throughout the entire singing session.[7] The child's mother, Shiv Puri's daughter-in-law, also participated as one of the lead singers in this group sing. Everyone, including my field associate Manvendra Singh, gathered in Shiv Puri's personal room, which was hidden behind the ashram compound where it was cool and dry, and where we found a much appreciated reprieve from the construction activities happening at the ashram at the time (Shiv Puri was in the process of expanding her ashram). Manvendra's presence prompted the younger women, including Shiv Puri's daughter-in-law, to shield their faces with the edges of their skirts (*ghūṇghaṭ*), so that only their mouths were visible through their veils. Shiv Puri, mindful of her modesty in front of non-kin men, pulled her *ghūṇghaṭ* to the edge of her hairline, without fully concealing her face.

In this context of *bhajan satsang*, I recorded the Rupa Rani narrative that is analyzed below. The story, however, emerged not from a *bhajan* (although after its telling, Shiv Puri and her devotees performed a Rupa Rani *bhajan*), but rather from an incident representative of how women employ various methods to negotiate religious activities, even meeting the guru, with domestic obligations—a key theme of Shiv Puri's Rupa Rani story. After an hour of singing, several of the *bhakts* said that they had to return to their domiciles. The tinkling of anklets (*pāyal*) resounded in the room as the women rose from the floor, repositioned their clothing, and made their way toward the door to leave. As they exited, Shiv Puri shouted, "Listen, don't tell anyone that [she named the *bhakts* remaining in the room] are here singing *bhajans*!" I asked her why she prohibited these women from speaking about their activities to others. Her answer fell hard on my ears. I discovered that Shiv Puri spoke to her *bhakts* not as a sadhu, but as a *female* sadhu who acutely recognizes the sometimes unavoidable difficulties women who worship God endure in a patriarchal society. In response to my question, Shiv Puri told this Rupa Rani story:

> Have you heard of our [i.e., India's] Rupa Rani? OK, she used to leave the palace [in secret] to meet with her guru. He would call her to come in the assembly [*jhamle*] of *sants* and sadhus to sing *bhajans*. She had to walk through the jungle in the night. On the way, she encountered fraudulent people who emerged on the path [that she took to her guru's place]—[frightening characters who] would stick out their tongues and release a terrible laughter. A lot of frauds appeared on the path. Rupa Rani used to go to meet her guru. He [the guru] would say, "You come in the assembly," and she went, OK. She had to go, right? But her husband, what did he do? He put a snake on the lattice [on which Rupa would climb to enter the palace in order that her husband wouldn't know she had gone to meet her guru], and in this way he learned Rupa Rani came home [because she had to enter through the front door instead]. The women of India endure so many restrictions [*pratibandh*]. In our Rajput community, too, there are so many difficult customs [*muśkil bandhan*] which women have to follow. But [by enduring these obstacles] they have developed so much *śakti*. Some [Rajput] women in our community [have become so powerful that] they took baths of fire with their husbands [i.e., they immolated themselves on their husbands' funeral pyres].

Very little scholarship on the life of the *bhakt* Rupa Rani is available. In consulting the works of other scholars, I have found only one essay, written by Sonal Shukla, that discusses Rupa Rani's life in any illuminating detail (Shukla 1989, 63–73). In this informative piece focused specifically on the religious lives of several legendary female saints from Gujarat, such as Jaisal and Toral, Loyal, and Gangasati, Shukla briefly discusses the importance of Rupa Rani, not because she hailed from this region, but rather because she is considered by Indians familiar with her story to be a *satī*. In her explication of this term, Shukla elaborates, "Some other *bhakta* women...who sacrificed their lives in the interest of their communities are also called Sati. An unusual and glorified life qualified a woman to get the title of Sati" (Shukla 1987, 72).

While Shiv Puri does not explicitly use the word *satī* in her narrative, she implicitly ascribes this religious status to Rupa Rani by associating her with Rajput women who have taken what she calls, "baths of fire," that is, women who immolated themselves on their husbands' funeral pyres, *satīs* (after she told Manvendra and me Rupa's story, Shiv Puri, also from the Rajput community, proudly mentioned that in her family several women had become *satīs*). Although she is a Rajput, Rupa Rani is not a *satī* in this sense of the term. Harlan explains: "In the minds of Rajputs...[to become] a *sati* does not, as is often assumed, result from the act of self-immolation. The word *sati* means 'a good woman' and not, as English speakers tend to think, an act" (1992, 115). In other Indian caste communities, too, *satī* connotes a woman (or wife) of "good" or "virtuous" character. In this religious framework, we should understand Rupa's devotional asceticism to be illustrative of her "glorious" life as a *satī*, because, as Sonal Shukla concurs, she sacrificed her life "in the interest of" her *bhakti* community (1987, 71).

A similar view of sacrifice underpins Shiv Puri's Rupa Rani narrative performance. However, for Shiv Puri, Rupa Rani's implied *satī* status stems not so much from the sacrifices she has made as much as from the *śakti* (power) she has developed in making those sacrifices for her *bhakti* community, her guru, and by implication, God. But how does Shiv Puri understand the source of this power? By stating that, "[t]he women of India endure so many restrictions [*pratibandh*]...But [by enduring them] they have developed so much *śakti*," Shiv Puri makes poignantly explicit her view that female power and inner strength derive from the sufferings and difficulties women experience in having to follow, sometimes reluctantly, traditional customs which intentionally restrict females on the basis of their subordinate gender status. A common perception shared among the female sadhus is that, regardless of her religious propensities and marital status, a woman has (and is expected) to "endure so many difficulties [*bahut hī kaṣṭ uṭānā*]" or "suffer so many problems and pains [*duhkh bhognā*]" on account of the more orthodox attitudes and practices, implying that gender is directly related to women's social experiences of suffering. I understand Shiv Puri's use of the phrase, "to endure great difficulties," to mean, more specifically, the concept of struggle (*kaṣṭ*). As Shiv Puri suggests, Rupa Rani's experience of oppression and danger parallels Shiv Puri's female devotees leaving their "bounded" homes in order to participate in *bhajan satsang* and worship God, and their female guru, through song. Figure 3.1 illustrates this point in its depiction of the mother of twins negotiating a brief visit with her guru, Shiv Puri, with the demands of being a new mother. She came to the ashram so that Shiv Puri could bless the twins with happiness, success, and long-life. Thus, in this narrative performance, Shiv Puri invokes a gendered ideology of suffering as religiously empowering for women, implying that struggle (like suffering) is a foundational virtue of devotional asceticism.

Although Shiv Puri's selection of the virtue of struggle is explicitly based on a gendered ideology of suffering, her emphasis on this particular concept also implicates the influence of a dominant Brahmanical model of *sannyās*. Here too, struggle, like the virtues of suffering and sacrifice, constitutes an

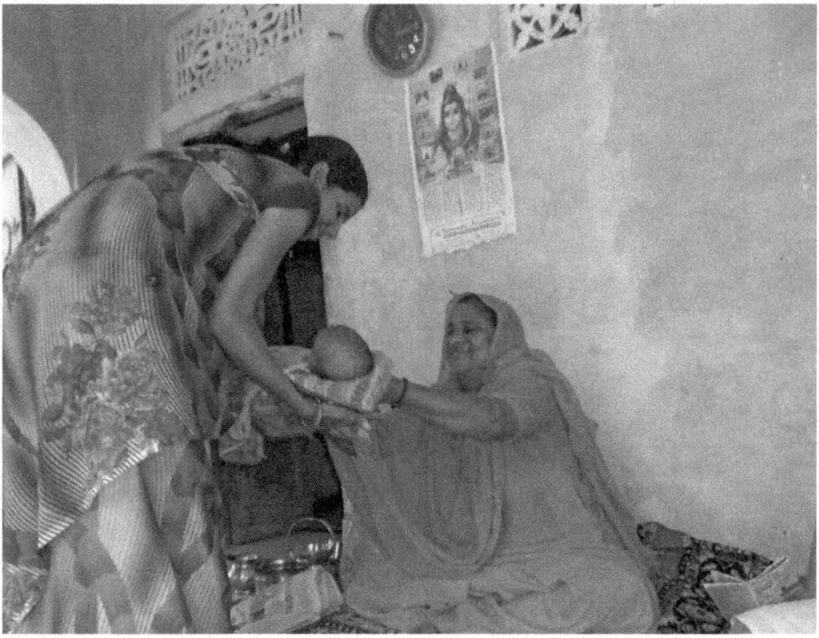

FIGURE 3.1 A mother offers Shiv Puri her newborn twins for blessings at Shiv Puri's ashram.
Photo by A. DeNapoli.

ideal integral to most traditions of orthodox renunciation, one through which the female sadhus understand and experience their renunciant identities and religiosities. Among the collaborators in my field study, the male sadhus and the female sadhus individually or collectively alluded to the *sannyās* notion of struggle in the context of either descriptions of their religious lives as "difficult," or definitions of renunciation as a path in which sadhus (are supposed to) make "great efforts [*bahut hī kaṣṭ/prayās*]" with respect to their religious practices and personal spiritual advancement. In both cases, the sadhus implied in these statements an underlying perception of the heroic nature of *sannyās*. Their ideas of *sannyās* as heroic is important to underscore, because the concepts of suffering, sacrifice, and struggle which index the motif of heroism embedded in the dominant model of Brahmanical *sannyās* are similarly extolled as ideals in Rajput and warrior frameworks (Harlan 1992; Martin 1999; Jain and Sharma 2004; see also Chapter 4). It is also significant to note that the founders of the *Śramana* traditions (radical *sannyās* movements from the sixth century B.C.E.) like Buddhism and Jainism, came from high-caste *Kshatriya* (warrior) backgrounds (Samuel 2010; Rodriguez 2006). We find a cross-fertilization of ideas between renunciant and warrior cultures: in matters of religiosity, sadhus represent themselves as warriors, and in the case of warriors, in matters of battle, they construct themselves as sadhus (Hawley 1987, 67; Smith 1991; Harlan 1992; Schomer et al. 2001; Jain and Sharma 2004). Although a sadhu, Shiv Puri is also a Shaktavat Sisodiya Rajput by birth, a fact of which she is proud (she mentions this detail in most of our meetings), and on which basis she constructs her renouncer identity. Shiv Puri's emphasis on struggle, therefore, may be as motivated by Rajput frameworks, in which the ideals of sacrifice and struggle define caste identity and female behavior, as by a model of Brahmanical *sannyās*.

In Rajput traditions, as Harlan has discussed, the ideals of sacrifice and struggle represent a "Rajput way of life" and constitute the social duty of all Rajputs, regardless of gender (Harlan 1992, 122; Jain and Sharma 2004, 147–154). However, "[t]he contexts and contents of these ideals," according to Harlan, are gendered (123). For example, the Rajput males whom Harlan describes understand sacrifice and struggle in terms of the notion of the *saka*, or "the battle unto death," which depicts a "symbolic summation" of these ideals (122). Harlan explains,

> Preparing for the *saka* (the cutting down), Rajputs donned the garb of ascetics, which showed that they intended to sacrifice their lives in accord with duty and with the reward of a place in warrior heaven. Today the *saka* remains a powerful symbol of caste identity and personal

integrity and represents to all Rajputs the idea that sacrifice is both a natural proclivity and a moral imperative. (Harlan 1992, 122)

Whereas the Rajput men associate the caste duties of sacrifice and struggle with the image of the *saka* who willingly gives his own life on the battlefield, the females Harlan interviewed situate these ideals specifically within the domestic context of family and home (123). From their perspectives, Rajput women fulfill their caste duties and preserve the honor and integrity of the larger Rajput community by selflessly serving their husbands and their families with love and devotion. Harland elucidates: "a Rajput woman gives to her family as her husband gives to his subjects" (123). Through a life of "sacrificial devotion to the husband" and the family (123), Rajput women acquire *sat*[8] (a term often glossed as "truth" or "purity," but which may also signify "moral goodness"), and prepare themselves to become *satīs*, the female equivalent of the male *saka*, who in an ultimate display of self-sacrifice (*balidān*), follow their husbands in death to an afterlife in heaven (123–124). Harlan contends, "by dying as a *sati* a woman acquires the insight and confidence that she has done her duty and done it well" (124).

How, then, might Rajput frameworks underlie and inform Shiv Puri's understandings of the ideals of sacrifice and struggle in her interpretation of Rupa Rani's life? Her perception that female *śakti* derives from enduring gender-related struggles and sacrifices may also refer to the Rajput notion of *sat*. Harlan elaborates, "*Sat* is essentially an autogenerative moral fuel. Produced by good activity, it generates good activity" (1992, 129). By struggling *through*, rather than against, the myriad restrictions enforced on her because of her feminine gender, Rupa Rani acquires not only renunciant devotional power, but also *sat*, or moral power, which enables her to struggle and sacrifice in her everyday life. In doing so, Rupa Rani further manifests and fulfills her duty as a Rajput woman. But duty to whom, and for what purpose? This proposition remains incomplete. We need to consider here the principal reason behind Rupa Rani's daily struggles and sacrifices, and then we must consider how Shiv Puri conceptualizes the concept of duty.

Implicit in Shiv Puri's narrative is an understanding that Rupa Rani's struggles and sacrifices emerge from a direct sense of duty. However, in this particular case, unlike Rajput female householders, Rupa Rani channels her duty neither to the husband nor to the family, not even to the larger Rajput community. On the contrary, Rupa Rani struggles through traditional restrictions and intentionally sacrifices worldly concerns on the sole basis of a religious duty to her guru—and by extension, to her *bhakti* community of sadhus and *bhakts*. Shiv Puri's statement in the context of "Rupa Rani used to go to meet her guru. He would say, 'You come in the assembly' [so] she *had* to go, right? (emphasis mine)," supports this view of her life as one of religious duty. In this description, Shiv Puri uses the compulsory form of the Hindi verb, "to have to go," implying that Rupa Rani's actions pivot on an underlying perception of duty to the guru. In the same vein, Rupa Rani's going into the assembly in order to sing *bhajans* relates the corollary notion, which we saw earlier in the Mira story, that singing *bhajans* enacts renunciant duty. The theme of duty to the guru, and not to husband and family, evokes a motif paramount to both the Sanskritic and vernacular *bhakti* traditions—that is, the daily struggles and sacrifices that devotees (male or female) endure on the grounds of duty to the guru and the *bhakti* community illuminate, more broadly, their devotion to the divine. By means of the *bhakti* frameworks embedded in this performance context, Shiv Puri, like Ganga Giri in her Mira Bai narrative performance, understands duty to be constitutive of radical *bhakti*—i.e., singing *bhajans*, the highest priority for a *bhakt*. In the Rupa Rani sing, too, Shiv Puri's translation of struggle wraps tightly around a *bhakti* vision of a *sannyās*/heroic concept. Although her emphasis on struggle and sacrifice in the narrative is based on ideals drawn from multiple and coexisting religious frameworks, which also remain embedded features of the performance context, by interpreting these virtues through use of *bhakti* frameworks, in particular, Shiv Puri constructs singing *bhajans* in a manner that compassionately acknowledges gender-related experiences of suffering on path of devotional asceticism and, in doing so, indicates the exceptionalism of female *bhakts*.

"*More of a Sadhu than We Are*": The Karma Bai Paradigm

Our final narrative, about Karma Bai, illuminates the theme of females as ideal devotees of God on account of a popular perception woven into the story of women's "natural" or inherent ability to love. The sadhus perform this ideal as the foremost quality of devotional asceticism, which makes it possible for them to construct singing *bhajans* as a feminine religiosity. On a crisp early morning in January 2006, before Ganga Giri narrated the story of Karma Bai to me and my Brahmin host sister, Kalpana—who accompanied me to Ganga Giri's ashram for the purpose of assisting me with transcription questions—she sang a *bhajan* that she attributed to the famous Gujarati *bhakti* saint Narsi Mehta.[9] In the *bhajan*, Narsi Mehta lovingly pleads with God, begging to "meet" him, and then proceeds to ask God why, when He has met *bhakts* like Mira Bai, Kabir, and Karma Bai, does He not meet Narsi, who also loves Him? Hearing the *bhajan* refer to Karma Bai, another of God's female *bhakts* about

FIGURE 3.2 Ganga Giri telling Karma Bai's story. Kalpana transcribes her narrative.
Photo by A. DeNapoli.

whom I knew little at the time, inspired me to ask Ganga Giri about her life and work. To my question, "Who was Karma Bai?" my Brahmin host sister replied, "Sister (*dīdī*), Karma Bai was one of God's greatest devotees." But why is this so? I asked. "[Karma Bai] had real faith [*sahi śraddh*] in God," Ganga Giri interjected in response. She continued, "Not everybody has faith like this [faith especially in the midst of difficulty] but she did. So, God came to her." Then Ganga Giri told me and Kalpana this story of Karma Bai (see Figure 3.2, which shows Ganga Giri telling Karma Bai's story while Kalpana transcribes her narrative):

> Karma Bai had a lot of land. All the people in her house died. She never married. Her mother and father died, and she didn't have any brothers or sisters. She was alone. But she was awakened [*jāgṛt*]. She had a lot of land. From what she earned in her fields, she gave half of it away [to others], and with the other half she made different kinds of sweet dishes [*khīnch*], and brought them to the temple [to feed the sadhus and the gods]. She made sweet dishes of millet and wheat and corn. She pounded the grains, added the sugar, ghee, oil, and then boiled them.

She made so many [different] sweet dishes [that] she gave half of it away to anyone who came, and the other half she gave to the temple.

One day, eight, ten, fifteen sadhus came [to Karma Bai's home]. They had to go on a pilgrimage, but had to walk because there were no cars in those days. They wanted someone to serve [the temple gods]. They thought, "We have to go [on a pilgrimage], but someone has to take responsibility [for the temple]." They said to Karma Bai, "Sister, you serve the temple and feed the gods. We're going on a pilgrimage. You stay here and serve [the temple]." "If I have to serve, I'll do it from here [my home]," thought Karma Bai. "Take whatever you need from the store, and we'll give the money [to the storekeeper] when we return," said the sadhus. The sadhus spoke like this to Karma Bai and left [for their pilgrimage].

"I'll make sweet dishes and feed [the gods]," said Karma Bai. She spent the whole day serving the deities. She pounded and threshed the grains; she filled [separate pots] with [the different] grains, and then boiled them. [Karma Bai] thought, "I should buy plenty of sugar, ghee, and oil [because] if five members [of God's family] come today, ten will come tomorrow." God has a big family, OK. And those sadhus told her, "Whatever you need, take it from the store, and we'll pay [the storekeeper] when we return." But [Karma Bai] spent a lot of money. She bought ghee, sugar, cane, oil, incense, and so forth. The sadhus returned [from pilgrimage] and asked the storekeeper, "How much do we owe?" The storekeeper said, "She spent this much money." "How could you have spent so much money? Who came to the temple [and ate all the food]?" the sadhus asked Karma Bai. She said, "You told me to serve God, so I did. God and his whole family came [to the temple]. They ate a lot; God ate a lot of food." Karma Bai explained. Those sadhus replied, "But we also serve God, and he doesn't eat [the food]. God doesn't eat the food, sister. How can we believe what you say? We serve God every day and we've never seen God eat the food." "But it's true! God eats," said Karma Bai. The sadhus told her, "We'll believe it when we see it! We'll believe it when we see it!"

Later on, Karma Bai said to God [who was at her home], "You have to come [to my house tomorrow] and eat." God said, "You have faith in me, so I come here to eat. But I won't come to eat while others are watching me [because they have no faith]. If you alone call me, I'll come. But I won't come and eat while everyone else watches." Karma Bai pleaded, "But those sadhus are questioning my honor [*izzat*]! If you don't come, they'll call me a liar [*jhūṭī*], and think I ate all the food myself! You have to come." After all, this was an issue of [her] honor [*izzat kī bāt*]. When the devotee calls [God] with such love in [her] heart, God has to come, right? God said, "OK, I'll come; but you have to put up a curtain [*pardā*]." "Alright," said Karma Bai. So, the next day, God came [to her home] and ate. He brought his whole family, too. Everyone came, and they ate [the sweet dishes Karma Bai had prepared]. In the curtain that was hung was a hole. Karma Bai had put that hole there so the sadhus could see God eating the food. She told those sadhus, "Look through the hole. They're eating, right?" They looked through the hole and saw she was right. "It's true!" they said, "All the gods have come to her place, and they're eating [the food]." Those sadhus fell at her feet and said, "Sister, you're not a sadhu, but you're more of a sadhu than we are. We serve God, too, but he doesn't come to [the temple] to eat. But you make sweet dishes [with love] and God and his whole family come [here] to eat." This is the story of Karma Bai.

In contrast to Mira Bai and Rupa Rani, who are Rajputs, Karma Bai was born into the Jāt *jātī*, a community of cultivators, and was thought to have lived in the city of Pūrī in Orissa near the famous Jagganath temple where the *mūrtīs* of Krishna, his sister Subhadra, and his brother Balarama, as Ganga Giri explains, are housed and worshipped daily by Brahmin priests.[10] In framing her performance, Ganga Giri says that what makes Karma Bai "one of God's greatest devotees" is her "real faith in God." But what does she mean by "real faith"?

In light of our conversations, Ganga Giri's use of the phrase "real faith" implies the *bhakti* value of love. That is, according to Ganga Giri, Karma Bai is an ideal devotee because, like Mira Bai, "she really loved" God. In the sadhus' views, just as singing *bhajans* distinguishes sadhus as "real" renouncers, Karma Bai's love distinguishes her as a "real" *bhakt*. What is more, as with Ganga Giri's portrayal of Mira Bai, Karma Bai similarly models "real" love through voluntary acts of charity and service: she distributes free grain to others; she offers the sweet dishes that she herself prepares to the sadhus and deities. Food plays a pivotal role in Karma Bai's radical *bhakti*—much more so than in Ganga Giri's Mira narrative. Caroline Walker Bynum (1987) and Grace Jantzen (1997) have discussed the significant role that food has in the renunciation of the medieval Christian female saints. Bynum explains,

> food was a powerful symbol. Like body, food must be broken and spilled forth in order to give life. Macerated by teeth before it can be assimilated to sustain life, food mirrors and recapitulates both suffering and

> fertility. Thus food, by what it is, seems to symbolize sacrifice and service. (Bynum 1987, 30)

Food was not only a "powerful symbol," it was also a gender-related symbol. Jantzen elucidates,

> women's preoccupation with food was by no means all to do with renunciation. The everyday reality was that women on the whole were the ones who prepared food and were responsible for feeding men and children. Holy women extended this in their efforts to serve Christ by feeding others, especially those who were too poor to be able to feed themselves in the famines of the late medieval period. (Jantzen 1997, 211; cf. Bynum 1987, 30)

Bynum's and Jantzen's insights help us to put into perspective Karma Bai's asceticism as it is practiced. A prosperous and magnanimous landowner, she donates half of the grains which she receives from her fertile fields to the poor and destitute, and the other half she gives to the sadhus and deities at the Jagganath temple. Although wealthy, Karma Bai still lives, by her own choice, a simple religious existence. Without any material concerns, she spends her days preparing multiple sweet dishes (*khīnch*),[11] bringing these to the temple and offering them to the sadhus and the deities there. The food Karma Bai offers to God symbolizes her body, that is, the female self whose own sacrifice feeds and nourishes many others, including the gods. But Karma Bai's symbolic self-sacrifice, as the performance frame suggests, also represents an expression of her love for God and others. By feeding others "with love," Karma Bai serves God; and by feeding God "with love," she creates an intimate relationship with God and with his "big" family.

Thus, Karma Bai's delicious daily food offerings, as expressions of her love to the divine, constitute an exemplary hallmark of her devotional asceticism. Even the *bhajans* attributed to Karma Bai that I recorded from the sadhus in other contexts affirm the importance of food and its preparation for God's daily worship. In these *bhajans*, Karma Bai describes to God in great detail the ways that she has prepared the sweet dishes, and obliquely expresses her love for him. And, as one Karma Bai story I recorded from Shiv Puri emphasizes, when God does not come to eat her food, Karma Bai becomes emotionally distraught, threatening to break his image into small pieces (see also Gold and Raheja 1994 for similar stories about householder women's devotions). God not eating the sweet dishes signifies a rejection of Karma Bai's love. However, as Shiv Giri maintains in that performance, "God had to come right" implying that God appears to Karma Bai and eats her *khīnch*, drawn to her because of her love, and not by his hunger. By feeding God, then, Karma Bai demonstrates the power of her "real faith"; she "really" believes "in her heart and mind," as Ganga Giri foregrounds in other conversations, that God will come, eat the *khīnch*, and enjoy it. Not surprisingly, every day God and his "big family" arrive at Karma Bai's home and feast on the delectable sweet dishes she has prepared for them. Yet, in an unpredictable twist of fate, this blessing becomes the very source of her troubles with the sadhus.

As the narrative dramatically shows, the group of male sadhus who asked Karma Bai to serve the temple and the gods during their absence on pilgrimage now suspect her of foul play. Without expressly saying as much, they accuse Karma Bai of being greedy and gluttonous, and attempt to tarnish her good name, or honor (*izzat*). The sadhus base their erroneous claims on the fact that Karma Bai spent more money than they had initially anticipated on the purchase of food and supplies for the temple. Unlike the sadhus, however, in the expectation that not only God, but his whole family would also come and eat, Karma Bai carefully decides the amount of ghee, sugar, and oil she will need to make the *khīnch*, and therewith purchases these materials on the agreed understanding that the sadhus will pay the storekeeper upon their return to the temple.

When the sadhus return to the city and inquire about their debt from the storekeeper, consumed by a mixture of shock and anger, they immediately confront Karma Bai by asking her, "How could you have spent so much money? Who came to the temple [and ate all the food]?" In response, Karma Bai tells them only what she knows—the truth: "You told me to serve God, so I did. God and His... family came to the temple. They ate the food. God ate the food." But the sadhus find this answer unacceptable and unconvincing. "How can we believe what you say? We serve God every day and we've never seen God eat the food," is their callous reply to Karma Bai. "But it's true! God eats," she exclaims, her pleas of course falling on deaf ears. Beyond their perceptions of her as greedy and gluttonous, the sadhus further imply that Karma Bai is a liar (*jhūtī*). And, as if to humiliate her more than they have already, the sadhus challenge Karma Bai to prove that God and His family really do eat the *khīnch* in her home: "We'll believe it when we see it," are the sadhus' last words to Karma Bai as they set off from her place.

Karma Bai's ordeal with the male sadhus leaves her an emotional wreck. "After all," Ganga Giri says in her performance, "this was an issue of [her] honor." In their questioning of Karma Bai's honor, the male sadhus fail to comprehend that her seemingly miraculous power to attract God and his family as honored guests to her home by offering them delicious sweet dishes stems from nothing less, and perhaps nothing more, than her unshakable faith in and love for God.[12] But the amazing devotional power that Karma Bai has managed to create and wield through her fierce love becomes confused with duplicity by the male sadhus, because of which they suspect her good name and accuse her of greed, gluttony, and lying. In the face of these serious accusations, Karma Bai, as the narrative intimates, suffers a great deal of emotional pain.

And yet, Karma Bai's suffering is neither unnoticed nor unappreciated by God. Implicit in Ganga Giri's narrative is the message that God is drawn to her like a magnet, both by the daily sacrifices Karma Bai makes on behalf of her strong faith in God by donating food and grain, as well as by the emotional suffering and conflict she experiences in the expression and defense of that faith. Importantly, in this story we encounter both the idea that women's suffering stems from their subordinate female gender status, and that women's ability to feel and acknowledge their pain is a direct result of their feminine gender. This gender-related power endows Karma Bai with the ability to feel "real" love, and as such, this makes her, in God's eyes, a better sadhu-*bhakt* than the male sadhus. In her analysis of *bhakti* from a Tamil perspective, Egnor has discussed the powerful role gender plays in females' ability to attract God through their love:

> *Bhakti* is a religion of emotion, of feeling (*unarcci*) as Tamils say, and without it all religion is empty. The emotion of the devotee, the pain of his longing and his love, give him a genuine power over the god he loves, the power to make the god come to him. It is this emotion alone that gives him that power. Women are regarded as inherently more religious than men, because they have naturally this power of feeling, of suffering for others, of love. It is said that male worshippers who seek union with the deity must "soften," that is, they must become like females, before their desire will be consummated. (Egnor 1991, 20–21)

On account of her love, God listens to and "meets" Karma Bai; however, he only agrees to grant her request to show up at her home once more and eat the *khīnch* in front of the disbelieving sadhus on the stipulation that she hang up a curtain (*pardā*). But why would God ask Karma Bai to place a curtain between him and the male sadhus? How might we understand God's seemingly unusual request to Karma Bai? As several scholars have variously discussed, more than just a tool for restriction, the curtain, in its role as a shield, creates distance between the viewer and the viewed, and by so doing, protects the privacy of its female wearers (Gold and Raheja 1994; Harlan 1992). In her examination of the concept of veiling or purdah (*pardā*) in women's oral traditions in North India, Ann Grodzins Gold maintains that it "is not a monolithic prison, but a subtle, fluid, and often highly manipulable bundle of precepts and practice" (1994, 169). For instance, in the case of male deities like Dev Narayanji, Gold suggests that purdah is used by devotees to protect and shield him from the "unpleasant sight" of liquor, a substance required by the lesser deity Bhairuji, and imbibed by his worshippers. From this perspective, purdah, as Gold argues, "gives license to perform displeasing or insubordinate acts" (1994, 169).

Gold's theory of purdah is similarly applicable to our analysis of Ganga Giri's Karma Bai narrative. In this story, the curtain may shield not so much God from the "unpleasant sight" of the sadhus, but rather the sadhus from God's displeasure. As God says to Karma Bai, "You have faith in me, so I come here to eat. But I won't come to eat while others are watching me [because they have no faith]." But there is another possibility. In making her request to God, Karma Bai remains motivated by the desire to redeem the perception of her honor in the eyes of the male sadhus. As the use of purdah also signifies the protection and maintenance of female honor, God's request to Karma Bai for a curtain indicates not only his understanding of, but also, perhaps, his identification with the emotional suffering Karma Bai experiences at the thought of losing her honor. In a reversal of the idea implicit in the Mira Bai and Rupa Rani narratives (namely, that female devotees acquire devotional power and "meet" God by means of their own mental or physical suffering), in this story we find that God "meets" Karma Bai through his identification with her pain and suffering. Ganga Giri's statement in the narrative to the effect that, "When the devotee calls [God] with such love in [her] heart, God has to come, right?" implies that God not only recognizes and understands Karma's love, but also empathizes with the suffering she experiences on account of her "real" love for him and her gender. God's request for a curtain intimates his identification with Karma Bai's pain and his intention to do something about it. Hence, while the curtain creates distance between God and his male devotees, it simultaneously creates intimacy and relationship between him and Karma Bai—a reward for her endearing faith in him. And God certainly ameliorates Karma Bai's suffering and her mounting fears by coming with his whole family to her home to eat the different sweet dishes she has prepared for them.

Witnessing this divine event through a mere hole in the curtain, the sadhus exclaim in amazement, "It's true! . . . All the gods [are here] and they're eating!" Once they realize the power of Karma Bai's faith in God, the sadhus immediately prostrate at her feet and say, "Sister, you're not a sadhu, but you're more of a sadhu than we are." This is a strong statement of renunciation implying *bhakti*/love. And the sadhus are right. Karma Bai is a "better" sadhu than they are because she "really loves" God; through faith she recovers her honor in the eyes of the male sadhus and empowers herself within that community of male religious authority. The image of the sadhus genuflecting before Karma Bai therefore evokes a theme central to the message of this narrative: that of the submission of male religious authority to female spiritual power.[13]

Performing Female Sadhu Authority and Lineage through Narrative

Performing vernacular stories serves as an effective rhetorical means through which the sadhus construct their female sadhu tradition and create themselves as virtuosi. Apart from establishing their spiritual power, performing *kahāniyān* also links the sadhus to a recognized tradition of devotional asceticism as expressed in medieval North Indian *bhakti*-saint religiosity, while also imbues their roles with credibility. Although scholars date the emergence of North Indian *bhakti* to over five hundred years ago, the sadhus perform the "ancient" historicity of their path by describing the people and events in their stories as belonging to a time period locally seen in terms of the glorious *satya yug* (literally, "the age of wisdom").[14] Similar contextualizations occur through means of keying their performances with the phrase, "this is an old [*purāṇī*] story that happened when people survived on truth alone." The sadhus' practices (re)create that perceived venerable history in the present milieu, and infuse received representations of *bhakti* with new life for themselves and their audiences. Their *sannyās*-as-practiced offers a meaningful possibility for how the *bhakts* lived and interpreted their everyday worlds and the complex negotiations they had to make in building those lives. The sadhus' bridging of vernacular religious imaginaries with daily realities shows the emergent potentialities of their performative practices to sustain continuity with, and effect the innovation of, *bhakti* traditions in vernacular contexts.

Furthermore, their performances not only connect the sadhus to a broader *bhakti* phenomenon, but also provide them a specific lineage with which to claim and craft the historical authenticity of their asceticism as practiced. Performing stories of female devotional asceticism, such as those analyzed earlier in the chapter, are especially crucial to authorizing oral lineage histories, as the sadhus cite the *bhakts*' femaleness to explain why women possess the right at all to become sadhus in a society where they are expected to be mothers and wives. According to the sadhus, *bhakts* like Mira Bai, Rupa Rani, and Karma Bai represent brave pioneers in the constructing of female lineages of devotional asceticism in North India. Many of the sadhus told me that by virtue of the omnipresent "grace" (*kṛpā*) of Mira Bai, they, too, have been able to renounce as sadhus of her particular lineage, through whom they receive power and authority as female sadhus. An illustrative conversation with Shiv Puri underscores this idea:

[S]HIV [P]URI: A long time ago, during Lord Krishna's time, there lived Mira Bai... She was the daughter of a Rajput [and] the Rana's wife. She was the wife of the Rana of Chittor. So after that [i.e., after Mira Bai's time], and by her grace, in our Rajput community 'ladies' have [been able to] become sadhus [like her].

[A]NTOINETTE: So, as far as you know, was Mira Bai the first Rajput woman to become a sadhu?

SP: Yes, Mira was the first lady sadhu. She was the first [woman] to become a sadhu in our Rajput clan.

A: Alright, and after that?

SP: Because of her grace, we have a lot of lady sadhus... In our Rajasthan, there are at least two hundred lady sadhus. There are two hundred lady sadhus that are Rajput. I counted them in the *Kumbh Melā*.

A: Do you know each other?

SP: Yes. We know each another... We all gather together at the *Kumbh Melā*. [This festival] happens every twelve years.

This passage relates that Mira's gender and her being from Rajasthan have the most social capital to the sadhus in legitimating their singing *bhajans* as *sannyās*. Shiv Puri traces the modern, regionally based female sadhu tradition to Mira Bai, and uses her femaleness to compose an ancient genealogy of female devotional asceticism in Rajasthan on account that Mira lived "a long time ago during Lord Krishna's time." In Shiv Puri's view, as "the first lady sadhu" from the Rajput community, Mira Bai's example allowed other "Rajput ladies" to turn away from the more accepted roles of wife and mother and sing *bhajans* to God. Shiv Puri's emphasis on the significance of Mira's devotional asceticism for Rajputs alludes to the inherent obstacles that women in this conservative caste group experience in their efforts to break away from established gender roles. She counts two hundred Rajput women who have taken *sannyās* through Mira's grace. Shiv Puri does not specify the types (or traditions) of their *sannyās*—only that "a lot" of these women exist. In my field study, I worked with female sadhus residing in three separate districts of Mewar, spread across a radius of approximately one hundred and fifty square kilometers. I encountered nothing near the number of female sadhus that Shiv Puri cites. At that time, though, I was searching for not only an "ideal type" of *sannyās* (that is, the kind illustrated by the mainstream imagination), but also the typical sadhu who belonged to an "official" *sannyās* organization, whether Shaiva or Vaishnava. Hence, I was not able to see the state of *sannyās*-as-lived in this region beyond my initially rigid conceptual parameters. For the female sadhus, *sannyās*-as-lived describes a much broader phenomenon with fluid boundaries. Shiv Puri's statement about there being two hundred Rajput sadhus in Rajasthan signals her understanding that *sannyās* is flexible enough to incorporate a dynamic tapestry of types, including the sadhus' singing *bhajans*, by which sadhus, *bhakts*, and *sants* reconfigure what *sannyās* means.[15]

The sadhus' attributing their *sannyās* to Mira Bai is significant. While they have taken initiation as Dashanamis or Naths from gurus who are considered as legitimate preceptors by the leaders of those monastic orders, the sadhus instead recognize Mira as their spiritual progenitor. Their initiations into Shaiva-based institutions provide a gateway for their ritually entering into the largely male-dominated world of *sannyās*, in which female sadhus are all too frequently seen as insignificant and marginal. By sharp contrast, Mira's vernacular example gives the sadhus something that Brahmanical *sannyās* does not—a *female* model of *sannyās* conceived as singing *bhajans* to God. The Brahmanical model's exclusion of women from *sannyās* leaves no room to consider singing *bhajans* a viable option. But Mira's model allows for this possibility. Her example establishes female asceticism as lived in Rajasthan and beyond as a both real and an acceptable life alternative to the dominant patriarchal imaginings of womanhood.

An Alternative Kind of Alternative Femininity? Reconsidering the Implications of Singing Bhajans *in Vernacular Asceticism*

If, as Chapter 2 and this chapter suggest, the sadhus view female *bhakts*' practices of singing *bhajans* as a traditional way of life, how alternative are their models of femininity? This is a critical question, given that the scholars who study the family of Mira traditions in particular mostly employ the term "alternative" in their common descriptions of her life to connote notions of resistance, subversion, defiance, and rebellion. For many scholars, Mira specifically illustrates an alternative to the more "traditional" (i.e., orthodox male) constructions of womanhood, because, in their view, she defiantly resists, subverts, and overcomes domesticity by becoming a renouncer. Mira's *sannyās* speaks clearly and loudly as a symbol of her resistance to patriarchal social norms, which, in turn, establishes her model as a gendered feminine alternative. In this construction, Mira's alternativeness constitutes a function of her resistance to patriarchy. With notions of resistance as its bulwark, Mira's alternative model reads, therefore, as transgressive womanhood. In making my claim, I am not questioning the fact that Indians, particularly Indian Hindu women, have seen Mira's model as transgressive (Harlan's 1992 study of Mira has provided an excellent example of this phenomenon among Rajput women in Rajasthan), or that the scholarly interpretations of Mira's behavior as a gendered form of resistance to hegemony are not persuasive on the basis of their evidence. Scholars of Mira Bai and the traditions attributed to her have supplied significant interpretations of this *bhakti* saint, and her role in the development of Hinduism and its constructs of gender and caste in Indian society. Nonetheless, such views have produced a dominant discourse (and model) of Mira Bai that privileges readings of resistance to the exclusion of other potentially empowering meanings of what "alternative" might also be to the women (and men) who draw on Mira's example.

What I am questioning, then, is the predominant scholarly tendency to graft the concept of resistance or its corollaries as the signifier for "alternative," in order to represent the lives and practices of women who do not themselves see or experience their worlds through categories such as feminism, resistance, power, and agency, or for whom such terms have markedly different significations than their Western (academic) meanings (cf. Knight 2011; Mahmood 2005; Mohanty 1991). Tracy Pintchman, too, questions the dominant association between "alternative" and "resistance" in academic interpretations of women's religious lives. She writes,

> While concerns about struggle or the dynamics of social dominance/resistance to domination certainly can be helpful for thinking about women's empowerment in traditional religious contexts, however, I would argue that the term "resistance" has been used overly broadly and in an unnuanced way to encompass too many types of discourses and practices. In particular, discussions of "resistance" tend sometimes to lump together alternative discourses, practices, representations, ideologies, and so forth, that do not conform to those associated with institutionally dominant groups with teleological discourses and practices that concretely envision or advocate an end goal of social change. (Pintchman 2005, 181)

The majority of the sadhus I interacted with are nonliterate and do not identify with the meanings or messages that scholars typically attribute to notions like power, for example. While the sadhus talk about power (*śakti; urjā*)—it is, indeed, a word in their vocabulary—for them the concept connotes the combination of *bhakti* and *tapasyā* (devotion and *sannyās*), by which they overcome adversity, fear, and chaos, and construct purposeful lives. From their perspective, power signifies neither a desire for social reform, nor a grand vision for gender equality (cf. Erndl 1997). Similarly, the sadhus' representing the singing of *bhajans* as a traditional way of life in their practices does not constitute a personal plea for all women to leave everything behind and become renouncers. Promoting this idea could be construed as an act of resistance and, hence, transgressive by the sadhus. To them, singing *bhajans* qualifies neither as resistance nor as transgressive, as it enacts divine duty. That *sannyās* occurs at all, by virtue of destiny, suggests, too, the sadhus' perceptions that, regardless of gender, not everyone is meant to be a renouncer.

Therefore, I am pushing for an alternative way to think about "alterative," in a manner that corresponds to the views articulated in the sadhus' practices. If "alternative" is equivalent to "resistance" and "subversion," then Mira's model is not an especially empowering example of alternative femininity to these sadhus, as they have a very different idea of this concept. But, if "alternative" connotes one who surrenders to God's will, sacrifices everything for God, and is prepared to suffer in order to manifest the fate God intends for her, Mira's example depicts an effective model of alternative femininity for them and other women in comparable life situations. When constructions of alternative femininity also mediate interpretations of living in the world in a traditional way, as the sadhus say in connection with Mira's and their *sannyās*, they open a dynamic space for women to pursue alternative life scripts and legitimate those realities.

The sadhus' female *bhakt* models of gender do not appear, then, to illustrate what Judith Okely refers to as "resistance to the conditions of subordination" engendered by normative patriarchal social structures and institutions (Okely 1989, 3–22). At the same time—and Okely persuasively contends this point in her discussion of individuals' "fragmented" and "momentary" resistance in cultures—even though the sadhus do not emphasize resistance in their practices, this alone is not an indication that they are oblivious to the reality of women's "fundamental subordination" in a patriarchal Indian society (Okely 1989, 6). Rather, they are hyperaware. Explicit or partially submerged critiques of the patriarchal structures and practices that subordinate women whose religious lives pose another possibility to normative life scripts for feminine gender appear in the form of a commentary threaded into the sadhus' narrative performances. After one narration of Mira's life, Ganga Giri offered this acerbic critique:

> Mira isn't respected in this Mewar. There is an image [*mūrtī*] of Mira in Chittor, but no one considers it... The people of Mewar lack faith.... Mira Bai's country [Mewar] is like this; Maharana Pratap's country is like this. The people are lazy [*alasi*] and ignorant [*ajnānī*]. [Manvendra Singh asks, "But, in Mewar, however many sadhus there are, they will consider Mira, right?" to which Ganga Giri responds:] If they have knowledge. But people don't know anything. They just eat and shit! And what else do they know? How to make babies. That's it. They don't know anything apart from this. This is hardly a big thing, isn't it? It's such a small thing. Even dogs produce babies! This is no big thing... Even birds make babies. There's nothing special in this. [But] people live in ignorance, in darkness.

By passing this stinging judgment on Mewari society, which, in Ganga Giri's view, remains submerged "in ignorance [and] darkness," she obliquely verbalizes her awareness of the structural patterns of women's subordination in a patriarchal culture. While not explicitly discussed in this passage, social castigation and approbation, as Ganga Giri intimates, are just some of the destructive ways that normative social structures attempt to control the minds and bodies of women dedicated to singing *bhajans* to the divine—women like Mira Bai, Rupa Rani, and Karma Bai. More significantly, beyond individual recognition of the underlying social forms of female subordination, the point Ganga Giri seems to want to make by means of this poignant criticism is that Mira Bai receives little or no respect in Mewar because "people" perceive her in the wrong way; that is, they do not see Mira Bai's true spiritual status because all they can think about is procreation. Such people, as Ganga Giri says, "are ignorant" and "don't know anything." Ganga Giri's statement implies the oppression of patriarchy—though it is not a term inherent to her or the other sadhus' conceptual apparatus—in thinking of women simply as reproducers.

Thus, the sadhus' performing of singing *bhajans* serves in a capacity similar to what Barbara Newman has characterized in her study of medieval female Christian renunciation, as a "modesty formula" (1987, cited in Jantzen 1997, 170) for enacting gendered expectations associated with the typically feminine ideals of humility and self-effacement as a means to authorize their positions in an androcentric religious institution, and construct themselves as respectable women in a society that views them with suspicion. Even the sadhus' self-abnegating representations as the "beggars" of God signify a rhetoric of humility that allows them to bridge competing renunciant and gendered expectations in a meaningful way. The scholarship on women and ethnography shows that women who serve in unusual roles of power and authority negotiate those positions by representing themselves as "good" women (Knight 2011; Flueckiger 2006; Hallstrom 1999). South Asian women locate their practices in the concept of modesty (*lajjā*), by which they perform their respectability.[16] Knight's work on Baul women in East India and Bangladesh offers an example of this process. She argues that Baul women navigate the rift between Baul and local gender expectations by constructing themselves as "good Bengali women" through use of the concept of *lajjā*, in order to gain the respect and protection of their non-Baul neighbors in the event that they are abandoned by their partners.[17]

Performances of modesty enable women to safeguard their reputations as good women, while accomplishing their religious goals. The writings of medieval Christian female mystics indicate that use of modesty formulas undercuts cultures and milieus. As cited by Grace Jantzen (1997), Newman has discussed the ways in which female mystics like Hildegard of Bingen, who deployed self-descriptions such as "a poor little figure of a woman," or Julian of Norwich, who apologetically wrote "though I am a woman, ignorant, weak, and frail," adopted modesty formulas in written discourse addressed to male ecclesiastical authorities as a means to claim spiritual authority in a religious tradition managed by men (Jantzen 1997, 170). In her interpretation of Newman's modesty theory with respect to Hildegard's life, Jantzen explains,

> This and her other formulas of humble self-description were part of a necessary self-abasement, a 'modesty formula' obligatory on medieval women writers. But, as Newman points out, these were also ideas that made it possible to compare her with Mary, the humble handmaid of God who was exalted to be the mother of Christ. If it was the very fact of Mary's humility that made her a suitable recipient of God's favour, then, it is implied, perhaps it is precisely Hildegard's lowliness as a 'poor little figure of a woman' that allows her to be exalted by the divine gift of visions to a position of spiritual authority. (Jantzen 1997, 170)

Similar self-representations of "lowliness" are expected of the sadhus as both women and sadhus. Let me stress that their modesty rhetoric constitutes a culturally gendered habit of mind, and not a conscious, strategic manipulation of others' perceptions of them. The notable difference between the Christian mystics described in the works of Newman and Jantzen and the sadhus is that the latter do not refer to their femaleness in statements implying female humility. Rather, their rhetoric appears to be gender-neutral, even though their use of these statements is gender-related. And yet, much like the examples of the Christian and Baul women, by signaling modesty formulas in their practices, the sadhus authenticate themselves without risking being seen as transgressive or morally loose, because *sannyās*, too, expects this behavior from its practitioners as a sign of their spiritual advancement and detachment. While the expression of humility underpinning their rhetoric would seem to contravene the sadhus' exerting agency, they continue to promote themselves as receptive agents of their worlds through the use of such idioms. In their view, only as the lowly "beggars of God," whose sufferings model their unconditional love for all beings and the divine, might the sadhus realize the ideals peculiar to their *sannyās* and prepare themselves to meet God, as they cross over the precarious ocean of worldly existence.

Conclusions: Vernacular Asceticism as "This-Worldly" Sannyās

In this chapter, we have investigated the vernacular narrative performance genre of *kahāniyān* in order to understand another expressive dimension through which the sadhus construct singing *bhajans* as *sannyās*. In these performances, the sadhus take the Brahmanical renunciant values of suffering, sacrifice, and struggle and selectively adjust their meanings in light of multifaceted *bhakti* frameworks to craft vernacular asceticism in Rajasthan. Moreover, by telling their stories, the sadhus perform the relevance of gender for the ways that both *bhakti* and *sannyās* are lived. The gender-related troubles that women who sing to God face transform the quality of their *bhakti*, which gives them superior moral power over men (i.e., women make better sadhus than men) and creates them as "real" sadhus who are able to overcome hardship.

Narrative performance makes it possible for the sadhus to place their *sannyās* within an ancient tradition of female devotional singing, à la Mira Bai; by telling the stories of female *bhakts* they claim authority and credibility as female sadhus and situate themselves within an exceptional lineage of female devotional asceticism. On account of the eminent examples of Mira Bai, Rupa Rani, and Karma Bai, who left behind "all happiness" for God, the sadhus say that they, too, have received the compelling inspiration and the spiritual wherewithal to do the same. By the same token, to leave everything and sing to God hardly signifies to the sadhus an intentional act of resistance to normative patriarchal social structures. Rather, their performances comparably show that a life of singing enacts a divine call of duty and devotion to God, to one's spiritual community, or to one's guru. Locating their *sannyās* in a female lineage indicates that the sadhus do not see their devotional asceticism as competing with the dominant male traditions of *sannyās*. Their emphasis on a regional female sadhu tradition indexes their views of *sannyās* as flexible and heterogeneous. Vernacular asceticism depicts the features of multiplicity and fluidity, a bricolage, in fact—a phenomenon in which many types of *sannyās* (co)exist, and in which *bhakti* plays a much more substantial role than the mainstream imagination suggests.

Finally, the values and virtues that the sadhus accentuate in their narrative performances serve in the capacity of modesty formulas for enacting humility that helps them to navigate gender-related and renunciant expectations productively and undermine prevalent societal perceptions of their lives as transgressive. In this way, the sadhus construct themselves and their *sannyās* as traditional, ensuring their spiritual status and social reputations in their communities.

Although carefully positioned within the larger sphere of renunciation, the dynamic world of devotional asceticism that is performatively constituted by the sadhus in *satsang* is not an "other-worldly" *sannyās* structured by the extreme ideals of penance, denial, and bodily self-mortification illustrative of the orthodox Sanskritic model. Rather, consisting of "the virtuous" people—i.e., sadhus, *bhakts*, and others who gather to remember God—the sadhus' asceticism as practiced performs a "this-worldly" or deeply engaged *sannyās*, shaped by a combined sense of love and compassion for the world. In Chapter 7, we will explore the sadhus' constructions of *sannyās* as interpersonal and celebratory. For now, however, this chapter leaves readers with the understanding that, at the levels of experience and practice, singing *bhajans* performs and establishes, as the sadhus' narratives show, a way of life that is grounded in-the-world and oriented by *bhakti* interpretations of suffering, sacrifice, and struggle. In the next chapter, we will consider the role of caste status in the sadhus' constructing of singing *bhajans* as *sannyās*.

4

"*On the Battlefield of* Bhakti"

GENDER AND CASTE IN VERNACULAR ASCETICISM

No two sadhus are the same. Everyone's nature is different.

—GANGA GIRI MAHARAJ

If a sadhu lives in Mewar people say, "Oh, that's Mira's country. His sannyās is glorious!"

—SHARDA PURI

The Conceptual Topography of Rajasthani Values in the Sadhus' Sannyās

LIVING IN THE land of Rajasthan gives the sadhus a sense of pride and satisfaction. Many of them extol its virtues by characterizing the region as "Mira's land" or "Maharana Pratap's country." The sadhus tend to speak about Rajasthan as a unified cultural-political entity, but they also distinguish Mewar from the former princely state of Marwar (Jodhpur district), and from other districts such as Jaisalmer, Barmer, Bikaner, Jaipur, and Ajmer. To the sadhus, Mewar is unlike any other place in Rajasthan. "There is such a big difference," Sharda Puri says, between Mewar and the other areas of Rajasthan. Her guru, Nityananda Puri, concedes: "The difference is like that between the earth and the sky." Sharda Puri continues: "The people who are from Mewar, the honor they speak with, the respect they speak with, you do not find that in Marwar." Unlike Sharda Puri, who was born in Mewar, Nityananda Puri, with the permission of his guru, came to Mewar in 1952 from "outside"—he was born in Delhi and was living in an ashram in the city with his guru before arriving in Mewar. He feels, however, that living in Mewar for the last fifty-three years—first as the abbot of an ashram near Suraj Pol gate in Udaipur city, and later as the abbot of his own ashram in Losingh village, Udaipur district—has made his mind "strong." Nityananda Puri says that "the influence [*prabhāv*] of the land" has permeated his mind-body and turned him into a "Mewari sadhu": that is, a fierce and heroic sadhu.

The idea of Rajasthan as the land of "very brave people [*bahut hī jordār log*]," which the sadhus emphasize in their statements, is related to the popular regional perception (which anyone who has ever spent time in the state has likely encountered in image, myth, and symbol) that Rajasthan constitutes the "land of kings," and that Rajputs (lit., "son of kings"), a community related to the Kshatriya class, represent its rightful heirs (Lodrick 2001; Meister 2001; Harlan 1992; 2003; Kolff 1990; Rudolph and Rudolph 1984). The widespread association made between Rajasthan and Rajputs, between a specific land and a specific class of people, has perpetuated a distinctive ethos of the martial Rajput, in which the "peculiarly and uniquely" Rajput ideals of bravery, self-sacrifice, honor, and the protection of truth in the name of a generalized Hindu *dharm* are seen as having made Rajasthan the heroic land that many Rajasthanis and non-Rajasthanis imagine it to be (Hitchcock 1959, 10; Harlan 2003; D. Gold 2001).

In this ethos, Mewar has pride of place. The heroic myths of the bardic traditions of Rajasthan, for example, have played a formative role in the transmission of the notion of Mewar's renowned martial status (Meister 2001, 144; Smith 1991; Tod and Crooke 2010, vol. 2). Riveting tales about legendary, and royal, Rajput figures such as Bappa Rawal (ca. eighth century), who is credited with establishing the kingdom of Mewar at the fortress of Chittor,[1] and Maharana Pratap Singh Sisodiya (ca. sixteenth century), Maharana Udai Singh's[2] eldest son, who is thought to have defiantly resisted Mughal imperial forces in the battle at Haldigathi[3] when Rajput kings in other principalities of Rajputana surrendered to Akbar's power, have validated ideas of Mewar's uncommon heroism. Influenced by those bardic compositions, which were commissioned by the princely courts, nineteenth-century British civil servant Colonel James Tod, in his classic three-volume work *Annals and Antiquities of Rajasthan*, eulogized Mewar as the land embodying what he and others, British and Indian, perceived as authentic "Rajputness." In Tod's estimation, Mewar's elite Rajput exemplified "conquest, sovereignty, and superiority over inherently lesser subjects" (Harlan 2003, 63; Tod and Crooke 2010, vol. 2). Tod's idea of the real (and hypermasculinized) Rajput, though relished by many Mewaris today as an accurate depiction of their ancient history, expresses a relatively recent ideological construction in Rajput historiography (Kolff 1990, 71–116; Bayly 1999; Schomer et al. 2001). The work of historian Dirk Kolff (1990) has shown that, in the late sixteenth century, Carans and Bhats employed as bards in the service of the royal Rajput courts constructed a "new Rajput Great Tradition," in which the concept "Rajput" became synonymous with an orthodox aristocratic genealogy (i.e., "Rajput" was seen as a closed-status group and genealogically defined landed class) characterized by radical militaristic vigor and uncharacteristic boldness, particularly in connection with resistance to Muslim authority (73; Harlan 2003, 31; Bayly 1999, 25–63). As Kolff observes, by the seventeenth century, "Mewar had become the seat of this new Rajput genealogical orthodoxy" (1990, 73; cf. Bayly 1999).

The martial characteristics that distinguish Rajasthan and Mewar, in particular, as a sociocultural and political region signify the high-caste attributes of the dominant Rajput class (Harlan 2003, 45).[4] Thus, the association that many Rajasthanis make between Rajasthan and Rajput status, implying that being Rajasthani is equivalent to imagining oneself as Rajput, continues to support the preeminence and superiority of Rajputs as a ruling class entitled to receive the loyalty and subservience of the perceived lower ranking Rajputs, the lower-castes, *and* the Brahmins. While the reign of the ruling Rajput families in Rajasthan and elsewhere in India ended in 1949, two years after the country's independence from Britain, and India's Congress Party required that the former princely states integrate themselves into the newly formed Republic of India, the idea of royal authority and the principles it stands for still have cultural currency for many Rajasthanis. The householder acquaintances with whom I spoke, for instance, recall wistfully the time in which India "was ruled by great kings." Whenever the erstwhile Maharana of Udaipur, Arvind Singh Mewar Sisodiya, is seen in any one of his classic vintage cars on the streets of Udaipur city, people bow reverently and say "*Mahārāṇa kī jay* [victory to the King]." The sadhus, too, reminisce about the glory of India's former monarchies. Sharda Puri explains that "[n]ow it is the time of the Public [the Congress Party]. It is the Public who makes us win, and it is the Public who makes us lose... Earlier, everybody was scared of the kings. Earlier, the kings used to give their heads for their people." In response Nityananda Puri says, "Today, there is neither a king nor a subject. We have to be the kings of our own bodies." Thus, when we consider that the sadhus' *sannyās* is practiced, and just as vitally, is evolving "in a region that idealizes royal authority" (D. Gold 2001, 255), the impact of regional culture and princely regional traditions on constructions of their religious worlds invites examination.

The Royal Rajput as the Ideal Sadhu: Merging Caste and Sadhu Identities

To that end, let us return to the sadhus' statements about the exceptional rulership of kings. Sharda Puri suggests the idea of the martial Rajput in connection with her understanding of the warrior-king who sacrificed his "head" for his people. Her words recall widely known ancient mythic stories featuring Vedic/Brahmanical sacrificial imagery, on which the sadhus draw in their interpretations of caste, rank, and status. Notice that the king's head functions as a trope for his life. In the Vedic ritual texts, and in the subsequent (Epic and Puranic) Hindu cosmological mythologies, the head symbolizes the best of all things—intelligence, wisdom, purity, truth, and life essence (Heesterman 1985, 45–58; Olivelle 1992). A classic example of this concept is featured in the *Rg Veda* (RV) 10.90, "Hymn to Purusha," a text with which the sadhus are familiar. Here, the god Purusha offers his body as the ultimate sacrifice, and from his great sacrifice emerges the entire cosmos, including the four hierarchically arranged caste (*varna*) communities. More specifically, the sacrifice of the Purusha's head produces the Brahmin *varna* (priests, scholars, and teachers); the sacrifice of his arms produces the Kshatriya *varna* (warriors/soldiers); the sacrifice of his thighs produces the Vaishya (or Baniya) *varna* (merchants, businesspeople, and land cultivators); and, finally, the sacrifice of his feet produces the Shudra *varna* (service-based laborers) (*RV* 10.90, Doniger 1981, 29–32). The correspondence of the four *varnas* with the specific body parts of the Purusha symbolically alludes to their perceived levels of purity or impurity. In this framework, the Brahmin (head) has the highest degree of purity, whereas the Shudra (feet) has the highest degree of impurity.

The connection that Sharda Puri makes between kings and heads, though, is noteworthy. Her comment indicates that royal power is not limited to the temporal realm, but rather extends into the spiritual realm as well (see also D. Gold 2001 for a discussion of this idea in connection with the Dadu-*panth* religion). Although the warrior *varna* is cosmologically identified with the Purusha's arms, symbolizing the mighty Kshatriya attribute of martial protection and, hence, a lower purity level than the Brahmin's, the king's offering of his own head—and by extension, his own body—in battle in the fulfillment of his cosmic duty (*dharm*) of protection likens him to the cosmic Purusha itself. In her study of contemporary Rajasthani hero cults, Lindsey Harlan (2003) observes, "In the myriad hero stories in which the heroes cut off their own heads, the sacrifice and the sacrificed are succinctly represented as one" (52). To that extent, the warrior-king's self-sacrifice appears to neutralize, or erase altogether, the karmic impurity acquired from his intentional (and expected) taking of human life in battle. His self-sacrifice, therefore, elevates him to same level as the Brahmin's, and, as a result, places these two status systems in perennial tension, "equaliz[ing] the religious potential of Brahmins and Rajputs" (D. Gold 2001, 254).[5] As with the Purusha's sacrifice, the warrior-king's violent sacrificial death brings about renewed life. The blood that the warrior dutifully spills on the battlefield in defense of his people, his principles, and his *dharm* doubly signifies the offering of his life in exchange for the protection of others' lives and, as a result of his selfless sacrificial exchange, the promise of everlasting life for him in heaven. Thus, embedded in the transactional symbology of the Vedic sacrificial imagery—which, as the work of Harlan (2003; 1992) shows, the Rajashani hero cults invoke via their symbols, ideologies, and rituals par excellence—is the notion that by virtue of his peculiar ability to sacrifice himself for the benefit of others, the warrior-king manifests a living god on earth (cf. Harlan 2002; 2000). Indeed, the reverence shown to Arvind Singh in both non-ritual and ritual contexts is linked to the popular Mewari belief that he represents the human form of Shiva (Eklingji). The interplay of the royal and the sacred constitutes a hallmark of Hinduism(s). The idea of a god as ruler and king of the universe, and vice versa, illustrates a prevailing theme in many of its theologies and literary and oral traditions. Sharda Puri's statement intimates, then, shared Mewari views of the innate power, heroism, and divinity of their former Rajput rulers.

Moreover, Sharda Puri's comment tacitly distinguishes the selfless rule of India's former kings from the selfish rule of the current democracy of the Indian Congress Party. Nityananda Puri concurs with Sharda Puri. His statement that immediately follows Sharda Puri's signals his perspective of the Congress government as weak and ineffective, inept in its purported capacity to lead and help the people. This image of India's present leadership effectively contrasts with that of, as Sharda Puri says, the "earlier kings," whose uniquely Rajput attributes endowed them with the authority to rule and the ability to be competent and truthful rulers. Furthermore, notice that Nityananda Puri's saying that "we [sadhus] have to be the kings of our own bodies," and his earlier comment in the same conversation that his living in Mewar has turned him into a "Mewari sadhu," constructs sadhus as the "new" kings: that is, as the new royal Rajputs. While the idea of controlling the body constitutes a common trope in renunciant discourse, if we allow that the sadhus' *sannyās* has absorbed the dominant cultural (and religious) elements of its geographical surroundings, it is likely that Nityananda Puri interprets and adapts that idea through the prism of the self-control that a brave warrior is thought to exhibit in battle. The particular virtues of sacrifice, suffering, and struggle that they underscore as illustrative of asceticism parallel Rajput attributes. In constructing *sannyās* in this way, Nityananda Puri and Sharda Puri conflate high-caste characteristics with renunciation. As this chapter will show, many of the female sadhus I worked with engender and enact this same kind of conceptual fusion in their practices.

The Peculiar Place of Caste in Ideal and Lived Models of Sannyās

In the dominant model of Brahmanical *sannyās*, a renouncer ideally leaves behind his or her previous caste identity in his or her radical renunciation of the world (Olivelle 1992). This lofty ideal is typically expressed in the sadhus' use of a well-known vernacular-language idiom, their version of which represents a reconfiguring of an oft-cited phrase widely attributed to the illustrious anti-caste (and anti-Brahmanical) guru Ramananda (ca. fourteenth century), founder of the renowned Ramanandi movement: "Don't ask a sadhu his caste; ask him about knowledge instead."[6] The work of Richard Burghart (1978; 1983), Robert Lewis Gross (2001), Sondra Hausner (2007), Ramdas Lamb (2002; 2008), Wendy Sinclair-Brull (1997), Kirin Narayan (1989), and Peter van der Veer (1988) has shown, however, that the phenomenon of *sannyās*-as-lived in North and South India diverges considerably in its ideologies, institutions, and practices from the standard Brahmanical model. Ideas about caste are no exception. Many of the sadhus with whom these scholars worked not only continued to underscore their caste identities (*jātī*) from birth, but also reproduced in their practices with householders *and* other sadhus the hierarchical structures and exclusionary patterns of behavior that are based on, and informed by, common cultural understandings of the inherent purity or impurity of caste communities. As Narayan (1989) has observed in her fieldwork with the storyteller sadhu Swamiji, "All Indian sadhus were, after all, born into a particular caste, and the indoctrination of upbringing does not altogether vanish with initiation" (77). She goes on:

> Watching Swamiji, it struck me that in certain arenas of interaction he did indeed continue to act like a Brahman concerned with purity: his small kitchen was always scrupulously cleaned, and though he welcomed people from low castes he nonetheless saw menstruation as polluting and asked that women not touch him, his food, or his altar when they "sat apart" (a common euphemism for menstruation). (Narayan 1989, 77)

My research with female sadhus in Rajasthan supports the trenchant findings of other South Asia scholars on the importance of caste status, caste ideals, and caste values to sadhus' *sannyās*. The significance of this pattern on the relevance of caste in vernacular asceticism cannot be overemphasized. Because the Brahmanical representations of *sannyās* privilege the value of itinerancy—that is, the transcendence of geographic boundaries—the mobility afforded to sadhus often encourages scholars to assume that not only textually based renunciation(s), but also *sannyās*-as-lived reflect and reproduce the pan-Hindu (i.e., Sanskritic) goal of transcending the social boundaries of caste and gender, as well, in the ultimate quest for *mokṣ*. The implication here is twofold: First, regardless of their sects, sadhus' goals of "salvation and renunciation" override caste and gender concerns (D. Gold 2001, 261). Second, upholding and maintaining caste customs and values, in particular, illustrates the this-worldly orientation of regional (or localized) Hinduisms, which "are more likely to offer relief from this-worldly distress" (D. Gold 2001, 261) than the supposed otherworldly Sanskritic traditions of *sannyās*. Such assumptions, therefore, reconstitute and reinforce the schematic conceptual binaries of the "Great" and "Little" Hindu Traditions. Through their syncretism of both Sanskritic and regional ideals, institutions, and practices—a phenomenon illustrative of what I have characterized as "vernacular asceticism"—the sadhus' *sannyās* challenges these dichotomies.

On the issue of the impact of regional traditions on *sannyās*, my research further supports the exploratory observations that Daniel Gold (2001) makes in the context of his findings of the pervasiveness of "Rajput institutions and ideals of martial valor" on "religious traditions that have developed in Rajasthan," like the unorthodox Dadu-*panth* (literally, "Dadu's way" or "Dadu's path"), a medieval *sant* movement originating with the Rajasthani poet-saint Dadu Dayal (ca. sixteenth century) (Gold, 242). This *panth*, unlike other competing *sant panths* during its heyday, such as those deriving from two of the best known poet-saints in North India's *sant-bhakti* conglomerate, Kabir and Nanak, developed under the royal patronage of the Jaipur state and, as Gold explains, became integrated "into the Rajput political order" (242). Similarly, "the predominance of celibate soldiers and scholars in the Dadu-*panth*," many of whom—like the warrior-sadhus—came from respectable Rajput backgrounds, indicated the crucial role of royal power in this sect's construction of a distinctive martial Rajput identity (Gold, 248). The institution of the warrior, or Naga,[7] sadhu of the Dadu-*panth*, which was much in favor with the Jaipur court, began in 1797 and was officially disbanded in 1938 (242).

Thus, as Gold argues, the Dadu-*panth* reflects, in its history, ideologies, and institutional structures, the high-caste standards of its former ruling Rajput patrons. What my data contributes to Gold's historical analysis concerns new ethnographic evidence that non-institutionalized as well as non-patronized expressions of *sannyās*, like the female sadhus' devotional asceticism, are as susceptible to Rajput cultural influences as are the more established, patronized, and institutionalized forms, such as the Dadu-*panth*. My research shows that, as with gender, caste also matters to the sadhus. It shapes their experiences of *sannyās*; it structures their interactions with householders and other sadhus as they live it; and it can help validate their "right" to serve in their unconventional roles. Moreover, regional and Mewari ideals, values, and customs affect the sadhus' ideas about gender and caste, which, in turn affect their conceptions and constructions of *sannyās*. We will explore the questions of why and how caste matters to these sadhus, and the extent to which their caste identities shape their sadhu identities. Furthermore, we will examine the ways that the dominant Rajput influence impacts the sadhus' craftings of their caste and renunciant identities, and the associations made between those identities on its basis. The data that I document and analyze below brings into sharp focus a fascinating pattern with respect to the sadhus' perceptions of the relationship between caste status and sadhu status in vernacular asceticism, and the role of the regional ethos of the martial Rajput in forming this perception, performed in their rhetoric of renunciation, and in their public feasting ceremonies (*bhaṇḍāra*), which are attended by householders and other sadhus, and which are held in commemoration of their gurus' *mahāsamādhi*,[8] their completion of a ritual vow (*vrat*), or the establishment of their ashrams or a new ritual image, temple, or shrine at their ashrams.

This chapter suggests that the female sadhus' practices perform a renunciant ethos of ambivalence in regard to the perceived relationship between caste status and sadhu status. While both the male sadhus and the female sadhus speak about their castes and, to varying extents, follow caste purity codes in their everyday social relations with householders and other sadhus, the female sadhus associate sadhus' caste status and the purity it implies with sadhus' ability to sing *bhajans*, i.e., with their inherent capacity to endure (or not) the hard life of *sannyās*. The ethos described here has two competing sides to it—the inclusive and the exclusive. The inclusive side of this ethos—the side one might expect to find in *bhakti*-inspired movements (but cf. Burchett 2009; see also Prentiss 1999, 27 for a similar discussion)—suggests that sadhu status overrides and negates caste status. Here, the question of a sadhu's caste remains irrelevant. In this framework, sadhus distinguish themselves as authentic by singing to God and, also, due to the knowledge that results from singing. Viewed from this socially democratic angle, the sadhus' practices support the observations of scholars that "renunciation can allow one to side-step social hierarchies" (Khandelwal 2009, 1011) and "offers social solace in a non-discriminating community and a deliberate inversion of the dominant power structure" (Hausner 2007, 184).

By contrast, the exclusionary side of this ethos—the aspect addressed in this chapter, and that aspect one would not expect to find in *bhakti* traditions—argues, sometimes vehemently, that sadhu status and caste status are inextricably related. Here, sadhu status is determined in large part by caste status. That is, rather than sadhu status overriding (or lessening the significance of) birth-given caste status, it can be enhanced or authorized by caste status. The castes to which the female sadhus attribute notions of legitimacy and efficacy concern the high-caste (and high-purity) Rajput and Brahmin communities. Recall, for example, Sharda Puri's merging of high-caste (Rajput) status and sadhu status ("Mewari sadhu") in her description of *sannyās*. Sharda Puri comes from a noble Rajput caste, which she brings up in conversation. All of the high-caste sadhus I know talk about their caste identities. They say, "I am a Rajput sadhu" or "I am a Brahmin sadhu." Some of them go so far as to discuss the specificity of their *jātī* within their *varnas*, e.g., Sisodiya Rajput, Jhala Rajput, or Goswami Brahmin.

On the flip side, I never heard a sadhu say, "I am a Baniya sadhu"[9] or "I am a Shudra sadhu." For those sadhus belonging to the low(er) castes, they simply say, "We are sadhus." It seems incongruous to them to speak about their former caste identities *because they are sadhus*. And yet, these sadhus also seem hyperaware of the exclusionary renunciant ethos in and around Mewar that measures a sadhu's authenticity on the basis of her *jātī*'s ranking. The incongruity perceived by the low-caste sadhus never appeared to be an issue for those sadhus born into the purportedly high-ranking Rajput and Brahmin "houses." Some of these sadhus occasionally seemed—usually at public gatherings like *bhaṇḍāras*, where strategic sadhu displays of status and prestige are quite common—preoccupied with informing other sadhus, including friends, acquaintances, and me, of their respectable statuses. By announcing their *jātīs* before others, these sadhus are by all accounts "pulling rank" in their communities. Such sadhus claim that the innate character traits associated with their elevated caste status, like wisdom (*jnān*), courage (*himmat*), self-sacrifice (*kurbān*), and truth (*satya*), increases, strengthens, and sustains their *sannyās*. They also consider these preeminent caste-based characteristics to be common *specifically* to both Rajputs and Brahmins. I am convinced that such a discriminatory and hegemonic ethos exists in the sadhus' *sannyās* on account of the popular regional association between Rajasthan and Rajput.

Thus, in the framework of the exclusionary dimension of this ethos, Rajput and Brahmin-born sadhus represent the ideal sadhu. Note that the ambivalence implied by the association between high-caste status and the *ideal* sadhu in this ethos opens up a sliver of a space to allow the possibility of low-caste people also taking *sannyās*. Be that as it may, such a claim simultaneously reinforces and replicates an exclusive ideology of essentialism that, in turn, promotes an attitude of high-caste entitlement in *sannyās*-as-lived in Mewar and, as the data of other scholars indicate, elsewhere in India. But Mewar's unique social-political and cultural context illuminates the regional (or Rajasthani) contours and nature of such an ethos. Specifically, the pursuit of truth and religion, as I was told, is thought to come "naturally [*svabhāv se*]" to high-caste sadhus. Similarly, because the sadhus who expressed this ethos see their role as that of protecting and defending *dharm*, they believe that sadhus born as Brahmins or Rajputs feel especially compelled "from inside [*andar se*]" to save their religion from "corruption [*bhraṣṭācār*]." A conversation I had in the summer of 2005 with Maya Nath, a noble Rajput, in which we discussed the significance of Mira Bai's example for female sadhus in Rajasthan, makes explicit this understanding: "Mira Bai was a Rajput. See, originally, only Brahmins and Rajputs took renunciation [*sannyās liyā*]... They will never cheat their religion... A Brahmin's nature [*prakṛti*] and a Rajput's nature are the same. That's why they had the right [*adhikār*] to renounce in the beginning, because they would give their lives for their religion."

Maya Nath's representation of *sannyās* as "originally" for Rajputs and Brahmins has text-based parallels. The phenomenon of vernacular asceticism, as this book shows, often constitutes at the levels of theory *and* practice a creative mixing and modulating of multiple religious-cultural resources. The sadhus' *sannyās*-as-lived in Mewar, for example, draws on classical Brahmanical resources, which may have *bhakti*-inspired elements, and classical-medieval *bhakti* resources, which may either promote or challenge Brahmanical ideologies and institutions. Despite its myriad forms and varieties "on the ground," historically, though, renunciation has been represented in a number of authoritative texts on the subject (e.g., *Mānava Dharmaśāstra, Samnyāsa Upaniṣads Yatidharmaprakāśa* and *Yatidharmasamuccaya*) as an originally high-caste Brahmanical institution that privileges orthodox Brahmanical theologies and worldviews (Olivelle 1992; 1996; 1983; 1975; Heesterman 1985; Dumont 1960).

One way that the underlying elite Brahmanical "spirit" of renunciation is illustrated in such writings involves the "connections between theologies of sacrifice and renunciation" made by the mostly male Brahmin authors of those texts (Olivelle 1992, 3–18, 71). In his analysis of the *Samnyāsa Upaniṣads*, Patrick Olivelle demonstrates that the dominant Brahmanical constructions of *sannyās* invoked and expanded on the logic of the ancient Vedic imagery of the ritual sacrifice (cf. Heesterman 1985, 26–44). In this framework, the ideal renouncer not only internalized the sacrificial fires within himself,[10] the renouncer actually became the ideal Brahmin. As Olivelle observes, the majority of these texts took for granted that the person (i.e., the man) who renounced the world had the authority to perform the Vedic sacrifices in the first place (Olivelle 1992, 83). The virtues of independence and individuality that identify the Brahmanical renouncer's radical life of detachment, in turn, constitute a function of his internationalization and perfection of the Vedic sacrificial performances, by which he is symbolically reborn as the perfect Brahmin (Olivelle 1992, 69). The message of the Brahmanical texts is transparent: *sannyās* transforms sadhus into ideal Brahmins. Moreover, it suggests that a Brahmin is most fit to renounce *sansār* and become the ideal sadhu. But Mewar's vernacular asceticism shows a shift of perspective occurring with respect to the royal Rajput as equaling the superiority of the Brahmin. Thus, a sadhu's renunciation pushes him to the top of the hierarchical caste system, not outside of it, on par with the best of Brahmins, and in Mewar, with princely Rajputs. The ideals that define the perfect Brahmin's or Rajput's life structure the extraordinary sadhu's life. While renunciation, in theory, enables a sadhu to shed (or loosen) his caste identity, it ritually establishes him as the high-ranking member of the highest caste at the same time.

Another way that the institution of *sannyās* presents its elite Brahmanical origins concerns the exclusion of those who are not "twice-born." Brahmanical *sannyās* intentionally limited its membership to high-caste Brahmins, Kshatriyas, and Vaishyas. Olivelle explains,

> With regard to caste, it is obvious that people not belonging to the three upper classes (*varna*) are not permitted to perform the rite of renunciation.... Even though *Śūdras* and other low-caste persons are *clearly excluded*, there is some uncertainty as to whether persons from all three upper classes or only Brahmins could perform this rite... It is nevertheless evident that even though these *Upaniṣads* do not explicitly exclude others, they address themselves principally to Brahmins. (Olivelle 1992, 83; emphasis mine)

This high-caste elitism of Brahmanical *sannyās* still exists today, particularly in the Shaiva-based forms of renunciation, such as the orthodox Shankaracarya Dashanami Order.[11] With two exceptions in my research, all of the low-caste sadhus sought their initiations from the Nath tradition, which generally espouses a much more inclusive religious ideology in connection with sadhus' caste status than that of the Dashanamis. Not all of the high-caste sadhus I worked with, however, were initiated into the mostly elitist Dashanami tradition. For example, Rajput sadhus like Maya Nath, Devi Nath, Saraswati Nath, and Ganesh Nath as well as the Brahmin sadhus Lehar Nath and Prem Nath, as their *dīkṣā* names suggest, all took renunciation from within the Nath tradition. Besides the Dashanami's exclusionary practices, there are also administrative branches (*akhāḍhā*),[12] such as the Niranjani Akhara, within the hierarchical structures of Shaiva *sannyās* that only offer twice-born sadhus membership in their sadhu organizations (Hausner 2007, 39).

The ethos of ambivalence established in the female sadhus' asceticism resonates with the Brahmanical orthodoxy's ideology of the sadhu as exemplifying the perfect Brahmin. But the reason that the Brahmanical texts give in legitimating their elitist ideology contrasts with the sadhus' rationale for their exclusionary ethos of the well-born sadhu as illustrative of the best of sadhus. Whereas the Brahmanical texts cite an individual's Vedic initiation and right to perform the requisite Vedic sacrificial rites as *prima facie* qualifications for initiation into *sannyās*, the sadhus locate their claims in their perceptions of the peculiar nature of *bhakti* itself as the criterion that makes *sannyās* possible. *Bhakti*, they argue, is not for the faint of heart. In making these kinds of statements, the sadhus accentuate the idea of *the bhakti of renouncers*, and not a generalized or generic notion of *bhakti*, as both arduous and uncommon. Renunciant *bhakti*, as this book suggests, represents a distinct category of *bhakti* in the sadhus' practices. In this context, doing *bhakti* is a lot like being a warrior, and the characteristics associated with the high castes are thought to make it work. Hence, for most of the female sadhus, *bhakti* represents "a difficult path." In Ganga Giri's words: "*Bhakti* is not so easy. It's not lying on the road. It is very precious... It is something which is round and slippery [*gol-mol gaṭṭā*] and there's no place to hold it. It is the most expensive thing [*sab se mahangī cīz*]; the best of all things [*uttam vastu*]."

The sadhus' understandings of *bhakti* as a difficult path are, therefore, embedded in their renunciant ethos of caste ambivalence. Note that their rhetoric of renunciation performs a similar ambivalence about *bhakti*. While, ideally, the concept provokes an attitude of disregarding social distinctions, the sadhus invoke *bhakti* to distinguish between householders and sadhus, as well as between sadhus. As an example, "It is equal for everyone," Ganga Giri explains in her *satsangs*. "Anybody can serve God, humans, sadhus, Brahmins. The path of *bhakti* is the same for everyone. Whether you are a girl [*corī*] or a boy [*corā*]; whether you work in the fields; whatever work you do. Everyone has the same right [*adhikār*]. It's not that only sadhus and Brahmins have a special contract [*ṭhekā*] for *bhakti*. Everyone's right is the same." But, as we saw in Chapter 3, *bhakti* hardly signifies a singular phenomenon to the sadhus. Even if "everyone's right" to practice *bhakti* is "the same," everyone's *bhakti* surely is not the same. *Bhakti* expresses an expansive spectrum of practices, and householders and sadhus typically occupy opposite (but not opposing) ends of this continuum of religiosity. For the sadhus, householder *bhakti* represents a relatively "easy" path, and their ideas complement the more dominant view expressed in classical or medieval, and Sanskritic or vernacular-language literature; namely, that *bhakti*'s inherent power and efficacy lies in its simplicity (e.g., the *Epics; Purāṇas* and the vast medieval *sant* literature). It is this generic *bhakti* that Ganga Giri describes as that which "doesn't cost anything." Sadhus' *bhakti*, however, is a different type of *bhakti* from that of householders. This *bhakti* is engendered and embodied through the paradigmatic idiom of singing *bhajans*, which, to these sadhus, signifies devotional asceticism. From their perspectives, singing *bhajans* requires sadhus to sacrifice everything, including their "heads" (i.e., to die for one's *dharm*), to suffer and struggle selflessly and courageously on the unconventional road that leads to *bhagwān*.

Thus, if at its most elementary level *bhakti* constitutes an effective and widely accessible path to God, singing *bhajans* represents the highest, and an extreme level of *bhakti*, "a difficult path," involving a specialized practice of worship *and* knowledge enacted with the ultimate intention of transcending the illusory and blinding power of *sansār*. No doubt, it takes a special type of sadhu to withstand the myriad and unexpected difficulties that the unconventional life of singing *bhajans* demands—specifically, the ideal sadhu. The female sadhus' ambivalence on *bhakti* constitutes a discourse for establishing dominant definitional boundaries around *sannyās* that aim to weed out the real from the fake sadhus, locally and elsewhere.[13] Also, this ambivalence on *bhakti* complements and condones their ethos of caste ambivalence, by suggesting that that Brahmin/Rajput sadhus represent the perfect ideal for the superior life task of singing *bhajans*, because their high-caste attributes, which parallel the traits that distinguish singing *bhajans* as renunciant *bhakti*, endow them with all the "right stuff" to live such *bhakti*.

"Bhakti is like a Lioness's Milk": *Performing Ambivalence in the Sadhus' Rhetoric of Renunciation*

"A sadhu is the king of India," Ganga Giri tells me. "A king is only the king of a town. But a sadhu rules over the entire country of India [Hindustan]," she says. On this mild February afternoon in 2005, Ganga Giri sits beneath a *rudrākṣ* tree and, like a king, holds court with her devotees. Three elderly householding women from the oil-pressing community (*ṭhelī*) have come to Ganga Giri's hermitage for her *darśan* after having made their weekly *darśan* rounds of the gods enshrined at the nearby Mahakaleshwar Temple. They, along with Nem Singh, a village Rajput who comes to Ganga Giri's place daily and fills her clay water pots as part of his *sevā* to her, sit respectfully around Ganga Giri, while Sohan Lal (Dadaji), my Baniya "grandfather" who has been hosting me at his guesthouse since my arrival in Udaipur two months ago, and who brought me to Ganga Giri's ashram, stands a few feet away from the rest of the group on the path leading to Mahakaleshwar. "Even kings go to sadhus and touch their feet," Ganga Giri says. "The king sits below the sadhu and says 'guruji, guruji,' and the sadhu sits there [she says laughing]. A sadhu is higher than a king." Dadaji concurs: "Absolutely. They're just like kings [*rājā kī tarah*]," he says, inching his way closer to the group. Everyone gathered in this *satsang* seems to understand and accept the association that Ganga Giri makes between royalty and *sannyās*. In my attempt to make sense of this perception, which is shared by the *satsangīs*, I ask Ganga Giri to explain her idea of this similarity. She says, "Sadhus are like oceans. The deeds [*krīyā*] of sadhus are as deep as oceans." After pausing briefly, she recites the lines of a *bhajan* that she afterwards identifies as song verses from the epic of Gopi Chand,[14] a renouncer-king: "Sadhus are born by their own wishes; they bear the pain of the thunderbolt [*vajra*]; they have the fierce [*raudra*] mentality of *sādhanā*. Sadhus die before they die. They reach heaven alive."

Ganga Giri's reciting of a *bhajan* from the Gopi Chand epic, a popular vernacular-language narrative tradition performed throughout Rajasthan (A. Gold 1992; 1991), performatively depicts that sadhus and kings are related in her mind (though her comments, unlike Dadaji's, express her view that sadhus are superior to kings on account of their special powers, which she attributes to their "singing *bhajans*"—see Chapter 8). They share the same uncommon martial qualities, which the *bhajan* intimates: fierceness of mentality, the strength to endure pain in both the physical and spiritual senses, and the courage to die to one's ego-self, which, in turn, enables the selfless sacrifice of one's body and mind. Both classes of persons represent God's warriors—the sadhu on the path of *bhakti*, and the solider on the path of *dharm*. In defining her idea of "sadhu" through performance of a regional bardic tradition of song that establishes the martial nature of *sannyās*, Ganga Giri constructs it through the lens of elite Rajput traits. She makes explicit the connection between sadhus and warriors in the context of another conversation, in which she explains that taking *sannyās* does not itself a sadhu make. Ganga Giri says,

> A sadhu isn't made by wearing the ochre robes, or by taking *sannyās*. When warriors go to fight on the battlefield, they put so many weapons on their bodies and then they fight. A sadhu's life, too, is a battlefield of *bhakti*. A sadhu has to bear the pain of the *vajra*. A sadhu's nature is fierce: she has to die before dying... but gets heaven while she's still alive. We are talking about *bhakti* here. This is our heaven, our gateway to the Lord.

Ganga Giri's commentary suggests that the sadhu's "battlefield of *bhakti*" and, as implied in this passage, the warrior's battlefield of *dharm* are equivalent. Her words engender an ideology of the ideal sadhu (i.e., the sadhu who fights on the "battlefield" illustrative of the "difficult" *bhakti* path) by distinguishing, through comparison with the notion of the perfect warrior, the unique characteristics, such as those elucidated earlier, that are thought to constitute the ideal sadhu's nature. But where do such extraordinary attributes come from? One response that the sadhus accentuate has to do with action (*karm*) and practice (*abhyās*). In a *satsang* that Tulsi Giri sponsored at her ashram in Shyalpura village on November 17, 2005, Ganga Giri explains that "[s]adhus have to make the practice of *sādhanā*. They have to worship [*pūjā karnā*]; they have to concentrate their minds [*dhyān lagānā*]; and, they have to chant [*tap-jap karnā*] the God's name. This is our duty, our work [*karm*], as sadhus. Why should I leave it?"

The practices that Ganga Giri associates with sadhu-*sādhanā* (*karm*) in this particular statement are not all that different from a generically conceived householder *bhakti*. Even the Brahmin and Patel (Baniyas) householders participating in this *satsang* (they hail from the village where Tulsi Giri's ashram is located, and are predominantly Patels who financially support and maintain that ashram, and who requested that Tulsi Giri come and live there) claim that the "karm" of sadhus resembles the "yog" of householders. Sukh Lal, a participant in that *satsang*, explains in response to Ganga Giri's comment that "householders have two kinds of duties: *karm* and *yog*." He describes *karm* as the duty of householders to "make families [*parivār banānā*]" and to teach their children "right from wrong [*burāī se saccāī jnān karānā*]." Here, Sukh Lal differentiates between householders and sadhus by clarifying that the former engage in worldly activities, such as sex and procreation, while the latter do not. To that extent, the *karm* of householders distinguishes them as "sansaris"—that is, people immersed in and consumed by, as Ganga Giri says, the dream-like *māyā* of *sansār*. However, according to Sukh Lal, householders' *yog*, as with sadhus' *karm*, brings them close to "the face of God." His definition of householder *yog* parallels word-for-word, in fact, Ganga Giri's interpretation of sadhu *karm*: "Householders have to do the *pūjā-pāṭh*, put their minds on God, and take the name of the Lord [*bhagwān*]."

While Ganga Giri recognizes the legitimacy of Sukh Lal's understanding of the differences and similarities between householders and sadhus, she quickly expands on it by making clear to everyone present at that *satsang* that, unlike householders, "Sadhus have three duties: *karm*, *yog*, and *tyāg*." In doing so, Ganga Giri returns sadhus to what she and the other sadhus at this event see as their rightful place at the apex of the social hierarchy. The audience members, content with Ganga Giri's explanation (after all, they and the other sadhus there publicly recognize her as the most qualified among them to speak about "these things"), exclaim "That's correct," "That's true," or "So be it [*tathāstu*]." Sukh Lal, too, agrees. He rhetorically surrenders to Ganga Giri's final authority on the matter with his reverential statement that "a true scholar [*vijnānī*] has spoken today." Sensing my confusion, Tulsi Giri elucidates further the meaning of Ganga Giri's explanation. She says, "We [sadhus] serve the people. We take the sins of the people. That is [our] *karm*. We serve *bhagwān*. We do *bhagwān*'s *pūjā*. That is *yog*. We sing *bhajans*. That is *tyāg*. We abandon everything. We don't need anything. That is *tyāg*." In response, Ganga Giri performs this idea of *tyāg* by reciting, in Hindi, a verse from chapter twelve of the *Bhagavad Gītā* (12.12): "*jnān* is better than *karm; dhyān* is better than *jnān*; and *tyāg* is better than *jnān*. Oh Arjun! You are a yogi. Lord Krishna says this to Arjun, 'You are a yogi!' "

Ganga Giri's representation of *tyāg* through use of the renowned example of the warrior-yogi Arjun shows, once more, that sadhus (or yogis) and warriors are intimately linked in her view, and that *tyāg* not only involves, but also requires, the kind of fearless (and selfless) act of self-sacrifice that Arjun makes on the battlefield of Kurukshetra in order to restore *dharm* and, by extension, cosmic harmony in the universe. Ganga Giri's use of Arjun to illustrate her view of *tyāg* is significant. In the *Gītā*, Arjun's sacrifice on the battlefield signifies more globally the idea of the devotee who releases attachment to the "fruits" of his or her actions, and whose acting in the world without desire for those fruits constitutes an offering of devotion to Krishna (Bh.G., Patton 2008). The text characterizes this type of "giving up" as *tyāg*, that is, renunciation of the fruits of action, and represents it as "real" renunciation, distinguishing *tyāg* from its well-known competitor, *sannyās*, defined in the *Gītā* as the renunciation of action itself. More importantly, Arjun demonstrates, through his abandoning of the results of his actions on the battlefield (i.e., the question of whether he lives or dies in the war), renunciation as a path of fierce and courageous self-sacrifice in the name of truth: as renouncer/yogic *bhakti* to *bhagwān*. Ganga Giri's defining *sannyās* and, to that extent, her life practice of "singing *bhajans*" as *tyāg*, then, expands the dominant Brahmanical notions of *sannyās* as the renunciation of action and, hence, as the "throwing down" of the world beyond its standard parameters, and constructs it through emphasis on Arjun's *tyāg* as the "most difficult" path of sacrificing those cravings that create an illusory and destructive attachment to an impermanent world, and not the world itself.

Moreover, Ganga Giri's use of Arjun as an example indicates that he illustrates the perfect sadhu (or yogi) because he has what it takes to make the greatest sacrifice of all for Krishna: his own life. The *Gītā* would hardly pack its prescient theological punch if the dialogue unfolded between Krishna and a Brahmin, a Vaishya, or a Shudra. That would turn the signal message of the *Gītā* topsy turvy. Why is this? The *karm* of fighting to the death and fearless self-sacrifice on the battlefield of *dharm* is thought not to come naturally to these classes. Of the four *varnas* that God created, only the Kshatriyas were born with the peculiar ability to fight to the death in order to defend and protect against "corruption" of "the Hindu religion." Recall from our discussion earlier that in the *Rg Veda* text, "Hymn to the Cosmic Person," the Kshatriyas emerge from the arms of the god Purusha. Such an image, which the *Gītā* employs in its teaching on the nature of the relationship between caste and *dharm* (Patton 2008, 3.10, 38–39), creates and communicates the Kshatriya's cardinal role as one of defense and protection. Krishna explains to Arjun: "as you discern your own *dharma*, you should not waiver. For the warrior there can be found nothing greater than battle for the sake of *dharma*" (Patton 2008, 2.31, 24).

The Kshatriya's capacity to fulfill the requirements of his prescribed warrior *dharm* relates to the Sankhya-influenced ideology expounded in the *Gītā* of the three essential qualities (*gun*) of the material world (*prakṛti*), namely: *sattva* (wisdom/truth/goodness), *rājas* (passion/energy), and *tamas* (darkness/inertia). In this framework, everything in the entire universe possesses all of these qualities, but in different proportions. The quality that dominates determines the "mentality" or essential nature of a living organism, including human beings. In the Kshatriyas, *rājo gun* reigns, whereas the dominant *satto gun* constitutes the nature of the Brahmin; all three qualities stand in equal proportion in the Vaishya; and the *tamo gun* dominates and, thus, influences the essential nature of the Shudra. In her study of the oral narrative traditions of noble Rajput communities in Mewar, Lindsey Harlan (1992) has observed that the prevalent view—that Rajputs have the natural capacity to sacrifice their lives for their *dharm*, an ethos of protection that manifests in gendered ways in the practices of the Rajputs she knew—is related to the belief that Rajputs possess *sattva* as well as *rājas*. She notes,

> Despite the formal distribution of the three qualities among high-caste groups, Rajputs with whom I conversed on the topic said that Rajputs have both *rajas* and *sat* and that both are essential to the performance of caste duty. It is tempting to speculate that this double identity arises from the fact that Rajputs are both warriors and rulers. As warriors they require *rajas*, but as rulers they require *sat*. A ruler who is good at being a ruler governs as a king who is generous and good, in accord with *sat*. Thus, the attribution of *sat* to Rajputs explains the frequently voiced Rajput contention that by caste tendency and duty they were best suited to be kings and are now well suited to be politicians. (Harlan 1992, 126)

Thus, because of Arjun's status as Kshatriya, "sacrifice is both a natural proclivity and a moral imperative" (Harlan 1992, 122). He represents a sure thing for Krishna's mysterious battle plan of restoring cosmic *dharm*. Krishna knows as much and implores Arjun: "Stand up, and gain honour! After conquering enemies, enjoy abundant reign. You who sling arrows from the left and the right, be an instrument and nothing more" (Patton 2008, 11.33, 132). Even if Arjun tried to resist the warrior nature with which his birth endows and entitles him (in the beginning of the *Gītā* this is exactly what Arjun tries to do), his natural "killer" instincts would kick in and force him to fight to the death. In Krishna's words: "There is no being on earth, or in heaven, or among the gods—no being who is free from these three *gunas* born of nature (18.40)... If you take refuge in the sense of 'mine', and think, 'I will not fight', your resolve is hopeless, and the force of nature will command you" (18.59; Patton 2008, 195 and 200). Arjun's internal "wiring" as Kshatriya makes it impossible for him, as Maya Nath speaks in her description of Brahmin and Rajput nature, to "cheat" his birth and his duty to his *dharm*.

Ganga Giri herself makes the connection between the *guns* constitutive of Arjun's warrior nature and his status as the ideal sadhu (an identity that results from, as well as manifests, his inner martial character) in a commentary she gave in the evening at her hermitage after she and I returned from Tulsi Giri's ashram on November 17, 2005 (see Figure 4.1): "The three *guns* are within everybody. *Sato gun, rājo gun*, and *tamo gun*—everyone has them... Everyone's nature is different [*sab kī prakṛti alag se hotī hai*]. No one has the same nature. No two people are alike. The *guns* play differently in everyone. Everything is written in the *Gītājī*. It's all in the *Gītājīi*."[15]

On the one hand, then, *karm, yog*, and *tyāg* serve as the practices by which sadhus develop the characteristic virtues that Ganga Giri and the other sadhus associate with "singing *bhajans*": fierceness of mentality, strength to endure pain, and courage to die "before dying." On the other hand, however, Ganga Giri's *Gītā* performance also suggests that those sadhus born into Brahmin or Rajput "houses"—that is, those high-castes communities in which such virtues are thought to arise automatically—possess the requisite moral nature and wherewithal that distinguish them as ideal sadhus precisely because their innate proclivities prepare them, from the moment of conception it seems, to "fight" on the extremely difficult "battlefield of *bhakti*."

To that extent, another idea that the sadhus' practices communicate as concerns the sources of sadhus' attributes has to do with their individual natures. Ganga Giri emphasizes that "No two sadhus are the same. Five brothers from the same family will have different natures. So, how can unrelated people have the same nature? Everyone's nature is different. Sadhus have different

FIGURE 4.1 Ganga Giri Maharaj standing in the doorway of her ashram. Photo by A. DeNapoli.

natures." Sadhus' births in a specific class and caste group explain, in part, the specificity of their individual natures. Ganga Giri crafts the uniqueness of her own sadhu nature by talking about her birth as a specific kind of Brahmin. "I am a Goswami Brahmin," she emphasizes. She brings up her caste identity in the *satsangs* that happen at her ashram, which consist of a mixed but primarily high-caste householder audience. The other sadhus who attend Ganga Giri's *satsangs* hail from a variety of caste backgrounds; one sadhu, Jnan Nath, was born in a Shudra community of bricklayers (*Oḍh*). Nonetheless, as with most of the householders who gather at Ganga Giri's ashram for *satsang*, the sadhus, too, mainly come from the high-caste communities of Brahmin and Rajput. In the *satsangs* that Tulsi Giri attends at Ganga Giri's ashram, she also speaks at length about her Brahmin identity. "We [pointing to Ganga Giri] are Brahmins. We were born in the same house. I mean we our *jātī* is the same."[16] While their ochre-colored clothing identifies them as renouncers, Ganga Giri and Tulsi Giri talk about their Brahmin identities before they even mention their renunciant identities. Since our first meeting in 2001, Ganga Giri has stressed her Brahmin status. Her personal narratives suggest that her high-caste status serves as a source of her extraordinary *bhajan* proclivities. Explaining the distinctions between sadhus on the basis of their natures, she says,

[G]ANGA [G]IRI: I've been singing *bhajans* since childhood. I've had this practice since childhood. When I was pregnant, even then I use to bathe, do *pūjā-pāṭh* [scripture recitation], *dīpak* [lighting the lamp for *pūjā*], *agarbattī* [lighting the incense for *pūjā*]. I used to do everything. I used to do the *pāṭh* exactly like I do now. I used to read *Rāmāyan, Gītājī*. When I was pregnant, if I didn't get time in the day, I used to read [the texts] in the night.

[A]NTOINETTE: You read in the night, too?

[GG]: Yes. I used to read in the night, too. Lakshmi's [Ganga Giri's daughter] father was very strict. So I used to read very quietly. There were no lights at that time [there was no electricity], so I used to read *Rāmāyan* quietly, in the light of a lantern. I used to spread the bed, I used to feed him [her husband], and I used to make him sleep, because I thought he will yell at me. Although I used to read quietly and slowly, he used to say, "read loudly. I also want to listen." Then I used to read loudly, but I read whenever I wanted to.

[A]: Your husband told you to read loudly?

[GG]: Yes. But I used to read whenever I wanted to. And whenever I wanted, I would go to sleep. But he never said, "Stop reading and go to sleep." He never said that. He, too, was a knower. That's why he used to say, "Read loudly. I also want to listen." I've had this practice since the beginning. When my relatives used to come, they also used to listen to me sing *bhajans*. Even when I was a householder, I used to sing *bhajans*. I've been singing *bhajans* since my childhood. It's a practice that I've had from the beginning. I remember the *bhajans* from my childhood.

[A]: OK. So, Mairam, not all sadhus are the same. They are different from each other.

[GG]: Yes. They're different from each other. Everyone's nature is different.

In this narrative, Ganga Giri explains her understanding of the religious ways characteristic of the Brahmin *varna* with which she identifies. She begins by speaking about her widely recognized practice of "singing *bhajans*" since childhood. The idioms "since childhood" or "from the beginning" appear five times in this telling. Her life narratives, as we saw in Chapter 2, make explicit that the stage "childhood" represents Ganga Giri's life—or, more precisely, Kashi's life, as that is her birth name—at the age of five or six, a time when she was singing *bhajans* before she knew how to wear shoes. Ganga Giri also says that she constantly "read" *Rāmayān* and *Gītājī* and, in conjunction with that, conducted daily *pūjā* worship, before which she bathed to constitute her physical purity, and during which she lighted the *dīpak* (oil) lamp and the incense. While Ganga Giri's practices typify orthodox Brahmin-caste behaviors of achieving and maintaining purity in everyday life, she draws attention to the power and role of her Brahmin nature in shaping her actions by emphasizing that despite her circumstances (e.g., being pregnant with Lakshmi), she continued to uphold the rigorous standards of her *varna* and *jātī* in matters of ritual purity and religiosity. Ganga Giri tells me that she "used to do everything" that Brahmins are supposed (and expected) to do, because her nature predisposes her to act in this specific way.

Significantly, Ganga Giri underscores that even as her husband slept, "I . . . read whenever I wanted to" in the night by the light of a lantern. Twice she emphasizes that she engaged in her religious practices whenever she wanted, suggesting that she was (and still is) compelled from within to sing *bhajans*, regardless of what people might think or say, including her "very strict" husband, also a Goswami. Hence, even as Ganga Giri locates her practices within the boundaries of a Brahmin-caste universe, she distinguishes herself from members of her *varna* and her *jātī*. The conversational context of this telling accentuates that the compelling force behind Ganga Giri's uncommon religiosity relates not only to the implied idea of God calling her to be a sadhu, but also to her own peculiar Goswami nature. "Everyone's nature is different," she says.

From this vantage point, Ganga Giri's narrative indexes that her birth as a Goswami Brahmin establishes who she is as a class of high-ranking persons having a superior status and prestige level. In addition, it orients her behavior and attitude as a householder *and* as a sadhu, which, in effect, presents her well-born caste status and entitles her to that status and the respect that the society associates with her *varna/jātī*. But just as crucial, her story differentiates her as special among an already distinguished class of people on account of her individual Goswami nature. Thus, her unusual religiosity of singing *bhajans* at every life stage, which expresses a signal feature of her entire life history, creates continuity between her householding and renunciation. What is more, her unique nature constitutes the illustrative thread in this tapestry of continuity. Although *sannyās*, as Ganga Giri's personal stories intimate, signifies an intensification of an extraordinary and fierce life dedicated to singing *bhajans* from an early age, this narrative also suggests that devotion compelled "since the beginning" leads to *sannyās*.

Furthermore, Ganga Giri's emphasis on her birth as a Goswami Brahmin enables her to connect her atypical sadhu identity to a particular caste lineage (Goswami) that traditionally models, in its ideologies and practices, extraordinary religious and renunciant proclivities. Unlike Brahmin communities in general, Goswami Brahmins are viewed as extremely knowledgeable and religious people (they are often characterized as the "purohits" or priests and scholars of the Brahmin *varna*),[17] and the Gosains (Shaiva *sannyāsīs*), a term probably derived from *goswami* (lit., "lord of the senses" or "lord of cows"), are seen as the complementary renouncer "branch" of the Goswami *jātī* (Lutgendorf 2007, 80).[18] During our years of collaboration, Ganga Giri and I visited her only living daughter, Lakshmi Bai, and her family, who reside in a predominantly Brahmin village located on the western border of Udaipur district. Lakshmi Bai and her husband, Dev Puri, own a plot of land behind their domicile that they cultivate for food; they also have goats, cows, and buffaloes, whose milk (and butter) they sell in the village for cash. They earn their living by selling their animals' milk and from the life-cycle rituals they perform for people in the village. A large Shiv-Parvati temple sits at the front of their residence, and the villagers have access to it (Lakshmi Bai and her husband sometimes perform rituals for temple visitors). The ringing of temple bells consistently punctuates our conversations.

On the occasions that I spent time with the family, Lakshmi Bai, Dev Puri (also a Goswami Brahmin), and their eldest son Mahendra explained that "Goswamis" and "Gosains" come from the same caste community ("*ek hī samāj kā*"). Significant overlap exists in the life practices of Goswami householders and sadhus. Both groups wear saffron-colored clothes and engage in daily forms of *sādhanā* (Dev Puri was wearing saffron clothing when I met him again in 2005). What is more, as with sadhu communities in general,[19] Goswami householders also build *samādhi* shrines for their dead.[20] At the far south end of Lakshmi Bai and Dev Puri's property are three *samādhi* shrines, symbolizing the resting places of their three children: an infant who died in childbirth, and two adult sons who were killed in automobile accidents (one son was killed two months after his wedding). In 2011, when I returned to Rajasthan to conduct follow-up field research with the sadhus, one more *samādhi* shrine had been added to the family complex: Ganga Giri's (she took *samādhi* on July 26, 2008, five days after *Guru Pūrṇimā*). In Figure 4.2, Laksmi Bai and Tulsi Giri, seen in the foreground, remember Ganga Giri and discuss the building of her *samādhi* shrine at Lakshmi Bai's home.

Although Ganga Giri's family recognizes that Goswami householders and sadhus belong to the same community (which indicates that not all Goswami

FIGURE 4.2 Lakhmi Bai (seated on ground) and Tulsi Giri (seated on the cot) discussing Ganga Giri's *samādhi* shrine.
Photo by A. DeNapoli.

householders become sadhus), to Ganga Giri, Goswamis are categorically sadhus. There is no difference. "We Goswamis are sadhus," she says; with this comment, she foregrounds the inherent renouncer character of her caste and constructs her own sadhu identity as constitutive of the essential nature of that caste identity. Figure 4.3 illustrates Ganga Giri and her late younger brother, Prithvi Puri, both of whom took renunciation into two different branches of the orthodox Dashanami tradition after they completed their respective householder duties. To bring home her point, Ganga Giri explains that Prithvi Puri and her late paternal grandfather "were sadhus." Similarly, to establish the natural connection she perceives between her caste status and sadhu status, Ganga Giri says, "I have the *sādhanā* of the veins [*nāḍī*]. Everybody has veins, right? Everyone has them. Even dogs have veins. But I have the veins of *sādhanā*. This is the thing." Ganga Giri's sadhu religiosity, as her words make clear, is "in her blood." Ganga Giri's life of "singing *bhajans*" represents the living out of an innate proclivity characteristic of her caste identity's traditional way of life. Thus, the "thing" that she wants me to understand is that, although *sannyās* is atypical for people (and especially for women) in her society, it is actually quite common for people in her Goswami community. Ganga Giri's

FIGURE 4.3 Memorialized *pūjā* images of Ganga Giri and her brother Prithvi Puri. Photo by A. DeNapoli.

high caste status as Goswami authorizes her seemingly unusual identity as a sadhu as well as her right to sing to God (see Figure 4.4).

The matters of authority and caste status remain inextricably (and precariously) interwoven in the sadhus' *sannyās*. Upon greeting each other, the sadhus will ask "who is your guru," and then they will ask, "what is your community," using the terms *ghar, jātī* and *kul* ("family") interchangeably.[21] Sadhus can tell a lot about each other on the basis of who their guru is. "If I know who their gurus are, I can recognize real or fake sadhus from miles away," Ganga Giri says. "My guru is like the horns on the head of a bull. I live in the shelter of his protection." A sadhu's authority constitutes, then, a function of the guru who instructs and initiates her on the path of *sannyās*. "Everybody recognizes me wherever I go," Ganga Giri emphasizes. "I can sit in the queue of sadhus at the Kumbh Mela and no one will say '*tū*' to me. They will say 'āp'; they will say, 'She's the one from Rani Road. She is ripened'... They will see the family [*khandān*] of my guru when they see me." Thus, when I heard the sadhus asking about each other's "kuls," I initially thought that they were inquiring about their individual renouncer "families" and those networks of relationships. While this is sometimes the case, as I listened more carefully to the

FIGURE 4.4 Lakshmi Bai's keepsake photo of Ganga Giri meditating on the *Gītā*. Photo by A. DeNapoli.

sadhus' responses of "Brahmin," or "Rajput," for example, I realized that they were also inquiring about one another's birth groups. Like the "family" of the guru, the caste status that a sadhu biologically inherits from her family also establishes her authority in the eyes of other sadhus. The problematic underbelly to this claim, however, concerns the perception that low-caste sadhus do not possess the inherent moral tendencies required to live "on the battlefield of *bhakti*." Without those attributes, their authority to renounce remains tenuous at best. Moreover, without the authority of high-caste status, their *sannyās* becomes suspect by Indian society. "People won't trust them," Manvendra Singh says. He explains,

> Caste is something very important to us Indians. Sadhus' castes tell you a lot about them... Rajput women who take *sannyās* is such a big thing in our culture. The people will think, "Wow. A Rajput woman has taken *sannyās*," and they'll touch her feet. But the lower *jātīs* don't have the respect in our culture. People will think, "A Meghwal [low-caste] has taken *sannyās*? What nonsense!" There is a respect that comes with [high] caste. How many Brahmin sadhus do you know? How many

Rajput sadhus do you know? They're all high-caste, right? In India, in Rajasthan especially, you cannot forget caste. The Meghwals don't have the respect because they don't have the high-caste.

The reverence shown to high-caste sadhus corresponds in large measure to the recognized authority of their upper-caste statuses. Hence, as Manvendra's commentary makes explicit, the *sannyās* of a Goswami Brahmin like Ganga Giri, or a Shaktavat Rajput like Shiv Puri, evokes a sense of awe from devotees and non-devotees alike, because it represents their reaping of the naturally occurring spiritual "earnings" that their respective birth groups establish as uniquely and rightfully theirs.[22] Therefore, these sadhus and the other high-caste sadhus I know symbolize, in their communities, the human equivalents of the ferocious lion of the jungle.[23] On my journeys to various temples and ashrams throughout Rajasthan with Ganga Giri, whenever our vehicle drove through mountain passes she roared like a lion and exclaimed, "I'm the most ferocious lion in these jungles." Ganga Giri's comment signals a Rajput sense of identity, as many Rajputs across royal, noble, and village communities are characterized in name as lions by means of the suffix "Singh." Many of the high-caste sadhus share Ganga Giri's perspective. These lions of the sadhu world see themselves as having the inherent moral authority to "drink" and "digest" the "milk" of their difficult *sannyās*. In a *satsang* that occurred at Ganga Giri's ashram in April 2005, she told me, "Only cubs can drink the milk of a lioness." In most of her *satsangs* she emphasizes that "*bhakti* is like a lioness' milk." Ganga Giri sings this *bhajan* to make her point:

Whoever understands what love is,
Its taste [ras] stays in the heart.

Only a cub can drink a lioness's milk;
That milk spills out of every metal bowl,
But it will stay in a gold bowl.
Whoever understands what love is,
Its taste stays in the heart.

Sugar is always sweet;
But if a donkey eats it,
It will die.
Saltwater fish only like the ocean;
But if you put them in sweet water,
They will die.

Only Brahmins can sing the Sāmavālī [a Vedic ritual text] purely;
But if other castes are made into Brahmins,
They, too, will chant the [language of the] Vedas purely.

Whoever understands what love is,
Its taste stays in the heart.
Cranes like to eat fish;
If they see a pearl in the ocean,
They will never eat it.

Whoever understands what love is,
Its taste remains in the heart.

You can do anything in a million [crore] ways,
But if you do anything with love,
God [purushottam] will never show his back to you.

Because of the love and devotion [in his heart],
Krishna lifted Govardhan mountain.

Whoever understands what love is,
Its taste remains in the heart.

The context of Ganga Giri's *bhajan* performance suggests that the *bhakti* about which she speaks is not simply any *bhakti*, but rather the kind of *bhakti* that resembles "a lioness's milk"—that is, a strong, fierce, and powerful *bhakti*. Ganga Giri's *bhajan* performs her understanding of the nature of renunciant *bhakti* ("singing *bhajans*") as both extraordinary and difficult. In her commentary she says, "*Bhakti* is like a lioness's milk [*śerṇī kā dudh*]. It will only stay in a bowl of gold." Another Rajput-derived reference underlies Ganga Giri's statement, as (royal) Rajputs are commonly known as givers and wearers of gold (cf. Smith 2009; Harlan 2003; 1992). "The bowl should not have any sort of color. It should only be made of gold. If you pour the milk into a bowl of gold, it will stay. But if you pour it in any other bowl, the milk will leak out from under it. The lioness's milk is so strong. It can only be digested [*hazam*] by her children. Only her cubs can digest her milk. Can you catch a lioness? You can't. And nobody can take her milk from her. She will never let anyone take out her milk. It is so strong. It can only be poured into a gold bowl. If you put in any other metal, the milk will break the dish. *Bhakti* is like this."

The maternal imagery of this *bhajan* is significant. It stretches the hypermasculinized imagery and the virtues of fierceness, courage, and self-sacrifice implicit in the renunciant idiom of "the battlefield of *bhakti*" and makes space to include in that paradigm the maternal instincts of protecting, nurturing, and feeding one's children as also illustrative of a sadhu's "fierceness of mentality." The lioness gives birth to her cubs and feeds them her "strong" milk that nourishes and sustains them. Her symbol, then, expresses the inherent life-giving power and creativity of femaleness (and of all female species) and counteracts the androcentric and gruesome imagery of death and dying symbolized by the warrior-king's self-sacrifice on the battlefield. We might even contend that the lioness is superior to her male counterpart, the lion, because of her life-giving capabilities. And yet, like the brave warrior in battle, the lioness, too, will instinctually sacrifice her own life for the protection and safety of her cubs. Both her destructive and creative capacities signify her "strong" love for her offspring. In the Hindu traditions, love connotes maternal as well as martial meanings. Ganga Giri says that "this is a *bhajan* about love," and the *bhajan* itself equates the lioness's fierceness with her maternal love. The lioness symbol expresses that the high-caste martial traits that the sadhus associate with "singing *bhajans*" interface with, and can be enhanced by, their "natural" maternal attributes (cf. Khandelwal 2004). Thus, the maternal ethos suggested by Ganga Giri's performance constructs "singing *bhajans*" as gendered feminine in its concerns and values and locates the sadhus' *sannyās* in a female universe.

But the lioness shares her love only with her own kind. Hence, although the very idea of love seems all-inclusive—something that everyone, regardless of caste, has a right to—in this *bhajan* love is ambivalent. In its framework *bhakti*, milk, and love constitute metonyms for the sadhus' devotional asceticism. What is more, because everything in the entire universe has a particular allocation of the three *guns*, which determines that thing's purity or impurity in relation to other things in the cosmos, they signify the purest of substances. Ganga Giri's *bhajan* performs *sannyās* as a path of purity. However, even as her singing constructs the purity of her vernacular asceticism, it establishes constrictive parameters that limit sadhus' access to this distinct realm of purity on the basis of their caste status. To that extent, the *bhajan* expresses, in its content and performance, an exclusive ethos of high-caste entitlement in *sannyās*. Ganga Giri's framing of her performance with the statement, "[*b*]*hakti* is not so easy. It's not lying on the road. It is precious. Taking the name of God is very precious" cues her audience, which consists of Dadaji, Nem Singh, me, and the three Theli women, to understand not only the difficult nature of her *sannyās*, but also that she has the requisite moral authority to live such a "precious" life.

The *bhajan*'s content also distinguishes among the various types of species and describes what they can and cannot do on account of their natures. "Sugar is always sweet. But if a donkey eats it, it will die," it explains. Similarly, "[o]nly Brahmins can sing the *Sāmavālī* purely. But if other castes are made into Brahmins, they, too, will chant the Vedas purely," the *bhajan* claims. Here, and in the *bhajan* more globally, an elitist Brahmanical ideology of caste is transparent in its view that the low-castes become essentially pure by turning themselves into Brahmins. Such transformation is patently required before the low-caste groups can chant the holiest of *mantras*: the Vedas (that this *bhajan* allows the possibility of upward caste mobility for the lower-caste groups via their association with the Vedas speaks to its intended egalitarian *bhakti* spirit). Just as significant, this verse makes explicit the popular Mewari-sadhu view that caste status can either authorize or deauthorize a person's access to particular kinds of religious practices, like chanting the Vedas and, as Ganga Giri's performance signals, taking *sannyās*. Her commentary which follows her singing session articulates the contours of ambivalence:

> *Bhakti* is the most expensive thing. If you get the best thing without authority, then it's of no use. It has no meaning. Even if you take it, you cannot use it. The ones who practice agriculture [*kheti kā kām*], only they understand what they do. We [Brahmins and people not from the landowning caste] don't understand it. Only those who practice business [*vyāpār karnā*] know what they do; the businessman knows what he does, but we don't know.

Performing Ambivalence on Brahminhood in Mewar's Vernacular Asceticism

Based on the practices of the sadhus analyzed in this chapter, it would appear that "the brahmin stands supreme" (Heesterman 1985, 26). Just as the dominant textual model of Brahmanical *sannyās* constructs the sadhu as the ideal Brahmin, in a similar way Ganga Giri's performances express that the Brahmin—and, in her case, the Goswami Brahmin—makes an ideal sadhu. In her view, a Brahmin-born sadhu possesses the inherent moral attributes that enable her to teach and transmit, and to protect and defend Hindu *dharm*. Her idea of the sacred role of the Brahmin parallels her interpretation of the meaning of singing *bhajans* as illustrative of the selfless act of sacrificing to God all those destructive attachments, including clinging to one's ego, that trap individuals in *sansār*. Ganga Giri builds her concept of *sannyās* on the familiar foundation of Brahmin-based caste traits. By the same token, Tulsi Giri's comment that the *karm* of sadhus involves taking the "sins" of the people whom they serve also indexes a Brahmin-related caste function and shows her invoking the ideal characteristics of her caste to construct *sannyās*.

The Brahmin's caste role of absorbing the sins of others that Tulsi Giri describes is seen in the Vedic-Brahmanical ritual exchange between priest and patron (Heesterman 1985). The Brahmin priest accepts as his remuneration a "gift" from the patron and is expected to "eat" it in order to remove the sins which the patron transfers to the gift via physical contact, and thus bring about the ritual transformation of the patron or his family. Diane P. Mines (2007) concurs in her observation of the practices of a central land-owning caste (Pillaimar) with whom she worked in the village of Yanaimangalam, South India: "I found that in many contexts, but especially during life-cycle rituals such as weddings, puberty ceremonies, naming ceremonies, first ear-piercings, births, and funerals, village servants—especially Brahmans, barbers, and washermen but others as well—were regularly expected to accept gifts and payments that effected the removal of sins and other faults from those undergoing the ritual" (21). Thus, the roles associated with their Brahmin *varna* enable Tulsi Giri and Ganga Giri to represent their *sannyās* in a way that parallels their caste's concerns, as well as underscores its high rank in the stratified caste hierarchy. Nevertheless, by drawing on the ideals of their high-caste *varna* to configure *sannyās*, they create and perpetuate an ethos of caste ambivalence in their practices.

Although these sadhus craft their religious lives and identities through the guiding lens of Brahminhood, consideration of the specific sociocultural context of Mewar brings to light the equally salient role of the local (and elite) Rajput oral and caste traditions in their (re)fashionings of *sannyās*. More specifically, the image of the perfect sadhu as exemplary of the ideal Brahmin who fights for God and religion, which Ganga Giri creates through performance of her renunciant rhetoric, resembles and recalls the martial character of the dominant caste group of Mewar, the royal Rajput. To that extent, the ideal sadhu that Ganga Giri's practices evoke looks more like a mustached Mewari Rajput warrior who dons shield and sword than like the scantily-clad and shaven-headed orthodox Brahmin renouncer who wears the *janeu* and withdraws in a cave.[24]

Why is this? The tension between Brahmin and Rajput classes in perceptions of their *varna*'s superiority constitutes a salient factor in the sadhus' constructions of *sannyās* as constituting Brahmin as well as Rajput attributes. An illustrative example of this tension is the occasion in which I introduced

Ganga Giri to Shiv Puri at the latter's ashram. Both sadhus are seen as extremely knowledgeable renunciants in their individual religious communities, so I was surprised to learn that, although they had heard of one another's reputation as "real" sadhus from other sadhus and mutual acquaintances, they had never actually met before. Upon greeting each other, these sadhus made clear their individual caste statuses and, as the day proceeded, competed with each other in singing *bhajans* that represented their perceptions of the glory of their respective caste communities. Shiv Puri's singing of a *bhajan* attributed to Karma Bai catalyzed the most contention between her and Ganga Giri, as each argued for the Rajput or Brahmin origins of the composition. By the end of the evening, the sadhus had retreated to opposite sides of the ashram, annoyed by each other's presences. On the drive home Ganga Giri said, "Don't ever bring me there again! I didn't learn any *bhajans*. I know everything she knows. More, in fact."

But the issue hardly stops there. While Ganga Giri's notion of the perfect sadhu demonstrates a selective and creative blending of the best essential characteristics of the Brahmin and Rajput classes, the fact remains that popular Mewari cultural resources, like the ethos of the martial Rajput, on which her practices draw, and which posit royal Rajput superiority, structure her experiences of Brahminhood and mold her conception of that identity to reflect the values, ideals, and concerns of Mewar's dominant class. Viewed from this angle, the prestige associated with Mewar's Rajput elite helps to explain the seeming incongruity of Brahmin sadhus like Ganga Giri and Tulsi Giri—who come from a class typically seen as nonviolent and peaceful—employing violent idioms and imagery in their representations of *sannyās*.[25] These sadhus recognize that in Mewar, being seen as (or acting) Rajput has more "social capital" (Bourdieu 1991) than being Brahmin ever could. Harlan concedes: "The proliferation and predominance of Rajput elites has made Rajputs, more than Brahmins, targets of identification and association" (2003, 65). Thus, as Harlan explains, "in Rajasthan lower status groups have been more likely to share Rajput values and aspire toward Rajput status" (65).

In conclusion, the data documented in this chapter expands on Harlan's excellent insights by showing that high-caste groups in Mewar similarly adopt and adapt, mix and modulate princely Rajput values and "aspire toward Rajput status" in their practices. This pattern is particularly evident in connection with the sadhus' performances explicated in this discussion. Their ideas of singing *bhajans* are largely, but not exclusively, drawn from Mewar's royal traditions. Thus, while their *sannyās* constitutes a bricolage of Brahmanical, Rajput, and *bhakti* elements, the accentuated martial thread knitted in this synthesis suggests that becoming a sadhu is tantamount to becoming Rajput to these sadhus. Fusing renouncer and Rajput identities enhances their social status and validates their religious identities. Hence, the associations that sadhus like Ganga Giri, Tulsi Giri, Sharda Puri, and others make between Brahminhood and *sannyās*, and between *sannyās* and Rajputness, creates "unity and affinity" between Brahmins and Rajputs, but just as important, gives Brahmins like themselves the benefit of the revered social status typically reserved for Rajputs in Rajasthan (Harlan 2003, 63). In this framework, these sadhus use performance of their rhetoric of renunciation as an effective means to "Rajputize" their Brahmin identities and elevate their caste's already respected status in Mewar.

The Rajputization of their sadhu identities, however, remains only partial. The tension, both real and imagined, between these two status systems prevents the Brahmin sadhus from completely absorbing Rajput ideals, in order to preserve the perceived authenticity of their class status. After all, as these sadhus intimate, if *sannyās* is ultimately about realizing Brahman, the Brahmins who are thought to propagate and embody Brahman represent those "really" most suited for this path. Legitimation for this exclusive association between caste status and religious status lies within the dominant tenets of classical Hinduism itself, which portrays Brahmins "as embodiments of the renunciatory Great Traditions" (D. Gold 2001, 269; cf. Heesterman 1985).

5

"*I Myself Am Shabari*"

A TRIBAL SADHU'S JOURNEY OF SINGING *BHAJANS*

The bhagwā *belongs to* bhagwān. *It doesn't belong to the people who give or receive it.*

—CHETANANANDA SWAMI

THE LOCATION OF Shabari Ashram recalls the idyllic surroundings of the mythical forest-dwelling anchorites of the *Rāmāyan*.[1] Nestled in the foothills of the Aravalli Mountains, and surrounded by ancient banyan trees that form a protective barrier around it, and without any villages or people in sight for miles, Shabari Ashram has the peace, privacy, and solitude that identify ashrams as sacred spaces of spiritual refuge, as is clear in Figure 5.1. In this ashram lives an elderly Bhil sadhu by the name of Chetanananda Swami (seen in Figure 5.2). Bhils constitute one of several indigenous tribal communities in India (others include Minas and Gonds) that are collectively known as *adivasis* (lit., "original inhabitants"). James Tod referred to Bhils as *vanputra* (lit. "sons of the forest"), as illustrative of their ancient practice of living in dense forests (Mathur 1988, 4). While found throughout the Indian subcontinent, Bhils predominate in the areas of southern Rajasthan, including Udaipur district (Mathur 1988; cf. Jain 2011). In 2011 Chetanananda Swami, whose *dīkṣā* name means "the bliss of consciousness," turned sixty years of age. I met her in the summer of 2003. She belongs to the conservative Dandi Swami branch of the Shankaracharya Dashanami Order and took initiation into *sannyās* forty-five years ago. Her guru, a Goswami Brahmin by the name of Bhumananda Swami, lives nearby in an ashram in the town of Chirva.

Chetanananda was born in Maruvas village, Chirva, Udaipur district, in 1951. She has been living at Shabari Ashram (also in Maruvas), which, as she says, "we built with our own hands," for over four decades. The "we" to whom she refers is Manor Singh, a village Sisodiya Rajput in his seventies; he can be seen in Figure 5.3. Together, Manor Singh and Chetanananda manage the entire temple complex and care for Chetanananda's four buffalo, all of

FIGURE 5.1 The land surrounding Chetanananda's ashram.
Photo by A. DeNapoli.

whom she named, and whom she keeps at the rear of the temple's property. Chetanananda and Manor Singh sustain themselves on the milk produced by these buffaloes and on the grains and vegetables (corn, wheat, millet, and sugarcane) that they grow in their fields. Manor Singh has ten adult children: three sons and seven daughters. His wife and two of his daughters died three years ago, "within twenty four hours of each other," he tells Manvendra Singh and me. Like Chetanananda Swami, I met Manor Singh in 2003. These days, however, he prefers to be called by his *dīkṣā* name, Prakashananda Swami. He took initiation into the same Dandi Swami lineage of *sannyās* as Chetanananda two years ago, after he arranged his youngest son's marriage. He explains, "I got the last [child] married and left my home completely." After a pause, Prakashananda says, "We are both disciples of the same ashram—Chirva Sannyas Ashram." "My guru is Agananandaji, and hers is Bhumanandaji. We're disciples of the same ashram." Although Prakashananda has been a sadhu for just two years, he has been serving Shabari Ashram for over forty-five years.

The emphasis that Prakashananda Swami places on him and Chetanananda Swami being "disciples of the same ashram" is important. This indicates that their spiritual ranking in the ashram is equal and that their religious roles

FIGURE 5.2 Chetanananda Swami.
Photo by A. DeNapoli.

are commensurate. As disciples of the Chirva Sannyas Ashram (though not of the same guru), their relationship constitutes one of spiritual kinship as guru-brother and guru-sister.[2] Both spiritual siblings serve Shabari Ashram in the capacity of "*dīvāns* [caretakers]" of the temple's principal deity, Gangeshwar Mahadev, a form of Shiv. While the name "Shabari Ashram" represents the nomenclature given by Chetanananda's devotees, the ashram-temple complex is more formally known as Gangeshwar Mahadev Mandir, signifying the god who resides there, and whom both Chetanananda and Prakashananda serve.

The Gangeshwar Mahadev image established in the temple at Shabari Ashram is thought to be related to the Ekling *mūrtī* (lit., "One Ling"),[3] also a form of Shiv, enshrined in Mewar's famous Eklingji Temple in Kailash Puri. The town of Kailash Puri serves as a popular pilgrimage destination. The name Kailash Puri means "city of Kailash" and alludes to Shiv's abode in the Himalayas. Mewari oral traditions construct Kailash Puri as a regional *tīrth-yātrā* (pilgrimage place); as Rajasthan's equivalent of Badrinath, a nationally recognized *tīrth-yātrā* in northern India believed to be one of the sources of the Ganges River, which, according to classical Hindu mythologies, descended to earth from Shiv's matted locks.[4] Mewari oral traditions also trace

FIGURE 5.3 Prakashananda raising his hands in praise.
Photo by A. DeNapoli.

the founding of Eklingji at Kailash Puri to Bappa Rawal (ca. eighth century). They credit him with the establishing of the Sisodiya dynasty at the fortress of Chittor in Mewar: the earliest kingdom of the Sisodiya rulers (Harlan 1992, 28–29; 2003, 64; Mathur 1988, 8; Sharma et. al. 1966, 374).

Prakashananda tells a story about having a dream in which Gangeshwar Mahadev reveals the location of a map that gives instructions on the building of a temple complex where the *dīvāns* will serve the god, and the exact place in the temple where the *dīvāns* have to enshrine the god's *mūrtī*. That dream changes the course of Prakashananda's destiny. Up until the time that he has the dream, Prakashananda, in his incarnation as Manor Singh, works as a supervisor of construction in Chirva. Following his dream, however, Prakashananda becomes so transformed by his visionary experience that, convinced of his new role as Gangeshwar Mahadev's *dīvān*, as portended in his dream, "from that day" he leaves behind his work and dedicates himself to establishing Mahadev's *mūrtī* at Shabari Ashram. Here is Prakashananda's account of his dream:

> This all happened in a dream. It's my own dream. It's my own experience. This is not written in any text. It's my own experience. In my

> dream I saw the map [of the temple complex]. The way that we have built this ashram is according to how it was laid out in the dream that I had. We built the ashram exactly as I saw it [in the dream]. The next morning I copied everything I saw in my dream in this copy book [shows the notebook to Manvendra Singh and me]. This is the map [pointing to his copy book]. Everything here [at the temple complex] fits exactly according to this map. This [pointing to the map in the copy book] is where the foundation [for the *mūrtī*] is; this [now pointing to another area on the map] is where the *mūrtī* is; this is where the ashram is. It's all here in this map. Well, [the map] came in a dream, but this is how everything was made. Slowly we made all this according to the map. Later, we brought the *mūrtī*. It appeared on the thirteenth day [after the dream]. I marked it on the map on the day it came out of the ground. You can see the marks [pointing again to the map]. It's all here.

Despite having his dream-inspired blueprint for the enshrinement of the *mūrtī*, Prakashananda does not know where it is. The dream only gives him instructions on where to establish it at the temple, but not where to find it. How does he know where to look for the *mūrtī*? While the dream Prakashananda has tells him where to put the *mūrtī*, Chetanananda experiences the vision of the *mūrtī* itself and its location. "Ekling Nath," she says, "came into my dreams…[He]…showed me the path." It seems, then, that the destinies of Chetanananda and Prakashananda are intertwined. In fact, they know each other before their visions start happening. Chetanananda works for Prakashananda as a manual laborer. She explains,

> This is how we met. My elder brother used to work for him [Manor Singh]. I, too, worked for him. I used to work as a laborer. I took stones in my hand. I don't know. Maybe I climbed up the stairs [of a ladder]. I don't know anything. Something wrong happened to me on that day. I would keep sleeping for six months. Then they took me to the gods. They thought I had some ghost in me or something. Then, Ekling Nath came into my dreams. I went to his temple. Ekling Nath was the one who showed me the path. At that time he [Manor Singh] would ask me to do something and I would do something else. [Manor Singh interjects here: I asked her to bring bricks and she brought stones.] Then my brother said that he would slap me. He thought I was crazy. I would get scared. Then, they all came to the place I saw in my dreams. They recited *Gītā pāṭh* at the shrine at Brahm Raj, and then they lit the *jyot*.[5] The *Gītā pāṭh*[6] happened for two and a half months. God himself

> started talking to me directly [*bhagwān svayam mene bāt karvā lāgi giyā*]. Then people started talking about this Bhil girl digging out money. So, the police came. People from twenty villages came here to see. We called someone to do the *havan*.[7] The police came, too... Imagine what would have happened to me if the *mūrtī* did not come out. But the *mūrtī* was found and the people said, "Oh ho! There's a *mūrtī*." Then I said, "The work is done." They brought it here and did the *havan*... The chief of police in the village said, "Now take the [*mūrtī*] out and let this girl do its *pūjā*. The *mūrtī* is hers, her father's, and her grandmother's [*dādī-mā*]." I did the *pūjā* here only. We did the *pūjā* here. The god wanted to be established here. We didn't decide. He decided.

Eklingji reveals himself to Chetanananda Swami. But the road to their inevitable encounter is bumpy in the beginning. Chetanananda becomes sick. She cannot explain why she feels the way she does, but she knows that "something wrong happened to me on that day"—that is, the day that Eklingji decides to manifest himself in the world through Chetanananda. Her physical and emotional instability portends Eklingji's appearing to Chetanananda and settling permanently at the place that people now call Shabari Ashram. Until then, "they"—the villagers, including Manor Singh and her brother—see Chetanananda as crazy. Her brother even threatens to slap her if she doesn't get her act together. "They thought I had some ghost in me or something," she says. On the day Chetanananda starts to dig the ground to unearth Ekling's *mūrtī*, which he, as her story suggests, commands her to do, the villagers patently misinterpret her actions and think that "this Bhil girl" is stealing buried money. Suspecting her of foul play, they call the police. Chetanananda's poignant comment, "Imagine what would have happened to me if the *mūrtī* did not come out," tacitly verbalizes the common Mewari (mis)perception of Bhils as petty thieves and scavengers. Robberies, a common occurrence in Mewar, are almost always viewed by the (non-tribal) locals as the work of "greedy" and "dangerous" Bhils. Mewar's topography consists of steep mountain ranges and peaks, and dense forests and jungles, in which Bhils are thought to reside and hide. Most of the sadhus who live in such areas, which remain tucked far away from the nearest village (and police station), often dissuade me from staying overnight at their ashrams by saying, "Bhils live in these areas," and implying that they constitute a dangerous (and uncivilized) population whom I should fear. Whenever a theft or a murder occurs (in 2011 several sadhus living in Mewar's jungles were murdered and their ashrams plundered), the blame falls on the Bhils. "You cannot trust Bhils," many Mewaris say.

Chetanananda's story signals that the villagers view her in a similar way. The *mūrtī*, however, "was found," and Eklingji's arrival validates Chetanananda's seemingly duplicitous behavior. "People from twenty villages came," she explains. The emergence of Eklingji's *mūrtī* evokes from the suspicious crowd veritable surprise: "Oh ho! There's a *mūrtī*," they exclaim. The police chief similarly authorizes her strange behavior to the villagers. "Now take the *mūrtī* out and let this girl do its *pūjā*. The *mūrtī* is hers, her father's, and her grandmother's," he declares publicly. His recognized position of authority makes it possible for him to set the record straight with the villagers about Chetanananda's and, by extension, her family's integrity. They are good people, and the crowd should feel ashamed for doubting Chetanananda's actions. The combination of the god's and the head policeman's maleness and power works rhetorically in the narrative to vindicate Chetanananda's innocence and reputation in her village as a "good" Bhil and, at the same time, as a "good" woman, because she acts merely as Eklingji's dutiful servant. She acts on behalf of Eklingji's intentions, and not her own. Notice that Chetanananda's story suggests that, when Eklingji works through her, she is not in her right mind. Her senses become confused to the extent that she has no idea about "anything." She simply goes through the motions, but does so incorrectly. "I told her to bring bricks and she brought stones," Prakashananda says, confirming Chetanananda's view of her senselessness at that prescient juncture in her life.

In her telling, Chetanananda refers to the *mūrtī* as Ekling Nath, and not as Gangeshwar Mahadev. Convinced that Ekling Nath appeared to her, Chetanananda constructs the deity whom she worships at Shabari Ashram as the same god whom the Mewar royal family worships at Kailash Puri's temple complex. Her visionary experience enables her to integrate her personal history with the royal history of the Sisodiya dynasty of Mewar. Bhils and Sisodiya Rajputs share a "sense of solidarity" in terms of their being "kindred martial spirits," that is, suitable allies, in their having forged together Mewar' s illustrious history (Harlan 2003, 63). Harlan observes that "Rajputs have referred to Bhils as rugged and worthy opponents, and frequently expressed admiration for their ability as hunters, warriors, and bandits . . . they also represent Bhils as brave and kindred martial spirits and even close companions to Rajputs" (2003, 64). Some Bhils communities, as L. P. Mathur has suggested, even claim Rajput origins (Mathur 1988, 8). Bhils, along with Rajputs, then, have played a definitive role in bringing about the Sisodiya dynasty's sovereignty in Mewar since before Bappa Rawal's time (Sharma 1966; Mathur 1988).

To illustrate, in the legends about Guha, the scion of the Guhila (or Guhilot) dynasty (*kul*), from which the Sisodiya branch (*śakh*) of Rajputs originates (Harlan 1992, 27; 2003, 63; Mathur 1988, 21; Sharma 1966, 234–249), he was entrusted to the care of Brahmins by his mother who, after she learned that her husband was slain in battle, "determined to become a *sati* right away" (Harlan 1992, 125; Mathur 1988). On account of his innate Rajput tendencies, Guha found life with his meek Brahmin foster parents awkward, to say the least (Harlan 1992, 120–29). Guha realized that he was better suited to a martial life in the forest among the Bhils, who befriended and, in a sense, raised him (Harlan 1992, 28). Harlan has written, "Guha grew up in a forested area populated by members of the Bhil tribe. Enormously popular, he was eventually elected king of the Bhils at Idar[8]... He was officially invested with royal authority when a Bhil cut his own finger and with his blood applied to Guha's brow the red mark (*tika*) of sovereignty" (Harlan 1992, 28; cf. Mathur 1988, 8–9, 20–21). Similarly, Bappa Rawal, eighth in the generation of Guhilot kings, though Rajput by birth, was raised by simple, cow-herding Brahmins residing in a forest. Bappa's mother, in an effort to safeguard her son's life, entrusted him to the care of a Brahmin couple shortly after the queen's husband, and Bappa's father, was killed in a battle attempting to protect his kingdom (Harlan 1992, 29, 78; 2003, 64). Bappa Rawal gained the friendship and loyalty of the Bhils whom he met in the forest while grazing his cows. Moreover, the other people, apart from Bappa and his Brahmin parents, who witnessed Eklingji's *mūrtī* emerge from the ground were two Bhils: Baleo and Deva, Bappa's confidants (Mathur 1988, 8).

Thus, like the legendary Guha, "Bappa Rawal and his descendants were helped by Bhils in the process of the consolidation of their kingdom in the Mewar region" (Mathur 1988, 9). The dynamics of association between Rajputs and Bhils is further expressed iconographically in the royal emblem of Mewar: a Bhil and the Maharana together holding Mewar's royal seal (Figure 5.4), inside of which shines the magnificent sun illuminating the royal Sisodiya's connection to the *sūrya vaṃś* (sun dynasty) of the illustrious Kshatriyas of yore (Harlan 2003, 65; Meister 2001; Bayly 1999; Rudolph 1987). The forms of comportment associated with both images—on the viewer's left side stands the brave and rugged Bhil wearing his tribal-style *dhotī* and holding in his right hand his bow weapon, and on the right side stands the mighty Maharana sporting his regal garments, with his royal sword and shield draped across his left shoulder—stylize their respective personalities as Bhil and Rajput. This image, and the legends of Guha and Bappa Rawal, articulate the message of Bhil-Rajput "unity and affinity" in regard to the resonance of their character traits and their ability to give their lives for their *dharm* (Harlan 2003, 63).

Chetanananda's and Prakashananda's caring for Gangeshwar Mahadev's *mūrtī* at Shabari Ashram, as well as Eklingji's, the divine king of the Sisodiyas,

FIGURE 5.4 Popular Mewari image of Bhil (on left) and Royal Rajput representing unified forces.
Photo by A. DeNapoli.

revealing himself and his plans to both of them narratively, ties into the popular Mewari ideology of Bhil-Rajput compatibility. Chetanananda's telling performs the idea that Eklingji considers her worthy of carrying out the task of the worship of his *mūrtī, because she is a Bhil* and, as a Bhil, has all the "right" virtues that the divine Sisodiya king himself expects of his Rajput *dīvāns*: strength, courage, and fierceness of mentality. What seals the "kindred" relationship between Chetanananda and Prakashananda has to do with Eklingji making his divine desires known to them concurrently.

Prakashananda explains that his dream of the map of the *mūrtī's* location and the temple complex starts when Chetanananda's dreams of Eklingji "showing [her] the path" begins. Initially, he believes that Chetanananda is slipping into a state of madness, until she confides the contents of her dreams to him. Hearing that, Prakashananda knows that "this Bhil girl is not crazy," but rather that she "is speaking the truth." Hence, while Prakashananda's dream of receiving Ekling's instructions for the building of his temple confirms Chetanananda's strange experiences, her dreams about Ekling's whereabouts in the local village landscape supports his unusual experiences. God is calling both of them. As in Guha's and Bappa's times, Eklingji is again joining the destinies of Rajputs and Bhils in the humble forms of Chetanananda and Prakashananda in order to actualize his mysterious plan. On the day that Chetanananda goes to dig the ground at the spot where Eklingji tells her to dig in her dreams, Prakashananda stands beside her, with his sketched map in hand. He informs the police about their concurrent dreams and shows them the map as evidence. When the *mūrtī* finally emerges from the earth, Eklingji makes Prakashananda and Chetanananda—a Rajput and a Bhil—as the (co) *dīvāns* of his *mūrtī*. Of course, he also gets himself established through their spiritual "union" at Shabari Ashram.

In the wake of this momentous event, Prakashananda leaves his position as a supervisor of construction in the village, and Chetanananda abandons her work as a manual laborer. In becoming one of Eklingji's (co)*dīvāns* along with Chetanananda, Prakashananda does not renounce his family. His *sannyās*, as explained earlier, happens only after he finalizes his householding duties—arranging the marriage of his youngest child. "He took care of both places, his house and the ashram," Chetanananda says. Up until his son's marriage, Prakshananda's routine involves living at the ashram during the day and returning to his home in the village at night. In the day he assists Chetanananda with ashram tasks, and in the evening he goes home "to sleep." However, once he becomes a sadhu, Prakashananda shifts permanently to Shabari Ashram. There, he and Chetanananda have their own separate quarters. Prakashananda's children come regularly to see him and Chetanananda and bring them supplies from nearby Chirva. But without any income, how did Prakashananda and Chetanananda get the funds to build and maintain Shabari Ashram?

The Brahmin, Rajput, and Kumavat (Baniya) villagers of Chirva and Maruvas village in particular have provided a constant source of financial, organizational, and emotional support to Chetanananda and Prakashananda. Chetanananda speaks frequently about the magnanimity of her Kumavat devotees. They donated the land on which Shabari Ashram sits, as well as the Hanuman *mūrtī* that is also established at the ashram, along with Gangeshwar Mahadev, in the main temple room, and the funds that went toward building the road that leads to Shabari Ashram. One of the people who helped raise funds for the road is a local politician. Chetanananda says, "This road was made by him... He heard about the temple. He came here to see it and take *prasād*. He came walking from the crossroads to the temple. He said, 'This is a nice temple. Who's building it?' We told him that we want to make a temple for Mahadev, but there is no road. After a few days, he sent some people to construct the road. He came here before the road was built. He gave the money for the road. He told them, 'Bring the materials,' and that's how the road was made."

The people of Chirva and Maruvas hold Chetanananda and Prakashananda in the highest regard and show their devotion through their material support of Shabari Ashram. The villagers helped them in building a tube well on the ashram's property several years ago, so that Prakashananda and Chetanananda (and, as the latter points out, "the buffaloes" and "bhakts" of the ashram) could have access to fresh drinking water. Locally, the villagers characterize Prakashananda and Chetanananda as "Mahadev's servants [*dās*]" and as "Eklingjī's *dīvāns*." While the villagers respect both of them, and their spiritually equivalent roles at the ashram, in my experience, the people seem to have bonded more intimately with Chetanananda than with Prakashananda. Her devotees know that she is special and express their feelings on the matter. "*Bhagwān* showed himself to Maharaj" or "*Bhagwān* chose Mātājī," most of them say, men and women, their eyes sometimes welling up with tears. Chetanananda's response, in turn, performs her humility as Eklingjī's co-*dīvān*: "The *bhagwā* [saffron-color that distinguishes Shaiva sadhus] belongs to *bhagwān*. It doesn't belong to the people who give or receive it. The sun is very beautiful when it rises in the morning. This *bhagwā* is the form of that rising sun. God decides if we take *bhagwā* or not. God gives the *bhagwā*. Because of *bhagwān*, I am here on this earth. God is standing on this earth and carrying me. I am at his feet. We are the dirt [*dhūl*] of God's feet."

In telling her life story, Chetanananda accentuates her uniqueness as a human being; in particular, she emphasizes the special divine assistance needed to brook her inordinately difficult life circumstances, such as her mother dying twelve hours after giving birth to her and the extreme poverty of her father's family. Here is the narrative as Chetanananda told it to me on June 25, 2011 at Shabari Ashram:

[C]HETANANANDA: I am from this village [Maruvas]. I was born here.

[P]RAKASHANANDA: They got her married, too, in this village.

[C]: In the morning at 5 a.m., I was born. In the evening at 5 p.m., my mother died. She died at 5 p.m. in the evening.

[A]NTOINETTE: Oh ho! She died the same day?

[C]: The same day. They tied the baby and put it aside. And they shifted it under a bed.

[M]ANVENDRA [S]INGH: Who?

[C]: Them.

[MS]: Who did it?

[P]: The ladies [of her family].

[C]: Because my mother died. They shifted me [under the bed]. For three days I was there. Then they started looking for me. I was all dirty. In the month of *Ashād* [April], there is so much filth everywhere. I had so much filth on me. But let me tell you one thing: The ants did not eat my eyes. If they would have eaten my eyes, what would have been the use of my life?

My *dādī-mā* [paternal grandmother] washed me after three days. Then she fed me goat's milk. Then on *Dev Julni Gyāra* [a festival that takes place on the eleventh day after the month of *Sāvan*, the fifth month of the Hindu lunar calendar in July-August], a girl spilled milk in the fields. My *dādī-mā* was also there. [To Antoinette]: Do you understand the fields?

[A]: Yes.

[C]: The girl spilled [the milk] in the fields. Then my *dādī-mā* went to bring water. When she returned she found me crying. She asked the girl, "Where's the milk?" But the girl was small. I was crying there. My *dādī-mā* started crying. "I will feed some pigeons with corn, and God, you take her away," my *dādī-mā* said to *bhagwān*. "You should take care of her." She kept saying, "You should take care of her." All of a sudden she started sweating. At the same time, my *dādī-mā* had milk come out of her breasts.

Then what happened, I was seven years old. When I was seven, my *dādī-mā* said, "I will die one day. I should get you married with my own hands and then you will keep growing [i.e., Chetanananda will continue to be provided for after her *dādī-mā* dies]." My *dādī-mā* got me married when I was seven. They waited for another three years before sending me [to the groom's home]. But he married someone else.

[A]: Your husband married someone else?

[C]: Yes. I was not sent to live with him because he married someone else. So, then I started working as a manual laborer. This is how [I] met [Manor Singh]. My elder brother used to work for him. I, too, worked for him. I used to work as a laborer. I took stones in my hand. I don't know. Maybe I climbed up the stairs. I don't know anything. Something wrong happened to me on that day. I would keep sleeping for six months....

Chetanananda pairs the telling of her life story with performance of the story of Eklingji making her his *dīvān*. Notice that the last segment of Chetanananda's narrative presents the same Eklingji story documented earlier.

The two narratives rhetorically support each other. Chetanananda's story of her unusual birth and childhood illustrates that everything that happens to her—from her mother dying twelve hours after she was born, to the "ladies" of the family placing the newborn Chetanananda under a bed for three days and the ants not eating her eyes, to her *dādī-mā* miraculously producing milk from her breasts in order to feed the infant Chetanananda—represents the mysterious workings of Eklingji. By the time she gets to her dream encounter with Eklingji, her narrative has already given Manvendra Singh, Prakashananda, and me the "contextualization cues" that enable us to understand that God has all along been the centripetal power shaping her destiny from the beginning of her life (Briggs 1989). This segment confirms the atypical events of Chetanananda's birth and youth by situating them in a global narrative of divine intentionality. It verifies that what happens to her happens because that is exactly what Eklingji intends. The details of Chetanananda's mother dying on the day of her birth, before she ever knows her mother, her family's neglecting her for several days, and their life of poverty (a common phenomenon for Bhils in Rajasthan) work to elicit from the audience a sense of awe and respect, rather than pity, for Chetanananda. Telling her story helps her to mold others' views of her in a positive light and challenges the more dominant views of Bhils as poor victims who steal, lie, and murder in reaction to their forced oppression.[9]

Furthermore, Chetanananda's shifting into the telling of the Eklingji episode—the segment of her story that she spends the most time narrating—performs an "a-ha" moment in the larger progression of the narrative's construction; that is, the narrative shift itself cues an internal recognition on Chetanananda's part of her own realization of her uniqueness. By telling her story—which constitutes at the levels of structure and content the story of Eklingji revealing himself and her true destiny as his *dīvān* to Chetanananda, a "simple Bhil girl"—she convinces herself as much as she convinces those who hear it that she is special. Her story portends and promotes her unique status, because God himself selects her to be his sacred vehicle in the world.

The telling of her narrative also suggests Chetanananda's awareness that her life signifies the mercy of Eklingji. She often says in her self-descriptions, "Look at this child? What can she do?" by which she indexes the simplicity of her character and Eklingji's cardinal role in sustaining her life on earth. In the view of her narrative, Chetanananda exists because Eklingji needs her to care for him by establishing him properly in a temple and performing his worship, by which he manifests his blessings for the benefit of everyone in the world, and not just the royal Rajputs. Her story expresses that her life is precious to God, because without her, his *mūrtī* would still be lying in the ground. But just as significant, Eklingji needs Chetanananda's love. Although established at Kailash Puri, the sacred womb of Mewar's royal "house," perhaps Eklingji has grown tired of (or bored with) all of the ritual formalities regulated and maintained by the orthodox Brahmin priests employed in the service of the Sisodiyas at the temple complex.

Chetanananda's story expresses that her simplicity of character draws Eklingji to her, because he knows that she will shower him with the love that he desires from his *dīvāns*. He also knows that her low tribal status imbues Chetanananda with the special Bhil fortitude to love God, even at the cost of her own precious life. In this way, the story hints at Chetanananda's understanding that love constitutes the defining essence of her Bhil nature. Like the lioness in Ganga Giri's *bhajan*, whose fierce maternal love distinguishes her (and her species) as innately capable of drinking the strong milk symbolic of devotional asceticism, Chetanananda intimates through the telling of her life story that she (and, by extension, Bhil people in general) has the requisite character traits that enable "a simple Bhil girl" like her to worship God in her specific role as *dīvān* and to serve him more globally in her sadhu role on the battlefield of *bhakti*.

Therefore, in her narrative Chetanananda links her religious status to her caste status by claiming that Eklingji purposely chooses her on account of her love, as well as two other "natural" proclivities commonly associated with Bhils—fierceness and honesty. Her idea of Bhils contrasts sharply with G. Morris Carstairs's classic representation of them. He writes,

> Here was clearly a people whose values were strikingly different to those cherished by my Hindu informants, as the latter indeed insisted. The Bhils were boisterously demonstrative. They shouted, sang, laughed aloud and were unashamedly drunk in the public gaze. All these, I was told, were indications that they were nearer to monkeys than to men. But there was worse to tell: had I not seen that they would dance together, men and women? They were even so shameless that Bhil husbands and wives could be seen walking hand in hand, talking and laughing together. This open display of affection was profoundly shocking to an orthodox Hindu. (Carstairs 1967, 126)

And,

> They are as uninhibited as the Hindus are restrained. Meat, drink, love, and laughter are all enjoyed without reserve. A Brahmin once remarked to me: "look at them, dancing and enjoying themselves, although they

are so poor that they often do not know whether they will have anything to eat for their next meal—isn't that a strange thing!" (1967, 135)

For Chetanananda, however, her birth story invokes the notion of Bhils' fierce physical heartiness and strength by emphasizing the various obstacles that she surmounts, despite the incredible odds stacked against her, from the moment she is born. It is a miracle that she survives her first three crucial days as a newborn without any food and water under a bed where her women kin place her, after they wrap her in a blanket, so that they can deal with the more urgent issue of her mother's death. Her mother had already given birth to a son a year and a half before Chetanananda; perhaps, the birth of another (and a female) child hardly seems an occasion worth celebrating to Chetanananda's family, especially since her birth remains contiguous with her mother's untimely death. On the day that she tells her life story Chetanananda also says, while sweeping the marble floor outside of Eklingji's temple, that after her mother's passing her father married another woman, with whom he had three more children.

The responsibility of raising Chetanananda and her elder brother, however, falls hard on her *dādī-mā*'s fragile shoulders. Poor and economically dependent on her son's meager income, which he earns from his work as a farm laborer, Chetanananda's *dādī-mā* does not have the financial resources to care for the two children of her son (with whom she also resides). Not only that, the *dādī-mā*'s old age makes it physically difficult for her to look after them. The day that the young village girl accidently spills all of the goat milk meant for baby Chetanananda, her *dādī-mā* loses her wits. Recognizing her miserable situation, Chetanananda's *dādī-mā* cries to God and beseeches him to end Chetanananda's life (for which she intends to repay him by feeding corn to the pigeons in the fields), believing that the child would be better off with him than with her. Hearing her plea, Eklingji eases the *dādī-mā's* almost intolerable burden by making her breasts "all of a sudden" produce milk, so that she can breastfeed the hungry infant and ensure her survival in the world. The miraculous nature of this event is expressed by the story's suggestive portrayal of Chetanananda's *dādī-mā* as postmenopausal.

But there is more to the story. Recognizing her advanced age, and wanting her child to be cared for after her passing from this world, Chetanananda's *dādī-mā* arranges Chetanananda's marriage at the age of seven to a Bhil boy in the village (a common Bhil practice). Three years later, when Chetanananda is expected to leave her natal kin and live with her husband in his natal home, she and her *dādī-mā* learn that he has married someone else. In narrating this episode, Chetanananda seems emotionally unaffected by the unexpected twist of events. That this telling of Chetanananda's life story occurs forty-five years after Eklingji emplaces her and Prakashananda in the temple that they built with his assistance puts the indifference with which she speaks about her husband into clearer perspective. Her attitude performs her view that Eklingji himself is behind the foiling of her marriage. Only ten years old, and with her marriage over before it ever started, Chetanananda moves on with her life and finds work in the village as a manual laborer for Manor Singh. Thereafter, Chetanananda's life takes a sharp turn. As she cleans the floor outside of Eklingji's temple, she explains that her visions of Eklingji began when she was fifteen years old. Despite her tender age, the tale that Chetanananda narrates next depicts the idea, woven in her performance, that her Bhil status explains, in part, why Eklingji selects her, along with her guru-brother Prakashananda, to be his *dīvāns*:

> Now let me tell you another thing. That police chief said, "Listen to me. I will tell you [the villagers] one more thing." This is what he said: "There was a Muslim emperor [*bādshāh*] who had no faith in the Hindu *dharm.* Since he didn't believe in the Hindu *dharm,* he came and destroyed all the *mūrtīs* [in the temples of India]." That emperor came through this village. He broke the *mūrtīs.* He went from temple to temple breaking *mūrtīs.* They [the Muslims] destroyed all kinds of temples. [Chetanananda asks Manvendra Singh and me if we have seen the broken temples in the area]. They broke the *mūrtīs*; they destroyed the temples. They broke the hands and legs of those *mūrtīs.* Even at Ekling Nath's temple [in Kailash Puri] everything is broken. Even after [they] broke the *mūrtīs,* they did not stop [destroying Hindu temples]. Later, though, Akbar asked for Eklingji's mercy. Akbar said, "I can no longer escape [your wrath]. You [Ekling] walk with your army behind you and I'll do the same [i.e., Akbar proposed a truce with Eklingji]." After that, Akbar said that he would never fight again. He said he would never touch anything again. And Eklingji's army stopped killing them [Akbar's army]. Akbar gave all that gold to Eklingji. He gave so much gold [to the Ekling's temple]. This is why the armies stopped fighting.
>
> At that time there was a sadhu who lived here and cared for the *mūrtīs.* But that sadhu died. He died after he hid the *mūrtīs* [in the ground]. Since this is a hilly region, the *mūrtīs* sank deeper and deeper into the ground. A tree grew there. "That is why Eklingji has come into the dreams of this girl," the police chief said to those villagers. "Let this girl do the *pūjā.* The *mūrtīs* belongs to her, her father, and her *dādī-mā.*" I was still living with my *dādī-mā* then. The Brahmins and

> Rajputs had to hide the *mūrtīs*. They fought to protect the *mūrtīs*. I am telling you this so that you know that this is my feeling [*anubhav*] since the last forty-five years. Look at this child! I am Shabari Bai and no one else. [Manvendra agrees with Chetanananda]. It's written here [pointing to the sign above the temple]. Shabari Bai's name is written right here... We named the ashram after Shabari Bai because of the story from ancient times.

Chetanananda's "breakthrough into performance" happens after she frames her narrative as based on what she has heard from the police chief (Hymes 1975). She wants her listeners to understand that her telling performs a retelling of a story she learned from a perceived power figure on the day that the *mūrtī* "was found." Thus, Chetanananda's "disclaimer of performance" performs not only the credibility of her story, but also her authority to tell it to others (Bauman 1977). According to her story, the Gangeshwar Mahadev *mūrtī* must be almost five hundred years old. It configures the date of the *mūrtī's* worship (its construction and establishment remain unknown) to have been during the medieval period, in which the Mughal (Muslim) emperor Akbar (a descendent of the ruling Turko-Mongol tribes of Central Asia), who reigned in north India between 1556 and 1605, battled the rulers of the erstwhile feudal states of Rajputana in order to bring this independently governed region under Mughal state control. The story emphasizes the massive destruction of Hindu religious-material culture wrought by Akbar and his army in Rajasthan and Mewar specifically. The Mughal emperors, beginning with Akbar, perceived Hindu idol worship on the Indian subcontinent as inconsistent with Islamic teachings (Rodrigues 2006). One strategy that the Mughals employed in discouraging such a practice in their larger campaign for sovereignty was to demolish Hindu temples as a way of demonstrating publicly the superiority of Islam vis-à-vis Hinduism, and of one dynasty over another. In that spirit, when the Mughal army arrived in Mewar, as Chetanananda's story observes, it "broke" the *mūrtīs*, desecrating their "hands and legs," and ransacked Hindu temples, including Eklingji's in Kailash Puri. Another significant temple complex in Mewar that Akbar's army purportedly plundered concerns Nagda (now more popularly known as the Sas-Bahu temple), in the town of Ishwal, where Bappa Rawal is thought to have become a sadhu (Sharma et al. 1966). Chetanananda implies that the Mughal Army destroyed Nagda's *mūrtīs* in her question to me and Manvendra Singh: "Did you see the other broken temples around here?"

Despite the widescale ransacking of Hindu temples in Mewar, one *mūrtī* that dodges the Mughal army's indiscriminate acts of destruction is

Gangeshwar Mahadev. "At that time," Chetanananda says, a sadhu (most likely an orthodox Brahmin), was caring for the *mūrtī* in the place where Shabari Ashram sits today. To protect it from being destroyed, he buried the *mūrtī* in the ground near a tree. Over the course of time, and due to ecological changes, the *mūrtī* became submerged in the earth. Chetanananda tells Manvendra Singh and me that it took many hours of digging before Eklingji emerged. Importantly, the story stresses that the sadhu "died after he hid the *mūrtī*." It is possible that soldiers in Akbar's army killed him as part of the Mughal's military strategy of cultural domination on the subcontinent. In the Hindu traditions, sadhus are often venerated as human *mūrtīs*, that is, as living manifestations of salvific truth (Heesterman 1985). Also, sadhus symbolize, through their practices (e.g., performing rituals for *mūrtīs* established in temples), living representatives of the truth of Hindu *dharm*. Chetanananda's narrative suggests that the Mughal army, in its annihilation of Hindu culture, did not distinguish between human and material forms of Hindu *dharm*: rather, it destroyed them both. Her story reinforces popular perceptions of Muslims' antagonism against Hindus, despite the peaceful coexistence between these groups in this part of the Indian subcontinent for centuries. The performance of the structure of her story seems to guide the listeners in the direction of that conclusion. In this way, the narrative creates and communicates, by means of performance, the idea that the sadhu died for his religion.

The performative shift to the sadhu episode occurs in the context of Chetanananda talking about the people, namely the Brahmins and Rajputs, who "fought," presumably with their lives, "to protect the *mūrtīs*," a metonym for Hindu *dharm*. These caste groups, as Chetanananda's story makes explicit, "had to hide the *mūrtīs*" because they wanted their religion to survive beyond the imminent cultural destruction of the Mughals. Chetanananda's story suggests that the Brahmins' and Rajputs' nature had everything to do with their courageous and selfless acts of hiding and protecting the *mūrtīs* from foreign powers, as well as sacrificing themselves for their *dharm*, like the sadhu who died after hiding Gangeshwar Mahadev. More significantly, her story constructs a tight connection between caste status and sadhu status by indicating that the sadhus who lived in Mewar during the time of Akbar and the Mughal Empire, and who were responsible for the care and worship of the *mūrtīs* at various temples in that region, had to have been high-caste sadhus, for their innate proclivities would have inevitably forced them to hide and protect the *mūrtīs*. Chetanananda could locate Gangeshwar Mahadev's *mūrtī* only because six hundred years ago, a Brahmin sadhu risked his life to ensure its survival. The sadhu probably thought that the *mūrtī* would be discovered eventually, and that Mahadev himself would contact that person(s) whom he trusted to continue the tradition of his worship. Eklingji's intention for Chetanananda to find his *mūrtī* makes apparent that she has, as she says in her telling, the "*anubhav*" to serve in the difficult *dīvān* role. Like the high-caste sadhus of medieval times, she, too, will sacrifice herself on the battlefield of *bhakti* for her religion.

The "Rajputization" of Bhil Identity: Performing Shabari's Caste Status

But what is the connection that Chetanananda crafts between Shabari Bai, a forest-dwelling anchorite featured in many versions of the *Rāmāyan* epic, and the high-caste sadhus of medieval Mewar? Both seem to be linked in her mind. But how?

As an elderly female Bhil sadhu who spends her life "singing *bhajans* to *bhagwān*," Shabari's example offers an apropriate mythic model for Chetanananda to represent and validate her way of life (for a discussion of female mythic models as resources for women's empowerment, see Falk and Gross 2001). Chetanananda's *sannyās* is atypical not only for Hindu women situated within the parameters of the caste system, but also for Bhils, and especially Bhil women. Apart from Shabari, I know of no other literary example in the Hindu traditions of Bhil women becoming sadhus and dedicating themselves to singing *bhajans*. Moreover, besides Chetanananda, I have not located any other female Bhil sadhu in Mewar. The unusual nature of Chetanananda's *sannyās* recalls Carstairs's poignant assessment that, among Bhils, there was no "desire to emulate the Hindu ideal of celibacy and asceticism" (1967, 132). Shabari's example, therefore, effectively blunts the strangeness of Chetanananda's life path. She herself says, "I am Shabari and no one else," suggesting both the formative influence that Shabari has had on her life, and that no other (female) sadhu in the region lives out Shabari's exemplary model in India like she does. Chetanananda identifies so completely with her idea of Shabari that, as her comment expresses, she claims special ownership of that identity: Chetanananda *is* Shabari. This exact mythic relationship is what Chetanananda wants people who come to the ashram to understand. She constructs herself through means of Shabari's renowned example. Because of Shabari, Chetanananda and Prakashananda have named their ashram after her.

The first time I heard Chetanananda share her version of the Shabari story was on June 25, 2011. Her telling arose in the conversational context of her speaking about the naming of the ashram after Shabari to Manvendra

Singh and me. While sitting on the cool marble floors in the shaded courtyard of Gangeshwar Mahadev's temple, I ask her, "Maharaj, do you know Shabari's story?" "I don't know the whole thing. I only know what I've heard," Chetanananda says. "Tell us what you've heard," Manvendra Singh says. "I'll tell you what I've heard," she says. Below, I document Chetanananda's narrative of Shabari as she performs it for Manvendra Singh and me, so that the reader may understand the ways in which she uses her telling of that story as a constructive means in representing the linkage between her sadhu and Bhil identities. We will also explore Chetanananda's performance for the clues it provides into her idea of the connection between Shabari Bai and the Mewari sadhus. Here is the story that Chetanananda has heard, and performs for Manvendra Singh and me:

[C]HETANANANDA: I've heard about the queen of the king.
[M]ANVENDRA [S]INGH: Tell us what you've heard?
[C]: Correct me if there's any mistake.
[MS]: OK.
[C]: She [Shabari] was the queen of a king. And she had a beautiful body. She had a very beautiful body. She was the queen of a king.
[A]NTOINETTE: She was the queen of a king.
[C]: Now, she didn't come out of the palace. She would keep sitting and she would think, "If I had been born in a small house [*cote ghar*] I would be free to wander. God has made me born in a big house [*bahut mote ghar*], and I cannot see anything."
[MS]: OK.
[C]: "I grew up in my *pīhar* [natal home] and I was brought here in *pardā*. So, I could not see the world." This is what she accepted. Nobody told her this. She accepted it as a fact [that the queen's high position prevented her from moving around in public]. Then she asked her maidservants to go and bring her some wet clay. She made a big *ling* [aniconic form of Shiv] from clay in her house.
[MS]: In the palace?
[C]: Yes. In the palace. Then she served that *ling* for twelve years. Twelve years. After twelve years, Shiv appeared and said, "Yes, girl, tell me what you want?" The queen told Mahadev, "This is what I want: I want to be ugly so that nobody looks at me. I want to be born in a small house so that I can do all the *darśans* of God. So that I can do the *bhajans* of God. Give me such a body."
[MS]: Is she talking about her last birth or her present birth?

[C]: In the next birth. Then God said, "Alright, child. OK." After one hundred years she was born in a Bhil's home. She was born black [and] with yellow teeth. She grew up slowly. Then they [her parents] got her engaged when she was young. So they decorated her and made her sit far away when they arranged the engagement. Then they got her married by doing this and that [after much effort]. After getting married, she went to live in the house of her in-laws. In the morning she went to the jungle [Shabari went to the toilet]. [To Antoinette]: Do you understand the jungle?

[A]: Yes.

[C]: Then her sister-in-law brought her in the house, but she [the sister-in-law] didn't know. [Shabari] had three sisters-in-law. Her sister-in-law said that her *bhābhī* [elder brother's wife] is so black. She went home and told her mother "How could you bring such a black *bhābhī* for my brother? She's no good." Her mother said, "She's a human being, after all? She's OK." But the husband heard this. After looking at her he said, "I'm not going to live with her." This is what happened. He started fighting with her. Then he said, "blah, blah, blah. Go back to your father's house." She went back to her father's house. They said, "Why did you come back?" She said, "They fought with me. They said, 'You're no good. Our boy is so good.' Even the boy said, 'Why did you bring someone like that for me?' That's why I came back here." Her mother said, "You whore! Why the hell were you born at my house. We got you married so many days ago and now they're saying they can't keep you?" They started yelling at her. She started crying. It was the same *ātmā*. But there was a secret. Actually, she was a queen with hundreds of thousands of rupees. She started crying. Since it was evening, while crying and crying she fell asleep. Then God came and said, "What are you doing here? Let's go!" She woke up and saw nothing. She went back to sleep. God returned and said, "Why are you still sleeping? Come on, let's go! Why are you still sitting here?" God gave her *darśan* many times. They went twelve plus twelve miles in the jungle. Then he gave her a drum and asked her to do one thing: "Keep singing *bhajans*. Keep singing *rām-rām* and live here in the jungle. Eat fruits and flowers and plants. Right now it's the season of blackberries. Soon the red berry season will start. Different fruits will come at different times. Right now there are seventy-eight sadhus who are doing *tapasyā* [*sannyās*] around here. I will take you there in the night. Take some wood from here. Take some wood from the jungle."

[MS]: God was saying this?

[C]: Yes. God is speaking. Since she had done the *bhakti* before already. She took some wood. "When all of these seventy-eight sadhus go to sleep, you go there. You don't need to be scared. Nobody will hurt you. You have *śakti* so you don't need to be afraid." God gave her *śakti* [power] so that she wouldn't get scared. "The wood that you bring from this jungle, place it on this *dhūni* [fire pit]. After you place it on the *dhūni* clean everything. There is a stepwell which you should use to drink water. Fill this pot with water and go back [to your place in the forest]." God left after telling her what she has to do every night.

[MS]: She started going every night?

[C]: She used to go every night and serve those seventy-eight sadhus. But they wanted to catch her.

[MS]: They were wondering who does the cleaning?

[C]: So that day what happened was the sadhus kept themselves awake to catch her. They cut a sadhu's hand so he doesn't fall asleep. Then Shabari came. She came and put wood on the *dhūni*. She did all the cleaning. She filled water from the stepwell. They all came around the stepwell. Shabari was in there. They asked, "Who are you?" She said, "I am a Bhilni." "You made our water dirty!" Some of them kicked her. Some of them punched her. She yelled, "I'll not come back again!" She left crying. They used to use that stepwell for their drinking water, to bathe, and to wash. They used to drink water from there. When she left the sadhus came back in the morning and saw blood. They thought, "Where will we wash? Where will we drink water?" That stepwell was filled with blood and vermin. They said, "That Bhilni spoiled all the water. It never happened before it happened today." They went thirsty for three days and the news reached the crown of God. I'm telling you what I've heard, OK?

[MS]: Yes.

[C]: The news traveled all the way up to God's crown.

[MS]: I've never heard the version of the story that you're telling us.

[C]: Since the news reached the crown of God, he thought, "It has been three days. They have been punished enough. Let's go to Shabari Bai now and give the verdict. Though I don't want to give *darśan* to them."

[MS]: Who? The sadhus?

[C]: Yes. The sadhus. But they were dying of thirst for the past three days. They were punished enough for three days. "I should go and find out what's up with Shabari." He knew everything that had happened. He took some books in his hands and took the form of a Brahmin. He went [to the sadhus] to ask for wheat flour. It was hot. He got tired. He said,

"I've walked a long way from the village. Give me enough water so that I can make some bread [*rotī*]."

[MS]: But there wasn't any water.

[C]: "I have already collected some wheat flour. Just give me enough water so that I can make my food here." "Oh Maharaj! We have been thirsty for the last three days. There's no water. There's nothing." "What are you drinking, then?" "We are drinking nothing." "What happened to your water?" "A Bhilni came and spoiled the water." "A Bhilni came and spoiled the water? How can a Bhilni spoil your water?" "There's blood and vermin everywhere." "Really? Tell me the truth. What did you do to that Bhilni? You have to tell me the truth. You must have done something wrong [to her]. After all, the Bhilni has been coming here since all these days. How could this happen on that particular day?" They said, "We made a small cut on one of the sadhu's hands and we caught her. We beat her up; we kicked her; we punched her. Then she ran away, crying." God said, "OK, my children. Do what I say. I will find the Bhilni and bring her here. I will go to her and ask for wheat flour and I will bring her here. But you will have to do exactly as I say. Then your water and yourselves will become pure again." They said, "O.k., Maharaj. Bring her." The Maharaj knew everything that had happened. He took the form of a sadhu. God didn't take the form of a Brahmin. He took the form of a sadhu.

Shabari was picking up berries. Shabari was tasting the berries, and she was throwing away the sour ones and keeping the sweet ones for God because she knew he was coming. She knew God would come. She saw the sadhu coming. She thought, "The ones who have beat me up are coming back." She started walking away slowly. God was following her from behind. She started running and running. God also kept walking and walking in the form of a sadhu. But then she got tired. She got really tired. She said, "Oh, Owner of all the Worlds! I am going to die." She threw her berries in the air. Then God, with all his hands, caught those berries and held Shabari. She was falling down. After holding her, he took away the form of a sadhu and showed her his true form as God. She said, "Oh, Datta! It's you? I thought it was one of those sadhus, and that's why I ran away. Look where you have sent me! What have you done? Oh Surya Narayan Bhagwan! They beat me to death. I just ran away to save my life. This happened and that happened." God said, "OK, my child. Now I have come." She gave those berries to God. She didn't keep them for herself. He ate them like they were special to him.

After talking together for some time, God said, "Let's go. Come on, let's go!" "Now what will we do there? They'll beat me, Datta!" He said, "Would you beat you if you were with me?" After explaining everything to her, God brought Shabari to the seventy-eight sadhus and said to them, "Wash her feet with the water of the stepwell and drink the immortal nectar [*amṛt*] of that water. You should have her bathe completely with this water." Then Shabari bathed there and the water became as clear as a mirror. Then God showed his form in front of the seventy-eight sadhus and gave his *darśan* to them in front of Shabari Bai. And from that day Shabari Bai has been recognized [in India].

[MS]: It's a great story.

[C]: I've heard it.

[MS]: Yes, you've heard it. But it's a great story.

[C]: Now, correct me if there was anything wrong. I don't know. How did it go?

[MS]: The stories we know are the ones we've heard. There's nothing wrong with telling the story that you've heard.

[C]: I've told you everything I've heard.

Here, too, Chetanananda's breakthrough into performance occurs in the context of her rhetorical disclaimer that the Shabari story she knows constitutes the story she has heard, and that is the story she tells Manvendra Singh and me. The Shabari story has been told and retold in a plethora of ways in the Sanskritic and the vernacular-language *Rāmāyan* traditions (for an analysis of the various representations of Shabari in the *Rāmāyan* traditions, see Lutgendorf 2000). Those versions consistently represent Shabari as a "low-born" Bhilni who, at the command of the great sage Matanga (also from a low-caste community), spends her time in the forest serving the sadhus,[10] singing *bhajans*,[11] and desperately waiting for Ram to come and bless her with his *darśan*.[12] In whatever way it is told, Shabari's tale is explicitly rooted in the larger *Rāmāyan* universe. Chetanananda's version, however, diverges considerably from the more dominant literary and oral versions of the tale. Manvendra Singh's comment, "I've never heard the version of the story you're telling us," expresses the uniqueness of Chetanananda's narration. Her performance gives Shabari a mythic life outside of the narrative boundaries of the *Rāmāyan* by constructing a broader interpretive framework beyond that of Shabari's current Bhilni incarnation with which to understand Shabari's life circumstances, past and present.

To that extent, Chetanananda performs a remarkably different story from the more standard versions, because her tale presents a regional example that blends the dominant Mewari cultural-religious elements (i.e., Rajput) with the typically well-known pan-Indian details of the Shabari narrative. The result of her performative bricolage exemplifies a fascinating narrative tapestry. Notice that in Chetanananda's version, before Shabari was Shabari, the Bhilni, in her prior birth she was "the queen of a king" who had "hundreds of thousands of rupees." The queen's royal status distinguishes her as Kshatriya. But that alone hardly identifies Mewari and, more globally, Rajasthani influence. How do we know that the queen is Rajput? The Mewari cultural context in which Chetanananda's narrative performance is situated constructs the queen's identity as Rajput, thus joining her to Mewar's dominant caste group. In addition, certain narrative elements cue the specificity of the queen's Rajput status, such as her arrival in her conjugal home in *pardā*—(lit., "curtain") a characteristically Rajput custom of female modesty that restricts royal women's movements in the palace. Furthermore, the queen's worship of Shiv, and not Vishnu (the major god of the *Rāmāyan*), around whom the tale's events orbit, and whom the royal Sisodiyas worship as their supreme deity, suggests that the religious traditions of Mewar's Rajput elite are implicitly at work in Chetanananda's adaptation of the Shabari story.

The intimacy that Chetanananda feels for Eklingji, and her emotional identification with Shabari, as reflected in her statement, "I myself am Shabari," help to explain why, in the narrative that she tells, Shabari has a relationship with Shiv, rather than with Vishnu (or Ram). The god who calls Chetanananda has to be the same deity who carves Shabari's destiny. The parallels, then, between Chetanananda's and Shabari's stories are strikingly similar. Shabari's life experiences seem very similar to those of Chetanananda. Comparison of the two narratives shows that Chetanananda crafts Shabari's life in her image as much as she creates her life in Shabari's image.

To take an example, Mahadev (a title for Shiv) initially appears to Shabari in a dream-like experience, much like Eklingji approaches Chetanananda in her dreams. After Shabari's quarrel with her parents, who are so distraught over her abandoning her husband (who does not want her) that her mother calls her a "whore," she cries herself to sleep and, while sleeping, hears Shiv saying, "What are you doing here? Let's go!" When Shabari wakes up, she sees nothing and falls back asleep. But Shiv abruptly awakens her again, approaching her directly this time, and says, "Why are you still sleeping? Come on, let's go! Why are you still sitting here?" Shabari immediately knows Shiv's identity because, as the performance indicates, she retains in her present life an awareness of her identity as a queen in her past life and knows that, in that birth, she made a solemn wish to Mahadev to be reborn not only in "a low house," but also "ugly [and] with yellow teeth." The consciousness of the continuity of experience from life to life, therefore, stays with Shabari in her Bhilni incarnation. And, Mahadev grants her wish. There are, however, severe consequences in store for Shabari. Notice that Mahadev appears to Shabari after a personal and marital crisis. Her husband refuses to live with her because of her "black" skin, a sign of her physical unattractiveness. "Why did you bring such a black *bhābhī* for my brother," Shabari's sister-in-law cries to her mother. By virtue of Shabari's unsightly dark skin and yellow teeth, her in-laws decide that "she is no good" and quickly send her back to her parent's home.

As with Chetanananda's marriage, Shabari's also ends before it begins. Chetanananda's husband rejects her on the grounds that he has married someone else. Someone better looking, perhaps? Could it be that, like Shabari's husband, Chetanananda's husband similarly deemed her "no good," due to her physical features and, therefore, without even consulting her (or her *dādī-mā*), married another woman more attractive to him? On the day that Chetanananda tells her Shabari tale, she mentions, in the context of showing Manvendra Singh and me the photos of the consecration of the Gangeshwar Mahadev temple, that she looks "ugly [*badsūrat*]" in her pictures. "I always come so black in them," Chetanananda laments. "My teeth are so yellow." "But this is how God made me." She resigns herself to the physical form that God presents her with in this life. Shabari, too, accepts the body that Mahadev gives her. The Bhilni body that Shabari receives as a result of the queen's request to Mahadev, who actually determines the exact components and assemblage of that form, makes her a pariah in the dominant society. No one wants her. But that same Bhilni form that everyone shuns gives Shabari the freedom of movement to do what she could never do in her "very beautiful" body as a queen. "I [want] to be free to wander," the queen says. "I [want to] do all the *darśans* of God. I [want to] do the *bhajans* of God." The queen desires to spend her following life rapt in singing *bhajans* to *bhagwān*. That is, she intends to renounce the world in her next birth. But, she knows that such a life demands independence from the illusory (and expected) trappings of householding. For that to happen, the queen needs Mahadev to make her so "ugly that nobody looks at her." She hopes that her next incarnation's ugliness will serve as a protective shield against anyone proposing marriage to her, as marriage would only keep her from her life's goal of singing *bhajans*. Indeed, Shabari's marriage occurs simply because her face remains covered during the entire engagement and wedding ceremonies. Once her in-laws see her body, they release her from the binding ties of marriage and householding.

Both Chetanananda's and Shabari's foiled marriages pave the way for their new lives of singing *bhajans*. Neither, however, proceeds on their paths until Mahadev himself tells them to leave everything and sing to God. That happens after Chetanananda's and Shabari's marital crises, at that moment in which Mahadev enters their dreams and guides them in their new roles as sadhus. Mahadev's divine command constitutes the requisite permission that directly grants Chetanananda and Shabari the moral authority to practice their *sannyās*. Who can question their way of life when God himself has given them that right? In some of the vernacular-language tellings, Shabari's guru Matanga bequeaths her the authority to sing *bhajans* and serve the other (male) sadhus in the forest. According to the Shabari story featured in Priyadas's *Bhaktirasbodhinī*, in which, as Philip Lutgendorf (2000) observes, "seven of [the 630] stanzas are devoted to Shabari" (127), Matanga "initiates her in the divine name" (Lutgendorf 2000, 127). Similarly, the widely popular religious journal *Kalyān*, a Gita Press publication, illustrates its version of Shabari's story in a special issue on the lives of the *bhakti* saints entitled *Bhakta Caritānka* (Bh. C). Here, following Matanga's and his sadhu-disciples' discovery of Shabari in the forest, and moved by her extraordinary humility and compassion, Matanga permits the Bhilni to stay and live in *their* forest singing the divine name of Lord Ram. The text states:

> Hearing the faithful and courteous words of Shabari...Matanga thoughtfully reflected for a little while and then lovingly said to her, "Prosperous Woman! Do not fear. Live here and chant the name of Lord Ram." With the support of the sage, Shabari dressed herself in the tattered clothing and matted locks of ascetics and began living at the ashram immersing herself in the *bhajans* of the Lord. (Bh. C. 292, author's translation)

In sharp contrast, in Chetanananda's telling, Shabari's dwelling in the forest near (but hidden from) the sadhus and singing *bhajans* signifies a function of Mahadev's permission, not Matanga's (who is never mentioned). Likewise, Eklingji consecrates and establishes Chetanananda in her *dīvān* role, not her guru, Bhumanandaji. For both Bhilnis, God serves as their first guru long before they encounter their human gurus. Thus, Chetanananda's narratives emphasize Mahadev as the power behind both her life and Shabari's life. After giving Shabari "*darśan* many times" and walking "twelve plus twelve miles" with her "in the jungle," Mahadev instructs her to "[k]eep singing *bhajans*. Keep singing *rām-rām* and live here in the jungle. Eat fruits and flowers and plants...Right now there are seventy-eight sadhus who are doing *tapasyā* around here. I will take you there in the night." He also tells her "don't...be scared. Nobody will hurt you. You have *śakti* so you don't need to be afraid." To convince Shabari of her power, Mahadev transmits his *śakti* to her, doubling her *śakti*. The transmission of *śakti* represents Mahadev's empowering Shabari with the divine right to sing *bhajans*. By his ultimate authority, both Chetanananda and Shabari have the strength and fierceness of mentality to endure life on the battlefield of *bhakti*.

Once the other male sadhus learn of Shabari's existence, her life becomes a veritable battlefield on the path of *bhakti*. She needs all the courage she can muster against the suspecting male sadhus. The physical violence to which they subject the innocent Shabari is disturbing. These sadhus hate her, given that they mistakenly perceive her to be a low-born and, hence, impure Bhilni purposely polluting their sacred environs, their *sādhanā*, and their bodies. Hence, they waste no time taking their anger out on her. "Some of them kicked her" and "some of them punched her." Several of the vernacular-language tellings, such as Priyadas's, Kalyan's, and Ramanand Sagar's televised rendition, depict the sadhus verbally abusing, berating, or mocking Shabari (Lutgendorf 2000; c.f. *Bhakta Caritānka* 1952, 293). Chetanananda's telling, however, intensifies the violence and, in doing so, performs in narrative high relief the selfless sacrifice that Shabari makes for the love of Mahadev. Chetanananda's performance cues her audience to recognize that virtue as demonstrative of Shabari's (and her own) Bhil nature. And, on account of that nature, just as Chetanananda endures the harsh accusations of the local villagers (they accuse her of being a thief), Shabari, too, bears the sadhus' beating. But, she also dishes it right back at them. Shabari does not just run away after her altercation with the sadhus; instead, she screams at them, saying, "I'll not come back again!" before she takes off into the jungle.

Thus, Chetanananda's tale performs an alternative Shabari to the predominant Shabari figure usually featured in *Rāmāyan* narratives.[13] In most of those tellings, Shabari fears the sadhus and cowers before them. The *Bhakta Caritānka*, for example, uses the following adjectives to characterize Shabari's emotional state of mind as she stands in front of the jury of her sadhu-peers: "afraid," "terrified," and "trembling" (Bh C., 292). Such descriptions tacitly reinforce Shabari's low-caste status in relation to the sadhus' high-caste status. The *Bhakta Caritānka* discusses Shabari's low-caste identity six times in its four and a half pages of narrative. Not only that, Shabari internalizes the shame that the Brahmanical orthodoxy illustrated by the well-born, elitist sadhus attributes to her Bhil status, for she, too, views her birth as the manifestation of a "misfortune" from the deeds of a previous life. In her words: "Because of some misfortune, my birth happened in a low-community" (Bh. C., 292). Later on in the text, and citing Tulsidas' *Rāmcaritmānas* as evidence, Shabari says to Ram, "I am from a low-community and very dull-witted. The lowest among the low will always be low" (*Mānas* 3.34.1 cited in Bh. C., 293).

Chetanananda's telling challenges these representations in several crucial ways. First of all, the Shabari she crafts is fierce. This Shabari hardly depicts a self-deprecating and apologetic Bhilni. Not once in Chetanananda's telling are the words "afraid," "trembling," or "terrified" used to describe Shabari. She stands up to the sadhus and makes known her anger over their reprehensible behavior before she abandons them. Hence, Chetanananda's telling articulates that Shabari's running away from the sadhus signifies her punishing them, and not simply her fearing them. The blood-stained, vermin-filled water corroborates this view. Chetanananda's story suggests that the sadhus' water becomes spoiled not by Mahadev's doing, but rather by a combination of Shabari's *śakti* and the sadhus' obfuscating arrogance. Mahadev's descending to earth so that he may "see what's up with Shabari" and "give the verdict," occurs as a result of the news of their tainted water and three days of thirst traveling "all the way up to the crown of God." His comment that "they have been punished enough" suggests that the sadhus' fate lay in the lap of Shabari's *śakti*, not his. When Mahadev brings Shabari in front of the confused and pitiful sadhus, giving them *darśan* with her as his witness, he verifies her actions, much like the police chief and Eklingji authenticate Chetanananda's behavior to the villagers. Mahadev publicly declares that Shabari is not responsible for the sadhus' spoiled water. Nor, as Mahadev's relationship with Shabari intimates, is she robbing them of the merit of their *sādhanā*.

Shabari's dilemma resembles Karma Bai's. Those sadhus, who initially trusted Karma Bai to perform Krishna's *pūjā*, accuse her of stealing their money when those ritual expenses turn out to be more than they had expected. Had they known that Karma Bai spends their funds feeding Krishna and, as Ganga Giri says, his entire "big family," they never would have doubted her character. Similarly, the sadhus whom Shabari confronts once more, this time with Mahadev at her side, behave as those other sadhus acted in their genuflecting before Karma Bai. By washing Shabari's feet with the polluted water from the stepwell, and by drinking the "immortal nectar" of that water, they show that Shabari is more of a sadhu than they are. But the dilemmas that Karma Bai and Shabari face testify to their strength of character, a Bhil trait par excellence.

Second, through her alternative narrative construction of Shabari, Chetanananda performs the idea that Bhils, and Bhil women, in particular, are just as, if not more, capable of singing *bhajans* to God as high-caste male sadhus are. Bhils' strength, courage, and innocence of character à la Shabari and, by extension, Chetanananda, distinguish them as exceptional *bhakts* of *bhagwān* vis-à-vis the more typical well-born (and male) candidates. Perhaps, for this reason, Shabari refuses to cower before the haughty sadhus, because she views herself as their spiritual *and* social equal. Her Bhil nature authorizes her to live as Mahadev's sadhu-warrior on the battlefield of *bhakti* as much as the high-caste status of the sadhus gives them their right to do so.

Chetanananda's telling thus expresses the notion that, despite their upper-caste status, if those sadhus were "real" sadhus they would have recognized Shabari's purity of character and the power of her Bhil nature. They would have considered her as their religious equal and, perhaps, on account of her uncommon sadhu-*bhakti* and selfless service to them, their spiritual superior. Mahadev's question, "How can a Bhilni spoil your water?... You must have done something wrong to her," alludes to the sadhus' ignorant clinging to their individual high-caste statuses as an obstacle that paralyzes their ability to discern between true and crooked sadhus, and between real and false sadhu *bhakti*. These seemingly spiritually elevated sadhus are so attached to their high-caste status that, after they learn about Shabari's Bhil identity, all they can say is, "Where will we bathe?" For them, maintaining their caste purity through their regular ritual ablutions trumps all other concerns. At the same time, Shabari's gender (after all, what woman would dare to sing *bhajans* alone in the jungle?) and purportedly low birth prevent the sadhus from seeing a fierce lion(ess), much like themselves, standing before them. Indeed, the Bhil woman who retrieves water from the stepwell is really a Rajput queen (Singh), but the sadhus' stupidity blinds them from figuring out the "secret" that Chetanananda reveals to her audience: that Shabari and the queen are, in fact, "the same *ātmā*"; that the "ugly" Shabari with the "black" skin and "yellow teeth" is really the gorgeous and wealthy queen who, through her devotional asceticism, beseeches Mahadev to cause her to be reborn "in a Bhil's house" so that she can sing *bhajans*.

Finally, in constructing Shabari in this manner, Chetanananda performatively questions the dominant (and classical) Brahmanical Hindu theologies that frequently interpret external physical attributes such as birth in a low-caste community, unattractiveness, and, to some extent, unsuccessful social relationships (e.g., marriage and family), as the inevitable (and deserved) ripening of the "sins" of the negative actions (*karm*) of previous births. Her performance persuasively flips the standard equation of high-caste birth, beauty, wealth, and progeny as illustrative of a person's good past life *karm*. In the view of Chetanananda's story, Shabari's birth in the Bhil community hardly represents, as the predominant *Rāmāyan* perspective suggests, the manifestation of the misfortune accumulated from her past lives. Rather, it constitutes the intended result of the queen's twelve years of penance and pleas to Mahadev to be able to renounce the world in her next birth. Chetanananda's telling, therefore, constructs Shabari's position in a low-status Bhil community, and her unpleasing physical form, as karmic rewards—blessings, in fact, for her precious and powerful *bhakti* to *bhagwān*. Chetanananda's statement to Manvendra Singh that Shabari "had done the *bhakti* before already" signals her understanding (which, in effect, shapes the audience's interpretations of her tale) that Shabari's birth and harsh life circumstances represent the positive consequences of the renouncer *bhakti* of her previous life's incarnation as a queen. In her new Bhil form, the queen *qua* Shabari has the independence of movement to make God's *darśan* everywhere she travels and sing *bhajans*. She can worship Mahadev without the need (or expectation) to uphold the restrictive traditional Hindu customs of female modesty (*pardā*) that circumscribe high-caste women's behaviors and interactions with (male) non-kin others. Hence, Chetanananda tacitly connects (non-Bhil) women's obstacles in their becoming sadhus to their higher caste statuses.

The perspective on the interface between caste identity and past karmic influences that Chetanananda suggests through her Shabari performance pushes back at the claims of the majority of the high-caste sadhus with whom I worked. These sadhus argue that the good *karm* of their previous births made it possible for them to be reborn, as Tulsi Giri says in the context of talking about her life, "in a Brahmin's house." In this way, sadhus like Tulsi Giri imply that women from the high caste stand a much better chance of being able to practice their unusual *bhakti* and, later on, take *sannyās* than those born in the low castes, by virtue of the common cultural perception that associates *sannyās*, including its female expressions such as the devotional asceticism illustrated in this study, with high-caste privilege and authority. In contrast, in the viewpoint of Chetanananda's narrative, birth in a "big house" serves as a karmic slap in the face. Her telling questions Tulsi Giri's and the other sadhus' perspectives by asking, to play on Ganga Giri's words, "What sort of renouncer *bhakti* can women from upper-caste communities practice?" Therefore, Chetanananda's performance buoys the social status of Bhils to a level that competes with that of the Brahmins and Rajputs and aligns the perceived martial attributes of her tribal identity with her idea of *sannyās* as a difficult path of singing *bhajans*. Through her narrative construction of Shabari's birth and life as constitutive of the workings of the mixture of good *karm* and divine beneficence, Chetanananda crafts her birth and life as a Bhil in a similar light.

But Chetanananda's telling of the Shabari story is not without the tell-tale signs of an ethos of caste ambivalence characteristic of the practices of most of the high-caste sadhus. As with Ganga Giri's *bhajan* performance analyzed in the last chapter, Chetanananda's narrative performance similarly expresses ambivalence about Bhil social status. That is, while her telling creates and communicates an alternative (and positive) image of Shabari to her more usual incarnations, and while her telling compellingly reconfigures the standard logic underpinning the mysterious dance between *karm* and caste status in human birth, what we have to remember as we attempt to make sense of Chetanananda's vision of the links between caste status and sadhu status concerns that signal secret that she shares with her audience in the construction of her *exemplum*—Shabari's Bhil birth functions as a clandestine karmic disguise for the queen's brilliant strategy of actualizing her intention to sing *bhajans* in her next life.

In her telling, Chetanananda clarifies that Shabari is originally Rajput. That caste identity provides the ultimate and underlying conceptual backdrop in light of which she and her audience interpret Shabari's uncommon strength, courage, and fierceness of mentality in conjunction with not only her uncommon sadhu devotion, but also her living in a jungle populated by spiritually immature sadhus. This is not to say that Shabari's Bhil nature has no bearing on her authority and ability to sing *bhajans* to Chetanananda. Nonetheless, the queen's Rajput nature—which is evident in her peculiar capacity to renounce, without a second thought, the status and privileges attached to her royal birth—constitutes the karmic substratum that shapes and fortifies Shabari's Bhil nature.

From this perspective, the connection that Chetanananda appears to make in her association between the sadhus of medieval Mewar, who fought bravely with their lives against Akbar's Mughal forces to protect Hindu *dharm*, and Shabari, a Bhilni sadhu of yore who fiercely devoted herself to Mahadev on the battlefield of *bhakti*, has to do with her perception of Shabari's Rajput origins. Chetanananda's telling of the Shabari tale, therefore, depicts a regional (and renunciant) example of the process of "Rajputization," by which she creates Bhil sadhus like herself as ideal Rajputs by incorporating the dominant royal idioms, symbols, and values into her practices, in an effort to enhance Bhil social status (Mines 2009; Harlan 2003; Bayly 1999; Kolff 1990; Srinivas 1989). Thus, by representing herself to her interlocutors with the statement, "I myself am Shabari," Chetanananda suggests her understanding that she, too, was once Rajput.

The powerful model of Shabari presents an immediate mythic example with which Chetanananda Swami creatively carves and (re)constitutes her caste and sadhu identities through means of performance. Moreover, her innovative narrative adaptation of Shabari as originally Rajput performatively synchronizes Bhil status with the power and prestige associated with the royal Rajput. But what happens in those cases in which the sadhus born in low castes or as outcastes (i.e., formerly "untouchable" communities) do not have the support of a legitimating mythic model? On what do they draw to authorize their *sannyās*? Do those sadhus adopt the values and practices of the dominant high-caste groups as a way to transform their society's perceptions of their low-caste or outcaste status? In Chapter 6 (the last in our series of explorations on gender, caste, and vernacular asceticism in Mewar), we will examine the life and practices of a sadhu born into a (formerly) low and underprivileged caste in India, so that we may be able to see from her vantage point the complex and ever-changing relationship, as well as the ongoing tensions, between caste status and sadhu status in contemporary North India.

6

"Even the Black Cuckoo Sings Beautifully"

CHALLENGE AND RECONFIGURATION IN THE PRACTICES OF A KHATIK SADHU

Don't die for the body. Why do you see the flesh? See the words. See the ātmā. That's the real beauty, and the only truth.

—SAD GIRI MAHARAJ

THE SAFFRON-COLORED SEA of movement in the foothills of the Aravalli Mountains signals the location of the *bhaṇḍāra* at Bholenath[1] Ashram in Gogunda village, Udaipur district.[2] Large orange tent-like structures, protecting the participants from the rays of the harsh summer sun on this June morning, have been erected on the western side of the ashram complex as shelter for the hundreds of sadhus, of many genders, sects, and traditions, in attendance at this ceremonial event. Five long years have passed since I last visited this sacred place and its resident sadhus in 2006, when I was conducting field research for my PhD dissertation. Forty days earlier, the sadhu who built and managed this ashram for a quarter of a century, Maya Nath, passed away from a heart attack. She was sixty-eight years old.[3] Her daughter Paras Bai, and her grandson Shankar, with the assistance of the local sadhu *maṇḍal* (an administrative organization that oversees sadhu affairs, initiations, and institutions in Mewar), organized the *bhaṇḍāra* sending out hundreds of invitations (*nimantran*) to sadhus throughout Rajasthan and elsewhere in North India, in order to sponsor the ritual consecration of Maya Nath's *mūrtī* at the place of her *mahāsamādhi* shrine. To the right of the shrine, on an elevated concrete platform below the ashram's century-old mango tree, groups of householding women dressed in brightly colored saris imprinted with traditional Rajasthani designs—most likely devotees of Maya Nath and the ashram—are singing *bhajans* and observing the ritual festivities (see Figure 6.1). Their menfolk—husbands, brothers, sons, and fathers—who are congregated

FIGURE 6.1 The *bhaṇḍāra* festival held on the occasion of Maya Nath's *mahāsamādhi* ceremony.
Photo by A. DeNapoli.

on various parts on the property, serve the guests food and drink, monitor the parking, or talk business with the other attendees. In the midst of this activity, the caterers, a Brahmin man who owns a restaurant in Gogunda and his team of employees, prepare the day's delicious food, consisting of fried breads (*pūrī*), *dāl*, vegetables, and *halwā* (sweet meat) cooked in huge vats over wood-burning fires in their makeshift kitchen set up below the platform.

Three hundred feet away from the outdoor kitchen, the sadhus are gathered in the shade of the tarpaulin and conducting their own affairs. Some read newspapers, while others are fast asleep; some wait for the food to be served (*jalebīs*,[4] *pūrī*, and chai are on the breakfast menu), while others debate the rules of the procedures for the ritual consecration of Maya Nath's *mūrtī* about to take place at the shrine; some sit quietly in meditation, while others enjoy the company of old friends, laughing and telling jokes (see Figure 6.2). The female sadhus are easy to spot in this predominantly male collectivity. On this occasion, all eleven of them, dressed in ochre robes (or a mixture of ochre and white clothing), and wearing the symbols of their sect or order on their foreheads and bodies, sit together and discuss their lives and sing *bhajans* when the desire arises, and to heighten the mood of the ceremony. Sad Giri,

FIGURE 6.2 Sadhus holding court at the *bhaṇḍāra*.
Photo by A. DeNapoli.

the youngest participant in this group (depicted in Figure 6.3), situates herself on the outer cusp of this vibrant, all-female *maṇḍalī*, and observes her elders in action; she also observes me, the American ethnographer with her camera, notebook, and tape recorder gingerly taking her place in the circle among the welcoming and curious sadhus.

A thirty-two-year-old sadhu (as of 2011) who took initiation into the Giri branch of the Dashanami order two years earlier (one of the only four branches that initiate women), Sad Giri is as unique as she is noteworthy in the more global context of the population sample of female sadhus with whom I have worked in Mewar during the last decade. Apart from her much younger age (in 2006, the average age of the sadhus was sixty-eight years), she is the only sadhu I know who comes from the *jātī of* Khatiks, a low caste of animal butchers, within the Shudra *varna*. At the same time, her views and practices distinguish her as a new and emerging class of sadhus in Rajasthan.

Significantly, unlike the other sadhus, Sad Giri lives with her parents (more about this below). She is also an entrepreneur who has professionalized her asceticism by starting a *satsang* "business," for which she earns two thousand rupees ($40 USD) for each performance (she gets more money if she uses her

FIGURE 6.3 Sad Giri attending the *bhaṇḍāra*.
Photo by A. DeNapoli.

own sound system and brings her own people to perform with her), which starts around dusk and runs for the entire night. She travels four times a week in and around Mewar, performing for well-off Hindu patrons primarily from the Jat (or Mahajan) castes.

The entrepreneurial attitude demanded from Sad Giri's *satsang* business parallels the entrance of Khatiks elsewhere in North India into nontraditional occupations (Gold 2012; Gill 2009).[5] In her recent study of a Khatik community in the small market town of Jahazpur in Bhilwara district, Rajasthan, Ann Gold (forthcoming) observes that, with the exception of some families (five to ten people), the Khatiks in this municipality, which consists of two hundred households, have largely adopted new and respectable professions outside of their caste's traditional occupation in meat selling and trading. Characterizing this community as "entrepreneurial go-getters,"[6] she says that, "Many Khatiks work at the vegetable market both as vendors and as brokers or middle-men for vegetables shipped in from the countryside" (11). And, based on information she found on a Google Web site (Khatiksamaj.com), Gold notes, "members of this now global community have moved into modern professions [doctors, engineers, teachers, advocates, management/administrative staff]; in

Jahazpur, too, as we have learned, they have taken up several alternative forms of employment available to them in the cash economy" (13).

From the moment she learns of my professional interest in the religious practices of sadhus, Sad Giri speaks at length about her business. "I run things by playing the instruments, like the drum [*dholak*], I bring the 'sound' system, I set up the tent, etc. A lot of this I do myself. Later, when the public comes, I give *pravacan* [religious discourses], *kathā* [narrative recitation and explanation], *sangīt* [singing with music and dancing], *kīrtan* [singing *bhajans* and hymns of praise to a deity], whatever they [unspecified] want. I perform everything. Wherever I go, I sing and play instruments [*gānā-bajānā*]." Sad Giri pauses the conversation and asks her youngest brother Kamlesh, who has accompanied her to the *bhaṇḍāra* and sits behind the *maṇḍalī*, listening to our talk, to show me her business card. Against a bright, sky-blue background appear the words, "Satgiri Maharaj," under which it reads, "Mewari Storyteller" in even larger letters (the business card is visible in Figure 6.4). A heavenly halo of white light encircles Sad Giri's image, imbuing her with divine radiance. The names written at the top left of the card are those of her younger brothers Ramesh and Kamlesh, who are her business associates, and the phone numbers listed at the top right of the card are Ramesh's, Kamlesh's, and Sad Giri's, respectively.

With the earnings she has received from her *satsang* business, which she has been operating for the last twelve years with the help of her family (i.e., her

FIGURE 6.4 Sad Giri's business card.
Scan by A. DeNapoli. Used with permission.

father and two brothers), Sad Giri purchased the land on which the ashram sits, which, as she says, she "built with her own hands." She bought the land ten years ago for 35 thousand rupees (approx. $750 USD). "I purchased this land myself. Nobody helped me. I never asked anyone for anything, not even my parents," Sad Giri tells me and Manvendra Singh as we walk on the road leading to her ashram. Impressed by our first meeting at the *bhaṇḍāra*, Sad Giri invited me to come and see her ashram (which is visible in Figure 6.5), and Manvendra Singh and I made the hour-long trip two days later. The ashram and the business, as the bottom of Sad Giri's business card states, are located in Gadavara village, Mavli (sub)district, which borders Udaipur district. Like many ashrams in India, a faded salmon-colored flag tied to a bamboo pole and raised high above the building, and a burning *dhūni* (fire pit) located in the shaded front courtyard, distinguish Sad Giri's ashram as a sacred place amid the chaos of *sansār*, and as a working ashram. The inner space consists of a single, rectangular-shaped room that measures sixteen feet wide by eighty feet long. Two wooden doors have been placed on the east and west sides of the structure, and Sad Giri keeps them open in the summer to allow the cool breeze to circulate inside the ashram. As of this writing (2012),

FIGURE 6.5 The front entrance to Sad Giri's ashram.
Photo by A. DeNapoli.

no *mūrtīs* have yet been established, but mass-produced images of the gods on calendars and posters embellish the whitewashed walls. A large poster of baby Krishna mischievously reaching for a type of sweet called *laḍḍūs,*[7] with the logo "Kelwa Marble" written across it (probably a gift from one of Sad Giri's patrons, several of whom work in Rajasthan's leading marble industry), adorns the south-facing wall. Kamlesh joins the three of us and we sit and talk for a while. The ashram, according to Sad Giri, remains in an "unfinished" (*kaccā*) state. "I have to build a kitchen and a bathroom. And there's no running water," she explains. "Otherwise, everything an ashram needs is right here. The pots, cups, utensils, bed cushions, the gas stove—it's all here."

Inner and Outer Forms: Knowledge of the Ātmā *as Grammar for Challenge*

In her relations with members of higher status groups, Sad Giri reproduces hierarchical, caste-determined codes of behavior. But Sad Giri's practices express more than her conformity to hegemonic caste hierarchies. Accommodating to constrictive caste customs and norms demonstrates that Sad Giri's everyday behaviors are embedded in a complex matrix of shifting cultural structures that shape, and are shaped by, her interactions with higher caste communities. By working within those structures, however, Sad Giri not only "maneuvers and negotiates conditions that are often inherently disempowering" for low-caste groups (Jassal 2012, 8), but also creates a space within which she critically reflects on and challenges the shared cultural norms of caste exclusion that her practices appear to legitimate (cf. Knight 2011). As Lisa Knight observes in her study of Baul women in West Bengal and Bangladesh, "We can look at moments of contradiction for what they might reveal about discourses that are debated rather than merely accepted" (8).

In her study of the song traditions of women from the disadvantaged and marginalized laboring castes in the Northeast Indian states of Uttar Pradesh and Bihar, Smita Tewari Jassal (2012) makes the compelling claim that "Limited views of agency in western feminist discourse" assume "that women's actions emerge from their own free will, rather than from the dictates of custom, tradition, or direct coercion" (13). The frameworks that women in nonwestern and nonliberal traditions in particular use to organize their lives demand that scholars represent their dynamic gendered and social worlds through lenses beyond those that promote the more standard feminist narrative of "resistance and subversion" or "acceptance and conformity"[8] (Jassal 2012, 13). Citing the groundbreaking work of Saba Mahmood (2005) on the women's piety movement in Cairo, Egypt, Jassal suggests that "women's practices may be understood as spaces for subordinate discourse that cultivates women's consciousness"[9] (14). In this light, Jassal observes that more accurate conceptualizations of agency, defined as "the socio-culturally mediated capacity to act," can be reached by considering the variety of ways in which "specific relations of subordination create and enable" women's capacities for action (2012, 14). Thus, as Jassal states, "[A] notion of agency that is socially, linguistically, and culturally constrained is a more effective one when trying to understand how women are sometimes complicit with, while also making accommodations for or reinforcing, the status quo—often all at the same time" (2012, 14).

Constrained by the "dictates of custom," Sad Giri yields to established caste structures in her practices as a means to comply with, as well as to critique, the dominant forms of knowledge, value systems, and ideologies that such an embedded cultural system constitutes and enacts. In one conversation, Sad Giri reflects thoughtfully on the social discrimination, engendered by exclusive caste structures, which she experiences in *sannyās*. "Sadhus don't keep cleanliness, and they just wear one piece of clothing. If you are uneducated you do nothing. But if you are educated, you get dressed up. This is what I do. Still, nobody takes water from my hands. I don't know why, but sadhus don't bathe for two days. Why do they do this? Well, it's all God's blessings." In this constructive statement, Sad Giri's goal is not to critique the inequalities of the caste system. Rather, it is to draw attention to the exclusionary caste-based practices, and the common systems of knowledge on which they are based, that operate in a religious institution that is supposed to be blind (and deaf) to the social distinctions of caste, class, race, and gender.

Speaking about her personal journey on the difficult path of *sannyās*, Sad Giri invokes the pan-Indian renunciant idiom of knowledge of the *ātmā* as a potent grammar for challenging the dominant (and competing) exclusionary renunciant ethos of caste ambivalence illustrative of vernacular asceticism in Mewar. The triple signification of meanings suggested in her earlier statement (i.e., "Sadhus don't keep cleanliness...") distinguishes Sad Giri as clean, pure, and educated, and carefully crafts her authenticity for her audience. Moreover, the personal narrative performances in which she talks about her cataclysmic experiences of "meeting" (*milnā*) her *ātmā*, serve as constructive "spaces for subordinate discourse that cultivates women's consciousness" (Jassal 2012, 14). Her narratives represent her *ātmā*, which she equates in these and other performances with the *paramātmā*, as the absolute authority that allows her to interrogate the local ethos of caste ambivalence. Thus, by drawing on the provocative grammar of *ātmā*-realization, Sad Giri performs her divinely legitimated challenge to the mainstream and engages in a converging system of practices constitutive of her life of *sannyās*. These are: (1) her adopting of a ritual state that she terms "white *sannyās* [celibate studenthood]," which prepares her to take "full" *sannyās*; (2) her starting of a *satsang* business, (3) and her participating in the annual pilgrimage (*yātrā*) to Ramdevra, a regional shrine dedicated to the hero-god Ramdev, revered by Hindus *and* Muslims alike, and viewed as a deity par excellence for the downtrodden.[10] The next section analyzes Sad Giri's personal narratives, in which she crafts a grammar of *ātmā*-realization, and which make specific claims about female agency and personhood in *sannyās*-as-lived. It also discusses the three aforementioned practices, which are informed by that grammar, in an effort to understand the ways that Sad Giri pushes back at the caste hegemonies she faces everyday in vernacular asceticism.

"Dyed in Two Colors": Sad Giri's Personal Narrative Performances

"There are two types of knowledge [*vidyā*]," Sad Giri tells me. "What are they?" I ask, my curiosity piqued. "*Bhed* and *ved.*" She takes my pen and writes these words using Hindi script in the blank pages of my notebook. In this corner of Maya Nath's *bhaṇḍāra, satsang* begins. The other female sadhus observe our interaction. Eyes watch us carefully. "She writes everything down in her book," Jamuna Bharti remarks about me to the rest of the group. With a handkerchief, she wipes beads of sweat from my cheek. "It's too hot," the sadhus complain. Several yards away at Maya Nath's *mahāsamādhi* shrine, the chief sadhus of the *maṇḍal*, with Maya Nath's grandson Shankar by their side, prepare for the ritual consecration of the *mūrtī*. "*Bhed* exists within [*andar*]; it cannot be seen with the eyes. This is called *bhed.* This is the *ātmā-jnān* [knowledge of the self]. *Ved,* however, exists outside [*bāhar*], like the qualities of the mind [*sir-gun*]. It's outside, and it can be seen. *Ved* is only a curtain [*pardā*]," Sad Giri explains. "It hides *bhed?*" I ask for clarification. "Correct! It hides *bhed.* But it can be seen." Pointing to the tape recorder I keep positioned between us, Sad Giri says: "This machine has two switches, an outside switch and an inside switch. The outside switch turns it on, and the inside switch makes the tape run." Both of us stare at the running recorder. "Isn't that right?" she asks. "Yes, Maharaj," I reply. She continues, "The outside is black [*kālāpan*], and the inside is white [*safed*]." Pointing now to her body, Sad Giri says, "This form here, like that switch there, is black. But that within is white. Do you understand? The *ātmā* is white, but the curtain is black."

Drawing on the non-dualistic (and widely popular) mystical theology of Advaita Vedanta through which she articulates common *nirguṇī* understandings of the *ātmā* as genderless, formless, and thus, without any distinguishing qualities or characteristics, Sad Giri nonetheless constructs a dualism between "inner" and "outer" phenomena, between the esoteric and exoteric, respectively (cf. Knight 2011 for a similar discussion, situated in the context of Baul ideology). While the latter characterizes the body, which, as Sad Giri suggests, represents a global signifier of gender, skin color, and caste for the constituents, the former describes the *ātmā*, the color of which she stresses is "white." Similarly, the outer—what people see and base their ideas on—acts as a "curtain" that conceals the *ātmā*, shielding their realization of its potent truth: that what is outside is insignificant. Hence, the emphasis she places on the *ātmā* being white and everything else being "black" expresses her perception of there being two fundamental colors in the whole universe, and that every person (and every species in the cosmos), despite gender, class, and caste status—the guiding lenses of human experience—is white on the inside and black on the outside.[11] Since all humanity, as described in a Mira *bhajan* that Sad Giri sings in *satsang*, is "dyed" in the eternal shades of white and black, everyone essentially stands at an equal level.

The verbalizing of her statement in the ritual context of the *bhaṇḍāra*, where gender and caste distinctions among the sadhus are performed via specific actions, serves as a prescient meta-commentary that reveals as much as it criticizes an ethos of caste ambivalence in *sannyās*. The female sadhus and the male sadhus at this *bhaṇḍāra* sit separately throughout most of the gathering, and the low-caste sadhus eat in the *panghaṭ* (queue) only after the high-caste sadhus have been served their meals.[12] Occupying the periphery of the sadhu *maṇḍalī*, Sad Giri indicates her ascribed inferior position within the larger sadhu hierarchy (even among women), and her perceived status as an outsider in a male-dominated and high-caste Brahmanical institution. By invoking the grammar of knowledge of the *ātmā* in the presence of the other sadhus to distinguish between two types of truth and, by extension, two kinds of color, she speaks against the dominant practice of sadhus' reproducing established gender and caste-based norms and ideologies, and points out their own blinding ignorance in treating them as anything but real.

The stories that Sad Giri tells about experiencing the *ātmā* have enabled her to legitimate her *sannyās* by emphasizing her intimate connection to the real. They frame her interactions with many of her (often skeptical) interlocutors, both householders and other sadhus. From the time of our first meeting at the *bhaṇḍāra*, Sad Giri employs such narratives to represent and interpret the difficult choices she makes, and is frequently forced to make, on the basis of the options resulting from the marginalizing cultural conditions and power structures in which her world is rooted. What follows is a transcription of a conversation that took place at her natal home in the company of her family; Sad Giri shared this story with me in our second meeting on June 23, 2011:

[SG]: The *ātmā* is the guru. I live by the grace of the guru. [sings a *bhajan*].

The sadguru has come as a guest. What shall I offer?
Shall I make rice?
The sadguru has come as a guest. What shall I offer?
What should I cook?
O Salviji!
Wash the feet of the sadguru.

This is a Marwari *bhajan*. I didn't sing it in Hindi. The *bhajan* speaks about the guru within [*andarūni gurudev kā bhajan*]. Do you understand? Remember there [i.e., at the *bhaṇḍāra*] I told you about the knowledge of the *ātmā* ? The *ātmā-jnān* lies within. And, the knowledge of the material [*sir-śarīr kā*] qualities exist outside.

[A]: Yes, I remember. One is outside, and the other is inside.

[SG]: What kind of knowledge is outside?

[A]: *Ved.*

[SG]: And the one inside? What is that called?

[A]: *Bhed.*

[SG]: These are two different things.... Now you understand... The *ātmā* opened my mind [*buddhi khul gayī*]. It was all "automatic." The *ātmā* gave me divine vision [*divya dṛṣṭī*]. Because of the *ātmā* I can recognize letters [i.e., she can read]. I saw everything. I saw all the letters. S, V, T, N, everything was written there [in *divya dṛṣṭī*]. Now, I know the letters.

[A]: You recognize what is written?

[SG]: Yes. And, I remember what I hear. If you speak English, I'll remember it. I don't have to see what you're saying, I only have to hear it to remember it. I sing *bhajans* in Gujarati, all languages, because I heard them [sung] in those languages. Remember at the *bhaṇḍāra* I sung Gujarati *bhajans*? I sung Hindi *bhajans*, too.

[A]: Uh-huh.

[SG]: You're educated [*paḍhe hue*]. You went to school. You have "files" of degrees. I, however, never went to school. I didn't study in the school. This is the grace of the guru.

[A]: You mean, the guru who initiated you?

[SG]: No. I didn't learn this from him. I learned it all on my own [*akele hī*], from the *ātmā*. I never asked my guruji to teach me anything. I didn't ask him to teach me this or that. I never stayed at any single place for a minute to learn what I have learned. I never took help from anyone. My guruji only gave me one word [*śabd*] that I chant when I turn the *mālā* [i.e., she recites the mantra given by her guru in meditation using a *mālā*, a string, or necklace, of beads, to keep count of her repetitions].

[A]: OK.

[SG]: I learned all by myself how to play the harmonium, too. [Striking the keys of the harmonium that Kamlesh has brought so that she can demonstrate, Sad Giri chants the notes]: *Sā re gā mā pā dha ni sā. Sā ni dha pā mā gā re sā.* I remember the sounds forwards [*sīdhā*] and backwards [*ultā*]... My *ātmā* has given me the "power" to do this. It's all "automatic." [Sad Giri's father repeats, "it's automatic."]

[A]: What do you mean?

[SG]: I didn't know [pointing to her saffron clothes] this would happen.

[A]: You mean you didn't know you would take *sannyās*? You had no idea?

[SG]: I had no idea at all. I was only a child. I didn't understand anything. I was just a child.

[A]: You were just a child?

[SG]: I never thought when I was a child that I would take *sannyās*. What did I know? I was a child. I didn't know what I had to do. It was seventeen years before I took full *sannyās* [*pūrā sannyās*]. Before that I lived in [a state of] white *sannyās*. I lived alone in white *sannyās* for seventeen years.

[A]: Then you took full *sannyās* ?

[SG]: Yes, two years ago. But seventeen years passed before taking full *sannyās*.

[A]: So, you were twelve years old when you started living in white *sannyās* ?

[SAD GIRI'S FATHER]: Yes. She was twelve years old. It happened in childhood.

[SG]: I was twelve years old when I began living in white *sannyās*. But I didn't know that I would take full *sannyās*. I was young. More and more the path became clear to me. I just kept practicing and my understanding [*siddhī*] increased. I kept putting one foot in front of the other. I kept moving forward step-by-step and I never looked back. As I moved forward, so did my practice. As my practice developed, so did my understanding.

[A]: OK, but why take full *sannyās*, then? If you [sentence unfinished]

[SG]: [Interrupts Antoinette:] I never decided! My *ātmā* did. The decision came from my *ātmā* alone. Didn't I tell you that earlier? [she sings this *bhajan*]:

> You called me, Oh Lion-riding Goddess!
> I came, I came, Oh Lion-riding Goddess!
> Oh Lion-riding Goddess who lives in the mountains!
> You called me and I came. I came, Oh Lion-riding Goddess.

FIGURE 6.6 Sad Giri showing a *bhajan* she recorded in a journal.
Photo by A. DeNapoli.

...I do what my *ātmā* tells me to do. I listen to my *ātmā*. I speak from my *ātmā*. People should listen to their *ātmā*.

This narrative delivers a mighty moral message: caste status plays no role whatsoever in the emergence and development of spiritual virtuosity. Rather, access to the *ātmā*, and to the wisdom it transmits in that transformative encounter, constitute the sources by which sadhus gain and sustain the strength, fierceness of mind, and courage to die to worldly illusions and become sadhus. Figure 6.6 illustrates this idea with respect to Sad Giri showing me a record of the knowledge that she has received from her *ātmā* over the years (like the *bhajans* she sings for her public performances), and which she has written down in a book. Note that these mental and physical virtues ("*sir-śarīr kā*"), which the sadhus represent as upper-caste attributes and associate with their superlative path, are relegated to an entirely superficial realm. Hence, the traits that the high-caste majority see as indicative of their essential natures, Sad Giri views as veiling their real nature. Through use of the keen example of the *ātmā*, her story thus constructs in light of that signifier a series of dichotomies between inner and outer knowledge, superior and inferior modes of experience, and real and immaterial and ephemeral and material natures, by which she in turn performs the notion of caste irrelevance in *sannyās*. Moreover, her performance distinguishes between the two types of sadhus elucidated earlier, on the grounds of their connection to the *ātmā* and their realization of these dichotomies.

The practices that define Sad Giri's *sannyās* constitute the products of her *ātmā*'s will. Ever since she was twelve years old, she has been led on a path delegated by this higher power. Sad Giri matter-of-factly reminds me in our exchange that "I never decided!" to become a sadhu. More specifically, she never decided to live in the state of white *sannyās*, by which she means the life of *brahmacārya* (celibate studentship), nor to take what she terms "full *sannyās*," that is, ritual initiation into *sannyās*, distinguishing the latter from the former category. As she presses on, during that early stage in which her *ātmā* teaches and empowers her, Sad Giri has no idea of herself as an agent, much less of the actions she would take and the consequences those actions would have. She spends an equal amount of time talking about having "no idea at all" about the radical road on which her *ātmā* would lead her as she spends discussing being "just a child" when her unusual experiences started. "What did I know…I was young." In this way Sad Giri denies what anthropologists have referred to as "complex agency" in her *sannyās*.

In an astute essay that explores the idea of women's agency in a genre of ancient Vedic domestic ritual texts known as the *Āśvalāyana Gṛhya Sūtra* historian of religion Laurie L. Patton (2004) discusses complex agency in light of the explications provided by Mark Hobart (1990) and Corinne Kratz (2002).[13] She observes that "Different kinds of persons are culturally defined in part by the various rights, abilities, and responsibilities associated with them, including the right to undertake certain kinds of action and responsibility for their effects" (295). Using the same texts, Patton further explains, in a more recent analytical reflection on this issue but as concerns the relationship of complex agency to notions of subjectivity and personhood, that "by agency, I mean the capacity to act with discernment—that is, the capacity to choose a path of action and understand, according to the cultural norms of the day, the consequences of one's actions…To put it another way, 'self' focuses on the simple distinction between one subjectivity and another; 'person' denotes one complex subjectivity interacting with another or others; and 'agency' is the capacity to discern, plan, and act in that process of interaction" (2012, 369).

Denying complex agency in her becoming a sadhu, Sad Giri, like the other sadhus, uses personal narrative performance to situate her seemingly transgressive actions within the normative male-constructed parameters of gendered feminine behavior. That is, because she herself does not intend to renounce, her *sannyās* may be seen as "receptive" rather than "active" and, therefore, within the bounds of acceptable (but unusual) feminine social behavior. Her performance thus restricts anyone who hears her story from perceiving her as transgressing norms, by constructing herself as an exception to the norm (cf. Khandelwal 2004). And yet, the fact that Sad Giri's telling is organized around the tacit theme of caste insignificance, which in effect cues her exceptionality as a sadhu, indicates that her denying complex agency in *sannyās* may in fact express a meta-signifier in her narrative construction for Brahmanical orthodoxy's denying people of her caste and similar caste groups the right to renounce. As her father suggests in his statement that Sad Giri is the only person in their family and caste group to have taken *sannyās*, and, as suggested by the actions of the *maṇḍal* who refused her entry into their exclusive organization, the Brahmanical mainstream not only denies Sad Giri's right to take *sannyās* and her responsibility for the effects associated with it but, on the foundation of that rejection, also denies her capacity for *sannyās*, because *she is Khatik*. In the dominant framework of the classical system, as discussed in Chapter 4, Sad Giri's caste defines her as a specific kind of person with a certain status, as well as certain rights and responsibilities. Not surprisingly, she sees her own capacity to act and discern the consequences of those actions in terms largely perpetuated by the constrictive cultural and religious structures in which she operates, and which she navigates. To that extent, Sad Giri's use of a specific vocabulary of agency to describe her *sannyās* constitutes a social (and not only a linguistic) function of oppressive caste structures. However, by linking her *sannyās* to "the various rights, abilities, and responsibilities" (Patton 2012, 295) granted by the power of her *ātmā*, Sad Giri disputes the established parameters of complex agency assigned to the different caste and class groups in that hierarchy by providing, with demonstrated aplomb, an alternative paradigm of the concept.

The way that Sad Giri thinks about her "capacity to discern, plan, and act" as a sadhu says something significant about her understandings of self and personhood (Patton 2012, 295). At several points in the crafting of her narrative, she insists on her own pivotal role in determining the course of her life. One area in which she makes this point concerns her learning to read and play the harmonium, as she says, "all on my own." Sad Giri emphasizes that she "learned all by myself" to do these things, highlighting her accomplishments as well as drawing attention to her individual ego-self instead of the global *ātmā*-self as the agent of her *sannyās*. Her emphasis on her ego-self becomes particularly pronounced in her explanation that her (human) guru only taught her the *mantra* on which she meditates, and not those activities and skills that distinguish her as special from the other sadhus, regardless of their gender and caste, in her locality. "I never asked my guru to teach me anything. I never stayed at a single place for a minute to learn what I have learned. I never took help from anyone." Recall that Sad Giri echoes a similar view in her descriptions about building "with her own hands" a personal ashram without soliciting either financial or physical assistance from others, kin and non-kin alike. "Nobody helped me build this ashram. Not my parents, not anyone. I did this all by myself."

In these ways, she signals the range of obstacles that people in her position experience everyday as a result of established caste customs which discriminate against disadvantaged groups. At the same time, Sad Giri articulates a strong sense of her own independence as a sadhu to do what others would try and prevent her from doing. Despite the constellation of forces working to disempower her in life, Sad Giri relies on her own strength as a resource to overcome them. The unusual degree of freedom she enacts with respect to her traveling "here and there" in order to meet other sadhus and for her *satsang* business sets her apart from the other female sadhus.

But even as she emphasizes her independence and strength of mind as causal factors in shaping her destiny, she reminds me in the same breath that the "*ātmā* has given me the 'power' to do this." Sad Giri stresses that "I do what my *ātmā* tells me to do. I listen to my *ātmā*... People should listen to their *ātmā*." On the one hand, then, she claims and identifies with the power of her limited ego-self as the source of her actions ("I did all this"). On the other hand, she trivializes that power by citing the *ātmā*-self as the ultimate actor ("The *ātmā* alone does all this"). We are left with the understanding that Sad Giri does and does not act in her world. Her narrative constructs a tension between the activities and the motives underlying them, engendered by two competing selves. How are we to understand this seeming contradiction? What does this tension suggest about Sad Giri's views of self and personhood? How might her perceptions of these concepts express an indigenous model of complex agency illustrative of female *sannyās*?

Ideas of selfhood and personhood represent, as Patton (2012) observes, "two distinct but overlapping modes of conceiving an individual ritual actor" (368). As Patton says, "I use 'self' when an individual ritual actor is considered as a single subjectivity distinct from others and the world... I use the term 'person' when that subjectivity is presumed to overlap with other subjectivities as well as entities in the world" (369). Patton's explication of these notions supplies a lens through which Sad Giri's actions can come to light. The emphasis that she places on the "I" in her narratives suggests that she distinguishes between her ego-self and the *ātmā*-self. That is, she has a keen sense of her individual subjectivity and, thus, of her separate identity as Sad Giri, which she perceives and experiences as distinct from the *ātmā*'s. To her, their different subjectivities create them as discrete entities, as discrete forms of consciousness, in the world.

By distinguishing between her ego-self and the *ātmā*-self, Sad Giri engenders a strong sense of the autonomy she feels, expresses, and enacts in her life. The degree to which one recognizes a distinct subjectivity appears to be linked to the level of one's awareness of autonomy. Unlike Sad Giri, the other sadhus do not speak at any length about their autonomy (which is not to say that they do not recognize that they have it). Rather, in their personal narratives, individual subjectivity remains fused with divine subjectivity. The statement "I did all this myself," much less the attribution of action to a separate "I," rarely appears in their stories. Here, the "I" plays more of a receptive than active part in their narratives, in that God acts on and ultimately consumes their individual subjectivities. The experiences of states of craziness (*pāgalpan*) that the sadhus underscore suggest shared perceptions of their individual subjectivities melding into God's. Chetanananda describes it best in her illustrative statement that "We are the dirt of God's feet." This pattern of surrendering the ego-self to the God-self in order to displace the role of autonomy in *sannyās* exemplifies the experiences of the high-caste sadhus. While Chetanananda is a Bhil, the ambiguity of that group's social status in the caste hierarchy, and her blurring of the boundaries between Bhils and Rajputs, locate the former within a predominantly high-caste sphere of influence. What this pattern also illuminates is that caste status plays an eminent role in the sadhus' use of a renunciant grammar of humility and surrender to conceptualize their subjectivities and experience their autonomy. The high-caste sadhus imagine and construct their worlds within ideological parameters that constrict (and restrict) their sense of autonomy more so than they limit the awareness of that experience for sadhus like Sad Giri.

But autonomy is not tantamount to agency (Patton 2004, 295; 2012, 370). Notions of agency must consider the interface between ever-shifting conceptions of self and personhood in human beings' capacity to act, and discern the motives for and consequences of their actions (Patton 2012, 369). By accentuating the role of the *ātmā* in her behavior, Sad Giri suggests that she conceives of her personhood as constituting the motivations and actions of two different subjectivities—hers and the *ātmā*'s—coming together in unison in her self-consciousness. The extent of overlap in the process of interaction between complex subjectivities affects her capacity to discern (or plan) her part as an individual actor—her actions and their motivations and consequences. In this framework, the higher the degree of overlap, the less complex agency Sad Giri experiences. Furthermore, the less the recognition of complex agency, the more her actions interrogate normative gender and caste boundaries and their supporting ideologies, precisely because of her perception that the *ātmā* has all the agency. Here, the subjectivity of the *ātmā* governs her sense of personhood and, as a result, obscures her self-identity as Sad Giri. However, insofar as her own subjectivity dominates her personhood—her subjectivity, as her stories attest, never monopolizes her personhood to the extent that the *ātmā*'s does—she remains cognizant of a separate ego-self that acts in conjunction with, or in opposition to, the *ātmā*-self. Thus, Sad Giri understands her capacity to act, plan, and discern her life and its results within the parameters set forth by dominant cultural customs and by the power of the *ātmā*. Divine forces play as significant a role as cultural ones in both constricting and enabling Sad Giri's complex agency. She explains, "I can become a lawyer in one second if it is the grace of the *ātmā*. I can become a soldier, a teacher; I can even fly an airplane. But it has to be the grace of the *ātmā*."

The ruling influence of her *ātmā*-self compels Sad Giri to become a *brahmacāriṇī* (celibate student) and, thus, to manifest the religious path that she characterizes as white *sannyās*; that decision represents her first crucial step in actualizing her life of full (or *bhagwā*) *sannyās*. For seventeen years, between the ages of twelve and twenty-nine, she lived in this constant state of ritual purity, following a "strict" (*sakat*) vegetarian (and low-spice) diet,[14] meditating daily on the *ātmā*, and restricting her interactions to kin as necessary means for maintaining her purity. During this time, Sad Giri mainly sequestered herself in the main living space of her home, occupying one of only two rooms in the entire domicile, absorbed in singing *bhajans* and *ātmā-jnān*. She says, "I started to wear white clothing. Those colorful clothes I use to wear are worldly clothes. 'I won't wear them,' I thought. I wore white clothing. My clothes were absolutely white in color. They were ordinary, simple clothes, like the ones doctors wear."

About a year after her religious experiences started, Sad Giri's *ātmā* pushed her in another direction, which once again altered her life course. A mysterious man whom she vaguely identifies in our conversations as "Ba" (literally, "old man") came to her village and ran all-night *bhajan* sessions for an unspecified length of time. "People from the village went every night to sing. I thought I too should go and sing because I know many *bhajans*." Because of her love of *bhajan* singing and other related activities, Sad Giri left her home in the evenings, accompanied by family members (usually her mother or Kamlesh), and participated in these *satsangs*, where she sat beside Ba. Over time, the other *satsang* participants, including Ba, praised her exceptional singing abilities, and soon enough Ba invited Sad Giri to travel with him and give public stage performances in Mewar. She jumped at the opportunity, for when she sings she feels the enervating "vibration power" of the *ātmā* coursing through her mind-body and transmitting *bhed*. Ba, of course, compensated Sad Giri for her expenses by paying her a nominal performer's fee. To Sad Giri, it is her *ātmā* that sang every night with Ba, and not her. Ironically, the more Sad Giri performed with Ba, the more she felt compelled by her *ātmā* to sing on her own, without Ba. "That was the first time I was told [by the *ātmā*] to sing on my own. Then I started the business."

Thus, the *ātmā* drove Sad Giri to adopt the state of white *sannyās*, attend nightly *satsangs* in her village, sing as a paid performer with Ba, and eventually establish a *satsang* business in order to earn the money to build an ashram, where she could devote herself to singing *bhajans* to God. By the age of fourteen she began operating her fledgling business with the help of her brothers (and occasionally her father), who travel with her, set up the equipment, and book her performances. Coordinating her every step by compelling her actions at epochal junctures the *ātmā*, manifested its plan for her destiny. Sad Giri's statement "I kept putting one foot in front of the other" implies her view that the *ātmā* commanded her movements and motivations, which she neither questioned nor resisted. The farther along her path she moved, the more her knowledge increased. The *ātmā* continued to teach and guide Sad Giri as her practices developed. "As I moved forward, so did my practice. As my practice developed, so did my understanding." Her understanding about what? Certainly not that she would take *sannyās*? She refutes that idea every time I ask (and attempt to ask) her. "Didn't I tell you that earlier?" she chastises. The revelation of her taking full *sannyās* came much later in her journey—seventeen years later. Nonetheless, whatever insight she gained from her relationship with the *ātmā* while living as a *brahmacāriṇī* convinced her that renouncing the world represents the only valid option she has. What is it that Sad Giri discovered?

"*Bhakti* never happens when a person is stuck in the cycle [*cakkar*] of householding," she says. "It traps people in the snares of the illusory world [*māyā-jāl*]. *Bhakti* is impossible in this situation! Householders get stuck in the world, and how will they come out of it? Can they come out of it? They look this way and that way but they're stuck. When you become a householder you make a wife or a husband, you make babies, you buy a car, you get greedy for [having] more things, and in my estimation [*hisāb*], more troubles. All these relationships just keep people stuck in ignorance." The answer is transparent: "the snares of the illusory world," a popular renunciant trope for householding, tear people away from their "real" work of worshipping the divine (*ātmā; paramātmā; bhagvān; devī-mātājī*)[15] by burying them in worldly "troubles." Householding, as she implies, serves as an illustrative metaphor for the classic spider's web, in that from a distance it appears beautifully lustrous. Its magnificence draws unsuspecting (and unwise) observers to it. Its beauty is irresistible. But those who know its real nature stay away. But for those who do not know, its beauty becomes the agent of their demise. Once people come into its orbit, the web sticks to them and traps them until they are incapacitated. Looking "this way and that way," yet unable to move because "they're stuck," the spider, the god of death, finally arrives and ends their lives, sending them back into the vicious cycle (*cakkar*) of *sansār*. As cued by the conversational context, what Sad Giri realizes concerns the understanding that householding signifies death. That is, householders die to realizing the truth of their *ātmā*, simply because, as she highlights, "[*b*]*hakti* is absolutely impossible" to accomplish. Once a person becomes "stuck" in the duties of householding ("having babies"), she cannot "come out of it."

While Sad Giri stresses that her insight on the (spiritually) ruinous nature of the life of householding stems from the *ātmā-jnān* she receives through her practices, the context of our conversations also indexes the role of her living arrangements in catalyzing this realization. The home she shares with her family consists of three generations of kin residing under a single roof. A lot of activity happens here. In the main sitting room, children play their games while watching our conversation with amusement, an infant (Ramesh's eight-month-old son) cries for its mother, a group of female relatives pay an unexpected visit to relay the news of a family member's death, two of Kamlesh's friends stop by and join the action, and so forth. To be sure, the unusual presence of a foreigner "from America" in the village attracts more than the typical number of people to Sad Giri's home. Nevertheless, as I learn from our frequent meetings, the house often bustles and brims with this dynamic movement. Even Sad Giri, hyperconscious of the contradictions between her ritual vows and her living arrangement, comments on the chaos that comes with residing with her family: "The heart speaks freely when it's at peace." Our conversations are usually punctuated with her telling the children to "be quiet" or "be still."

But there is more to what Sad Giri discovers about householding than this vignette expresses. In another context, in which she, Manvendra Singh, and I sit in the ashram without the presence of her kin, she speaks at length about the deleterious effect of householding on women in particular. Although recognizing that women as well as men become trapped in and by their householding responsibilities (as she says, "sex[16] no bar in *sansār*"), she claims that it keeps women from doing what men have the freedom to do: namely, travel. Sad Giri explains,

> If it's not a woman's wish to marry, then she doesn't have to get married. If she marries her husband won't allow her to travel [*bhramaṇ karnā*] alone. [To Manvendra:] Will her husband allow her to travel alone? [Manvendra replies, "No Maharaj. He wouldn't."] Would you let your woman [i.e., wife] travel alone? People, too, will say, "Why are

> you traveling alone? Travel with your husband." If they say to her "you should get married," she should do what her *ātmā* wants her to do. Don't listen to anybody. Just do what your *ātmā* tells you to do. Hey brother, will you do what your *ātmā* tells you to do? Or will you do what people tell you to do? They will say, "What's wrong, girl? You don't have a place for a husband in your heart [*man*]?" But if you've decided not to make someone your husband, your parents cannot force you to marry. If you say no to your parents they should listen. I don't want to get married means I don't want to get married! Otherwise, it's their duty [*pharj*] to get the girl married. If the daughter has become young enough, she just says "husband." "We will get you married with him," the parents say. [To Antoinette:] Do you understand? If it's not your wish [*iccā*] to get married, you will say, "Papa, I don't want to get married." The father will ask, "Why daughter?" "Because I want to travel first." Hey brother, I want to travel first. I don't want to get married.

In this conversation, Sad Giri underscores the (male-enforced) constraints on women's freedom of movement in Indian society. Householding, as she makes explicit, restricts women's activities outside of the acceptable limits of the domicile. More importantly, husbands restrict "their women" from traveling "alone" beyond the boundaries of the home. It is not simply the idea of going anywhere, such as to the local bazaar or to the tailor's, that Sad Giri describes here. The idea of travel, and the unusual (but, for Sad Giri, welcomed) independence and mobility it produces, has to do with intra-regional and pan-Indian forms of religious journeying, typically known as *yātrā*, by which pilgrims connect with and worship the divine (cf. Gold 1988; A. Gold 2001). Sad Giri uses the word "bhramaṇ karnā" to signal her understanding of pilgrimage, and that traveling "alone" to the sacred dwellings of the divine, for whatever reason—whether in search of wisdom, comfort, healing, children, or *mokṣ*—transforms people. In this way she links the ultimate purpose of pilgrimage with personal transformation. What is more, Sad Giri's idea of traveling is largely connected to going wherever the *ātmā* desires one to go. To that extent, not only traveling alone, but also traveling at the automatic command of the *ātmā* (i.e., whenever and if the *ātmā* wishes to travel), constitutes and communicates Sad Giri's vision of freedom, which she feels women do not have. "Will her husband allow [his wife] to travel alone?" she asks. Her emphasis on the notion of women traveling alone for pilgrimage (i.e., without their *husbands*) is, therefore, significant. Traveling with family members, or a (female) friend seems fine, but not traveling with a husband. As she implies, it keeps a woman from focusing on her *bhakti*—that is, from developing intimacy with the *ātmā*—as she will only end up attending to her husband's needs. She will ensure that he eats, bathes, goes to toilet, and stays healthy on the trip. The other female sadhus I worked with voiced similar claims in the context of the practice of cohabitating male and female sadhus, which many of them strongly opposed. In Sad Giri's view, traveling with a husband turns a woman into a wife rather a pilgrim. For this crucial reason, a woman must travel alone, because that is the only way that *bhakti* is possible.

Another freedom that Sad Giri talks about involves women's decisions to marry or not. Again, she feels that women do not have the right to say no to marriage. She emphasizes that "your parents cannot force you to marry . . . I don't want to get married means I don't want to get married!" While she situates women's decisions about marriage within the context of the *ātmā's* wishes ("Just do what your *ātmā* tells you to do"), implying that a woman should marry insofar as she has the divine blessings of her *ātmā*, she also makes clear that women are coerced by their families, and in general by society, to marry against their desires. As Chapter 2 shows, most of the sadhus were forced to marry against their wishes, the planning of which often occurred without their knowledge, and regardless of their unusual (and demonstrated) religious proclivities. Sad Giri is no exception. At the age of sixteen her parents arranged her marriage to a man in her community. Her living in the state of white *sannyās* did not prevent them from "searching for a boy." "We wanted her to be happy, to have security," her mother says. For many women, marriage represents an expected form of security. Arranging her marriage was, as Sad Giri says, her parent's duty. But she had already sheltered herself in the security of her *ātmā*.

Although opposed to the arrangement, she went through with the ceremony. After the wedding, however, Sad Giri did not go to the groom's home. "I refused to live with him and my in-laws. I absolutely refused to live with them." Despite having gone through the ritual, Sad Giri did not see herself as wedded to *that* man. "Like Mira, I found Lord Krishna as my husband." Her parents tried to persuade her to change her mind, but to no avail. She returned to her natal home and continued with her ritual practices as if the wedding had never happened. Her father could not accept her decision. At some point he phoned the rejected husband and begged him to come to the house. When he arrived, the father dragged Sad Giri outside and forced her into her husband's car. " 'Take her,' I said. I pushed her into the car," her father describes, his voice tinged with pathos. In an interesting twist, the husband refused to take Sad Giri against her will. "He was a wise man [*guru-mukhi*]," Sad Giri says. "He saw no point in forcing me into the marriage." She, however, could not in good conscience leave such a "wise man" languishing defeated in the dust. She explains, "I said, 'I am not going to spoil your life. I will spend the money to find you another girl. I will organize another marriage.'" He said no.

The freedom that Sad Giri exerts in defiantly refusing what turns out to be a botched marriage is motivated and enabled by her own financial resources. Due to her *satsang* business, which had already been operating for two years, she had the money to find "another girl" and "organize another marriage" for her husband. That is, she had the financial power to say no to those social arrangements that, in her view, stifle women's independence. The other sadhus did not have that (financial) power at her age. Their families' high-caste values and orthodox attitudes would not have allowed them to pursue employment outside of their natal homes. It is difficult to say whether or not the sadhus themselves would have fathomed such a possibility. Most of them were born into strict Brahmin and Rajput homes. Not only that, most of the sadhus come from an older (and socially conservative) generation[17] that associates working women with loose moral character. Sad Giri, however, is different for two reasons. First, born at the end of the twentieth century and, in many ways, holding views and attitudes illustrative of her sociohistorical milieu, she understands that women's freedom of movement beyond the parameters of the domicile is to a great extent a function of their economic independence. Second, for many low-caste groups, including Bhils, a woman working outside of the home is not uncommon. Often, women in these communities have to work, simply due to economic necessity. In the same vein, because of embedded structural inequalities, low-caste groups such as Khatiks tend to occupy the lowest rungs of the economic ladder. Employment provides women like Sad Giri a strategy for survival. She uses her economic power to expand the sphere of possibilities available to her and construct her world with dignity and the freedom to move as her *ātmā* compels her.

Besides her becoming a *brahmacāriṇī* and starting a *satsang* business, the third way Sad Giri uses a grammar of *ātmā*-realization to validate her renunciation and, by implication, question caste hegemonies in *sannyās*-as-lived involves her traveling to the temple-shrine of the deified-hero, Baba Ramdevji in order to participate in the annual Ramdevra *yātrā*. Here, too, Sad Giri says she feels driven by her *ātmā* to make the two-hundred mile journey to Baba Ramdev's shrine from her village and worship him. Located in Runecha village in Jaisalmer district (northwest Rajasthan) in order to participate in the annual Ramdevra *yātrā*. Ramdevra (lit., "shrine of Ram") attracts hundreds of thousands of pilgrims every year, predominantly from the rural Meghwal and Muslim communities (Balzani 2001, 217; cf. A. Gold 2001). In recent years, urban and upper-caste Hindus have also become more involved in the Ramdevra festival for a variety of reasons, notably in times of "increasing communal tension" (Balzani 2001, 219). The annual festival, which runs according to the Hindu lunar calendar, happens in the month of *Bhādwa* (mid-August to mid-September) and lasts for a month, sometimes longer. Participating in the annual festival constitutes a means by which marginalized social communities and groups seek to make themselves visible in the society (see also Jassal 2012, 61 for a discussion of Dusadh Dalits in Bihar using festivals to forge a separate identity). "I walked all the way to Ramdevra on foot," Sad Giri says. "I walked twice on foot and the rest of the journeys I made by train." She shows me a framed photo of her and Ramesh taken in front of the Ramdevji *mūrtī* a decade ago, which she keeps in the main living room. Minutes later she takes my hand and leads me into the kitchen, where she reveals her recent project of stitching together an embroidered image of Ramdevji seated on top of his horse. "I traveled to Ramdevji's shrine while I was in the state of white *sannyās*," she tells me. "Why do you make the journey to Ramdevra?" I ask her. "Huh," she responds. "Is there any special reason for your journeying there?" I ask once more. "I go every year. People in my community go every year to Ramdevra. I leave from here, in the village."

The journey she makes to Ramdevra constitutes a central aspect of her *sannyās*. Sad Giri describes her journeying both on foot and by train to the shrine as *tapaysā* (renunciant penance). Ramdeviji is widely considered to be a human incarnation of Lord Krishna in his manifestation as Ranchor, a popular form of Krishna revered in the nearby state of Gujarat. In several of our conversations, Sad Giri links her worship of Ramdevji to Mira Bai's worship of Lord Krishna. Sad Giri's worship of Ramdevji illustrates the significance that this hero-god holds for her and, more broadly, low-caste (and untouchable) communities all over the Indian subcontinent. The image of the god-man located in the center of Sad Giri's business card is that of Ramdevji (see, again, Figure 6.4). Her use of his image in connection with her professionalizing of her *sannyās* through her *satsang* business signals to the sadhus in her local community, her patrons, and anyone else interested in her package of religious services, not only her low-caste identity, but also her attempt to reconstruct that identity in a more positive light by associating it with the powerful figure of Ramdevji. It further expresses her alternative view that *sannyās* is open to anyone, regardless of caste, gender, and class. For many pilgrims to his shrine, Ramdevji's symbol represents the fierce power of a divinity willing to listen to the voices of the oppressed (i.e., Dalits) and fight for their right to be heard in a society where they often do not matter.

But Ramdevji was not himself low-caste. Born into the royal house of Ajmal, a Rajput feudal king (Thakur) of Pokaran village, which lies close to Runecha, Ramdevji came from the dominant and most privileged of classes in Rajasthani society. What is more, he, too, despite his father's wishes—after all, Ajmal prayed to Ranchor for a boy child so that he could have an heir for the throne—took up the life of a sadhu, leaving behind his princely comforts and status, in order to spend the rest of his days rapt in singing *bhajans* and, as many of the sadhus told me, performing miracles for devotees through the power of his renunciant devotion. In this way, Ramdevji and Mira Bai are a lot alike. The narratives the sadhus tell and the songs they sing about these divine hero-saints imagine them as devoting themselves to the worship of God and, by virtue of the salvific insight gained from their practices, as pushing the orthodox boundaries engendered by established gender and caste norms. While Sad Giri did not tell me the story she knows (or has heard) about Ramdevji, relating a popular narrative told in the area in which I worked about this god-hero helps to frame the significance that he has for people in her community. Legend has it that once Ramdevji was traveling in the untouchable area of his village in the month of *Śrāvan* (July-August), in which the ritual of *rākhī* is celebrated.[18] During *rākhī* (lit., "protective talisman"), sisters tie pieces of raw cotton string on their brothers' wrists, and brothers give their sisters a small gift of money in exchange. The ritual represents brothers' and sisters' symbolically acknowledging their familial obligations to protect and safeguard each other's well-being. While traveling, Ramdevji came across a young Meghwal woman by the name of Dali Bai. She was crying. He inquired as to why she was crying, and Dali Bai explained that she could not tie the *rākhī* string because she did not have a brother. Touched by her humility, and recognizing that he neither had a sister to protect him, nor a sister to protect, Ramdevji told Dali Bai to tie the *rākhī* on his wrist and, by that compassionate gesture, made her, an untouchable, his sister. This narrative constructs Ramdevji as the brother of the untouchables and, because of that association, as a hero-god who challenges gender and caste boundaries.

"Don't Die for the Body!": Sad Giri's *Bhajan* Performances

Apart from the practices already elucidated, another effective means through which Sad Giri questions and resists exclusionary caste distinctions has to do with her song performances. The overtly pedagogical function and critical nature of *bhajans*, particularly the *nirguṇī* kind, make them an appropriate genre of renunciant performance with which Sad Giri can directly speak against a tradition of *sannyās* that reinforces normative caste and gender ideologies (Jassal 2012; Hess 2002; Lorenzen 1996; Henry 1988). As we will see, the *bhajans* she sings in her *satsangs* provide an alternative ritual code or grammar that emphasizes the potent message of the irrelevance of caste, gender, class, *and* color on the spiritual—and especially the sadhu—path. This grammar is similarly etched in her personal narrative constructions analyzed earlier. Moreover, because most of the *bhajans* in her repertoire are attributed to poet-saints who, like herself, are from the lower classes of society, the personal relationship this singer has to her songs, paralleling the intimacy she perceives having in her relationship with the *ātmā*, is cued by the performance context itself. Understanding the relation of singing communities to their songs helps to illuminate the range of goals that those singers have and the variety of meanings their songs express (Flueckiger 1996; Jassal 2012, 14). Hence, the "ideas, moods, and messages" (Jassal 2012, 7) that Sad Giri's songs contain as well as create must be seen in light of the backdrop of both her caste and renunciant identities. The alternative worlds constituted by her *bhajans*, therefore, offer an illustrative model of sadhu behavior in which she locates and legitimates her own oppositional actions and motivations vis-à-vis the dominant renunciant practice of caste exclusionism in Mewar. Below, I document and analyze three *bhajans* performed by Sad Giri on the basis of their texts, performance contexts, and elicited exegesis to depict her challenge to those norms.

Bhajan 1: "Oh Guruji, I Am Your Beggar"—July 5, 2011

Give me the alms of your darśan.
Oh guruji, I am your beggar.
Give me the alms of your darśan.
Oh guruji, I am your beggar.

The concentration of God has come into my mind.
Since then, I've become detached.
The concentration of God has come into my mind.
Since then, I've become detached.

I have given up the lust of sex,
And I am under your control.
Give me the alms of your darśan.
Oh guruji, I am your beggar.

I've applied ashes all over my body,
And then I kept wandering in the jungle.
I've applied ashes all over my body,
And then I kept wandering in the jungle.
I wish to have a glance of you in my heart.

Without your darśan, I'm in pain.

Give me the alms of your darśan.
Oh guruji, I am your beggar.
After doing all the pilgrimages
Of Kashi and Kedar,
After doing all the pilgrimages
Of Kashi and Kedar,

I still couldn't find you, Oh Avinashi [indestructible One]!
I've become very surprised,
I still couldn't find you, Oh Avinashi!

Give me the alms of your darśan.
Oh guruji, I am your beggar.

Where have you settled?
Come and purify me.
Why were you so late in coming?
Come and purify me.

Come and make your rounds and give me darśan.
I always keep remembering you.
Come and make your rounds and give me darśan.
I always keep remembering you.
Give me the alms of your darśan.
Oh guruji, I am your beggar.

This is how we sing this thing,
That we like your glance.
Bharti Kalyan sings this,
That we like your glance.
We don't wish for heaven or mokṣ.
All we want is a place at your feet.
All we want is a place at your feet.

Give me the alms of your mokṣ.
Oh guruji, I am your beggar.

In this descriptive song, the guru whom the sadhu beseeches for "the alms of your *darśan*" constitutes the indestructible *ātmā*. Just as Sad Giri understands the *ātmā* as the ultimate guru due to whose grace (or "glance") everything happens in life, so does the sadhu in the *bhajan* approach this absolute power within as the guru, whose salvific *darśan* removes all obfuscating worldly illusions. What is more, as the song indicates, the *darśan* of the *ātmā* purifies a sadhu of all mental/physical pollution, as well as the ritual pollution brought about by her caste status. The sadhu sees herself in relation to the *ātmā* as a "beggar" (a trope whose meaning we explored in Chapter 2). Like the other sadhus, Sad Giri, too, perceives and describes herself as God's beggar. The emphasis expressed by the refrain on the idea of sadhus as beggars ("Oh guruji, I am your beggar") illustrates this *bhajan*'s underlying egalitarian social ideology that a sadhu's caste status has no significance before the eyes of God. Why? Because the *ātmā* is inherently pure. Similarly, despite the caste status a sadhu receives at the time of her physical birth, the spiritual birth she experiences through initiation into *sannyās* and by extension, as the sadhus say, "into the family of God," nullifies her caste identity, so that she stands before God as God's beggar. That is, she stands in front of God naked, without the distinguishing marks of caste or class. As this *bhajan* intimates, by virtue of surrendering their ego-self at God's feet, sadhus occupy the lowest status in the social hierarchy. Their beggar status highlights their occupying the margins, the periphery, of society. And yet, the *bhajan* juxtaposes the loss of social status with the gaining of spiritual insight and status. The lowest are seen as the most precious to God. The divine spirit does not see a sadhu's caste, but rather her love and devotion. Singing this *bhajan*, then, provides a means by which sadhus express and engender their love for the Absolute. By singing this song, Sad Giri performs love to the divine and constructs herself as precious to God.

Importantly, the song hints that the intensity of a sadhu's love brings about God's precious glance. All of the outer ritual practices that distinguish and, thus, identify sadhus as religious virtuosi, such as developing their concentration on God, abandoning the lust of sex, keeping their emotions and desires under their control, smearing their bodies with ash—an act that signals sadhus' "death" to the world—wandering in the jungle, and making the sacred pilgrimages to Kedarnath and Kashi, are meaningless to the *ātmā*. Much like the irrelevance with which it regards the outer material form and its identifying characteristics, the *ātmā* hardly recognizes outer displays of renunciant religiosity. What the *ātmā* sees is the devotee's heart: her *ātmā*. As Sad Giri says in another context, "that's the real truth and the real beauty." The *bhajan* articulates a cautionary warning that sadhus should pay more attention to the voice of the *ātmā* guiding them from within, and not get caught up in the outer posturings of *sannyās*. In this light, the *bhajan* teaches, as Sad Giri stresses in her practices, that what is inside has far more soteriological significance than what is outside. To that extent, the song tacitly constructs the same dichotomies that Sad Giri crafts in her narratives between inner and outer wisdom; superior and inferior modes of knowledge; and immaterial/eternal and material/impermanent phenomena.

Bhajan 2: "Wake Up, Traveler! You've Been Asleep for so Long"—July 3, 2011

Traveler, it's been many days that you're asleep.
You've been asleep for so long.
Wake up, traveler.
Wake up!

In the beginning you slept comfortably in the womb of your mother.
When you came out, you made a promise. But you forgot it.

The second deep sleep was in the lap of your mother.
Your sister, aunty, and mother loved you, and everyone was happy.
Your sister, aunty, and mother loved you, and everyone was happy.

You've been asleep for so long.
Now wake up, traveler.
Wake up!

Who are we, traveler?
Who are we, traveler?

The third sleep was when you slept with a woman in the bed.
You cuddled in each other's arms.
You slept with her in the bed.
You cuddled in each other's arms.

You've been asleep for so long.
Now wake up, traveler.
Wake up!

The fourth sleep is in the cremation ground.
You're sleeping in the cremation grounds, traveler.
You're stretching your legs.
You have died.

Now it's time to wake up, traveler.
You've been asleep for so long.
Wake up, traveler.
Wake up!

This song, which Sad Giri attributes to the poet-saint Kabir, presses on the spiritually destructive effects of clinging to the impermanent and material body. If, as Sad Giri suggests, the outer form represents a curtain that shields people from realizing the *ātmā* lying within it, then identification with the physical body becomes akin to living in a perpetual state of ignorance and darkness, which the *bhajan* cues through use of the fitting motif of sleep. In this murky state, one travels through life in the dark and remains blind to the penetrating light (and truth) of the *ātmā*. Sad Giri sees the majority of the sadhus in her local *samāj* as living asleep, because of the importance they attach to the physical. If the outer form were seen as simply the clothing wrapped around the *ātmā*, the *maṇḍal* would never have denied her entry. Before she sings this *bhajan*, Sad Giri speaks about her perception of sadhus' attachment to material things. Using the example of two male sadhu acquaintances, she says that "they come here on their motorcycles and tell me that I shouldn't let all kinds of sadhus stay here. I ask why, and they say that these sadhus may take your rings, your blankets, your things. Why do they say this? None of it matters. If it's stolen, it's God's will. I have the *ātmā*. What else do I need?" Singing this *bhajan* immediately after making this statement frames her understanding of the incapacitating ignorance of those sadhus. Moreover, her poignant question, "Why do they say this?" cues her view of the inappropriateness of their attitudes toward the superfluous. According to Sad Giri and the *bhajan*, such ignorant sadhus spend their lives in a state of "deep" sleep. Although an ephemeron, it is difficult to awake from this slumber once a person becomes trapped in it.

Structurally, the song describes four types of debilitating sleep in the life of a human being: first, that which happens in the womb; second, that which happens in the "lap of the mother"; third, that which occurs in the act of making love with one's partner; and finally, that which happens in the cremation ground. Notice that through use of these tropes, the *bhajan* indexes four signal junctures through which the individual *ātmā* is typically thought to pass in its incarnations on earth: at birth, maturation into adulthood, householding and family, and death. The *bhajan* signals the idea of the *ātmā* in its phrase, "Who are we traveler?" Hence, in the song the sleeping traveler signifies the *ātmā* enmeshed in the sticky web of ignorance. This view is often articulated in the *bhajans* attributed to Kabir (Hess 2002; Lorenzen 1996; Henry 1995). And, as Sad Giri explains, this sleeping traveler "moves from first to last; from birth to death." In this way, she suggests that, in the *bhajan*, sleep serves as a prescient metaphor more globally for the illusory and impermanent *sansār*. She observes: "I'm being honest [*khulī bāt*] here. This teaching is like a sword [*talwār*]. The body [*tan*] feels pain from enjoyment [*bhog*] and illness [*rog*]. First enjoyment happens; then illness comes to the body. Illness happens when there is enjoyment. In householding the illness comes. The children are illness. They are born through [sexual] enjoyment. The child says, 'Papa, bring me clothes, feed me, bring me chocolate; Papa, do this; Papa, do that' . . . The family will be made. From the family everything expands and enjoyment and illness come. Whether enjoyment or illness, the body suffers."

In this illustrative commentary, Sad Giri implies not only that sleep is tantamount to being stuck in the snares of illusion, but also that living asleep is bad *for the body*. "The body suffers [*duhkhi huā*]" from actions done out of human ignorance. To that extent, and as I have explained elsewhere (DeNapoli 2011), in contrast to the dominant renunciant ideology of the body featured in the Brahmanical texts on *sannyās* (cf. Olivelle 1992; 1996; 2011), the sadhus' practices construct the body by representing it as an immensely valuable vehicle for their life's objective of "singing *bhajans*." Thus, it is neither bad nor dangerous. Rather, as Sad Giri intimates, the perceptions people have of the body, and the actions they perform with it on the basis of those perceptions (sexual intercourse, reproduction, householding), cause people to fall into a deep sleep, thereby ensnaring them in the endless cycle of *sansār*. Sad Giri, like the other sadhus, appears, then, to distinguish between the body and social constructions of it. To Sad Giri, though, waking up expresses the idea of penetrating beyond the limiting (and illusory) social significations imputed on the body and realizing the promise that the *ātmā* made to itself in the womb: to worship God. Our final *bhajan* accentuates this theme with even more urgency.

Bhajan 3: "Mira's Beautiful because of her *bhajans*"—July 5, 2011

Mira's beautiful because of her bhajans.
Oh, Mewari Rana!
Mira's beautiful because of her bhajans.

Mira's beautiful because of her bhajans.
Oh, Mewari Rana!
Mira's beautiful because of her bhajans.

Oh, Sanwariya!
There is loneliness without you.
I am just a ring on your hand.

Oh, Sanwariya!
There is loneliness without you.
I am just a ring on your hand.

Oh, Mewari Rana!
Mira's beautiful because of her bhajans.

My mother-in-law and sister-in-law,
My mother-in-law and sister-in-law,
[next line of bhajan is unclear]
Oh, Mewari Rana!
Mira's beautiful because of her bhajans.

Even if the cuckoo is black,
Her voice is still sweet.
Even if the cuckoo is black,
Her voice is still sweet.

[INTERJECTS]: Why do you see the body?
See the words! See the ātmā !
That's the real beauty, and the only truth.
Don't die for the body!
Don't die for the beauty of the flesh!

Oh, Mewari Rana!
Mira's beautiful because of her bhajans.

I met Krishna is a very narrow gulley.
I met Krishna in a very narrow gulley.

I met Kanheya in the street.
I met Kanheya in the street.
Now how can I turn back?
Oh, Mewari Rana!
Mira's beautiful because of her bhajans.

Sad Giri lodges her most direct challenge to the ethos of caste ambivalence in her singing of this song, which is attributed to Mira Bai. Through use of her exemplary model, it expresses and establishes the view that a sadhu's (or a *bhakt*'s) beauty constitutes a function of her singing *bhajans* to *bhagwān*, not of her physical body and material characteristics. Here, the body serves as a metonym for the outer forms of gender, caste, class, and color, whereas beauty signifies the inner purity of the *ātmā*. As the *bhajan* suggests, the Sisodiya king, possibly Mira's father-in-law or elder brother-in-law, sees only the outer (and, thus, illusory) manifestation of her feminine gender and, as Rajput royal customs dictate, tries to prevent her from leaving the security of the palace and mixing with "all kinds of sadhus" in her extraordinary practice of sadhu *bhakti*. But, as the *bhajan* also conveys, Mira meets her Lord Krishna, addressed by the names Sanwariya and Kanheya, "in a very narrow gulley" or "in the street." That is, Mira Bai defies the restrictions that the Mewari *rāṇā* places on her freedom of movement by leaving the palace and traveling outside of those suffocating parameters in search of divine truth. What is her rationale? She implores the ignorant and obstinate *rāṇā* to see the *bhakti* expressed through her singing of *bhajans* as the true essence of who she is, and as that which "really" makes her beautiful on the outside. As Sad Giri would have Mira Bai say, "Why do you see the body? See the words! See the *ātmā*. That's the real beauty, and the only truth. Don't die for the beauty of the flesh."

By interjecting this poignant commentary into her performance, Sad Giri attempts to construct her perspective as Mira's, and *vice versa*. It appears, on the basis of her narrative constructions, that Sad Giri's and Mira Bai's points of view are unified on this theme. Like her exemplum, Sad Giri has been defying the restrictions that the larger institution of Brahmanical *sannyās*—indeed her "Mewari *rāṇā*"— attempts to impose on her right and capacity to practice *sannyās* because of her low-caste status. We can hear Sad Giri shouting her challenge to its exclusivism with the sharp words, "Why do you see my caste? Why do you see my skin color? See the *ātmā* within me instead." Her performance critiques conflating a person with, and defining her by, her gender, caste, and color. It argues instead that for those who have "painted" the color of God on their bodies and in their minds, such distinctions no longer exist. She says,

> Mira Bai's Lord is Giridhar Nagar. And her head is painted with the color of truth. The *ātmā* is also painted with the same color. [To Antoinette:] Do you understand? The color has been applied. What is the word for color? *Rang*. This is the color. This is the color of Ram [i.e., the nameless and formless Absolute]. The color has been applied in the brain. Now, this color has been applied both inside and outside. It will never be washed away. This is how Mira Bai practiced. This is what you call love. Mira Bai loved God.

As her words make apparent, in singing *bhajans* Mira Bai "paint[s]" herself with the eternal color of God. In Sad Giri's and the *bhajan*'s views, singing *bhajans* as devotional asceticism constitutes the means by which sadhus strip themselves of their birth-induced caste, class, and gender distinctions and apply a divine coat of paint that, in turn, colors them "both inside and outside" in the transformative hue of the divine. In addition, Sad Giri associates the color of God with the color of love. Even the *ātmā* is dyed in the same color. But what is the color of love? Is it white? Is it black? Is it orange, the color of the resplendent morning sun that the other sadhus, such as Chetanananda, associate with the *bhagwā* color of (their) *sannyās*?

In this commentary, Sad Giri does not identify any color as illustrative of the color of love. Thus, the answer seems ambiguous. It could be, as she has explained in other contexts, that since there are only "two colors" in the whole universe, the *ātmā* being white, and everything else being black, that she sees the color of love as white. But I am more inclined to suggest on the grounds of this *bhajan*'s performance context that, for Sad Giri, all colors—white, black, orange, and others—represent the enduring color of love, as long as their outer hues reflect the inner power and presence of God. Even the cuckoo, though black, is painted in the color of love by the sublime beauty of her song. Thus, this song expresses that anything immersed in the love of God is essentially colored in and with that love, and is beautiful. That color and its beauty will never wash away. Like the cuckoo, Sad Giri sings *bhajans* to construct herself as beautiful and alter others' adverse perceptions of her. But even as she challenges caste exclusivism by singing *nirguṇī bhajans* and telling tales about her relationship with the *ātmā*, she redefines the nature of her caste identity through those practices. That is, performance enables Sad Giri to refashion Khatik parameters by abandoning the occupation that name signifies.[19] But how is she redefining herself? Furthermore, what are the implications of her efforts to reconfigure her caste identity?

Performing Khatik Identity with Dignity—Sad Giri's Life Practices

Sad Giri never hides the social fact of her being Khatik in our conversations, or in her interactions with householders and other sadhus. She is proud of her caste identity. Her use of the Ramdevji symbol on her business card, which signals her low-caste identity; her interrogating of discriminating caste ideologies and practices in *sannyās* in her performances; and her emphasis on building an ashram and buying land for it "all by myself" (in such statements, the implicit "I" indicates her being a Khatik) suggest the distinct pride that Sad Giri derives from her Khatik identity. In each case, she connects her capacity to overcome the struggles she faces on a daily basis to her being a Khatik. In doing so, she represents the notion of struggling in the face of difficulty *as an inherently Khatik trait.* As we learned in Chapter 3, the other sadhus commonly perceive this trait as a special virtue of their *sannyās* and attribute it to a combination of their (high) caste and gender identities. What this pattern indicates more broadly, though, is that low-caste sadhus are as likely to cite their low-caste status as a legitimating factor in their *sannyās* as are the high-caste sadhus likely to invoke their upper-status to validate their lives of *sannyās*. To this extent, Sad Giri, and to some extent Chetanananda, pose a signal counterpoint to Srinivas's (1962) classic theory that low castes, especially, tend to demonstrate the cultural pattern of changing their social identities by Sanskritization, that is, by emulating the values, ideals, and customs of the high-caste status groups in order to upgrade their own status in the social hierarchy. Kaveri Gill discusses a similar instance of this counterpoint in her study of Delhi's Khatik communities who work in the urban informal industry of the plastic scrap trade: "I would hazard a guess that in an inversion of Jayaram's (1996) observation, Sanskritization holds little currency in contemporary India, unless it is accompanied by a simultaneous improvement in a caste's economic clout, for Khatik traders who have achieved the latter, the former ceases to matter so much, or indeed at all" (2009, 166). For Sad Giri, as her practices clarify, she wants to become neither a Brahmin, nor a Rajput.

And yet, the satisfaction that Sad Giri derives from being a member of the Khatik community has much to do with her redefining the dominant conceptual parameters of her caste identity beyond its traditional association with the meat trade. In a society where being Khatik often evokes negative associations, on account of the varying degrees of violence (*himsā*) implied by that occupation, Sad Giri seeks to recast the dominant perceptions of that identity in a new light by tying it to notions of dignity, respect, and respectability (cf. Gill 2009, 160).[20] So, while she has renounced the standard societal association of Khatik with "unclean" animal butchering and, therefore, the attribution of *himsā* to her community, she has not renounced being Khatik. This tendency to reconfigure low-caste identity and status through association with nontraditional, alternative, and "clean" professions appears to be characteristic of the social milieu of postindependence India, in which, as Gill discusses, an economic liberation has occurred in informal market economies (2009) and, as Ann Gold suggests, "Identities are increasingly flexible and formerly disempowered groups push against old barriers" (forthcoming, 9). Rajasthan's strong and developing industrial economy has enabled Sad Giri to take advantage of new and emerging economic opportunities that not only make her business feasible, but also help it to thrive. Most of her patrons either own or manage businesses in the state's lucrative marble and granite trade.

Sad Giri is not alone in redefining her Khatik identity as a means of "status enhancement" (Gill 2009, 160). As Gold describes of the Khatiks whom she worked with in Jahazpur, "However paradoxical it may seem, to remove oneself as far as possible from commerce in flesh seems long to have been the desired trajectory for persons designated as butchers" (forthcoming, 10). Hence, that community has similarly infused its reworked identity with dignity by constructing a Satya Narayan (a form of Vishnu, a vegetarian god) temple for its own community on land it purchased. Much to her surprise, Gold discovered that this Khatik community had no Mataji temple (the Goddess accepts meat offerings and, thus, Gold had assumed that these Khatiks were non-vegetarian).[21] One of Gold's collaborators, Durga Lal Khatik, a senior leader of the Jahazpur Khatik society (forthcoming, 11), in speaking about the temple's history emphasized that the Khatiks themselves raised the funds to build their own Satya Narayan temple. A lot of the temple's maintenance expenses are covered by the rent collected from the (all) Khatik shopkeepers on the temple's property. In Durga Lal Khatik's words: "Only the Jahazpur Khatik donated the money for the temple. We wouldn't accept money from anyone else, even if they wanted to give it to us" (Gold forthcoming, 12). Even more fascinating, Durga Lal told Gold that, in his estimation, "80% of the Khatik community had given up eating meat out of devotion to Satya Narayan" (13). When Gold pressed him about meat stores belonging to members of his community, Durga Lal exclaimed, "There is only one such storekeeper and we despise him, and give him no regard" (11). In response to Gold's query about why the Khatiks built a temple to Satya Narayan instead of one to Mataji, Durga Lal said that,

> Brahmins didn't let us in their temple, and brahmins wouldn't let us touch the feet of God in *bevan* [chariot used in temple processions].

> Other people could walk under the chariot, but they wouldn't even let us walk under it. So we decided to build our own temple [to Vishnu]. Then the brahmins were ashamed. Brahmins from out of town came to see *our* temple. Then the Jahazpur brahmins wanted to see it too, and the Khatik said to them, "Hey, it's a Butcher's temple, why have you come to see it?" That shamed them. (Gold forthcoming, 12; emphasis in original)

As Durga Lal's narrative makes explicit, the Jahazpur Khatik community has struggled against numerous obstacles posed by the local high-caste Brahmin elites, in particular, in order to carve a respectable social space for itself within the broader Jahazpur community by also carving out a separate physical space for their deity, Satya Narayan.[22] Its crafting of self-respect is, therefore, linked to leaving behind its traditional caste occupation. Gold explains: "For Durga Lal and his community, both their successful struggle [to build the temple] and their temple's beauty are sources of immense pride and satisfaction. By worshipping Vishnu, a vegetarian deity, in such grand style, the Khatik in a sense deny the identity their name carries, but significantly not by erasure. A plaque prominently displayed announces the temple as the work of the Khatik Samaj. The name is retained with pride, even as its occupational associations are abandoned" (13).

In her practices Sad Giri similarly "den[ies] the identity [her] name carries" by refashioning its "occupational associations" in multiple ways. One illustrative way is through her *satsang* business, by which she reconstitutes the idea of Khatik to highlight its entrepreneurial spirit as innovative, creative, and intelligent. Khatiks, as Gold's and Gill's works also show, are crafting themselves as entrepreneurs. Describing the Khatik traders and laborers she worked with in Delhi, Gill says that they have "a perception of themselves, first and foremost, as entrepreneurs and risk-taking individuals riding the wave of market-based opportunities" (2009, 167). Sad Giri, too, seems to be riding the wave of new economic opportunities. Because her business exposes her to large numbers of people regularly, it makes an excellent vehicle for stretching the content of her Khatik identity. Perhaps in time, as her business develops, it will help to define Khatiks as a caste of professional singers, like the Manganiyars of northwestern Rajasthan (Kotari 2001).

Another method has to do with, as we learned with the Jahazpur Khatiks, adopting a vegetarian diet. Sad Giri emphasizes that she eats only "pure veg *śudh śakahārī*]"; that is, she follows a strict vegetarian diet consisting of vegetables, legumes, milk products, bread, nuts, and vegetable oils. Sad Giri's vegetarianism began prior to her living in the state of white *sannyās*. In our meeting at the *bhaṇḍāra* she told me that she was a vegetarian *long before* she became a sadhu. This is significant because, while exceptions exist, sadhus are normally expected to be vegetarian.[23] There is nothing exceptional about sadhus being vegetarians, or saying that they are. Hence, even if Sad Giri were not a vegetarian before taking *sannyās*, her initiation into the orthodox Dashanami order would have demanded that she become one. But that was not the case. She explains, "My whole family is vegetarian. We have been vegetarian since the time of my grandfather [*dādā*]." By tracing her vegetarianism to the lifestyle of her paternal grandfather, Sad Giri cues that she and her family—three generations of her family, in fact—remain free of the perceived state of pollution associated with her caste occupation. Although Khatik, her family has never worked as butchers. Rather, her father and Ramesh, also entrepreneurs like Sad Giri, own and manage a small bicycle repair shop located one hundred yards from their home. As a child, her father worked with his father in transporting camels throughout Rajasthan. Furthermore, Kamlesh, the youngest sibling, helps Sad Giri in the managing of her *satsang* business. Sometimes he performs with her. The clean state of her family's new occupation and her business, coupled with their strict vegetarian practices, enable Sad Giri and her family to claim high-caste purity as their inherent state as well as refashion their identity with the dignity often denied them.

A third practice through which Sad Giri creates her self-respect as a Khatik concerns that of gender modesty. I employ this term to describe specifically the fact that Sad Giri always travels with kin or a female friend, and not in the sense of women's veiling practices illustrative of the concept of female modesty in Asia.[24] While textual and popular discourse frequently represents sadhus as solitary wanderers, none of the female sadhus I worked with (and this applies across the age spectrum) ever wander alone. They travel with other female sadhus or with a group of householders. The sadhus connect their traveling with others to the orthodox practices of gender modesty observed in their own high-caste communities. Many of them express sentiments similar to those of Santosh Puri, who says that "Rajput women never travel alone," or like those of Tulsi Giri, who says that "Brahmin women should not travel by themselves."

Sad Giri, too, never travels alone. She mentions this detail in almost every conversation we have. Her emphasis on her being accompanied wherever she moves is important, as it is not all that unusual for low-caste women to travel by themselves in their local wanderings. Sad Giri, however, travels either with Kamlesh or with her much older friend Tulsa Bai. Kamlesh accompanies Sad Giri on her business travels and her journeys to local ashrams. Whenever Sad Giri and I travel by car or bus to meet other sadhus or to visit local temples, Kamlesh always comes with us. Once, while traveling to an ashram in Haldigathi, Sad Giri, referring to Kamlesh, said, "He is my shadow. He goes wherever I go. I will never travel alone." On the basis of my own fieldwork experience of often traveling alone in India, I have to admit that having Kamlesh accompany Sad Giri and me on our travels helped to deter curious young men from approaching me and asking all sorts of probing questions. Unlike Kamlesh, Tulsa Bai accompanies Sad Giri mostly on her intra-regional or pan-Indian journeys. A widow who lives with her son, Tulsa Bai has the freedom to move and wander that married women do not usually have on account of their householding obligations, and thus she makes an excellent travel partner for a young and mobile sadhu like Sad Giri. Tulsa Bai's son takes pride in the fact that his mother travels with a female sadhu and considers her journeying with Sad Giri to distant places as *sādhanā*. By having her brother or Tulsa Bai with her wherever she goes, Sad Giri has the security of knowing that, as she stresses, "my honor will never be looted [*izzat lūṭnā*]," by which she means that her reputation will not be tarnished or questioned, because of the sense of protection she experiences simply by having trusted people with her. It took several months of frequent meetings before Sad Giri sat alone with me and Manvendra Singh at her ashram. Otherwise, besides the devotees who visit the ashram, her mother or Kamlesh, or both, are often present during most of our conversations.

Finally, Sad Giri's taking full *sannyās*, after living as a *brahmacāriṇī* for seventeen years, suggests that she has drawn on this elite institution to reconfigure herself with respectability. From the time I first met her, I wondered why she did not continue to live as a *brahmacāriṇī*. While her narratives express that "the decision" to renounce came "from the *ātmā* alone," I asked myself, what it is that full *sannyās* accords her that white *sannyās* does not? Feeling that I had gained her trust, I revisited this issue in the short meeting I had with her at her ashram in the summer of 2012. In an illuminating conversation, Sad Giri told me, "I didn't want to be hanging like a loose thread in my parent's home. I took *sannyās* because some things you have to do for the world."

She makes two important points here. First, she conveys her understanding that her renouncing of the world has enabled her to reap the kind of religious prestige and respect for her, as well as her kin, that her earlier state of *brahmcārya* did not provide. Why is this? Although *brahmcārya* constitutes a well-regarded ritual state of purity, and despite the fact that many individuals, men and women, spend their entire lives in this state (Teskey Denton 1991; 2004; Sinclar-Brull 1997), it tends to be viewed as a transitional, and hence, impermanent religious commitment. Contributing to this pervasive societal perception is the fact that in the classical system *brahmcārya* signifies the temporary stage of celibate *studenthood*, which a person between the ages of twelve and twenty-five undergoes before moving into the more permanent householding stage (Olivelle 1993). As Manvendra Singh explained to me, "People will respect her as a *brahmacārī*, but they will also feel that she should get married at some point." Sad Giri's comment about "hanging like a loose thread" in her parental home cues her awareness of the mainstream perception of her liminality, that is, her being out of place as a *brahmacāriṇī* in the context of her natal home. Unlike the majority of *brahmacārīs* who live in the communal setting of an ashram and study under a guru, Sad Giri was living in her parent's house. Hence, her atypical living arrangements encourage both householders and the other sadhus to see her commitment to white *sannyās* as anything but permanent. As long as she lives as a *brahmacāriṇī* under her parent's roof, both her family and society will expect her to "make up her mind" and get married, or renounce completely so that no doubt exists on her character. Thus, societal pressures pushed Sad Giri to take full *sannyās*. By renouncing completely, Sad Giri indicates that she quelled suspicions about the sincerity of her commitment and engendered her self-respect.

Second, she expresses that her initiation into *sannyās* gave her the rare opportunity for people in her community to become part of an elite class of religious practitioners. Sadhus have a lot of prestige in India, and their presence often commands respect (Gross 2001; Narayan 1989). Their social capital is evident not only in the comments people make about them, but also in their behaviors toward them. I often heard the householders who came to see the sadhus for *satsang* say that, "sadhus cross over [*pār tārnā*] seven generations of family." Also, because sadhus are viewed as mediators of salvific merit and power—indeed, as human manifestations of divinity—Hindus typically touch their feet as a respectful sign of their elevated holy status, seek their *darśan* and blessings, and make donations as appropriate to their individual needs and spiritual rank.

Their prestige constitutes in part, then, the result of their intense religious practices. As this book shows, the sadhus, across caste, class, age, and gender differences, perceive their practices of singing, storytelling, and textual recitation as constitutive of their renunciant power and identity. At the same time, their prestige also has to do with their status as ideal Brahmins, as discussed in Chapter 4. In the orthodox framework, taking *sannyās* is equivalent to becoming an exceptional Brahmin. Sad Giri, however, patently denies this common association. For her, taking *sannyās* is tantamount to challenging the dominant perceptions of her community's identity as butchers and garnering the respect that she believes her people deserve. The emphasis she places on her Khatik identity *as a sadhu* shows that she clearly distinguishes her *sannyās* from the orthodox Brahmanical version, and that *sannyās* is not equivalent to the dominant Brahmanical representation of it in the classical texts. It further poses an ostensible challenge to the ideology of essentialism (i.e., high-caste sadhus are "essentially" better equipped to live the extremely difficult path of *sannyās*) and the attitude of high-caste entitlement it produces in *sannyās* (i.e., high-caste sadhus make better sadhus).

Thus, while renunciation offers women the potential of mobility (Knight 2011; Khandelwal, Hausner, and Gold, 2006; Khandelwal 2004), it provides low-caste groups a potent means of upward mobility in the social hierarchy by making it possible for them to imagine and define those identities in creative and empowering ways, retaining their caste names with pride.[25] For Sad Giri, taking *sannyās* gave her the benefit of both opportunities. Through her ritual initiation, she acquired a new (and raised) status and transformed static perceptions of her caste's social role by aligning it with *sannyās*. Also, her practices of professional singing, vegetarianism, and gender modesty heighten and support her reconfiguring of Khatik identity with dignity and respectability. Through these practices, Sad Giri adapts the standard definitional parameters of *sannyās*, by interrogating established caste hegemonies in that institution; she also expands the range of possibilities for what it means to be Khatik in a rapidly changing twenty-first century India. In Sad Giri's view, being a Khatik means leaving everything behind and singing *bhajans* to God.

Conclusions: Survival Strategies for Women Outside of the Mainstream

Like the other sadhus, Sad Giri constructs herself and her religious world through means of the paradigmatic idiom of singing *bhajans*. The *bhakti* ideologies invoked in her rhetorical practices press on the global theme of the social equality of all, regardless of gender or caste. To Sad Giri, caste status affords no special distinction in one's capacity to reach and experience the divine. Authentic sadhu status, as she contends, is determined on the basis of one's relationship with the *ātmā*. By the same token, for Sad Giri, caste remains a fluid and dynamic phenomenon, an identity that readily adapts to the changing values and contexts of a modernizing, contemporary India. Because she sees it as an elastic identity, she redefines her low Khatik status by linking it to her respected life of *sannyās*. In contrast, for the majority of the sadhus, caste status not only carries a more static valence in their practices, but is also thought to influence *sannyās*. It is seen as the essential ingredient that makes singing *bhajans* possible. In these sadhus' practices, *bhakti* is, thus, ambivalent. Their tendency of assigning salvific signification to upper-caste values in constructions of *sannyās* parallels the attitudes of the untouchable *bhakti* saints as featured in the hagiographies composed about them (Burchett 2009).

In an article that interrogates the dominant scholarly model of *bhakti* theory and practice as unequivocally egalitarian, Patton Burchett demonstrates, through his deft analysis of the hagiographies of four untouchable saints, that "it is not simply that there has been a failure to put the egalitarian *bhakti* theory of these 'untouchable' hagiographies into actual practice, but rather that the messages in these hagiographies are themselves far less democratizing and socially progressive than they might first appear" (2009, 116). He further observes that, "In other words, what appears to be egalitarian *bhakti* theory is itself, on one level, subtly working *against* the actual practice of egalitarian social relations and *for* the maintenance of the purity-based caste hierarchy" (117; emphasis in original). As this book similarly shows in the context of *sannyās* in Mewar, the low-caste sadhus as well as the high-caste sadhus "largely affirm the caste and purity restrictions of ordinary life in the world" (Burchett, 117). But why do the sadhus who have the most to gain socially from the potentially egalitarian ethos engendered by *bhakti* ideology reinforce these disempowering restrictions in their practices? How do we explain the incongruity between their use of *bhakti* to redefine *sannyās* in a manner that enables women to construct a valid space for themselves and their use of *bhakti* to reinforce caste exclusivism in *sannyās* ?

The intersecting themes of hierarchy, respect, status, and prestige are underscored in the lives and work of people who exist outside of the social mainstream. In her compelling and sensitive ethnography of the lives and practices of the *hijras* of North India—a transgendered community of individuals who make a living by performing "after the birth of a child, at weddings, and at temple festivals" and through prostitution— Serena Nanda (1999) demonstrates that *hijras* adopt and reproduce the ideologies and institutions (e.g., heteronormative marriage) that express the perspectives of the dominant class in order to create respectability for themselves as a stigmatized social group. Moreover, many of the mainstream beliefs and behaviors replicated in their practices actually work to disempower them socially, psychologically, and economically. However, by appropriating normative values, as Nanda suggests, the *hijras* craft a "voice" that makes it possible for them to be heard and, to that extent, to be seen as a legitimate "third caste" with a valid role in society (1999, 38–54).[26] She explains: "Although becoming hijra means making a commitment to a stigmatized identity in some respects, it is a commitment that nonetheless gives social support and some economic security, as well as cultural meaning, to their lives, linking them to the larger world rather than isolating them from it" (Nanda 1999, 54).

As a class of women who inhabit the social margins by virtue of their unusual religious commitments, the sadhus seek to link themselves to "the larger world" by affirming mainstream exclusionary views like caste and purity restrictions and high-caste superiority. Going against the social mainstream highlights their minority status and keeps them from achieving connection, by casting them as rebels. Knight describes a similar pattern in her study of female Baul identity: "For encumbered Baul women, resistance and defiance are not always the most useful or feasible ways to respond... In fact, challenging the status quo can create a very difficult life, a reality that should not be overlooked" (2011, 7). With these considerations in mind, in contrast to the Brahmanical model of renunciants as aloof to the world, the sadhus I collaborated with want to create and develop relationships with householders and other sadhus, and view those connections as crucial to their *sannyās*. Forming relationships with others expresses their desire to connect to the world, and not to escape it. By doing so, the sadhus soften the strangeness of their uncommon position, as well as perceptions of their transgression of gender norms, and, most importantly, gain the confidence and respect of the people who often become their devotees and provide them with essential economic and material support. Without that, the sadhus, who are not employed and thus do not earn a living (Sad Giri being a notable exception to the norm) would have no means of social or financial support, which would jeopardize their ability to survive *on their own* in the world as sadhus. As Sad Giri supports herself through the earnings from her business, she can unabashedly "push against old barriers" (Gold forthcoming, 9). For the other sadhus, however, their situation is different. Their capacity to survive independently (i.e., alone and away from family structures, which represent the two mainstream renouncer criteria that separate them from Sad Giri, who, by her own choice, continues to reside with her family)[27] not only distinguishes them as authentic sadhus in the eyes of their (male-dominated) *samāj*, but also can be disabled by their minority status, which compounds their social invisibility. The erroneous statements of my early fieldwork acquaintances that female sadhus "don't exist" in Mewar, or that they can only be found at noteworthy ashrams in popular pilgrimage sites, such as Haridwar/Rishikesh, contribute to the sense of female sadhus' social invisibility in the society.

As paradoxical as it might seem, the sadhus' affirming of exclusionary cultural practices acts as an "everyday survival strategy" (Dewey 2011, 51–85) for securing important resources in their society. I want to make clear here that this pattern depicts neither a tool of deception, nor a way to take advantage of others simply in order to get what they want. As women whose everyday lives are "situated amid the ordinary concerns of life" (Orsi 2003, 172), the hierarchical values articulated in their practices constitute what the sadhus have largely inherited from the myriad cultural processes in which their lives are entwined and, therefore, provide an interpretive lens with which they organize and make sense of their worlds. In this light, replicating the mainstream view on caste enables them not only to connect to those familiar worlds, but also to negotiate a respectable place for themselves in their society from within their peculiar position of being outside of the mainstream. For Sad Giri, her minority status is thrice emphasized: as a female sadhu, as a low-caste sadhu in a predominantly high-caste institution, and as a sadhu who lives with her kin. To that extent, for her, navigating her respectability in society, as well as in *sannyās*, occurs through her reformulation of Khatik identity. As for their survival on the path, competition for resources among sadhus constitutes a real, and yet underexplored, issue in *sannyās*-as-lived in modern India. Even—and especially—on the spiritual path, sadhus compete with each other for precious, and often limited, material (e.g., food, cash, clothing, goods), structural (i.e., buildings for ashrams and temples, or visitors' quarters), and social resources (cf. McKean 1996; Bayly 1999; Gross 2001). In the context of the latter, having a strong and reliable social network of support on which to draw bolsters sadhus' status and their sense of security, and thus enables them to live self-sufficiently.

By accentuating, then, those characteristics and dispositions that distinguish them as unique from other sadhus—such as for the sadhu majority, their high-caste status or, for Sad Giri, her connection to the *ātmā*—the sadhus secure their ability to access those resources and ensure their survival on the difficult path of singing *bhajans*. Indeed, they not only manage to survive, but also to adapt successfully in their constructions of meaningful worlds.

7

"*Write the Text in Your Heart*"

NON-LITERACY, AUTHORITY, AND FEMALE SADHUS' PERFORMANCES OF ASCETICISM THROUGH SACRED TEXTS

Keep reading Rāmāyan. Once you finish, read [it] again and again. It doesn't cost anything.

—GANGA GIRI MAHARAJ

THE TELLING OF stories, both personal and vernacular, and the singing of *bhajans*, become a way for sadhus like Chetanananda Swami and Sad Giri, who come from tribal and formerly disadvantaged communities, respectively, to perform their power, authority, and legitimacy in *sannyās*. As with the high-caste sadhus described in Chapter 4, Chetanananda Swami and Sad Giri perform their views that singing to God embodies *sannyās*-as-lived in Rajasthan. But the reciting of sacred texts, too, plays as meaningful a role as singing songs and telling stories in the establishing of the female sadhus' power and legitimacy, and in the constructing of asceticism as relational. The use of texts to perform *sannyās* as relational blunts, if not altogether erases, the sting of the ambivalent caste-based discourses that the sadhus' practices also highlight. Performing texts accentuates that vernacular asceticism exists as a network of relationships, and that the sadhus' identities are tied to, and shaped by, the spiritual communities of which they are integral parts, and on which they depend for their individual survival. Singing *bhajans* in this manner, as the performing of texts, further ensures the sadhus' well-being, happiness, and immortality.

As an example, at ten o'clock every morning, Ganga Giri recites the *Rāmcaritmānas*. She retrieves the book from the ochre-colored (*bhagwā*) cloth in which it is reverently wrapped and sits by the *dhūni* to perform her recitation, as can be seen in Figure 7.1. She does this every day, twice a day.

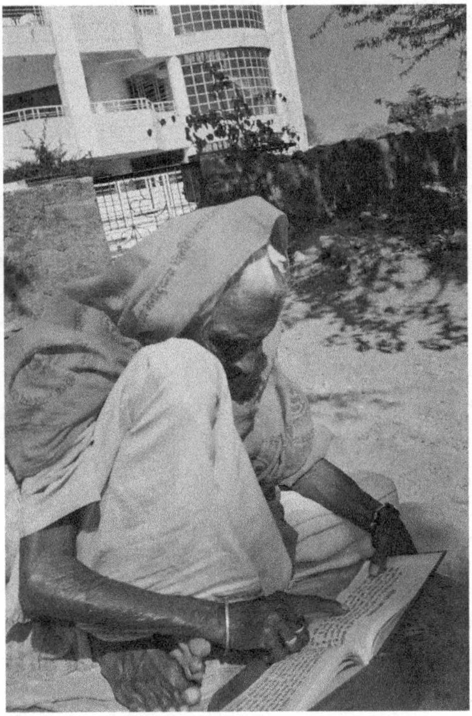

FIGURE 7.1 Ganga Giri reciting the *Gītā*.
Photo by A. DeNapoli.

Sometimes, in the evenings, Ganga Giri recites the *Bhagavad Gītā* instead of the *Rāmcaritmānas*. Even so, she performs, in her words, "*Gītā-jī*," in the same way that she performs the *Rāmcaritmānas*. One winter morning when Ganga Giri and I went to visit her daughter Lakshmi Bai and son-in-law Dev Puri, who live on the outskirts of Udaipur, Ganga Giri was not able to recite the text. During the long return trip back to her ashram, she complained that her whole day had been "spoiled" because she did not "read" *Rāmāyan*; and that she felt "tired [*ṭhak gayī*]" and "out of sorts [*behoś*]" because she skipped her recitation of *Rāmāyan*. In making these statements, Ganga Giri conveyed the important message that regular performance of this text helps her to organize and make sense of her world. It creates her power. She has said many times that, like her singing of *bhajans*, she started reading *Rāmāyan* "before [she] knew how to wear shoes." As a householder, too, Ganga Giri read the *Rāmāyan*. Often, after her recitations, she tells her audience to "[r]ead *Rāmāyan*. It's filled with knowledge. It doesn't cost anything."

Vernacular Textual Practice as Performance of Renunciant Legitimacy

The performance of religious texts marks a significant genre of renunciant practice in the sadhus' vernacular asceticism. While they perform a variety of devotional texts from their repertoires, including the *Bhagavad Gītā*, the sadhus' lives, worship, and rituals are predominantly structured around performance of the *Rāmcaritmānas* attributed to Tulsidas. Commonly known in Rajasthan as the Tulsi *Rāmāyan*, this text represents the most popular vernacular-language version of the Hindi *Rāmāyan* narrative tradition in North India. It is sung, recited, read, studied, memorized, and expounded by Hindus of all castes, classes, ages, and educational backgrounds. Its language, like the poetry of the medieval *sants* discussed in the next chapter, gives voice to the exceptional devotional fervor that many of the sadhus associate with singing *bhajans* and, by implication, *sannyās*. Its composition by the sixteenth-century Vaishnava Brahmin poet-saint Tulsidas, whom the sadhus regard as a paragon of sadhu *bhakti*—a *sant* par excellence—establishes the moral authority of the more general *bhakti* path that is practiced by householders in many strands of Hinduism, and the renunciant type of *bhakti* that the sadhus say they practice. Performing the Tulsi *Rāmāyan* illustrates another means, along with that of singing *bhajans* and telling religious stories, by which the sadhus perform their power, authority, and legitimation as female renouncers and construct *sannyās* in a gendered way. For them, the metaphor of singing *bhajans* is synonymous with performing the Tulsi *Rāmāyan*.

Moreover, the sadhus' performing of the *Rāmāyan* constitutes a performance of literacy by which they create their legitimacy and power. Literacy and legitimacy make an odd couple in the lives of the female sadhus. Many of these sadhus are uneducated (*anpaḍh*). They never learned to read or write, as their parents never sent them to school. In the few cases of female sadhus who went to school, their parents allowed them to be educated only through elementary school. Ganga Giri says that she is "only first-class passed." When she speaks about her youth, she tells me that her parents supported her brother's education even though he did not want to go to school; but they forbade Ganga Giri from attending school beyond the first standard. Similarly, Shiv Puri explains that she went to school through the fourth standard, but had to leave her studies behind in order to care for her younger siblings. Her mother was diagnosed as mentally unsound shortly after her birth and could not care for Shiv Puri and her siblings. Some of the sadhus were born in the early twentieth century, and the others—the majority of the women—were born in the 1930s and 1940s. Neither of these historical milieus was particularly sympathetic to female education.[1] Especially in the more conservative states like Rajasthan,[2] where most of the sadhus were born, and in orthodox Hindu families, sending girls to school was not a priority. Women were (and still are) expected to be selfless mothers and wives, and were (and still are) taught from a young age to construct themselves around these normative identities and roles. The sadhus are no exception. Education, in the eyes of society, would have distracted them from those goals.

The topic of literacy comes up a lot in my conversations with the sadhus. My own educated status that I "perform" in my role as ethnographer, by writing the sadhus' words in my field notebook in Hindi and English, no doubt contributes to their reflecting on their own literacy and education levels, or lack thereof. The sadhus appreciate my being educated insofar as they see it as a means to bring their stories, songs, and texts to people "in my country," whom they might never meet but can still teach. "Write [these songs] one hundred times and sing them in your country," Ganga Giri tells me. My being educated, however, does not automatically construct me as a "knower [*jnānī*]" to the sadhus with whom I worked. Recall, from Chapter 1, the description of Ganga Giri's dismissal of me because I did not sing *bhajans*. "What does she know? She doesn't sing *bhajans*." Similarly, in response to my documentation of their teachings in my notebook, Ganga Giri says: "Write the words here," pointing to her heart, "not here," implying my book. Being literate (or educated), therefore, does not a "real" sadhu make. The Indian hagiographical and vernacular-language *bhakti* literature undermines, or rejects altogether, the idea of literacy as a sign of authentic spirituality. Some of India's most famous sadhus and saints, men and women alike, were "unlettered" and still achieved remarkable religious status and leadership during their lifetimes. The writings of the sixteenth-century *bhakti* poet-saint Kabir, for instance, read as a catalogue of stinging critiques against educated religious specialists (both Hindu and Muslim) who can read and write (the *Veda* or the Quran) and know the ritual traditions, but who use their specialized training to exploit vulnerable others for their own materialistic gains.[3] A true sadhu, the words of Kabir suggest, is measured by singing to God.

While being literate seems to be irrelevant to the sadhus in connection with their views of renunciant authenticity, it matters a lot in the local Rajasthani perceptions of who "counts" as a sadhu. In my fieldwork experience, the literate sadhus are regarded (and treated) better than the nonliterate sadhus. I was told on numerous occasions (by male householders in particular) not to work with female sadhus on account of popular (and usually unfounded) perceptions that these women are simply "uneducated widows [*anpaḍh vidhvāen*]" who "ran away" from domestic hardship and "know nothing" that would be useful to my research. The younger married son of a householder collaborator who introduced me to some of the sadhus at the beginning of my field research consistently asked me, "Why do you want to work with them [female sadhus]?" Shaking his head in disappointment, he told me that "lady sadhus cannot be trusted" and that I should "work with men instead. They have knowledge"; female sadhus, his words imply, do not. I understand the commonly used phrase "knows nothing" to mean that the local female sadhus neither read nor write, nor have formal training in *sannyās*.[4] A few of the male sadhus echoed similar opinions. In those instances in which I challenged such claims by invoking the name of a specific female sadhu in my field study who appearred to me to hold a public position of authority (but not always of leadership) in the local community, I was told that that sadhu represents an exception to the rule. I was never told, however, by male householders or sadhus, and certainly not by the female sadhus, not to speak to nonliterate male sadhus. In the institution of Brahmanical *sannyās*, in which maleness and literacy signify authenticity and authority, female sadhus, and those without education, are generally perceived negatively. Moreover, because literacy legitimates sadhus in the dominant local perceptions, the female sadhus perform texts as a means to show their literacy, even as their statements challenge its authenticating value for *sannyās*-as-lived. Being *anpaḍh*, then, is largely, but not completely, irrelevant to the sadhus. They know that without others seeing them as "real" sadhus, they would not have the status, authority, or respect that they command in their communities. To that extent, the sadhus' *Rāmāyan* performances help them to create legitimacy by aligning them with an authoritative *literate* textual tradition and an established tradition of singing *bhajans* as *sannyās* (the sadhus see Tulsidas as a sadhu), and to navigate both societal and renunciant expectations.

Take, for instance, Ganga Giri, who recites the *Rāmāyan* every day. She is well respected by householders and other sadhus in her community. Recall that she was the first female sadhu to whom Dadaji introduced me in 2001. In his view, which he made explicit to me and Ganga Giri, she is "the best lady sadhu" in Udaipur district. Dadaji characterizes her as "*vidvān*" (learned) in *sannyās*. Like Dadaji, most of the other sadhus call Ganga Giri a "knower," and many of the female sadhus regard her as their informal guru.[5] Her religious status, I argue, constitutes, in part, a function of her textual practices. Significantly, Ganga Giri is functionally literate—meaning that she can read Gujarati (her "mother tongue"), Hindi, and Sanskrit, albeit with some difficulty and, with the exception of Sanskrit, she can comprehend what she reads. She cannot, however, write. Like Ganga Giri, most of the sadhus are nonliterate or semiliterate (meaning that they can read and understand printed words, but they cannot write words, including their names).[6] Also, like Ganga Giri, most of these sadhus performatively locate themselves within the literate textual tradition of the Tulsi *Rāmāyan*.[7] To the sadhus, the word "*Rāmāyan*" refers to the *written* text of the *Rāmcaritmānas*: an original vernacular retelling, written in Avadhi, a literary dialect of Hindi (Lutgendorf 1991, 3; cf. Flueckiger 1991b). But how do sadhus who have either no or little formal education, and are mostly unable to read and write, perform a *scriptural* text? What are the contexts and processes by which they become scriptural in their performances of literacy?

The Scripturality of Female Sadhus in Rajasthan

My use of the term "scriptural" is based on William A. Graham's (1993) use of the words "scriptural," "scripturality," and "scripture-consciousness" to describe the interpersonal phenomenon in which an individual or community engages the *written* text—i.e., scripture—and, in doing so, creates a personal relationship with it (cf. Levering 1989, 58–101). According to Graham, as a "relational phenomenon," scripturality arises "in the interaction of persons or groups of persons with a text or texts," to which they attribute claims of sacrality and ultimate transcendence and confirm "the boundaries of scripture" for specific faith communities (1993, 6).[8] In another vein, Jonathan Boyarin (1993) understands the practices of textual study and interpretation to be a relational phenomenon, in which a group of persons decipher together the meanings of texts in particular sociohistorical contexts. In his study of a yeshiva (traditional, all-male Jewish study group) on Manhattan's Lower East Side, Boyarin discusses the ways in which participants construct the meanings of given texts through a combination of textual strategies. He argues that the experience of textual study in community creates "a nonauthoritarian intimacy" among yeshiva participants, and more significantly, between readers and the text. Moreover, Boyarin suggests that participants create both Jewish identity and community through group textual reading. Boyarin's work aptly demonstrates that the written text and the social processes that underlie the individual's interaction with written texts and create their meanings constitute a function of literacy (cf. Patton 2007; Long 1986; Heath 1982).

Graham's and Boyarin's models of scripturality provide a conceptual foundation with which to understand the multiple means through which the nonliterate and semiliterate female sadhus create relationships with their written textual traditions, and through that, power and legitimacy. Most of their scriptural performances, including those of the Tulsi *Rāmāyan*, occur in interactive social contexts of *satsang*, in which the sadhus interpret written texts together through use of various textual or performative strategies. I describe these below. Although oral performance of the printed text enables them to participate in a specific tradition of scripture, it is not the only way the female sadhus connect themselves to the literate text of the Tulsi *Rāmāyan*. Most of them, and some of the male sadhus with whom I also worked, equate both their oral and performed versions of the Tulsi *Rāmāyan* with the medieval Hindi text composed by Tulsidas, and in so doing, perform their scripturality. While such *Rāmāyan* performances are not scriptural in the Western, academic sense of the term, they clearly are to the sadhus who undertake them.

Female Sadhus' Idea of the Text: The Flexibility of Vernacular Asceticism

The female sadhus are able to create an intimate relationship with scripture, and more broadly, with textual traditions, on the basis of their *idea of the text*. Western concepts of the text almost exclusively assume the physical book to be representative of "what constitutes a text of any kind, secular or religious" (Graham 1993, 9; cf. Doniger 1991; Coburn 1984). Graham states, "In our minds, a book is a written or printed document of reasonable length to which the basic access is through an individual's private, silent reading and study. For most if not all of us, the fixed, visible page of print is the fundamental medium of both information and demonstration of proof" (1993, 9). Historians of religion, however, have argued that in an Indian context a text signifies more than just the written or printed holy book. Thomas Coburn (1984) explains that the text exists in oral *and* written forms. He maintains, "[H]oly words... have been oral/aural realities at least as much as they have been written ones" (1984, 437). Coburn and other scholars also contend that the oral or aural text has been the primary means for encountering and embodying written sacred texts in an Indian, and more broadly, a South Asian context (cf. Lamb 2002, 183–184; 1991). Building on Coburn's and A. K. Ramanujan's insights, Wendy Doniger (1991) challenges the traditional Western notion of written texts as fixed and stable entities. She suggests that both oral and written texts have "fluid" and "fixed" forms, and that India's oral culture of written sacred texts offers an alternate view of textuality.

Furthermore, Joyce Burkhalter Flueckiger and Laurie J. Sears's (1991) coedited volume argues that the boundaries of the text in South and Southeast Asia extend beyond the written book. The contributors to Flueckiger and

Sears document and describe several oral and performative traditions of the *Rāmāyan* and the *Mahābhārat* and, more significantly, examine the relationship between those performances and the written texts in which these epics are recorded in order to understand indigenous concepts of the text. For example, in her essay on the women's informal and temple *Rāmāyan maṇḍalīs* (devotional singing circles) in Chhattisgarh, Flueckiger states that the women of the informal *maṇḍalī* groups, which consist primarily of nonliterate participants, "place themselves... within the *literate* tradition of Tulsidas" by stretching the boundaries of the idea of the "*Rāmāyan*" as a text (1991b, 49; emphasis mine). These women equate the *Rāmāyan bhajans* they sing with the written Hindi text. Flueckiger explains, "In their informal Ramayana *mandalī*, even if they do not sing from the written text or memorized portions of it, the women still claim, if asked, that they are singing Tulsi" (ibid.).

In the vernacular performances examined here, we encounter a similar phenomenon, where semiliterate and nonliterate female sadhus construct a relationship with the Tulsi *Rāmāyan* textual tradition by performatively reconfiguring the idea of the text *beyond the written book*. To this extent, the sadhus' textual practices not only suggest a new way to think about the category of scripture, but also provide an alternative model of scripturality to that of Graham's (cf. Griffiths 1999 and Holdrege 1996 for other models), as their shared understanding of scripture includes both the printed text and regional expressive traditions that are also equated with the written text.[9] Although Graham's model emphasizes the oral and performative aspects of textual practice in the formation of scripturality, he does not address what performance itself "does" to the written text (Flueckiger and Sears 1991), or how performance creates participants' relationship with textual traditions, that is, their scripturality. Furthermore, Graham's model of scripturality conflates the *written* sacred text with a textual tradition.[10] My data provides a counterpoint to this dominant view of scripturality. The sadhus' practices indicate that their scripturality is neither founded on, nor limited to the written text. Rather, it is based on what the text means to them. Textual meanings emerge and shift in performance. By reconceptualizing the parameters of the text, the sadhus situate themselves (and their practices) within a broadly conceived *Rāmāyan* textual tradition and perform their scripturality in the process.

There are a number of academic studies on the oral, performative, and written textual traditions of the *Rāmāyan* in South Asia (cf. Hess 2006; Flueckiger 1996; Flueckiger and Sears 1991; Lamb 1991; Richman 1991; 2000; Lutgendorf 1991a; 1991b). In their emphases on the diversity, hybridity, and fluidity of the "Ram" tradition, scholars have contributed a swath of alternative literary and vernacular-language *Rāmāyaṇas* to the classical (Sanskrit and Tamil) versions, and have expanded the discourse on the *Rāmāyan* beyond the classical tradition. With the exception of Ramdas Lamb's study of the Ramnamis of Central India, many of whom are low caste, the literature does not conceptualize *Rāmāyan* performance in any form as a rhetorical resource that participants use to imagine and articulate their religious identities, experiences, and traditions (Lamb 1991; 1994; 2002).[11] Spotlighting the sadhus with whom he worked, Lamb suggests that, through their textual practices, the Ramnamis create and participate in the larger North Indian tradition he characterizes as "Ram *bhakti*," which, like the female sadhus' asceticism, constitutes a vernacular and nonorthodox alternative to orthodox Brahmanical *sannyās*.[12] Similarly, the Ramnamis performatively equate their oral tradition of *rāmnām bhajan* (lit., "songs of the divine name of Ram"), which is the movement's signal *mantra*, with the *Rāmcaritmānas* text, and integrate these *bhajans* into their performances. Lamb argues that the Ramnamis utilize *rāmnām bhajan* to articulate Ramanandi philosophy and to construct the text as a divinely inspired (*śruti*), authoritative tradition that affirms the egalitarian social ideology of the Ramanandi movement. Besides Lamb's work, the few scholars who have analyzed sadhus' textual performances of the Tulsi *Rāmāyan* focus on the practices of male sadhus and represent those expressions as ritual worship, rather than as constructive and embodying practices of vernacular asceticism (Gross 2001; van der Veer 1988).

This chapter explores two different genres of *Rāmāyan* performance: the first is a group recitation of the written text of the Tulsi *Rāmāyan*, and the second is a *bhajan* from oral tradition that performs a regional version of the entire Ram story. The multiple genres of textual performance evident in the sadhus' practices convey the flexibility of notions of the text enacted and embodied "on the ground" in vernacular asceticism. I narrow my analysis to nonliterate and functionally literate sadhus' practices because almost all of the female sadhus fall within one of these two categories of literacy. Performing the *Rāmāyan* is as important to them as it is to the literate sadhus in crafting authenticity, authority, and *sannyās*. I also note here that regardless of their gender, the *Rāmāyan* performance styles of the male sadhus and the female sadhus are similar, as are their ideas of the text. Their practices integrate a combination of strategies for creating relationships with written texts and literacy in those textual traditions.

Nonetheless, the views of *sannyās* that the female sadhus perform in their use of the *Rāmāyan* are gendered. The sadhus' *Rāmāyan* textual performances reconsider and modify the dominant definitional parameters of *sannyās* as radically individualistic and as primarily concerned with detachment and one's own spiritual welfare. Rather, their practices construct *sannyās* alternatively, by locating it within a framework of meanings embodied in, and illustrated through, interpersonal symbols, values, and behaviors that index their gynocentric perspectives as illustrative of singing *bhajans*. I contend that the sadhus perform a female tradition of *sannyās* (what I have characterized in this book as *devotional asceticism*) by emphasizing cultural ideals, social roles, and moral subjectivities that are typically construed as feminine in their culture. Their practices construct, to use the social theorist Sandra Harding's (1987, 297) words, a "care orientation" model of *sannyās* that reinforces the interpersonal values of relationship and reciprocity—roles centered on caretaking, and subjectivities imagined through an acute sense of one's dependence on and accountability to others within a specific sociobiological network.

Therefore, this chapter further suggests that the sadhus' *Rāmāyan* performances provide an effective resource for their "domestication" of *sannyās* by making it possible for them to engender singing *bhajans* as intensely interpersonal and involved in the world (Sered 1992). A term coined by the feminist anthropologist Susan Starr Sered, domestication describes "a process in which people who profess their allegiance to a wider religious tradition personalize the rituals, institutions, symbols, and theology of that wider system... to safeguard the health, happiness, and security of... people with whom they are linked in relationships of caring and interdependence" (1992, 10; cf. Pintchman 2005; 2007, 5–6). In their practices, the sadhus' vernacular asceticism exemplifies "this type of personally involved religious mode" (Sered, 10). Their performance of texts to convey the message that care and concern for others constitute a moral imperative of *sannyās* sacralizes their everyday gendered worlds, concerns, and experiences, as well as establishes their ties with the communities that their practices help to create. Similarly, the sadhus' personalizing of a religious life largely seen as impersonal and otherworldly challenges these and other utopian representations of *sannyās* in scholarly and popular discourse.

"*The* Rāmāyan *is Full of Bliss*": *Female* Sadhus' *Recitation of the* Rāmāyan

Rāmāyan recitation is a renunciant vernacular practice that the sadhus categorize as *Rāmāyan pāṭh*. Known to them simply as the "Tulsi *Rāmāyan*," many of these sadhus consider the text to be one of the most important devotional scriptures ever written in India, one filled with "bliss." Every day, both early in the morning and late in the evening while they are alone in their ashrams, the sadhus recite from a printed book or, as is more often the case, from memory, either a specific chapter or specific verses of this text as part of their *sannyās*-as-lived.

Apart from generally individualized contexts of solitude and silence, *Rāmāyan pāṭh* also happens in *satsang* contexts, where a small group of female sadhus meets weekly during the middle-to-late afternoon to recite a chapter or more from the written *Ramcaritmānas* text (Ganga Giri's personal copy is visible in Figure 7.2). These recitation events are informal and impromptu. There is no prescheduled or predetermined day, time, or place for their occurrence in what is a loosely structured and widely scattered "community" of female sadhus. No single individual or group of individuals remains responsible for coordinating these events. Instead, whenever the sadhus visit one another (and the reasons for these visits range from "business" to personal), one, or perhaps all, of them will announce to the group her "desire [*iccā*]" either to perform or to listen to a recitation of the Tulsi *Rāmāyan*.

In most of the recitations I attended, Ganga Giri leads the performance. Many times, she is the only "literate" female sadhu in the group, and others acknowledge her "literary" or her "educated" status by telling her, "Maharāj [lit., "great king"], unlike us, you are educated [*paḍhī likhī*]; you know things," implying that because she has the knowledge of "letters [*akṣar*]," she should

FIGURE 7.2 A copy of Ganga Giri's *Ramcaritmānas* reverently placed on a wooden stand.
Photo by A. DeNapoli.

lead the group performance of the text.[13] While Ganga Giri initially undermines her "first class passed" education by responding, "What do I know? All this is God's doing," she runs the recitation. Even when highly literate and college-educated female sadhus participate in *Rāmāyan satsangs* with Ganga Giri, she still assumes leadership of the performance. Not only is Ganga Giri the oldest living female sadhu in Mewar, but her birthday also falls on the Hindu holy day of *Rām Nāvami*, the auspicious day on which Ram, the hero of the *Rāmāyan* epic, was born.[14] Due to the combination of the auspicious day of her birth, her advanced age, and her individually developed reading knowledge, the other sadhus usually defer to Ganga Giri in *Rāmāyan satsangs*, letting her determine the structure and content of these vernacular performances.

Textual Strategies in Female Sadhus' Rāmāyan Pāṭh

Most of the *Rāmāyan pāṭhs* of the female sadhus incorporate three converging text-based, performance strategies: those of *arthāv*, a word the sadhus themselves use in their descriptions of their textual practices, and which literally means "elaboration on the meaning [of the text]"; the *samput*,[15] or formulaic verses of praise; and various types of musical accompaniment provided by the use of cymbals, drums, or the synchronized clapping of hands. While *Rāmāyan satsang* performs a relational context in which the participants, both renouncer and householder, interact with the physical text, these performance strategies variously contribute to the overall process by which the sadhus individually participate in the literate tradition of Tulsidas.

Arthāv: Elaborating the *Rāmāyan* as Recorded Text

In the *Rāmāyan* recitations in which she participates, Ganga Giri acts as the principal elaborator on the text for the group, rendering in contemporary Hindi or Mewari the meaning of the medieval Avadhi Hindi dialect in which the text is written. Often without consulting the Hindi translation of the text she is reading, Ganga Giri provides her own retellings of or elaborations on the various *caupāī*, which consist of two lines of four equal parts, and occasionally the *dohā*, which consist of two lines of unequal parts (Lutgendorf 1991a, 15). She integrates her *arthāv* into the structure of her recitation in several ways. Either she recites the first half of the first line of a *caupāī* and provides a brief *arthāv* of that line before moving on to the next half of that line; or, she recites a single line of *caupāī* and retells the actions or scene described in the recited whole verse, in her own words. More often, Ganga Giri recites a full *caupāī* and elaborates on the sense of the whole unit, sometimes incorporating descriptions of events from the following *caupāī*. Here is an example of this dialectical process of recitation and *arthāv* from Ganga Giri's performance of the *Kiṣkindha Kāṇḍ*, the fourth chapter of the Tulsi *Rāmāyan*:

> [Ganga Giri starts the recitation and the rest of the group then chants along with her. This pattern is repeated throughout the performance. It, however, is interrupted only when Ganga Giri provides *arthāv* of the verses she and the others have already chanted, in which case, she speaks in a non-heightened mode]:
>
> *sakhā bacan suni haraṣe krpāsindhu balasīnva/*
> *kāran kavan basahu ban mohī kahahu sugrīva// dohā* 5
> [Ganga Giri's *arthāv* of the verse:]
> "Sugriva, why have you come to live in the forest? Tell me everything so I can understand what has happened [to you]."
> OK, now Sugriva is going to tell Ram what happened [to him].
> *nāth bāli aru main dvau bhāī/ prīti rahī kacchu barani na jāī//* [first half of 5.1]
> "Bali and I are brothers. We really loved each other." Sugriva is telling this to Ram.
> *mayasut māyāvī tehi nāum/āvā so prabhu hamaren gāum//* [second half of 5.1]
> "Mayavi was a demon. One day, he came into our town [Kiṣkindha]."
> *ardh rāti pur dvār pukārā/bālī ripu bal sahai na pārā//* [first half of 5.2]
> "That demon arrived in the middle of the night and challenged my brother [to a fight]."
> *dhāvā bāli dekhi so bhāgā/ main puni gayu bandhu sang lāgā//* [second half of 5.2]
> "When that demon saw my brother, he got scared and ran away; my brother ran after him, and I followed right behind [Bali], running."
> [Tulsi Giri and Jamuna Bharti together say, "*jāī ho, jāī ho.*"]
> *giribar guhān paiṭh so jāī/tab bālīn mohi kahā bujhāī//* [first half of 5.3]
> "That demon entered a cave, and then my brother entered it."
> *parikhesu mohi ek pakhavārā/nahi āvaun tab jānesu mārā//* [second half of 5.3]
> "Watch this place for fifteen days," Bali is telling this to Sugriva. My brother told me, "Watch this place for fifteen days. If I don't return,

then you understand that the demon has killed me, and you run away from here." My brother told me to stay for fifteen days, but I waited there a whole month.

Sugriva was telling all this to Ram. "I watched [the cave] carefully. There was so much blood that came out of there that I thought that demon had killed my brother. I thought, 'Hey, if I go inside [the cave], he'll kill me, too.' So I left from there for Kiṣkindha." Sugriva explained this to Ram…

mantrinha pur dekhā binu sāīn/dīnheu mohi rāj bariāīn// [first half of 5.5]
"The ministers of the city saw that the throne was empty and they forced me to sit on the throne [and become the king of Kiṣkindha]."
bālī tāhi māri gṛh āvā/ [first part of second half of 5.5]
"Bali returned [to Kiṣkindha]; he killed the demon and then returned [to the city]."
bālī tāhi māri gṛh āvā /dekhi mohi jiyan bhed baḍāvā// [second half of 5.5]
ripu sama mohi māresi ati bhārī/ hari līnhesi sarbasu aru nārī//
tāken bhay raghubīr krpālā/ sakal bhuvan main phireun bihālā// [5.6]
"My brother beat me badly; he got angry [when he saw me on the throne] and beat me like anything. Then he took my wife [away from me]."
ihān sāp bas āvat nāhīn/tadapi sabhīt rahaun man māhīn//
suni sevak dukh dīndayālā/pharaki uṭhīn dvai bhujā bisālā// 5.7
Ram heard Sugriva's distress and became enraged [with Bali].

As these instances demonstrate, Ganga Giri's verse-by-verse *arthāv* follows the recorded text. Through the means of her "retelling," the audience learns that Sugriva had a brother by the name of Bali, whom he loved and served dutifully as his master and king. However, their relationship took a sour turn when a demon by the name of Mavayi arrived at the gates of Kiṣkindha "at midnight" and challenged Bali to a fight. On seeing the formidable stature of Bali, the demon ran away, but Bali ran after him, and Sugriva followed behind him. Before entering the cave, though, Bali instructed his brother to remain there on the look-out for "fifteen days," and if after such time he did not emerge, Sugriva should understand that the demon has killed him and "run away from" there. But Sugriva waited "a whole month" for Bali to come out, and only after he discovered blood gushing from the cave did he assume that the demon had killed Bali, and therefore leave for Kiṣkindha. Once he returned to the city, the chief ministers forced Sugriva to become king. In the meantime, Bali returned to the city and found Sugriva ruling what was *his* kingdom. Consequently, Bali beat Sugriva, took away his wife, and exiled him from the city. In explaining the sense of the final *caupāī* in this segment, Ganga Giri says that, "Ram heard Sugriva's distress and became enraged," alluding to Ram's impending destruction of Bali.

To understand the ways in which *arthāv* enables the sadhus to create a relationship with the written text of Tulsidas, we need to examine more closely Ganga Giri's performance style. Notice that in her elaborations on the Avadhi, Ganga Giri does not provide word-for-word translations (*anuvād*)—or explanations—of the recited text. And, with the exception of the second line of the third *caupāī* of the fifth *dohā*, she moves rapidly through each of her *arthāv* in the recitations that I observed. The fact that neither Ganga Giri (nor any of the other sadhus) was trained in the academic styles of *arthāv* (or *anuvād*) accounts for her performance style. Apart from this, there are three other reasons for her textual (*arthāv*) practices. One reason is that most of the sadhus in this *satsang*—specifically Ganga Giri, Tulsi Giri, and Jamuna Bharti—have recited chapters from this *Rāmāyan* together many times before this particular event. And since Ganga Giri integrates *arthāv* into the structure of most of her *Rāmāyan* performances, we can assume that these sadhus are already familiar not only with the general narrative content of the *Kiṣkindha Kāṇḍ* (in particular, one of Ganga Giri's favorite chapters which she especially likes to recite for *satsang*), but also with the narrative content of the Tulsi *Rāmāyan*, more broadly.

To that extent, another reason for Ganga Giri's *arthāv* performance style is that Jamuna Bharti and Tulsi Giri already have a deep familiarity with the content as well as the narrative structure of the *Kiṣkindha Kāṇḍ*. That is, they comprehend the written text as they recite its verses. After some of the *Rāmāyan* recitations in which I participated, I asked the sadhus if they understood what they had read. Almost always, they told me that they understood (using the verb *samajhnā*) the text, and to demonstrate this, some of them retold parts of the story they had just recited from the text. *Samajhnā*, though, implies both comprehension and apprehension. To this extent, the sadhus not only comprehend, but also *apprehend* the written text through means of recognition of the names and epithets of the cast of characters that recur throughout the epic.

In his examination of scriptural performances of the Quran in the village of Tidore in Eastern Indonesia, James N. Baker has distinguished between the comprehension and the apprehension of a text. Baker characterizes comprehension as "an activity in which one has subjective transformational control over that which has been offered" (1993, 108). He also explains that,

"Comprehension can be thought of as an activity by which one takes control of something by way of linguistic competence" (1993, 107). In contrast, apprehension is "an activity…in which one confronts and takes hold of what there is to know and remember" (Baker 108). Citing Pierce's (1958) theory of the Symbol, Baker argues that the various names of God (there are ninety-nine mentioned in the whole *Quran*) recited during Quranic performance function as "indexical" signs which "have essentially evocative meanings rather than denotative (semantic) ones" for the participants (1993, 111–117). "[T]here is a sense," explains Baker, "that the uttering aloud of these words is revelatory, having the effect of not only evoking memories but also of impressing upon a collective memory an accepted order of things" (118).

Baker's theory provides a hermeneutic that can help shed light on the ways in which the "presence of the names" of the divine, including that of Ram, and the popular epithets for characters such as Ram, Sita, Lakshman, and Hanuman, for example, enable the sadhus to apprehend the *Rāmāyan* during recitation. How they might apprehend the text while chanting the *Kiṣkindha Kāṇḍ* becomes evident through an analysis of the following *caupāī*: "*dekhi pavansut pati anukūlā/hṛdayam haraṣ bītī sab sūlā//nāth sāīl par kapipati rahaī/so sugrīva dās tav ahaī* (3.1)." In this verse, besides the proper name, Sugriva, the sadhus would recognize the epithet, *pavansut*, literally meaning, "The son of the wind [god]," which signifies the monkey god, Hanuman, who is Sugriva's general and Ram's devotee. Similarly, common titles like *pati* and *nāth*, meaning "lord" and "master," respectively, would easily come into the sadhus' understandings, as these words are not only repeated throughout the text, but also refer to Ram. The repetition in recitation is crucial to the sadhus' apprehension of the text. Baker explains:

> If [the name] is repeated over and over, by itself, it will lose its denotative sense. A person is left then experiencing a foreign word. What has been lost is the value of a word in comprehending things; what can be gained is a new regard for it in its foreign state as a name by which something is apprehended. In this way the fundamental character of the name, as a word having a real relation to its dynamic object, can be had by any word when it is brought into a regimen of practice. (Baker 1993, 117)

Apart from proper names, epithets, and titles, this verse contains a number of verbs and nouns that would be immediately familiar to the sadhus. In the case of verbs like *dekhi*, the Avadhi correlate of the Hindi verbal root, *dekhnā*, or "to see," and the verbal form, *bītī*, the Avadhi parallel of the Hindi verb, *bītnā*, meaning "to pass" or "to come to pass," even though they might not recognize the particular tenses of these verbal forms, the sadhus, nonetheless, understand the types of action these verbs communicate. Avadhi nouns such as *hṛdayam, dās, haraṣ*, and *sab* almost exactly parallel common Hindi words such as *hṛday* ("heart"), *dās* ("servant"), *harṣ* ("happiness"), and, finally, *sab* ("everything"). The Hindi forms of these nouns and verbs comprise part of the everyday language of the sadhus, and to this extent, the recognition of their Avadhi correlates in the *Rāmāyan* allows them to grasp not only the evocative meanings of these terms, as Baker suggests for the names and epithets of the divine, but even the semantic meanings of other words during the recitation.

Finally, and perhaps most significantly, Ganga Giri's performance style must be viewed in light of the function with which these sadhus perceive their *Rāmāyan* recitation. For them, the recitation represents an expression of singing *bhajans* to God par excellence, a means to experience the divine through the vehicle of the written sacred text. These recitations are unlike other male reading groups, such as the New York City yeshiva reading group discussed by Boyarin (1993) or even the *Rāmāyan* recitations led by some of the male sadhus I worked with in Rajasthan. The reasons for which the female sadhus gather "around the text" have less to do with the need to interrogate and analyze the written text as an object of consumption, than with an intense desire to communicate their love and devotion for God through recitation of the text as an object of worship (Boyarin 1993). The sadhus' approach to the written text recalls the non-Arabic speaking Kalaodi, with whom Baker worked in Tidore, Indonesia. Baker says: "For the... Kalaodi, there is that much less of a question that reading scripture is an oral performance [of devotion] and aural experience that has value independent of any intellectual comprehension of content" (1993, 103). From the female sadhus' perspectives, the function of *Rāmāyan* recitation is to evoke feelings of *bhakti* to *bhagwān*, and Ganga Giri's *arthāv* serve this particular purpose.

For instance, in her elaborations on the recited *caupāī*, Ganga Giri more often speaks in the voices of the characters themselves. In this way she performs the particular emotions (*bhāv*) of both the verse and the characters, rather than simply speaks in the voice of an impersonal third person narrator. Illustrative of this method is her *arthāv* of verse 4.3 in the *Kiṣkindha Kāṇḍ*:

> *rām rām hā rām pukārī/hamhi dekhi dīnheu pat ḍārī//*
> *māgā rām turat tehin dinha/pat ur lāī soch ati kīnhā//*4.3
>
> In tears, Sugriva told Ram, "Hey Nath! Ravan has taken Sita; she was calling from the sky, [Ganga Giri raises her voice] 'Hey Ram, Hey

Ram!' " [Tulsi Giri and Jamuna Bharti respond, "hey Ram, hey Ram, oh Ram!"] Sita was calling out [to you], Ram. I myself saw all this happen. [To this Tulsi Giri and Jamuna Bharti reply, "*jāī* Sita Ram,[16] *jāī* Sita Ram, *jāī* Sita Ram."]

This performance strategy of speaking directly as the characters elicits from Tulsi Giri and Jamuna Bharti a series of responses related in the vocative case such as, "hey Ram, oh Ram," or responses of praise like, "*jāī* Sita Ram." Ganga Giri's performance of *Rāmāyan* characters' *bhāvs* indicates her ritual identification with those *bhāvs* and is not unique to the sadhus' textual practices. The work of Ramdas Lamb (1991; 2002) and Philip Lutgendorf (1991a) shows that Ramanandi sadhus and Ramayanis (male *kathā* performers), respectively, employ similar textual strategies in their *Rāmāyan* performances. These strategies represent the everyday ways that Ram *bhakti* is lived in North India.[17] It is interesting to note that Ganga Giri's and others' practices portray a specific (renunciant) *bhakti* approach that mimics the nonorthodox worship practices commonly found in Bengali Vaishnava devotionalism. In this system, devotees experience the love of Krishna by identifying with the intense emotions of agony or ecstasy that are experienced by any one of the Vrindavan personalities, particularly Radha, Krishna's favorite *gopī* (McDaniel 1989, 29–86). McDaniel deftly illustrates that, in Bengali Vaishnavism, the devotee's identification with Radha, which is viewed as the highest state of ecstasy (*mahābhāv*), engenders a relationship of love with Krishna. Thus, *bhāv* brings about relationship. Devotees' experiences of particular *bhāvs* (e.g., becoming Radha by identifying with her intense emotions of union with and separation from Krishna) ritually create relationship with deity.[18] The rationale that undergirds ecstatic religious practice in Bengali Vaishnava devotionalism provides a comparative frame for understanding Ganga Giri's performative identification with the *bhāv* of *Rāmāyan* characters. Her *bhāv* helps her and other *satsang* participants to create a personal relationship with the text.

Although Ganga Giri's *arthāv*, including her *bhāv* performances, promote basic textual comprehension for the participants, the varied emotional responses of the sadhus during recitation constitute more than just performative (or affective) demonstrations to indicate that they understand the text (or its particular episodes). They are, more significantly, intense, personal expressions of love and devotion, to God *and* to the text. By arousing *bhakti* to *bhagwān*—both to characters like Ram, Sita, or Hanuman, and to the text—Ganga Giri's *arthāv* empowers the sadhus to experience the *Rāmāyan* directly and, by "grabbing" it with their heart-minds, to construct a relationship with the text. But *arthāv* is not the only means through which the sadhus experience this text. Other performance strategies, such as the *samput* and musical accompaniment, also create intense and intimate feelings of *bhakti*, and in doing so, create the scripturality of the sadhus—that is, (1) their intense and personal relationship with the written text; (2) their participation in the literate textual tradition of Tulsidas; and (3) their internalization of the text in such a manner that it becomes part of the fabric of their vernacular asceticism.

The Samput and Musical Accompaniment: Female Sadhus' Recitation Strategies as Performative Translation of Recorded Text

Every *Rāmāyan* recitation of the sadhus follows a particular metric structure that arises from the specificity of the various verses, mostly *dohā* and *caupāī*.[19] In the recitation of these verses, *dohā*, which consist of two lines, receive thirteen beats for the first line and eleven beats for the second, while the *caupāī*, comprising two lines of four equal parts, receive thirty-two beats per line, or sixteen beats per quarter line (Lutgendorf 1991a, 14–15). In addition to the *dohā* and *caupāī* meters, the sadhus recite the *samput* (verses of praise and adoration) as part of their *Rāmāyan* performances. Unlike standard *samput*, which typically comprise a single line of praise to a pair or a panoply of deities (cf. Saunders 2005, 236; Flueckiger 1991b, 56), the *samput* chanted by the sadhus serve largely as a supplemental chorus verse and contain two separate components: a verse of praise to Ram and Sita which translates as, "Victory to the lotus feet of Ram and Sita, the source of all protection"; and two (or, in some cases, four) additional lines of prayer addressed specifically to Ram. These verses serve as propitiatory *mantras* and beseech Ram, as the lord of all creation, for protection from disease and affliction, as well as for happiness and good fortune in one's life. The following is an example of a *samput* that Ganga Giri, Tulsi Giri, and Jamuna Bharti chanted in the context of a *Kiṣkindha Kāṇḍ* recitation:

sīyāramacandra pad jay śaranam/ [line of praise]
mangal bhavan amangal hārī/dravau so daśarath ajira bihārī //
(1) [line of prayer]
dīn dayāl biridu sambhārī/haru nāth mama samkath bhārī// (2)

Victory to the lotus feet of Sita and Ram, the source of all protection.
May He who is the source of all happiness, the remover of all afflictions,
He who plays in the courtyard of Dasharatha, have mercy on me (1).
O Lord, who takes care of the poor and helpless all the time,
Heal and cure us of our afflictions, and take away our suffering. (2)

In the sadhus' recitation of the *samput*, the first line of praise to Sita and Ram and the first line of prayer to Ram remain the same throughout the performance, but the next line(s) of prayer often vary. If the content of the prayer verses (i.e., lines 1 and 2), in particular, seem familiar, it is because these are *caupāī* which the sadhus have taken from other chapters of the Tulsi *Rāmāyan*. The first line represents the second *caupāī* of the one-hundred and eleventh *dohā* from the *Bāl Kāṇḍ* (1.111.2), the first chapter of the text; the second line signifies the second *caupāī* of the twenty-sixth *dohā* from the *Sundar Kāṇḍ* (5.26.2), the fifth chapter.

During the performance, the sadhus recite the *samput* after every *dohā* and before the following *caupāī*. Whereas the praise component of the *samput* receives eleven beats, the prayer verses, as with *caupāī* in general, receive thirty-two beats per line. The *samput* not only signal for the sadhus the beginning of a new *dohā-caupāī* segment, but also connect each *dohā* to its constitutive *caupāī*. In doing so, the *samput* seamlessly join two different metrical units. For example, the *samput* line, "Victory to... Sita and Ram," wraps around the last line of a *dohā*, imitating its eleven-beat meter, while the next *samput* prayer verse, "May He who is the source of all happiness..." plugs into the proceeding *caupāī* sequence by following its meter. In the recitation of a *dohā* and the accompanying initial verse of the *samput*, the performance moves quickly; but the verses of prayer and supplication, because they receive thirty-two beats, noticeably reduce the pace of the recitation. This *samput* feature allows the sadhus to return to the metric structure of the *caupāī*, while preparing them for the recitation of the next *caupāī* sequence.

Importantly, the *samput* that the sadhus integrate into their recitation do not "reshape" Tulsidas's text, but rather heighten the importance participants performatively attribute to the literate Tulsi *Rāmāyan* tradition (Flueckiger 1991b).[20] Nevertheless, the sadhus redefine the boundaries of this text by performing Hindi *bhajans* or *mantras* at the start of every recitation of the written text. These *bhajans* and *mantras*, which beseech the divine for protection from evildoers, although not part of the Tulsi *Rāmāyan*, frame the recitation as a performance event, and the sadhus themselves identify these additional songs and prayers with the written text.[21]

In the sadhus' *Rāmāyan* recitations, a kind of spontaneity emerges in terms of which verse (or verses) is chosen to be recited as the *samput*. While the first line of praise and the first line of prayer remain relatively stable elements in every *samput* unit, no single *samput* unit dominates these performances. The sadhus' selection of the *samput* is rather arbitrary (i.e., any *caupāī* in the form of a prayer to Ram qualifies for inclusion in the *samput*), and happens while the participants are actively engaged in the recitation. For instance, following the recitation of a *dohā*, the sadhus chant in unison the praise line and the initial prayer verse, slowing down as they switch from one verse to the next, and thus, from *dohā* to *caupāī* meters. One of the sadhus then leads the chanting with another line of prayer—a verse chosen because it is, as they say, what "came to mind." Once a sadhu has selected a verse for inclusion in the *samput*, the others repeat it until someone else in the group decides what to recite for the next part of the chorus.

The spontaneity that arises from the quasi-random construction of the *samput* by the sadhus reveals the ways that their memorization of the text plays a key role in the recitation and, more broadly, in their scripturality. All of the *samput* that the sadhus chant are based on what they have memorized from the text. "Memorization is a particularly intimate appropriation of a text, and the capacity to quote or recite a text from memory [depicts] scriptural piety" (Graham 1993, 160; cf. Griffiths 1999). For the sadhus, the recitation from memory of the written text creates their participation in the literate tradition of Tulsidas and performs their internalization and embodiment of the *Rāmāyan*.[22] This, too, constitutes an aspect of their scripturality. During these performances, I realized that, due to their lack of reading knowledge, most of the sadhus relied more on their memory of the verses in the written text than on the words printed on the page. This was certainly the case for Tulsi Giri, who is nonliterate, and who cannot read the words of the text. But even Jamuna Bharti, a semiliterate sadhu who claims to have received knowledge of letters via the grace (*kṛpā*) of both God and her human guru, recited specific verses from the text in a *Kiṣkindha Kāṇḍ* recitation I attended with noticeable difficulty. Her participation, therefore, pivots primarily on her memory of the verses, and she looks at the book usually when she has forgotten the words of a verse.

The importance of memorization in their *Rāmāyan* performances suggests that affective performance features of the *samput* contribute to the larger performative (and interpretive) process by which the sadhus create and establish their scripturality in *satsang*. Both the repetitive chanting of the *dohā* and the *caupāī*, and the repetition of the *samput*, evoke feelings of devotion to God from the participants. At the same time, these performance features serve as mnemonic devices by which means the sadhus learn and memorize, and as such, embody the written text. By hearing the different meters of the verses in the *Rāmāyan*, and more precisely, by constantly repeating the *samput in the company of others*, instead of reading the text alone and silently, the sadhus individually and collectively "write" the text "letter-by-letter" in their hearts.

Along with *samput* recitation, the musical instruments the sadhus play during the recitations, including their synchronized hand clapping, enhance the devotional mood of the participants and of the performance. As with the *samput*, the instrumental accompaniment integrated into the recitation, too, contributes to the overall scriptural process whereby the sadhus create a relationship with the text. Tulsi Giri, for instance, depending on what instruments are available, likes to play the drums or the cymbals, while the other sadhus recite from the printed text. In doing so, she creates a steady rhythm of approximately three beats per second that undergirds the verbal performance. While playing the instruments, Tulsi Giri shuts her eyes and occasionally sways her body back and forth to the rhythm she creates with them. Sometimes, she drops the instruments and raises her hands in the air, chanting several times, "*jāī ho, bhagwān kī.*"[23] Despite being nonliterate, Tulsi Giri internalizes the *Rāmāyan* through musical accompaniment and repetition of the *samput*. As with *arthāv*, these performance strategies similarly arouse more than just devotion to a formless *bhagwān*; they also elicit devotion to the written text. It is also important to emphasize that *arthāv*, the *samput*, and instrumental accompaniment constitute *a form of textual study* for the sadhus I worked with. By the means of multiple performance features, the sadhus' *Rāmāyan satsangs* become, to use Graham's words, "a synaesthetic experience of communal worship" (Graham 1993, 163). Through performance, nonliterate and semiliterate female sadhus not only create a relationship with the written text, but also situate themselves within the literate tradition of Tulsidas.

Beyond Graham's Model: Tulsi Giri's Rāmāyan Bhajan *Performance*

The Tulsi *Rāmāyan* tradition encompasses more than the written text composed by Tulsidas for the sadhus. As discussed earlier, these sadhus frame their *Rāmāyan* recitations by singing Hindi *bhajans* and *mantras*, and many of these are identified with Tulsidas' text. In fact, most of the sadhus do not distinguish their oral or performed versions of the Tulsi *Rāmāyan* from the standard textual version. To them, it's simply the same *Rāmāyan*. The identification of their songs and stories with the literary tradition of Tulsidas constitutes an interpretive strategy by which the sadhus reconfigure the idea of the text and, more significantly, of scripture as the written book to include in that category Rajasthani oral tradition, which is also understood to be Tulsidas's written text. Another event that made explicit to me this vernacular notion of scripture as oral tradition was the *Rāmāyan bhajan* performance of Tulsi Giri, who can be seen in figure 7.3. The performance occurred on May 25, 2005 at Maya Nath's Gogunda ashram. Here is the song that Tulsi Giri sang for me under the ashram's ancient mango tree:

[Ram speaks]: "It's not your mistake, mother [Kaikeyi]."
"It's not your mistake, mother."

[Ram speaks to Lakshman]: "The one who has made the whole world
has written our destiny in this way, brother."

[Ram speaks to Kaikeyi]: "It's not your mistake, mother."
"It's not your mistake, mother."

[Ram speaks to Lakshman]: "It's just the fruit of our karm [actions], beloved brother."
"It's just the fruit of our karm, beloved brother."

[Ram speaks to Hanuman]: "Go to Sita in Lanka."
"Go to Sita in Lanka."
"Go to the place where Ravan rules."
"Go to the place where Ravan rules."
"Go to Sita in Lanka."
"Go to Sita in Lanka."
The three of them [Ram, Sita, and Lakshman] left the palace.
The three of them left the palace.
Ram is alone, Brother.

[Ram says to Hanuman]: "Go to Sita in Lanka."
"Go to the place where Ravan rules."

Sita says: "Ram and Lakshman are wandering in the forest."
"He hasn't found me yet";
"I have no happiness without him."
Ram is alone.
Without her son, Mother Sumitra shall beat her head
To the ground and die.
Both brothers are wandering alone in the forest.
Today, the brothers have fallen into trouble.
Ram and Lakshman are alone.
Ram is alone, brother.

[Ram says to Lakshman]: "O beloved brother, I keep yelling for Sita."
"O beloved brother, I keep yelling for Sita."
Ram takes permission from Kausalya to leave [for the forest].

[Ram says]: "My father has left his breath."
"O Lakshman, our father has left his breath."

"Thanks, Mother Kaikeyi for having us sent to the forest."
"Mother Kaikeyi had us sent to the forest."
"It's not your fault, Mother Kaikeyi."
"It's not your fault, Mother."

[Ram says to Lakshman]: "It's just the fruit of our karm, beloved brother."
"It's just the fruit of our karm, beloved brother."

After killing Ravan, Ram returned to the palace.
Ram returned to the palace.
Everyone lit lamps [dīpak] in their homes [to welcome Ram].
After killing Ravan, Ram has returned to the palace.
Ram returned to the palace.
Everyone lit lamps in their homes.
Mother Kausalya offers ārti [worship] to Ram.
Mother Kausalya offers ārti to Ram.
Tulsidas has sung this [story].

FIGURE 7.3 Tulsi Giri, who sang the excerpted *Rāmāyan bhajan*, preparing cow feed at her guru's ashram.
Photo by A. DeNapoli.

This *bhajan* narrates many events from the larger Ram story, and the signature line (*cāp*) at the end of the composition, that is, the line signifying (possible) authorship, indicates that this Ram story belongs to the Hindi tradition of Tulsidas. To Tulsi Giri, however, this is not just a *bhajan* about the *Rāmāyan*, it *is* the *Rāmāyan*. The conversation Tulsi Giri and I had after her performance expounds her view that this *bhajan* is equivalent to Tulsidas' written text:

ANTOINETTE [A]: *Māī rām*, is this from the *Rāmāyan*?
TULSI GIRI [TG]: Yes. This is the *Rāmāyan*.
A: Is it a *dohā* or *bhajan*?
TG: It's a *bhajan*. It's what Tulsidasji himself wrote. Tulsidasji wrote the *Rāmāyan*, right? He wrote the whole *Rāmāyan*. He was uneducated when he wrote it. He was uneducated. Even though he was uneducated, Tulsidasji wrote the whole *Rāmāyan*... He was uneducated like me... But, through the grace of my guru, I have been able to learn things. So, Tulsidasji wrote the *Rāmāyan* in seven months. He was not educated. He couldn't read; he couldn't write. But God made him learn. God transformed his mind.
A: Uh huh.
TG: So, Tulsidasji was able to write. And Valmiki, he was an Adivasi [tribal]. He, too, was uneducated. But Valmiki composed the whole *Rāmāyan*.
A: OK, Valmiki was uneducated like Tulsidas.
TG: He was uneducated.
A: But [they] were able to write the *Rāmāyan* by the grace of God? Is that what you're saying, *māī rām*?
TG: Yes. Tulsidasji could read and write because of God's grace. Before this [happened], he was uneducated. Now he could read and write. There are lots of sadhus like me [i.e., who are uneducated but who learned by God's grace]. From the grace of God and of the guru, we have received knowledge.
A: OK, and the *bhajan* you just sang, you're saying that—
TG: It's the *Rāmāyan*. What Tulsidasji wrote, that became the *Rāmāyan*.

This conversation calls to attention, as many scholars have noted, the fact that the *Rāmāyan* tradition is a heterogeneous narrative and textual tradition (Richman 1991; 2000). Tulsi Giri herself identifies two different *Rāmāyan* traditions by invoking the names of Tulsidas and Valmiki, implying her understanding that each of these poet-saints composed his own version of the Ram story. The emphasis she places on the notion that Valmiki and Tulsidas "wrote" the *Rāmāyan* indicates that Tulsi Giri perceives their texts as *written* textual traditions. At the same time, she associates her *bhajan*, which she learned from her guru, and which she believes was composed and transmitted by the guru par excellence, Tulsidas, with the text that he also wrote. To that extent, Tulsi Giri pushes the boundaries of the text beyond that of the written word. And yet, it is with the written word that she equates her *bhajan*. Notice that at the start of our conversation, I ask Tulsi Giri if this *bhajan* is "from" the *Rāmāyan*; she responds that it "*is*" the *Rāmāyan*, emphasizing that her song represents what she believes Tulsidas himself wrote. Intrigued by the implicit association she makes between her oral performance and the written text, I ask Tulsi Giri for further clarification if what she sang is a *bhajan* or a *dohā*. My question, however, reflects the fact that I, the analyst, distinguish between the performed and written versions of the *Rāmāyan*. This simply is not the case for Tulsi Giri. After explaining that her *bhajan* performance constitutes a *bhajan* and not a *dohā*, she makes explicit several times throughout the course of our conversation that what she sings is, in fact, the same *Rāmāyan* that Tulsidasji wrote.

Tulsidas's writing of the *Rāmāyan* is not the only detail Tulsi Giri emphasizes in her narrative. She also underscores that Tulsidas and Valmiki were uneducated at the time that they composed their texts. According to Tulsi Giri, the grace of God and the guru enabled both saints to become literate and compose their *Rāmāyans*. It is important to highlight this detail of Tulsi Giri's narrative for several reasons. First, most of the sadhus I worked with understand that Tulsidas, specifically, was nonliterate; and second, Tulsidas' non-literacy is not part of the standard narrative(s) of his life that have been told in the hagiographies (Lutgendorf 1991, 6).

Why, then, is Tulsidas's and Valmiki's non-literacy significant to Tulsi Giri's discussion about the *Rāmāyan*? Because she, too, is nonliterate. As Tulsi Giri tells me, "Tulsidasji was uneducated like me," and as with Tulsidas and Valmiki, Tulsi Giri has been able, as she implies, to become "literate" in the *Rāmāyan* by virtue of the grace of her guru. "From the grace of God," Tulsi Giri explains, "we [nonliterate sadhus] have been able to receive knowledge," including, she implies, "literate" knowledge, or knowledge of written sacred texts. Not only Tulsi Giri, but the other nonliterate and semiliterate female sadhus also perform equivalent narratives of literacy, and occasionally invoke Tulsidas' example in their performances. They say that their "literacy" stems from the power of two primary sources: their *bhakti* and the grace of God/guru. Tulsi Giri emphasizes these same themes in her narratives about Tulsidas's and Valmiki's development of literacy and in her own conversational narrative of literacy that follows. By telling stories about Tulsidas's and Valmiki's *bhakti* journey to literacy, Tulsi Giri in effect creates her own "literacy." She uses her idea of these poet-saints' lives as an explanatory model to perform her own literacy narrative and, thus, engenders her authenticity and authority as a female sadhu. Moreover, Tulsi Giri's performance of a *bhajan* that she identifies with the written text of Tulsidas allows her to construct herself as "literate" in this *Rāmāyan* tradition.

Performing Sannyās *as Relational through* Rāmāyan: *Motifs and Meanings*

How do, as I suggest, the sadhus' textual practices help them to create *sannyās* as interpersonal, as well as represent their gendered concerns, values, and experiences as legitimate to *sannyās*? What do the sadhus emphasize in these vernacular performances? Performing texts and *bhajans* like those analyzed in this chapter serves as a means for the sadhus I knew, and I would imagine for sadhus more generally, to articulate promises, demands, and expectations they might not otherwise express in light of the cultural expectations often placed upon them as seemingly detached virtuosi. By performing *Rāmāyan*, the sadhus teach (and remind) their constituencies of the relationships of reciprocity they share together and their duties to one another as a community of beings linked in a broader moral and cosmic universe. In the framework in which the sadhus imagine their tradition of singing *bhajans* as *sannyās*, the values they stress have to do with those of service and love, worldly engagement, and making connections with others. All of these convey the sadhus' interest in the welfare of those in their sociobiological networks.

Motifs 1 & 2: Selfless Service and Love

As an example, after Tulsi Giri asks me to turn on my tape recorder to record her *Rāmāyan bhajan*, she says: "Look, sister, this is a story about sadhus." Tulsi Giri's *bhajan* performs the entire Ram tale, but just as important relates her interpretation of *sannyās*. Immediately after our conversation, in which she equates the *Rāmāyan* as oral tradition with Tulsī's written text, Tulsi Giri explains the *bhajan*'s meaning by narrating her understanding of the Ram story, which, to use Flueckiger's (1991b) words, follows the "narrative grammar" of the Hindi text. She underscores that Ram and Lakshman "served [*sevā karnā*]" the sadhus of the forest, where the brothers were banished, by destroying the demons, including Shurpanakha, Ravan's sister, who tormented the sages night and day. Tulsi Giri's narrative emphasis identifies *sevā* as a renunciant value. Her focus on the value of *sevā* indexes, however, another concept integral to the sadhus' *sannyās*-as-lived: duty (*kartavya*).[24] Tulsi Giri's view of duty that she performs in her *Rāmāyan bhajan* has a wider connotation than duty to the divine. Here, *kartavya* also involves selfless *sevā* to the world, which the sadhus see as a manifestation of God.[25]

Many of the sadhus use the words "selfless," "service," and "duty" interchangeably in their renunciant expressive practices. They speak about selfless *sevā* as a form of renunciant duty. Despite the fact that, in the orthodox Brahmanical model, duty (*dharma*) implies a strong sense of obligation,[26] Tulsi Giri teaches that duty *as selfless service* should emerge spontaneously from a feeling of "pure love" for "the world," rather than from a prescribed notion of obligation. As Tulsi Giri explains, "My *sevā* to the world is a *sevā* of love. This is the *sevā* of sadhus."

Therefore, Tulsi Giri's *bhajan* performance pushes the Brahmanical concept of duty as obligation into a new renunciant *bhakti* framework, in which service and duty to others stand for love, as well as depict the moral values of the sadhus' *sannyās*. To Tulsi Giri, Ram's and Lakshman's *sevā* to the sages and the other forest dwellers illustrates the duty to love everyone. Ganga Giri concurs. In her practices, she not only teaches that "God is love" but also characterizes Ram as "the best kind of sadhu." When I questioned her about what makes Ram a model (or ideal) sadhu, she spoke at length about his love and compassion for all beings. Ram's incarnation on earth (he represents an incarnation of Vishnu) signifies to Ganga Giri and the other sadhus who also perform (and listen to others' performances of) the *Rāmāyan*, "his love for the world." In Ganga Giri's words, "They [Ram's devotees] called, and well, he had to come. This is love."

Moreover, Ganga Giri explains that Ram's love shows his dependence on his devotees ("*bhakt ke adhīn hai bhagwān*"). Ram needs his *bhakts* as much as they need him. Ram depends on the many beings he befriends in the forest (e.g., Sugriva, Hanuman, Vibhisan, and the sages) to help him fulfill his immediate goal of rescuing Sita from the ten-headed demon Ravan, and his ultimate goal of restoring cosmic harmony. Those same beings, in turn, depend on (and expect) Ram to keep his promises of protection. Ram's not keeping his promises to his *bhakts*, and vice versa, disrupts the cosmic cycle of interdependence within which the *Rāmāyan* characters function and live out their worlds. The bonds of love that Ram forges with others during his exile symbolize his attempt to restore a precarious equilibrium to his extended relationship networks, and remind the beings within this global network of their expected roles in sustaining these skeins of connections. Such a network requires right relations between all participants, human and divine, in order for it to work on everyone's behalf. Any disruption in the chain, intentional or otherwise, brings about chaos, disharmony, and death. Ram should never forget that, although he is a divine power, he, too, represents a member of a whole community of beings connected together in a moral and cosmic universe of his creation. The *Rāmāyan*, in the sadhus' vernacular practices, dramatizes this notion. Note that the traits they associate with Ram index sociocultural characteristics typically assigned to women. Hence, what the sadhus perceive to be love and *sannyās* are mediated through the lens of gender. Their gendered interpretations bring about the domestication of renunciation as a cultural phenomenon. To them, *sannyās* is a radically relational expression. The virtues that they equate with the actions of the *Rāmāyan*'s heroes suggest a gendered moral subjectivity informed by a combined sense of dependence on and responsibility to others, which the sadhus talk about a lot in connection with their own identities.

Motif 3: Engaging with the World

A third value that the sadhus emphasize, which overlaps with those of service and love, concerns worldly engagement. In the *Rāmcaritmānas* recitation analyzed earlier in the chapter, Ganga Giri discusses the ways that Ram helped Sugriva, Kiṣkindha's default monkey-king, during his exile in the forest. Recall that Ganga Giri spends most of her time commenting on the episode of Ram and Sugriva's initial encounter, particularly the scene where Ram promises to avenge Sugriva's pain and humiliation by killing his elder brother Bali, who kidnapped Sugriva's wife and exiled him to the forest. In narrating this event, Ganga Giri underscores that Ram's assistance to Sugriva constitutes not only an act of mercy (*dāyā*) and love, but also his duty to ease the suffering of others. Her performance suggests that Ram's duty *as a renouncer* is to serve and protect others. This requisite hardly diminishes in his forest exile, but rather becomes thematically heightened in the narrative in Ram's service to and protection of Sita, the sadhus, Sugriva (and his subjects), Vibhishan, Ravan's brother, and other divine and mortal beings.

Ram's duty must, therefore, be understood in relation to his high-caste Kshatriya status. He is a warrior prince, and accordingly, serving and protecting others is his requisite duty—especially as a warrior-king, whose *kartavya* is to safeguard everyone in his kingdom. Both sadhus and warriors involve themselves with the world, but they do so in markedly different ways. For the sadhus, worldly engagement constitutes a spiritual duty and daily commitment, and, to that extent, a fundamental value of their vernacular asceticism.[27] While there is no specific word they use to connote "worldly engagement," one term in their vocabulary that signifies this idea is a word we have already discussed: *sevā*. It requires involvement with others and caring for their pain and suffering.[28] Another term, on which the sadhus draw to describe Ram's worldly engagement, is *milnā*, ("meeting with others"). The sadhus emphasize that Ram "meets others" in the forest, suggesting that he became deeply involved in and concerned with their lives. From this vantage point, it is significant that in the *Rāmāyan* performances in which she participates, Ganga Giri stresses the behavior of the warrior princes, Ram and Lakshman, rather than that of the sadhus, sages, and rishis living in the forest. By invoking Ram, in particular, as an exemplary sadhu, Ganga Giri challenges the textual model of sadhus as withdrawn and aloof from the world. In the mainstream Brahmanical perspective, the reason that sadhus, sages, and other holy people enter the forest is to escape from the world. The forest symbolizes a rhetorical trope for the orthodox values of withdrawal, detachment, and solitude. Yet, Ganga Giri's performances create *sannyās* alternatively as a life of worldly engagement.

Motif 4: Making Connections with Others

Ganga Giri's emphasis on Ram's worldly engagement signals a final defining value in the sadhus' *sannyās*: the creation of connections and relationships with others. When Ram and Lakshman roamed the forest in search of Sita, they created many friendships and alliances with numerous divine, mortal, and animal beings or communities. Most of the sadhus who perform oral or written versions of the *Rāmāyan* emphasize the relationships that Ram and Lakshman formed with others. They consider the involved practice of relationality to be relevant to their everyday lives. The sadhus use several different words in their expression of this concept, like *samband karnā* (lit., "to make a relationship"), *yog karnā* ("to make a connection"), and *mitratā karnā* ("to make a friendship"). The sadhus say that, "Ram made a friendship with Sugriv," or "Ram formed a partnership/alliance with Vibhishan." Many of the sadhus understand that their *sannyās* involves—indeed requires—creating spiritual partnerships with others, particularly with disciples and devotees, and they rhetorically mark these bonds by addressing those whom they serve in the familial and kin terms of "brother," "sister," "aunty," and "child (Gold, Hausner and Khandelwal 2006; Khandelwal 2004)." Here, I present a narrative that Ganga Giri tells about the importance of creating connections with others:

> There's a *pūjārī* [priest] of Hanumanji. His name is Bansi. He has a friend who brought ghee for me. When I make roti on the *cūlā*, I offer

> it right away to God. For the offering [*bhog*] I need ghee. But I didn't have ghee. I told Bansi, but he didn't say anything. After two days, his friend brought the ghee. I didn't tell him to bring it. I told Bansi, and Bansi told him. God sent him to bring ghee to me. God does all my work. I have no suffering.

Ganga Giri's narrative depicts that she clearly depends on others in her local community for their friendships and the basic materials they provide her that, as a result, help her to survive in the world. More importantly, her story suggests that for her, God exists *in the form of her relationships with others,* such as Bansi and those in Bansi's social network. Similarly, as shown in the sadhus' *Rāmāyan* performances, the relationships of love and reciprocity, as well as the expectations and promises embedded in those relationships that Ram, Lakshman, Sita, Sugriva, and Hanuman make with each other—and with others in their worlds—speak to the sadhus' views that God manifests in a world of God's creation via the web of ties that symbolize that world. The sadhus' textual practices indicate their perception that God is located in the personal processes of interdependence between humans, humans and other beings, and humans and the divine, and that God fulfills *bhakts'* expectations through those myriad personal connections.

I draw out these points because sadhus, in theory, are expected to be removed from worldly concerns and desires. The classic renouncer who exists at the periphery of the world, who needs nothing and no one, constitutes a common metaphor in the dominant model of Brahmanical *sannyās* (Dumont 1960). Despite its ideological power, this image is nothing more than a "theological fiction" (Olivelle 2007). The reality is, as the sadhus' vernacular asceticism shows, that sadhus, like all humans, have needs: in the most basic sense, they need food and drink and some form of shelter; and, they need people. They further desire to be healthy and happy. For the sadhus, they desire others in their sociobiological networks to be happy, healthy, safe and secure. To be so concerned with others' welfare underscores what the sadhus see as their moral duty. To them, renunciant morality constitutes an acute awareness that one's own welfare is linked to that of others. Sadhus need others as much as they need God. They need their *bhakts* to serve them so that they can serve God and their *bhakts*, whom they, in turn, serve as God. None of the sadhus lives in a world without webs of connections that bind them to humans and to the divine powers. Singing *bhajans* in the way of performing texts helps the sadhus to create those connections. By the same token, just as the residents of the forest expect Ram to remember his promises to those to whom he pledges his assistance and to uphold his responsibilities to them, the devotees hearing the sadhus' *Rāmāyan* textual performances remember their individual promises and obligations to their sadhus. That God (or Ram) ultimately comes to those who "call" him and fulfills their wishes signifies the recognition of mutual responsibility, as well as a promised fulfilled. The sadhus perform *Rāmāyan* with the hope that their needs, too, will be fulfilled, even as their practices indicate their promise to provide for the needs of their constituencies. Performance helps Ganga Giri, Tulsi Giri, and others, as they told me, "to get [their] work done." "God," Ganga Giri says, "will get all our work done. We should have the kind of faith in God [that God has in us]. I am sitting here alone. I don't have a shortage of anything. Whatever I need comes here. I just have to tell God what I want, and God gets my work done."

Conclusions: Textual Performance as Vernacular Asceticism

We have explored two types of vernacular *Rāmāyan* textual performance in the sadhus' rhetoric of renunciation: namely, recitation and song and narrative genres. Both genres display female asceticism as practiced, interpreted, and experienced in Rajasthan. Thus, vernacular asceticism includes pan-Indian practices of performing written texts and regional practices that recast the notion of the sacred text as oral tradition. Textual performance shapes and structures the sadhus' ideas of *sannyās* as singing *bhajans*. *Rāmāyan* performance, in particular, enables the sadhus, many of whom are nonliterate, to perform a tradition of *sannyās* they can identify with, while connecting themselves to a literary textual tradition. Let us now review the contours of the sadhus' practices and the interpretations of *sannyās* that those practices help to articulate.

In recitation contexts, the sadhus chant from the written, printed text of Tulsidas and use multiple textual strategies, such as *arthāv*, or elaboration on the meaning of a verse or passage in the written sacred text, and the *samput* and musical accompaniment. Although their recitations largely follow the lexical text, the sadhus understand the Tulsi *Rāmāyan* tradition to be broader than the written book. Tulsi Giri associates the *bhajans* she sings in *Rāmāyan satsang* contexts with the same "text" that Tulsidas composed as a *nonliterate* sadhu. Her *Rāmāyan* performance challenges Graham's and others' models of scripturality as the oral performance of the written sacred text. The sadhus' idea of the written text as sung or spoken oral tradition, transmitted between guru and disciple, and perceived as constitutive of the literary tradition of knowledge and devotion that is thought to have been transmitted by Tulsidas himself, illustrates another understanding of scripture. The textual practices of the sadhus analyzed in this chapter offer an alternate model of scripturality as intense engagement with oral tradition that is equated with and embodied as the written text. Their idea of the boundaries of the text as fluid collapses the static binaries of oral tradition and written text often perpetuated in religious studies scholarship. In the sadhus' practices, both categories of text constitute scripture, and interaction with both kinds of texts confers legitimacy, power, and authority. To the sadhus, Tulsidas' *Rāmāyan* represents one dimension of a broadly conceived textual/narrative tradition.

Moreover, performing *Rāmāyan* together creates and affirms the sadhus' experiences of *sannyās* as relational. The values of service and love, engaging with the world, and forging connections with others that they call attention to in their textual practices offer an alternative to the radical (and masculine) ideals of detachment, solitude, and separation from the world that the mainstream imagination perceives as central to *sannyās*. The gendered worlds that the sadhus perform through their texts, their songs, and their stories allow them to construct not only a female vision of *sannyās*, for which love, reciprocity, and relationships constitute preeminent values, but also the communities on which they depend, and that depend on them. Through their textual performances, the sadhus articulate and reinforce the bonds of love, dependence, and responsibility that they believe they share with others and are, at the same time, shared with them. Furthermore, their practices recast the more common definitional boundaries of their unusual way of life, widening its parameters to include practices and symbols that sacralize their gendered realities and domesticate *sannyās* as an institution, making it a female world, as well.

8

"Real Sadhus Sing to God"

PERFORMING *SANT* ASCETICISM IN VERNACULAR SINGING

Bhajans are blessings for you, for me, for everyone. Therefore, we sadhus sing bhajans for the young and old people; for the healthy and the sick. If we don't sing bhajans, we commit a sin... This is our sevā as sadhus.

—TULSI GIRI MAHARAJ

One nirguṇī bhajan is worth a single one-hundred-rupee note. Everything else is small change.

—GANGA GIRI MAHARAJ

THE ORIENTING METAPHOR of singing *bhajans* that the sadhus draw on to represent *sannyās* as a relational path—in their words, as a " a carnival of meeting and parting"—and, more significantly, to describe a female way of being a sadhu in the world, embodies the totality of practices that constitute their rhetoric of renunciation. Telling stories about Mira Bai, Karma Bai, and Shabari Bai; singing Ram and Sita *bhajans*; reciting Tulsi *Rāmāyan*; and narrating personal experiences about the "spontaneous" arising of detachment and devotion in childhood, relate the sadhus' idea of singing *bhajans*. And, to them, singing *bhajans* characterizes asceticism as practiced. Up until now, this book has conveyed the spectrum of performances in the sadhus' vernacular asceticism, their contexts, and the power, authority, and legitimacy they confer on the sadhus. But because the sadhus perform *sannyās* as singing, and because singing creates what their *sannyās* is about, this chapter examines closely the *bhajans* that the sadhus sing as they construct asceticism, and explores exactly how they think about *bhajan* singing in terms of what it creates for sadhus. As we will see, the sadhus view *sannyās* as a glorious awakening to the power and presence of the divine, rather than as, in the dominant Brahmanical model, "dying" to the world. To become a sadhu means to celebrate, in the company of other "good people," the precious power that chanting the divine name bequeaths. That power, the sadhus say, is present everywhere in the world. "*Bhagwan* is standing wherever we look. In every seed, in every breath, in every being, in every moment, God is," Ganga Giri explains. Awakening to God, therefore, awakens within the *bhakt* a desire to serve the world in which God manifests "with love," and not, as mainstream imagination claims, disgust and a longing to escape it. The sadhus insist that their view of *sannyās* as a celebration in the *melā* of life is based on the practices of the medieval North Indian *sants*. They, too, the sadhus say, sang "lakhs and crores of" *bhajans* to God. Singing the *nirguṇī bhajans* that the *sants* themselves are thought to have sung becomes an effective way for the sadhus to perform *sannyās* as the asceticism of the *sants*. The sadhus prefer to sing *nirguṇī bhajans* because they see these songs as having a power that they say other kinds of *bhajans* simply do not have.[1] By singing *nirguṇī bhajans*, the sadhus also say that they generate *tapas*, which, in turn, creates their asceticism. *Tapas*, as I discuss below, makes sadhus powerful, and it is produced from singing *bhajans*. The sadhus' association of *bhajan* singing with *tapas*, rather than *bhakti*, is significant, because it suggests that they distinguish between *bhajan* and *bhakti*. This contrast allows them not only to differentiate between householder *bhakti* and sadhu *bhakti*, but also to establish sadhu *bhakti* as a "superior" and "difficult" path that only "real" sadhus can undertake.

"*My* Bhajans *are My Power*": *Performance and Efficacy in Singing*

The majority of the female sadhus view *bhajan* singing as an essential practice for their class of practitioners, because of the power it is believed to give them. It is considered to be necessary in the *kali yug* (the age of degeneration and darkness), which the sadhus identify with the current world age.[2] Ganga Giri observes that in the *satya yug* (the golden age), a time of truth, innocence, and wisdom, the minds of humans were so pure (*śuddh*) as to make religious practice superfluous. In the *kali yug*, however, human minds have become so corrupted (*bhraṣṭ*) with lust, deception, and greed that sadhus, as God's human representatives on earth, must cling to their *bhajans* to protect the world against evil. For this reason she says "my *bhajans* are my power [*śakti*]." She associates singing *bhajans*, which have the power to safeguard and transform a derelict cosmic age, with sadhus, who, by virtue of their singing, serve as trustworthy custodians of the world. Power, according to Ganga

Giri, manifests as and by means of singing *bhajans*. Even the mental power of wisdom is viewed as an effect of the *bhakti* practice of *bhajan* singing. Hence, Ganga Giri implies her perception of singing *bhajans* as devotional asceticism.

More significantly, Ganga Giri's statements suggest an underlying ideology of the inherent efficacy and power of *bhajan* singing for sadhus. This ideology is a significant theme in the sadhus' conversational narratives, and is usually related in terms of three overlapping motifs of *bhajan* singing: as transformative *ascetic* practice; as a symbolic medium of currency exchange; and as selfless service (*sevā*) to humanity. Here, I explore the contours of this ideology through analysis of these themes as they are performed in the narratives of two female sadhus and one male sadhu. I also tease out gendered patterns in their experiences and interpretations of this ideology in order to illuminate the central messages about singing and *sannyās* that it implies.

Theme 1: *Bhajan* Singing as Transformative Ascetic Practice

In her conversational narratives, Ganga Giri discusses a renowned Mewari sadhu, the late Bhole Nathji. According to Ganga Giri's stories of his life, besides living to an age of more than one hundred and fifty years (a detail most of my sadhu and householder collaborators considered as fact), Bhole Nath could transform his disciples into lions, talk to crows and send them on distant journeys in search of medicine (*jaḍī-bhūtī*) to heal his devotees of diseases, and make troublesome gods or spirits behave by binding them with his words. In her commentaries on these legends, Ganga Giri attributes Bhole Nath's extraordinary abilities to "the power of his [singing] *bhajans*." The following tale, which Ganga Giri told me at her ashram, presses on the theme of singing as empowering sadhu practice in its depiction of the relationship between Bhole Nath and his royal disciple, Fateh Singh (ca. 1884–1930), a *mahārāṇā* who, under the auspices of the Sisodiya dynasty, had once ruled the region of Mewar (cf. Harlan 1992).[3]

> [Bhole Nath] was a great *siddha*. He only sang *bhajans*. He only sang *bhajans*... He used to sit on his seat and receive visitors... Fateh Singh used to come to Bhole Nath... and sit on the floor. Bhole Nathji used to say, "Fatiya, you are the king of Udaipur, but I'm the king of the world. Fan me."... Fateh Singh would say, "As you wish, *andattā* [lit., benevolent one]," and fanned him. Fateh Singh used to fan Bhole Nathji.

Ganga Giri's story begs the question, "Who is the sovereign and who is the servant?" In this narrative not only the roles of, but also the hierarchy between, sadhu and king are reversed. Rather than Bhole Nath serving his king, Fateh Singh serves his sadhu—and as the legend implies, his guru—as a divine manifestation. The fan, a symbol of royalty in classical Indian poetry,[4] signifies Bhole Nath's royal and, thus, godly status vis-à-vis that of Fateh Singh's, who, in fanning Bhole Nath, enacts his own subservience to the sadhu. Even though he is the king of Udaipur, Ganga Giri's narrative makes explicit the point that Fateh Singh's secular ranking falls well below that of Bhole Nath's spiritual ranking, who, in this legend, describes himself to his humble Rajput disciple in an almost semi-divine manner, as "the king of the world."

At the beginning of her narration, Ganga Giri emphasizes that Bhole Nathji "only sang *bhajans*," making this statement twice in her performance. To that extent, *bhajan* singing provides an overarching frame within which Ganga Giri constructs this legend. Her specific framing of the story helps to explain the reasoning behind the switched roles and hierarchy between Bhole Nath and Fateh Singh. Being a sadhu hardly entitles Bhole Nath to an unusual life of power and authority equivalent to (or greater than) that of a king. On the contrary, his authority, power, and status derive from his singing practices. Through storytelling, Ganga Giri explains that sadhus who sing to God become more powerful than kings. Her emphasis on *bhajan* through use of the example of the sadhu Bhole Nath constructs singing as *sannyās*. Ganga Giri's story also suggests that singing *bhajans* empowers sadhus and transforms them into divine beings. Her narrative makes explicit that Bhole Nath's *bhajans* turned him into a *siddha*. This term typically connotes the idea of persons who, having developed supernatural powers and abilities on the basis of more standard practices like meditation, yoga, and fasting have become divine in their own right. Using the word *siddha* to describe Bhole Nath, Ganga Giri implicitly associates his remarkable ascetic power and spiritual transformation into a *siddha* with *bhajans*, suggesting that *bhajans* themselves function as agents of renunciant power and transformation.

Theme 2: *Bhajan* Singing as Symbolic Medium of Currency Exchange[5]

Ganga Giri underscores that Bhole Nathji acquired everything, from inner power to outer material items, as well as gifts like money, gold, and food. She indicates that singing *bhajans* functions as a type of symbolic currency: sadhus sing *bhajans*, and in turn receive (sometimes inordinate amounts of) material wealth from their householder patrons. This idea of singing *bhajans* as symbolic currency of exchange represents another motif embedded in the sadhus' ideology of singing as efficacious, and appears in our next narrative.

In this context, Ganga Giri attributes the financial success of Devi Nath's ashram (another sadhu I worked with) to the *bhajan* singing of her exemplary *dādā* (grandfather) guru, Bhole Nathji. This story came about on account of an audience member, Nem Singh, an elderly male Rajput devotee of Ganga Giri, who inquired as to how Devi Nath, a paraplegic at the time, "earned" so much money for her ashram. As with most of the sadhus, Devi Nath has no economic base, and as such, no independent income. And yet, as Nem Singh poses, "Her money must come from somewhere?" Some members volunteered that her earnings (*kamāī*) came from the donations of generous temple visitors and disciples. Others, however, believed that the donations came directly from the Mahakaleshwar Temple Trust. Ganga Giri refuted all these possibilities. In her view, "the whole world gives money [to Devi Nath and her temple]" because of the "brilliance of Bhole Nath's *bhajans*." She explains:

GG: That's why a lot of money and gifts still come [there], because of the brilliance of his [Bhole Nath's] *bhajans*. Bhole Nath used to have a pair of shoes with a sword pin [attached to] them. That sword [on both shoes] was made of gold. The cover of the swords was made of gold. He used to tie a turban on his head. It was saffron-colored [*bhagwā*]. On the top of that turban was this big, gold broach. Have you seen his photo?

ANTOINETTE: Yes. I saw it last year [when I visited Devi Nath at the temple].

GG: He used to wear a long coat over his clothes, and not only was that coat gold-colored, it even had real gold buttons.

MALE DEVOTEE: You're talking about Bhole Nathji?

GG: Yes. One prostitute and drummer used to visit Bhole Nathji all the time just to acquire his wealth. They came [to the ashram] without being called. The prostitute used to dance at [the front] door, while the drummer used to play his drums at the back door. Bhole Nath didn't come out [to greet them]. He used to call Jnan Nath [his female sadhu disciple]: "Jnan Nath, come here!" He used to say. He would sit on a high seat [*āsan*] in a meditative position and give gold coins [to Jnan Nath]. He told her, "Here, give this to the drummer; give this to the prostitute"... He would give a plate full of gold coins. He used to sit like a king; he sat high on his seat and distributed [to Jnan Nath] gold coins. He used to eat only one *pūrī* [deep-fried bread]. He didn't eat *roṭī* [plain wheat bread]; he ate one *pūrī*. He didn't eat vegetables; he ate only one *pūrī*.

A: Only one *pūrī*? That's it?

GG: He ate only one *pūrī*; he didn't eat any vegetables. In [a period of] twenty-four hours, he ate only one *pūrī*. That's it.

A: Where did Bhole Nath's power [*śakti*] come from?
GG: From his *bhajans*. Where else? There's a lot of power in [singing] *bhajans*.

Although without an economic base, Bhole Nath, according to Ganga Giri's narrative, was not without economic support. He lived like a king, a view the legend underscores through symbols, such as: his "high seat"; the golden swords on his shoes; his turban's "big" gold broach; his gold-colored coat with its "real" gold buttons; and, of course, the gold coins, which signal Bhole Nath's disposable income. Each of these images signifies Bhole Nath's royal status. Like a king, he had (and commanded) servants in the form of disciples, including four female sadhus, to serve him day and night. Even Bhole Nath's daily diet of *pūrī* (fried breads) conveys his economic wealth and prestige. As I learned from conversations with sadhus and householders, *pūrīs* are usually served on special occasions, such as religious holidays, birthdays, and festivals. Since they require oil—a precious commodity in many Indian households—for their preparation, *pūrīs* not only cost more, but also take more time to make than *capātīs* (unleavened wheat bread), for example, which are a staple food in most North Indian diets. But Bhole Nath only ate a single *pūrī*. This detail supplies an important narrative frame that intimates his ascetic discipline and power. Nevertheless, Bhole Nath's subsistence on this particular luxury food item, rather than that of simply *capātī* or *dāl* (lentil soup), attests to his material wealth.

How did Bhole Nath produce so much wealth? "From singing his *bhajans*," Ganga Giri says. Where else could the power to create and sustain such wealth come from? But Ganga Giri does not narrate this legend to glorify material wealth—a perspective that would contradict the purpose of her singing *bhajans*. Rather, she shares this story in order to emphasize the inherent power and efficacy of singing *bhajans* to God: "There's a lot of power in *bhajans*," Ganga Giri affirms at the end of her telling. However, the story effectively illustrates the idea that *bhajans* are literally worth their weight in gold, and thus constitute what historian of religion Laurie Patton calls "a medium of exchange" between sadhus and householders (1996a, 208).

Ganga Giri accentuates that "a single *nirguṇī bhajan* [song which praises a formless god] is worth a single one-hundred-rupee note," implying that Bhole Nath must have sung only *nirguṇī bhajans*. She suggests that *nirguṇī bhajans* have monetary value greater than that of *saguṇī bhajans* (songs that praise the different manifestations of God). Ganga Giri says, "One *nirguṇī bhajan* is worth a single one-hundred-rupee note. Everything else is small change." The high value of *nirguṇī bhajans* derives from the fact that they are considered to be the sound vehicles of revelatory knowledge of the soul and of God (*ātmā* and/or *brahma-jnān*). As her statement implies, *nirguṇī bhajans* are better than the *saguṇī* type because, firstly, the *nirguṇī* contain the precious (and thus difficult to come by) *brahma-jnān*, and secondly, by singing these *bhajans*, the sadhus in turn receive from God wisdom in exchange for their renunciant *bhakti*. Much like her *nirguṇī bhajans*, Ganga Giri characterizes the *Bhagavad Gītā* as a text "worth a single one-hundred-rupee note," implying that she perceives this text to be illustrative of the empowering and transformative *brahma-jnān*. Ganga Giri situates *nirguṇī bhajans* within a similar conceptual framework of salvific speech. Like Krishna's divine speech in the *Gītā*, *bhajans* represent agents of power and transformation because they release liberating or, as Ganga Giri says, the "very expensive" knowledge. By virtue of their soteriological value, *bhajans* qualify as currency of exchange, thus bestowing material wealth and spiritual status upon the sadhus who sing them.

Ganga Giri's representations of *bhajans* as valuable symbolic currency parallel early and late Vedic textual depictions of divine speech as a type of wealth and currency of exchange. In her examination of several narratives, or myths, about money, Patton demonstrates that in the Vedic world *mantras* (sacred poetic verses) constituted a precious form of wealth and currency for Brahmin priests, in particular, whose lives depended on the exchange of words for material wealth in the form of livestock (e.g., goats, horses, and cows), jewels, money, and even wives (1996a). As with Ganga Giri's understanding of *bhajan* singing, in the Vedic world, too, as Patton discusses, *mantra* utterance—considered a sign of exemplary knowledge and skill—conferred prestige on its performers. In this light, *mantras*, Patton says, not only "function as agents of transformation that affect the identity of the individual in the process of exchanging" (1996a, 216), but also represent "a valuable commodity in the system of Vedic exchange" (1996a, 214). Patton observes:

> [*Mantras*'] value...was placed within a context of exchange, as the Vedic poets themselves tell us. We must take the language of *mantra* at face value, and realize that the very self-reflexivity of the work—the references to *mantra* and *sukta* (hymn) in Rg-Vedic verses themselves—are more often than not explicitly linked to the expected return for the offering of the constructed word. It would be needless to multiply the staggering number of possible examples here. Suffice it to say that one might read the simplest Rg-Vedic expression differently: "The man who honors you today, Agni and Soma, with this speech, bestow on him heroic strength, an increase of cows and noble steeds" (RV 1.93.2) can be seen as a statement of a transaction between two kinds of value, wherein one agent bestows the word and the other bestows the wealth. (Patton 1996a, 215)

Ganga Giri's statement about the monetary value of *nirguṇī bhajans* has more spiritual than material connotations. Nonetheless, if, as Patton argues with respect to the Vedic language of *mantras*, we take Ganga Giri's words at "face value," she, too, cues that right speech (i.e., singing) has material consequences for its speakers; more importantly, that sadhus, like the Brahmins of the ancient Vedic world, create their wealth through their words.

This theme of words as wealth and currency of exchange underlies Ganga Giri's Bhole Nath narrative. Embedded in this story is the notion that in exchange for his *bhajans*, or his religious teachings, Bhole Nath received valuable gifts of money, gold, jewels, clothing, food, and, according to one legend, a donkey (which he named Fateh Singh!). He did not purchase any of these items for himself. Rather, Bhole Nath's devotees and disciples showered him with such donations as symbols of their gratitude and appreciation. By singing his *bhajans*, Bhole Nath had given his listeners, including Fateh Singh, salvific words of power and transformation, which, in turn, and as the legend implies, enabled them to prosper in their lives. He also provided an important religious service for his constituency, on account of which he acquired great material wealth. Bhole Nath's *bhajans*, therefore, have a double signification: they represent his spiritual assets, and become the means by which he creates his own materials assets. *Bhajans* constitute a precious commodity in the system of sadhu-householder exchanges (Narayan 1989; Gross 2001).

One of my earliest collaborators, Sohan Lal (Dadaji), an elderly male householder in his late seventies, who drove me from one field site to another, told me to leave donations (*dakṣin*) for the sadhus in the form of cash (coins), food, or cloth, after meeting with them. However, he also cautioned that offerings should reflect the amount of learning, or knowledge, I had received from the sadhus. In this context, knowledge meant not only the sadhus' personal information about when and why they had renounced the world, but more importantly, the spiritual teachings they brought out through their "utterances" (*vāṇī*), such as their songs, stories, and proverbs, which would help me to understand their individual ascetic worlds. Sadhus who gave "good utterances" should, according to this collaborator's estimation, have received between fifty-one and one hundred and one rupees, whereas sadhus who did not should have been offered no more than eleven rupees. Dadaji, who acknowledged the eloquence and value of Ganga Giri's utterances, referring to her on several occasions as a "poet," felt that I should have given her at least one hundred and one rupees for what he characterized as our "conversational exchanges" (*bātcīt*).

I also heard many other householders discuss the legitimacy of several of the sadhus with whom I had established working relationships on the basis of the quality of their utterances. For instance, one afternoon in December of 2005, while traveling in a car owned by a relative of my Brahmin host family, the subject of sadhus arose. Of the six people present, four of them agreed that Ganga Giri was a "true sadhu [*saccā* sadhu]" because she sang "beautiful *bhajans*." In fact, my host father, Jagdish, who knew many sadhus in Mewar region, and who had described his personal interest in their way of life as a lifelong hobby (*śauk*), introduced me to four sadhus whose extraordinary reputations, I soon discovered, pivoted on their *bhajan* singing, storytelling, or textual recitation (or some combination of all three). With these sadhus I observed a correlation between their utterances, the wealth of their ashrams, and their perceived status among their devotees and disciples.

To illustrate an example: from our very first meeting in October 2005, Barfani Baba, an elderly male sadhu[6] with a gentle, childlike disposition, was always surrounded by people at his ashram—and with good reason. He shared his religious teachings with his devotees, disciples, and visitors by singing *bhajans* and telling engaging tales of sadhus, *sants*, demons and gods, and wayward devotees of God. On account of his own devotion to God, which he performed through the means of song and story, Barfani Baba had become a well-known religious figure in Rajasthan. The state's prime minister, Vasundhara Raje Scindia,[7] as Barfani Baba told me, had visited his ashram in order to have his *darśan* and receive his blessings. Some of the audience members, too, have traveled from as far as Maharashtra to hear Barfani Baba speak. One individual, an articulate male sadhu in his early twenties, told me he came from his ashram in Mumbai at the command of his guru to be in the presence of Barfani Baba, whom he referred to as a "great saint." This same disciple explained to me that if I wanted to "interview" Barfani Baba, I would have to ask him questions. Otherwise, "Babaji" would just sing for the duration of the *satsang*, because, in the words of my acquaintance, "this is how [Barfani Baba] speaks."

Apart from the throngs of people who flocked to his side daily for *darśan*, Barfani Baba was surrounded by a large number of valuable, material things. These items—donations from his numerous and wealthy householder patrons—indicated that not only the wealth Barfani Baba has amassed, but also his prestige as a powerful, yet humble sadhu, are the results of his "beautiful" utterances. As with Ganga Giri's depiction of Bhole Nath in popular Mewari lore, Barfani Baba's *bhajans* function as a symbolic currency of exchange between him and his patrons. Almost everyone who came to his ashram brought him something useful. Some devotees, like my host father, brought milk and sugar for Barfani Baba's tea; some brought him cigarettes; others brought him ochre-colored fabrics. More wealthy disciples bequeathed him expensive gifts in the form of a silver Rolex watch, gold jewelry (e.g., necklaces and bracelets), and even a round-trip ticket to Russia (the country of origin of one of his foreign disciples). Though surrounded by wealth, Barfani Baba explains to his enrapt audience that he has no use for such impermanent things. After narrating a tale about the four *yugas*, Barfani Baba frankly discusses the topic of wealth.

[B]ARFANI [B]ABA: The *mahātmās* [here, sadhus and *sants*] of the *satya yug* were such that they used to give, not take.

[J]AGDISH [S]ANADHYIA [MY BRAHMIN HOST FATHER]: And, in the *kali yug*, they only take.

BB: Yes, they take money... [But] before [in the *satya yug*], the *sants* used to give.

JS: Yes.

BB: They [the *sants*/sadhus] had a lot. They were healthy, too. Today's *sants* don't have anything, and they're [physically] sick. They think, "We need to have wealth [*dhān*]." But I live like I'm in the *satya yug*. I tell myself that I don't need wealth. I only need what God has given: shade, work, and sun... I don't have any need for wealth. But [the accumulation of wealth] has become a hobby [for some sadhus]. That's why they wish for it. Otherwise, it has no meaning.

JS: That's right.

BB: I don't wish for anything. I don't wish for wealth, and if it shall come to me today, I'll chase it away.

JS: Yes.

BB: And then I can sleep [live without worries]... You see all these things [in the ashram], they have no meaning for me.

JS: OK.

BB: What love can you have with these [material] things? Some things, some objects are very beautiful, right? [Some disciples tell me], "Wear this gold ring," or "wear this gold necklace." But if I wore all these things, I'd become heavy! These [things] are useless [to me].

JS: Right!

BB: If I don't wear them, I'll be very light, indeed.

JS: [laughs] Yes.

BB: "Wear this ring," "wear this necklace," they say. But this is a habit, isn't it? I don't need anything. People [devotees] have painted [these] walls [of the ashram]; they have given clothes, silver... Look how many holes they put in the walls [in order to hang pictures]? They've put so many holes in the wall. Hai Ram! I've become very upset [by all this]. I told myself that I need to remove everything [from the walls]. Now the holes are gone, and pictures are gone. So, I'm happy.

[AUDIENCE MEMBER]: You've become content, Babaji.

BB: . . . I don't need anything. Now, he [Barfani Baba mentions the name of a Russian disciple who was not present in the audience] has brought me this big, gold bracelet. How can I wear this thing? How can I wear so much weight?

JS: Yes.

BB: Where is it? [He searches for the bracelet]. I know it's here someplace. And look at this ring [that this same disciple has brought me]. It has two-hundred fifty grams of gold. And how many necklaces he has brought! He has given so many things, but I don't need them.

JS: Yes.

BB: I become unhappy with such uselessness [*khāmo-khām*]. What's the value of these things to me? Over there [points to a section of the ashram] are many precious things . . . But I don't need any of it! I don't need anything. It's all right, because they [devotees] give these things with love. You [the audience] have come, therefore I have everything. I have your love, so I have everything. I'm happy.

JS: Yes!

BB: What is my work here? I have to sing my *bhajans*. From [singing] *bhajans*, everything happens.

Barfani Baba's public denouncement of wealth (*dhān*) is significant. Notice, however, that he does not reject wealth itself, but rather the sadhus and *sants* who have become attached to it. This narrative frame enables Barfani Baba to distinguish himself from the class of greedy sadhus whose obsession with money and material things has become, as he says, "a hobby." Barfani Baba is poignantly honest about the fact that he has acquired a lot of wealth at his ashram. He not only describes, but even shows, his audience the gold necklaces, the bracelets, and the rings that his Russian disciple offered him as a sign of his love for Barfani Baba. But Barfani Baba distinguishes himself from other sadhus who might also possess such items by emphasizing that these materials hold absolutely no meaning for him. "What's the value of these things to me?" he asks, implying that sadhus, who have renounced the world, "don't need wealth." Barfani Baba, in fact, states eight times that he does not "need anything," especially wealth. I have also observed the female sadhus make similar pronouncements in contexts where their devotees present them with material gifts.[8] Barfani Baba says, "I don't wish for wealth, and if it shall come to me today, I'll chase it away." He, of course, does not chase his wealth away, since, as he later notes, devotees give it "with love," and as such, "it's all right."

Nevertheless, by emphasizing that he does not need wealth, and that material goods lack both meaning and value for him, Barfani Baba implies a fundamental concept which repeatedly surfaces in the sadhus' rhetoric of renunciation: detachment. In this narrative, Barfani Baba performs his renunciant identity via an implied notion of detachment, and in doing so, establishes his legitimacy as a sadhu, despite his being surrounded by a lot of wealth. If Barfani Baba requires anything, it is simply his *bhajans*, and the love of his devotees who come to hear him sing. For him, love, rather than gold, money, and expensive gifts, identifies the "right" currency of exchange for sadhus, especially since, in theory, renouncers should neither keep nor touch these items. "What is my work here?" asks Baba; he answers his own question with "to sing *bhajans*." He himself tells the audience that "by [singing] *bhajans*, everything happens." This statement parallels the way that Ganga Giri has described her *bhajans*. Like her, Barfani Baba also views his songs and his love as "expensive" sadhu commodities. More significantly, he suggests that, unlike the sadhus whose wish for wealth attracted it into their lives, his *bhajans* themselves have created everything from his health to his material wealth. Barfani Baba further indicates that singing *bhajans* allows him to offer treasures of spiritual wealth to devotees as a sign of his own love—an act that, in turn, makes him a "giver" sadhu, rather than, as he points out, a "taker" sadhu, that is, a "svadhu."[9]

Theme 3: *Bhajan* Singing as *Sevā* to Humanity

Barfani Baba's representation of *bhajan* singing as a selfless means of giving devotees love and knowledge illuminates the third theme, of *bhajan* singing as *sevā* to humanity. However, unlike the previous two themes examined, that of *bhajan* singing as *sevā*, and more broadly, of *bhajan* singing as asceticism, appears more in the female sadhus' narratives than in those of the male sadhus. This is not to say that the male sadhus did not discuss *sevā*; they did. They did not, however, associate *sevā* with singing *bhajans*, or singing with *sannyās*. This difference speaks to the sadhus' gendered views of the meaning and purpose of *bhajan* singing and that of asceticism. While only two of the fifteen male sadhus made suggestions that singing functions as *sevā* to humanity (and God), neither of them explicitly defined asceticism in terms of *bhajan* singing or renunciant *bhakti* more globally. In contrast, most of the female sadhus, who equated *bhajan* singing with asceticism, described *bhajans* as a type of blessing (*āśīrvād; duā*) that should be offered to everyone, regardless of gender, caste, economic status. In the views of these sadhus, the efficacy and power of *bhajan* singing stems not only from its function as a blessing for humanity, but also from the sharing that occurs between the sadhus and their householder devotees in the process of singing. In this way, singing *bhajans* for others' benefit is what makes this renunciant *bhakti* practice an act of *sevā* to the world and to God.[10] Tulsi Giri explains,

> *Bhajans* are blessings for you, for me, for everyone. Therefore, we [sadhus] sing *bhajans* for the young and old people. If we don't sing *bhajans*, we commit a sin. If you go see some sadhu and he's just sitting there, he's wasting time. And if you sit with such a baba, you'll waste time, too. Every moment something dies. Whenever you grind wheat, flour, or corn, some creature [*jānwar*] dies; even if you bring water [from a well], a creature dies. [But] by singing *bhajans*, the sin [of killing creatures] is removed. [If sadhus don't sing *bhajans*], who will take this sin [away]? Someone has to take [away] the sin, right?

Although she does not mention the term, Tulsi Giri suggests that *bhajan* singing represents *sevā* in several ways. First, she equates *bhajans* with blessings and makes evident her understanding that "babas" or sadhus who sing them "for the young and [for] the old," bless humanity, whereas those who do not "commit a sin." Implicit in her words is the idea that *bhajan* singing constitutes the expected duty of sadhus, a practice they must perform as the "beggars of God." As with the female sadhus of Haridwar with whom Khandelwal (2004) worked, for most of the Rajasthani sadhus, too, *sevā* to humanity also signifies love for God and the world.

Second, Tulsi Giri further reveals her perception of singing *bhajans* as *sevā* when she emphasizes that this practice enables sadhus to remove the sins of humanity. From her perspective, sadhus have a duty not just to God, but to the world as well. If, as Tulsi Giri implies in this passage, sadhus do not sing *bhajans*, then, as she makes explicit toward the end of the discussion, "[w]ho will take [away] the sin[s]?" In this conversation we find associations between *bhajan* singing as *sevā*, and *sevā* as love, for all the moving and unmoving, seen and unseen "creatures" of the world. Importantly, for Tulsi Giri, sin is not simply intentional acts (murder or suicide), but also unintentional acts, such as eating food or drinking water, through which humans, in particular, take the lives of others so that they may continue to live on the planet. Though unintentional, these acts, in Tulsi Giri's view, fall within the category of sin, for which there must be some type of atonement.[11] She comments: "Every moment something dies. Whether you grind wheat, flour, or corn, some creature dies.

Even if you bring water [from a well] a creature dies... Someone *has* to take the sin [away], right?" Here, Tulsi Giri refers to the creatures which humans cannot readily see with the naked eye, those beings who sacrifice their lives in order that humans may live. Thus, for her, *bhajan* singing represents *sevā* because of its dual function: it serves equally as a blessing and an effective means for the atonement of sins. By singing *bhajans*, these sadhus understand that they bless the living as well as honor the dead.

In the following conversation, Tulsi Giri explicitly associates *bhajan* singing with *sevā*. Moreover, she describes this salvific *bhakti* practice as a "*sevā* of connection [*dorī*]," whereby sadhus create a relationship with God and with the people (or creatures) whom they serve as manifestations of the divine. Thus, Tulsi Giri indicates her understanding of singing as *sannyās*.

> I sing *bhajans*. I mean, we [sadhus] do God's *sevā* by singing *bhajans*. For the helpless people, we make them confident. We make their pain and suffering go away... It's like this, through *sevā* we become connected with God. For us, it's not like *sevā* doesn't happen until and unless we wash God's *mūrtī* and spread [God's] flowers. [Tulsi Giri distinguishes between *pūjā* and *sevā* here]. That's not *sevā* for us. Everyone does that kind of *sevā*; the world does that kind of *sevā*, [but] we don't. Our *sevā* happens from above. It's a *sevā* of connection, the connection we make with God [by singing *bhajans*]... We [sadhus] are at the feet of God. We are the ones who do the *sevā* of God. But when [householders] do God's *sevā*, they give water, flowers, and so forth. Their *sevā* happens like this, but our *sevā* is different... This is how we understand *sevā*: you are God for us [sadhus]. You are God for me. Even a child is God, and the old people, too... To us, everyone is the same. Everyone is God. This is *sevā*—the *sevā* of sadhus.

In her description, Tulsi Giri highlights some of the themes we have already discussed. She suggests the transformative power of *bhajans*, and her belief that they work as a vehicle of blessing and atonement, in the context of her statement that through *bhajan* singing "we [sadhus] make [the helpless people] confident and we make their pain... go away." But the time Tulsi Giri spends differentiating *pūjā* from *sevā* indexes her perception of singing *bhajans* as a renunciant *bhakti* expression through which sadhus experience and engender their asceticism as *sevā*. *Bhakti*, a term derived from the Sanskrit root, *bhaj*, which means not only "to worship," but also "to share," denotes the love that devotees (householders and sadhus) share with the divine and with each other. This idea of *bhakti* as "sharing" undergirds Tulsi Giri's view of *bhajan* singing as "a *sevā* of connection," through which she shares her feelings of love and devotion with *bhagwān*. And yet, as Tulsi Giri carefully points out, singing *bhajans* simultaneously allows sadhus to construct relationships with human beings, and thereby, to share their love and devotion, and even, as Ganga Giri contends, their "expensive" knowledge, with their devotees and disciples.

If *pūjā* and *sevā* both connote the notion of connection, of sharing love and devotion with the divine, why does Tulsi Giri distinguish between these two terms, associating the former with householders and the latter with sadhus? Several times in her discussion, Tulsi Giri characterizes householder *pūjā* as *sevā*, indicating her understanding that householder *bhakti* similarly illustrates an act of loving service to God. So what, then, makes householder *bhakti* different from sadhu *bhakti*? From Tulsi Giri's perspective, the difference is that, in addition to serving God's *mūrtīs*, sadhus also serve humans as they would serve God. This is the *sevā* of the sadhus. In Tulsi Giri's words: "It's not like *sevā* does not happen [for sadhus] until and unless we wash God's *mūrtī* and spread God's flowers... The *sevā* [of householders] happens like this, but our *sevā* is different." For Tulsi Giri, *sevā* involves seeing everyone, despite gender, caste, age, and class distinctions, as "the same," and treating everyone as she would treat God's *mūrtīs*. "To us," as Tulsi Giri says, "everyone is God," and for this reason she sings *bhajans* in the expression of her own *sevā* to the world. Her words allude to what Ganga Giri often has taught in *satsang*: *bhajans* "are for everyone," not only for God. Tulsi Giri's construction of *bhajan* singing as *sevā*/*bhakti* and as vernacular asceticism is, therefore, gendered. Unlike several of the male sadhus, who also suggested that *bhajans* are transformative and function as symbolic currency of exchange between sadhus and householders, and who sing *bhajans* to offer devotion to God, the female sadhus link this practice, and as such, renunciant *bhakti* on the whole, with singing *bhajans*. For these sadhus, singing *bhajans* qualifies simultaneously as *bhakti* and *tapas*.

Bhakti *and* Tapas: *The Interpretive Frameworks behind Singing* Bhajans

A broader interpretive framework of meaning informs the sadhus' ideology of *bhajan* singing as transformative, as currency of exchange, and as *sevā*. The foremost idea the sadhus emphasize in their practices is *tap* or *tapas*. In his study of asceticism in Vedic India, Walter Kaelber (1989) observes that *tapas* doubly refers to practices of self-sacrifice and to the heat resulting from such discipline(s).[12] As Chapter 3 discussed, *tapas*, a pivotal concept in Brahmanical ascetic/yogic frameworks, connotes asceticism. *Tapas* is also associated in these classical frameworks with practices of extreme self-sacrifice that sadhus are thought to voluntarily undertake in order to bring about the physical pain and mental discomfort that are seen as necessary for spiritual development and transformation (Lamb 2008, 584; Klostermaier 1996; Pearson 1996; Olivelle 1992; Stoler Miller 1996). This schematic of *tapas*, as Ramdas Lamb has said, is thought "to inspire renunciation . . . and the ability to transcend self-imposed limits that normally slow individuals from progressing on the path to the Absolute" (2008, 584).

This predominant understanding of *tapas*, however, captures a primarily masculine model and interpretation of asceticism. Although the female sadhus acknowledge the more orthodox and text-based notions of *tapas*, which hinge on extreme psychosomatic performances of sacrifice for self-realization and liberation from rebirth, they emphasize, nonetheless, verbal performances of singing *bhajans* in their representations of this concept (cf. Hausner 2007; Lamb 2002; Gross 2001). *Bhajan* singing is equivalent to *tapas* for these sadhus. Ganga Giri, for example, talks about traveling alone throughout India and "without a ticket" as a younger sadhu. When a female householder audience member in the group inquires how she was able to do this, Ganga Giri matter-of-factly replies, "It's all from the power [*tap*] of my *bhajans*." On another occasion, Ganga Giri characterizes the practice of speaking the truth as *tapas*. She says,

> There is no greater penance [*tap*] than speaking the truth. So tell the truth. People say, "Go to the jungle and practice penance." But I say, why go to the jungle for penance? Sit here and speak the truth. This is penance [*tapas*]. This is asceticism [*tapasyā*].

Implied in this passage is Ganga Giri's understanding that singing *bhajans* constitutes *tapasyā*, the act of speaking the truth.[13] She implicitly situates singing *bhajans* within the larger classical framework of *tapas*. In Sanskrit texts like the *Bhagavad Gītā*, for example (a text Ganga Giri recites daily, and which she invokes in her discourses), speaking the truth identifies an act of *tapas*, of asceticism.[14] It is equally significant, however, that Ganga Giri's statement "Sit here and speak the truth," indexes *satsang*, a *sant bhakti* concept, which the sadhus define as a "community of truth" where sadhus and *sants* (those who speak truth) gather to remember and praise God. Ganga Giri's words suggest her understanding of *bhajan* singing as *tapas* and of *satsang* as a ripe context for its practice. As she says, why escape to the jungle to do *tapas* when one can do so [by singing] in the company of saints? *Tapas* connotes speaking truth, and in Ganga Giri's view, singing *bhajans*. "This," she argues, "is *tapasyā*." Defining *bhajan* as *tapas* indicates that she draws on *sant bhakti* to construct singing as *sannyās*. In this framework, the "good people" praise God by singing *bhajans*, words of truth and power. This notion also implies that the female sadhus see sadhu and *sant* identities as equivalent. They say that the *sants* left everything behind so that they could devote their entire existence to singing *bhajans* and, by implication, to *satsang*. To them, the *sants* embody detachment, knowledge, and devotion—the three preeminent virtues that make it possible for the female sadhus to associate *sant bhakti* with *sannyās*.

The sadhus' views of *bhajan* singing as *tapas*, and by implication, *sant bhakti* as asceticism, shed light on the relationship these sadhus perceive between *bhajans, bhakti*, and power. For the sadhus, *bhakti* is an immediate and instrumental source of power behind their *bhajans*, infusing their songs with power and energy and making them reservoirs and agents of transformation. Because singing is thought to emerge from and enact feelings of *bhakti*, the sadhus do not distinguish between *bhajans* and *bhakti* in their descriptions of power. Both the medium (*bhajan*), and the intense emotion (*bhakti*) communicated through means of that medium, signify the same power source to them. This seems to be the idea Ganga Giri relates in her statement, "My *bhajans* are my power." We could interpret this to mean that, more globally, her *bhakti* empowers her and that, more specifically, her *bhajans* empower her as a sadhu. Both meanings are possible because, for Ganga Giri, *bhajans* and *bhakti* are "the same thing." And yet, her words, which the other sadhus also echoed, give the sense that *bhajan* and *bhakti* are different, that *bhajan*, as equivalent to *tapas*, displaces *bhakti*.[15] Or, to put it another way, that *sant bhakti* and the generic (householder) *bhakti* that Tulsi Giri differentiates between in her use of the word *pūjā* represent radically distinct categories of practice and experience. Recall from our earlier discussion that Ganga Giri insists that *bhajan*—especially in its *nirguṇī* form—has the powerful *brahma-jnān*, and that (knowledge) power establishes singing as asceticism. The sadhus' view of *brahma-jnān* as a transformative source for the ripening of asceticism is significant. Apart from knowledge, their idea of *brahma-jnān* signals the necessary attitude of detachment that they, like sadhus in general, associate with *sannyās*. *Bhajan*, therefore, not only creates asceticism as devotional, but also flags the two qualities that distinguish it from *bhakti*.

Moreover, while *brahma-jnān* may result from *bhakti*, to the sadhus, it remains distinct from *bhakti*. By this logic, *bhajan* has to be different from *bhakti* per se, and the *brahma-jnān* that *bhajan* contains creates *bhajan* as *tapas*, the power by which sadhus transform themselves. The sadhus' equation of *bhajan* singing with *tapas* further suggests that the power of *bhajans* comes from the singing itself, not only from the *bhakti* out of which it arises. Singing creates *bhajan* as something more than *bhakti*, because it releases *brahma-jnān* and develops detachment, and both transform singers (and listeners) of *bhajans*. Thus, singing creates *bhajan* as *sant bhakti*, which is synonymous with devotional asceticism. Since singing *bhajans* produces *tapas*, it may be seen as that activity in which *bhakti* (as the general emotion that stimulates singing) and *brahma-jnān* (as the power in the song) are "cooked" (*tapas*, after all, means "heat") and combined to generate a power that is more than the sum of its individual parts.

The power that emerges from this mixing of *bhakti* and *brahma-jnān* together embodies a *sant* kind of power that transforms singers (or *bhakts* in general) into sadhus and creates singing as *sannyās*. The sadhus' view of singing as *sannyās* synthesizes Brahmanical and *sant bhakti* models of power and the efficacy of practice. Whereas the classical model links *sannyās* with the production of knowledge and detachment, and with meditation, yoga, and fasting, by which it is produced, *sant bhakti* undermines the role of knowledge in divine experience and emphasizes the salvific power of love and relationship that singing *bhajans* is thought to evoke and create as the way to unite with God. Perhaps the distinction that informs sadhus' views of *bhajan* and *bhakti* explains why they insist on distinguishing between householder and sadhu kinds of *bhakti*: the former being that which "anyone" can do; the latter being what the *sants*, or "real" sadhus, do.

Although the male sadhus I know sing *bhajans* (Barfani Baba is a good example), they do not make the connection between *bhajan* and *tapas*, and singing and *sannyās*, that the female sadhus tend to make. Also, while the male sadhus talk about *tapas* in relation to *sannyās*, for them *tapas* signifies the "heat" or "fire" (*āg*) that asceticism generates. Their use of the language of heat models the masculine interpretation of *tapas* featured in the dominant textual discourse (Khandelwal 2001, 157–179). By contrast, the female sadhus say that *tapas* produces both revelatory knowledge and liberating detachment—what they refer to as the *ātmā-jnān* and the *brahma-jnān*, terms by which they mean the realization of one's true nature ("self") as the universal *brahman* ("Self"). Thus, knowledge and detachment signify as much a source of power as *bhakti* to the sadhus. Santosh Puri says, "from singing *bhajans* you receive knowledge... Without *bhajans*, you cannot receive the light of knowledge. It never blossoms in the heart." Without ruling out the possibility entirely, for the sadhus, the correlation between *tapas* and power has less to do with heat production than with "the blossoming of knowledge" in the heart and mind.

Bhakti, Brahmacārya, *and Power: Gendered Vernacular Models*

The female sadhus' views of *bhajan* singing as *tapas* index a signal perspective in their understandings of the relationship between *brahmacārya* and *bhakti* in asceticism as practiced. In her essay on the ways *brahmacārya* is gendered in Brahmanical textual discourse, Meena Khandelwal explains that this concept has been primarily understood as celibacy, and thus, associated with maleness and semen conservation (Khandelwal 2001, 157–179). For this reason, Khandelwal maintains, "celibacy has often been attributed with the purpose of obtaining ritual purity or magical power rather than moral goodness or virtue" (158). According to this dominant masculine model of *brahmacārya*, "women are... said to be incapable of celibacy" (158). Yet, *brahmacārya* constitutes much more than "abstaining from sex" (157). Khandelwal observes,

> [B]rahmacarya... has a primary meaning of "lifestyle to obtain Brahma" and is thus understood... when practiced by ascetics, as a means to spiritual liberation rather than an end in itself. Sexual abstinence is one essential aspect of an overall lifestyle that usually includes a strict vegetarian diet, the avoidance of most stimulants and intoxicants, and the practice of meditation or some other... spiritual discipline. (Khandelwal 2001, 157)

On the basis of her research with female sadhus in Haridwar, North India, Khandelwal moves beyond "the hydraulic model of semen retention," and proposes instead an alternative (female) model of the concept that argues not only for a psychosocial, but also an ethical, understanding of celibacy. Khandelwal states, "none of the women I interviewed suggested that women do not benefit from celibacy or that they are incapable of it" (2004, 159). She further explains, "In sannyasinis' understandings of brahmacarya, celibacy refers not to a strictly physiological control of seed but to the control of passions, attachments, and appetite, which are metaphorically and metonymically related to bodily fluids" (2004, 169). In proposing an alternative model of *brahmacārya*, Khandelwal does not suggest that it is exclusive to women. Rather, this "less physiological and arguably less androcentric" model of *brahmacārya* shows that celibacy, at least for the female sadhus with whom she worked, is not simply about the production of power, whether magical or ritual, because, as she argues, "brahmacarya focuses on moral [and] ritual purity, a lifestyle of self-restraint, and emotional detachment" (2004, 173).

Although the Rajasthani female sadhus do not explicitly speak about *brahmacārya*, their associating *bhajan* with *tapas* and, more broadly, singing with *sannyās* similarly contributes an alternative model of *brahmacārya* to the mainstream Brahmanical notion as a lifestyle of "singing to God"—that is, a path of love, devotion, and knowledge. Because *brahmacārya* in connection with *sannyās* intimates a life of *tapas* (including celibacy), I consider the sadhus' teachings on *tapas* to be indicative of their views on *brahmacārya*. To this extent, the sadhus' practices perform a devotional model of *brahmacārya* (as a lifestyle of *tapas*), by which they offer *bhakti* to *bhagwān*, develop knowledge, and share those qualities with their devotees and disciples whom they, in turn, serve as manifestations of *bhagwān*. Unlike the byproducts of heat and seminal fluid proposed by the dominant Brahmanical model, a devotional model of *brahmacārya* understands *bhakti* and *jnān* to be the immediate emotional or spiritual results of the sadhus' practices. And, although the sadhus use the language of power, rather than that of moral purity and emotional detachment, in their discussions of *tapas*, a devotional model of *brahmacārya* complements Khandelwal's psychosocial and ethical model. For the female sadhus, "power" is viewed in the *sant* terms of *bhakti*, and *tapas* (as singing *bhajans*) represents a form of *sevā* to humanity. In this respect, a devotional model of *brahmacārya* as performed in the sadhus' practices incorporates a moral-ethical vision and underscores emotional detachment.

Bhajans *as Resources for Vernacular Asceticism:* Nirguṇī *Themes*

Nirguṇī sant bhajans provide a significant resource in the female sadhus' vernacular asceticism. They speak about *tapasyā* or *sannyās* (terms they used interchangeably) through use of *nirguṇī* motifs like, "crossing one's boat over the ocean of existence," "keeping the precious diamond," or "holding *bhajans* tightly in the heart/mind." Even the largely, but not exclusively, *sant* idea that *bhakti* is "expensive," "precious," or "difficult," which are common themes in medieval *nirguṇī* poetry, surfaces in their rhetoric.[16] The asceticism the sadhus perform in the singing of *nirguṇī bhajans* is thus based on *sant* teachings (*sant mat*) (Vaudeville 1987; Schomer 1987; Hess 1987a; 1987b; 2002). The *sant mat*, related through poetic utterances (*dohā* or *pad*[17]) known as the *sant vāṇī*, supply the conceptual frameworks on which the sadhus draw to construct a female tradition of *sannyās* and, in doing so, craft singing as a female way of being a sadhu. Although singing *nirguṇī bhajans* in the transmission of *sant* teachings is not unique to the female sadhus (Henry 1995; Lorenzen 1996; Martin 2000,

2003; Hawley and Juergensmeyer 1988), their use of this rhetoric to perform *sannyās* as the asceticism of the *sants* reveals a new and dynamic context, in which *sant* poetry becomes embedded in everyday vernacular religion.

The *bhajans* that the sadhus attribute to the *sants* are synonymous with what they characterize as *nirguṇī bhakti*. In their *bhajan* sings, the sadhus perform *nirguṇī bhakti* as a life of fellowship (*satsang*), where "the good people" (*sants*) celebrate together the presence and power of the divine in the world. *Nirguṇī bhakti*, therefore, describes what these sadhus see as a life of devotional asceticism. They see *sant bhajans* as superlative sources of *nirguṇī* knowledge, and while *nirguṇī* and *saguṇī bhajans* are part of their performance repertoires, most of the female sadhus agree that sadhus, in particular, should sing and contemplate the *nirguṇī* type. In their views, these songs make explicit what asceticism is and how it should be lived. Because *nirguṇī bhajans* are key sources in the sadhus' crafting of asceticism, I limit my analysis to these songs.

But what comprises "*nirguṇī* knowledge" and *nirguṇī bhakti* for the sadhus? What are the outstanding *nirguṇī* themes that they accent in their performances? In constructing *sannyās*-as-lived, the sadhus underscore six major themes: (1) devotion to a nameless and formless *bhagwān*; (2) communion with the divine; (3) *bhakti* as "priceless" for asceticism; (4) *bhakti* as difficult or "expensive"; (5) complete surrender to and dependence on God for everything; and (6) repetition of the divine name for inner transformation.[18] Apart from these themes, the sadhus also stress that asceticism is above all a path of knowledge, action, and effort, and, along with these, love.

While I collected over fifty songs from the sadhus, below I examine only six *nirguṇī bhajans*. These *bhajans* illustrate the *nirguṇī sant* themes outlined earlier, as well as the broader themes of asceticism described in this book which the sadhus foreground or cue more globally in their performances. These *bhajans* also tend to be the songs from their song repertoires that the sadhus sing most frequently. These *bhajans* were all performed in or as *satsang*, and I discuss those contexts and the sadhus' interpretations of their songs as they emerged in and outside of *satsang*.

"Prabhu, You Have a Thousand Names": God as Nameless and Formless

In most *satsangs*, the sadhus describe their understandings of the divine through use of *nirguṇī sant* teachings of God as nameless and formless. For instance, in one *bhajan satsang*, Tulsi Giri and Ganga Giri speak about their perceptions of God in this very manner. Tulsi Giri says that while our parents "give birth to us... there is only one [God] who creates [everything in the universe].” She further explicates that God, though a single creator, has many names, such as Ishwar, Prabhu, and Gajananad (a name for Ganesh). In her words: “You can call [God] by any name, but God [*bhagwān*] is one.” Ganga Giri replies, “God is one and formless [*nirākār*].” Then she comments, “We say it like this,” and sings the following *nirguṇī bhajan*:

Prabhu, you have a thousand names.
Say the names Lakvi and Kankotri.

Hari, you have a thousand names.
Some call you Ram,
Some call you Radhesyam.
Some call you Ram,
Some call you Radhesyam.
Some call you Kishor of Nand.

Prabhu, you have a thousand names.
Say the names Lakvi and Kankotri.

In Mathura, you are called Mohan.
In Gokul, you are called Gwaliyo.
In Dwarka, you are called Raja Ranchor.

Say the names Lakvi and Kankotri.
Prabhu, you have a thousand names.

In this *satsang*, Ganga Giri keys her performance with the statement, “We say it like this,” a comment she makes immediately before she sings *bhajans* before a rapt multicaste audience (Bauman 1977, 15–24). By doing so, she provides an important performance frame that displays her use of *bhajans* as, to use Roger Abrahams’s words, “a tool for persuasion” that enables her to explain the concept of God as nameless and formless (1968, 146, cited from Narayan 1995, 258). Although the *bhajan* articulates the opposite notion of Ganga Giri’s and Tulsi Giri’s teaching—that God has many names and, thus, many forms—the context of their performance infuses the song with the underlying *nirguṇī* message that God is ultimately one and, therefore, nameless and formless. Both of the sadhus continue to make this idea explicit by means of their commentaries, which follow this sing. As Ganga Giri says, “In this way God is nameless [*anāmi*].”

But why do Ganga Giri and Tulsi Giri sing a *bhajan* with Vaishnava overtones to explain a *nirguṇī sant* conception of the divine? If we examine the names discussed in the *bhajan*, most of them either explicitly mention or allude to God in the forms of Ram and Krishna, two of the most popular incarnations of Vishnu. And yet, the *sants* (particularly the northern group) did not worship Vaishnava forms of divinity, but rather understood God in terms of the ineffable and all-pervading Absolute (cf. Vaudeville 1987, 26; Hess 1987a; 1987b). Also, neither Ganga Giri nor Tulsi Giri ever directly mention the *sants* in their commentary, and, unlike the *bhajans* we examine below, this song has no *cāp* (the signature line where the name of the *sant* who is thought to have composed the *bhajan* appears at the end of the poem) that would legitimize it as a *sant* teaching. How do we know, then, that *sant* views underlie these sadhus' interpretations and experiences of the divine as nameless and formless, and by extension, their constructions of asceticism?

In the discussion preceding the singing of the *bhajan*, apart from using the general term, *bhagwān*, Tulsi Giri refers to God as Ishwar, Prabhu, and Hari; the first term is a general one meaning "Lord," while the other two represent names for Vishnu. As we shall see in some of the *nirguṇī bhajans* later on, these are some of the same divine names that appear consistently in the poetry of the *sants*. The *sants* themselves, then, according to several scholars, imagined and communicated *nirguṇī* notions of the divine by borrowing both their poetic imagery and their God-language from the wellspring of Vaishnava *bhakti* traditions (cf. Schomer 1987). Vaudeville observes, "The Sants . . . cling exclusively to the Vaishnava names of God such as Ram, Hari, Govinda, Mukunda, Madhava, Murari, Sarangapani—with a special emphasis on the name of 'Ram' " (1987, 32). However, despite their use of such names, the *sants* neither conceptualized nor experienced the divine in the anthropomorphic manner implied by Vaishnava *bhakti* (Vaudeville 1987, 32; Lorenzen 1996). As Hess explains in relation to Kabir's poetry,

> Kabir's poetry is full of exhortations to recite the name of Ram, to devote oneself to Ram, to drop everything except Ram. It should be emphasized that this Ram is not the deity of popular Hindu mythology, incarnation of Vishnu and hero of the Ramayana epic. Though he sometimes addresses King Ram, Lord, or Hari (a name of Vishnu) in the songs, many references to Ram . . . indicate that his Ram is primarily a sound, a mantra consisting of the long and short syllables, Ra-ma. (Hess, with Shukdeo Singh, 2002, 3–4)

In their use of the names of Prabhu, Hari, and Ram to represent *nirguṇī* concepts of the divine, Ganga Giri and Tulsi Giri not only allude to *sant* interpretations about the nature of God, but also understand and explain these concepts much like the *sants* themselves understood and imagined them in their songs. As with the *sants*, the sadhus, too, teach that God is one, and nameless and formless, by singing *bhajans* that praise the various Vaishnava divine names.

In praising Vaishnava notions of the divine name, the female sadhus, again like the *sants*, further index a particular type of *nirguṇī* interpretation of God. While *sant*-constructed *nirguṇī* conceptualizations of the divine suggest that God is simultaneously impersonal and ineffable,[19] both the *sants* and the female sadhus understand and relate to a nameless and formless God in an intensely personal way. In this *satsang*, Tulsi Giri and Ganga Giri suggest that a *nirguṇī*-conceived *bhagwān*, though nameless and formless, also has the spiritual (and relatable) qualities of love and compassion that make a *bhakti*-driven relationship between deity and devotee possible. Commenting on the *bhajan*, Ganga Giri and Tulsi Giri together explain that

GG: When devotees have difficulty [*kaṣṭ*], so many evil [*duṣṭ*] things are spread [in the universe]. There are many reasons [for why difficulty/evil spreads]. There is not only one reason, but many [reasons]. For many reasons, then, *bhagwān* incarnates [as a particular form]. When [God] incarnates s/he take a name…

TG: So, if *bhakts* are in difficulty, Prabhu incarnates, I mean God takes birth [in some form].

GG: For this reason God has a name.

TG: Right. When God takes birth, he takes a name.

GG: [After he incarnates in a form] God kills the evil [ones] and crosses his devotees over the ocean of existence.

TG: And, like this, he gets a name.

Both Tulsi Giri's and Ganga Giri's explanations about the reasons for which God receives a name illustrate their perceptions that God incarnates in the world or, as Tulsi Giri says, "takes birth," in order to rescue his devotees from the difficulties and evil that spread in the world as a result of the lack of (or the decline of) righteousness (*dharm*) in the universe. Their commentary draws on classical Puranic *bhakti* views of divine incarnation (e.g., those found in the *Viṣṇu Purāṇas*)[20] and implies the *sant* view that God's actions in the world derive from his love and compassion for devotees.[21] Though not explicitly stated in this *satsang*, I have heard many of the sadhus describe God as love. "Love is what God is," Ganga Giri accentuates in our meetings. Hence, from Tulsi Giri's and Ganga Giri's perspectives, a *bhakt*-*bhagwān* relationship is entirely possible, because God still loves and cares for those who love and remember him. More significantly, he does so without concern for the gender, caste, or class qualities of his devotees.

An embedded social message of the inherent spiritual equality of all devotees thus underlies these sadhus' singing. Their commentary also indicates perceptions of *bhakt-bhagwān* duality. This interpretation of the divine-human relationship supports a classic *bhakti*-centered approach to God. As Vaudeville notes, "without some distinction between the Lord (Bhagvan) and the devotee (bhakta), the very notion of '*nirguṇa* bhakti'...would bring about the abolition of bhakti itself" (1987, 27). But just as important, the sadhus' implied perceptions of *bhakt-bhagwān* duality reflect the *sant* teachings about the divine-human relationship. *Sant*-conceived *nirguṇī* notions of God as nameless and formless coincide with Advaita Vedanta interpretations, "which den[y] any real distinction between the soul and God and urges man to recognize within himself his true divine nature" (Vaudeville 1987, 26). Nevertheless, as Vaudeville observes, the *sants* described their experiences in terms of "union with" God, rather than in Vedantic terms of the absolute dissolution of all distinctions between deity and devotee. They obliquely made known their perceptions of divine-human duality in the construction of *nirguṇī bhakti*. In performing devotional asceticism, most of the sadhus rely on the *sant* language of "meeting God" or "melting into God" often featured in their *nirguṇī bhajans* to articulate their understanding of the *bhakt-bhagwān* relationship as an encounter of love, devotion, and duality.

"Melting Into God": Divine Union

Another *nirguṇī* theme that the sadhus bring up in their sings concerns that of "melting into [*līn ho jānā*] God," or communion with God (*bhagwān se milnā*). For the majority of the sadhus, perhaps no *sant* or *bhakt* epitomizes the notion of divine encounter with God better than Mira Bai. She models the unconventional yet extraordinary life of devotional asceticism as a community-centered and celebratory path of remembering God "with the good people" to the sadhus. On one occasion, Tulsi Giri, Ganga Giri, and Jnan Nath gather at Tulsi Giri's ashram in Shyalpura for a *bhajan satsang* and perform a number of Mira *bhajans*. Before their group singing starts, Ganga Giri situates the meanings of the songs that they sing together in that *satsang* by sharing a popular legend about Mira's melting into Krishna at Dwarka[22] :

> Krishna and Mira used to talk to each other like we are talking to each other. God came to Mira. When Lord Krishna left for Dwarka, she followed him from Vrindavan[23] to Dwarka. She entered into his body.

> Only the corner of her *sari* remained... No one has ever had devotion like Mira's.

The three sadhus sing this Mira *bhajan* to accompany Ganga Giri's narration:

If I do not see you,
I shall not live till tomorrow.
My heart knows this.

If I do not see you,
I shall not live till tomorrow.
My heart knows this.
I climb higher and higher,
And I see your path.

I climb higher and higher,
And I see your path.

The whole night I spend crying [for you].
You are my partner through life and death.

The whole night I spend crying for you.
You are my partner through life and death.
I shall not remain another day and night separated from you.
You are my partner through the ages.

The whole world is false.
All the families are false.

The whole world is false.
All the families are false.
I request you to listen to me.
You are my partner through life and death.
I shall not remain another day and night separated from you.

You are my partner through the ages.
You are my partner through the ages.
This mind of mine is wicked,
Like a drunken elephant.

This mind of mine is wicked,
Like a drunken elephant.

You are my partner through life and death.
I shall not remain another day and night separated from you.
You are my partner through the ages.
I keep seeing your form each and every moment.
In seeing you, I find happiness.
I keep seeing your form each and every moment.
In seeing you, I find happiness.

Hey friend, Mira says: "Prabhu Girdhar Nagar."
I shall always remain at your feet.

Following their performance, Ganga Giri comments, "Mira was great [*mahān*]. She was so elevated [*aparam*] that no one could understand her... Her *bhajans* are full of devotion and knowledge."[24] Note Ganga Giri's mentioning of *bhakti* and *brahma-jnān* to suggest her view of Mira's singing as *sannyās*. In their commentary, the sadhus use the popular renunciant *bhakti* metaphor, with its monistic Vedanta overtones of "the light dissolving into the light" (*jyoti men jyoti milnā*), to represent Mira's experience of divine union. This implies that Mira, illustrating the individual soul (*ātmā*), merged with Krishna/God, the Supreme Soul (*brahman*). Since they perceive Mira's singing to be consistent with *nirguṇī bhakti*, the sadhus' use of her example to draw out *nirguṇī* light metaphors is not a logical contradiction. The following discussion among Ganga Giri (GG), Tulsi Giri (TG), and Jnan Nath (JN) heightens this point:

GG: Mira entered into God [*bhagwān*].
TG: She, well, the light dissolved into the light.
GG: Only the edge of her *sari* was left. Otherwise, she completely dissolved into God. People saw the edge of her sari and knew by looking at it that Mira had entered into God.
JN: Yes, the light dissolved into the light.

This conversation, including the narrative Ganga Giri shares prior to the sadhus' singing session, suggests that the theme of union with God underpins Mira's *bhajans*. This *bhajan* depicts Mira's intense desire for connection with Krishna, whom she addresses as the Clever Mountain Lord (Prabhu Girdhar Nagar). The lines "You are my partner through life and death," "You are my partner through the ages," and "I keep seeing your form each and every minute," each allude to this implied theme of the desire for divine union. Mira's desire to dissolve into her beloved Krishna reflects the emotional intoxication, the passion, she is believed to have experienced at the very thought of God. She says, "This mind of mine is wicked, like a drunken elephant." The sadhus themselves gloss Mira's intoxication as intense love for and devotion to God. To this extent, Ganga Giri not only comments that "Mira really loved God," but also emphasizes in her storytelling that "no one has ever had devotion like Mira's."

The sadhus' use of the model of Mira Bai to construct asceticism suggests that they perceive the experience of divine union in a holistic way. That is, not only their metaphors of "the light dissolving into the light," but also their emphasis that Mira's *whole being* merged into that of Krishna's supports a view of soul-body holism. Both Mira's soul and her *female* body "entered into" the Krishna's divine form. "Only the edge of her *sari* was left," Ganga Giri says. While their understandings of soul-body unification, with respect to the renunciant *bhakti* experience of divine union, resonate with the Advaita Vedanta philosophy often emphasized in Brahmanical *sannyās*, the sadhus' positive valuation of the body—and by extension, the female body—significantly contrasts with orthodox *sannyās* perspectives on the body and materiality. Classic literary sources on Brahmanical *sannyās* are replete with images that both devalue the human body and construct the female body, in particular, as the relentless locus of sexuality, suffering, and the illusory world of existence (Olivelle 1992; Wilson 1996; DeNapoli 2010; 2011; 2013a).

Despite the ideological misogynism of some Brahmanical texts, the sadhus' representation of divine union as an intimate and direct experience of wholeness enables them to engender their agency, legitimacy, and power as female renouncers. Their agency is additionally evident in the fact that, unlike male hagiographers who typically, but not always, eroticized the religiosity of female Hindu saints,[25] the sadhus refuse to use gender as a reason to eroticize their own or Mira's asceticism. Rather, they use Mira's feminine gender to craft a credible lineage of female devotional asceticism in Rajasthan. Apart from the implications of agency that their commentary evokes, Ganga Giri's, Jnan Nath's, and Tulsi Giri's singing indicates that the divine union that produces soul-body holism makes *bhakti* a "priceless" renunciant experience.

"Keep the Precious Diamond": Bhakti as Priceless

In the next song, Ganga Giri emphasizes the *nirguṇī sant* theme of renunciant *bhakti* as priceless (*anmol*). Frequently, she tells her audience that "[*b*]*hakti* is expensive [*mahengī*]," and then sings a *bhajan* to perform her understanding of this teaching. For example, Ganga Giri sings the following *bhajan*, which she attributes to Kabir, in order to underscore a point she makes earlier in this *satsang*—that *bhakti* comprises an invaluable aspect of a life of devotional asceticism.

Listen my crazy [bāvlā] mind,
Without bhajans, you lose the diamond [hīrā]. Keep [the diamond] safe.

Listen my crazy [bāvlā] mind,
Without bhajans, you lose the diamond. Keep it safe.
In this story, immortal rasas [juices] are filled.
Don't let your heart get attached with [worldly] things.

Listen my crazy mind,
In this story, immortal rasas are filled.
Don't let your heart get attached to [worldly] things.

Listen my crazy mind,
Without bhajans, you lose the diamond. Keep it safe.

Listen my crazy mind,
In this story, there is a quarry of diamonds.
Don't mix pebbles with the diamonds.

Listen my crazy mind,
In this story, there is a quarry of diamonds.
Don't mix pebbles with the diamonds.

Listen my crazy mind,
Without bhajans, you lose the diamond. Keep it safe.
In this story, unlimited water is filled.
Don't wash your clothes in mud.

Listen my crazy mind,
Without bhajans, you lose the diamond. Keep it safe.
Kabir says: "Listen brother sadhus."
Kabir says: "Listen brother sadhus."
It's only the sants who string one diamond after another.
Kabir says: "Listen brother sadhus!"
It's only the sants who string one diamond after another.

Listen my crazy mind,
Without bhajans, you lose the diamond. Keep it safe.

Ganga Giri describes the value of singing *nirguṇī bhajans* by referring directly to precious gems like diamonds (*hīrā*) and pearls (*motī*), sometimes including in this category precious metals such as gold (*sonā*) and silver (*cāndī*). Ganga Giri's drawing on gem imagery, in particular, to verbalize that *bhakti* is the *sine qua non* of vernacular asceticism (she often says, "*bhakti* is the only expensive thing") parallels the views illustrated in *sant* rhetoric that *bhakti* serves as the means through which devotees experience union with the divine. Jewels are common symbols in *nirguṇī sant* literature (Hess 2002; Hawley and Juergensmeyer 1988; Henry 1988; 1991; 1995; Lorenzen 1996). Kabir, for instance, spoke of precious jewels in his poetry and, in one poem, said, "A diamond fell in the market/lay in the trash/Many busy fools passed buy/A tester took it away" (*Bijak*, Hess, 2002, 109). Another of Kabir's poems reads, "You don't find: diamonds in storerooms/sandal trees in rows/lions in flocks/holy men in herds" (ibid.). For most of the female sadhus, too, the diamond is a poetically apt symbol with which they imagine and create devotional asceticism, because of the value that it signifies to them.

Several scholars have discussed and analyzed the meanings of polyvalent symbols, such as the precious diamond and gems in *nirguṇī sant* poetry (Henry 1988). For example, in his examination of three different versions of a *nirguṇī bhajan* attributed to Kabir entitled "Precious Gem" (the refrains of which resonate with that of Ganga Giri's *nirguṇī bhajan*, and which were performed by three different Jogi[26] mendicants of eastern Uttar Pradesh), ethnomusicologist Edward O. Henry glosses the diamond as "life itself, which here is seen as an opportunity to earn salvation or release (*mukti*), through devotion" (1991, 234). In a similar vein, in his analysis of one version of the "Precious Gem" *bhajan*, David Lorenzen identifies the diamond as "a symbol both of the difficult to achieve human birth, and of mystic illumination" (1996, 218).[27]

In her interpretation of these symbols, however, Ganga Giri underscores that the diamond and other precious gems symbolize the virtue of knowledge. While she does not explain the *bhajan*'s meaning in this *satsang*, Ganga Giri discusses the meanings of diamonds and gems in other *satsangs* and, in these contexts, almost always glosses such imagery in terms of salvific knowledge. In her use of the word "knowledge," Ganga Giri means precisely the revelatory and liberating knowledge that releases devotees from the chains of their own worldly illusions. According to Ganga Giri, "this whole world is an illusion [*māyā*]; it's a dream." She implies that the world of existence, which appears to be "real," is only illusory, and that knowledge enables devotees to awaken from their delusions and recognize that their happiness and well-being lie with God, and not with the world, which Ganga Giri characterizes as *māyā*. As she says, "the foundation of my well-being [*kalyān*] is not the world; it's knowledge." I use, then, the explanations Ganga Giri shares with me in her other *satsangs* to analyze this *bhajan*.

Ganga Giri distinguishes between knowledge and ignorance (*ajnān*). Notice that a similar distinction also occurs in the *nirguṇī bhajan* she performs about the precious diamond. The *bhajan* differentiates knowledge from ignorance through the use of three different rhetorical images. Addressing the "crazy mind," the first section of the *bhajan* uses the legitimizing voice of Kabir to caution, "Don't let your heart become attached to worldly things"; the second half similarly warns, "Don't mix pebbles with diamonds"; and finally, the third part of the *bhajan* declares, "Don't wash your clothes in the mud." Since Ganga Giri understands the diamond to signify clarity or knowledge, pebbles represent, in this song, the antithesis of knowledge, that is, ignorance. Relatedly, water represents knowledge, whereas mud symbolizes ignorance. Notice, though, that the poetic contrast between diamonds and pebbles illustrated in the *bhajan* implies further a distinction between light and darkness, respectively. Even the contrast between water and mud hints at an implied distinction between light and darkness. Ganga Giri speaks of knowledge and ignorance in terms of light and darkness. In one *satsang* she observes that

> Ignorance is darkness. But knowledge is light [*prakāś*]... Knowledge is light. Even if there are only stars and planets in the sky there will be light. Why? The stars and planets [sang] so many *bhajans*, so their light shines [in the sky]... Knowledge is priceless; it's hardly lying in the road.

While the association between knowledge and light and ignorance and darkness appears in classical mystical texts like the *Upaniṣads*, Ganga Giri performs her understanding of this ancient idea through use of *sant* imagery and language. But what makes knowledge priceless for Ganga Giri is that, in her perception, it helps devotees to free themselves from what she calls "the ocean of existence [*bhavsāgar*]." A common trope in *sant* poetry, the ocean of existence connotes the illusory and impermanent world. At the same time, attachment to the illusory world reflects a state of ignorance or darkness. Ganga Giri's *bhajan* makes explicit this idea: "Don't let your heart get attached to worldly things" and thus, as the song implies, drown in ignorance or darkness. She knows that wisdom enables devotees to cross over the turbulent ocean of existence and release themselves not only from the illusory world, but also from the emotional attachments that keep them trapped in *sansār*. Knowledge signifies light and lucidity because, according to Ganga Giri, it brings about understanding of the illusory, impermanent nature of existence within devotees' hearts and minds. Knowledge also leads toward spiritual awakening—an experience Ganga Giri describes as acquiring "peace in the heart," and as *mukti* or *mokṣ*, terms she uses to mean liberation from ignorance and the cycle of existence (*sansār*). She says,

> Until people understand [*māyā*], they remain fools [*mūrkh*]...When you understand you receive peace in your heart. Peace comes...If you understand the knowledge, you receive peace...Knowledge doesn't happen in one day. It takes the whole life to understand.

Implicit in Ganga Giri's teaching is the related idea that, in producing mental states such as peace or *mukti*, knowledge effects new life for sadhus and devotees of God; that is, knowledge provides a means through which devotees awaken to a life of radical devotion to God. Therefore, the distinctions Ganga Giri's *nirguṇī bhajan* poses between knowledge and ignorance signify symbolic contrasts not only between light and darkness, but also between life (awakening) and death (drowning). Like the precious diamond, the virtue of knowledge is priceless and expensive because it creates feelings of *bhakti*, and in doing so, leads devotees to God, the path of life. But let's not forget that, for Ganga Giri, *bhakti*, too, is priceless. The *bhajan*'s refrain—"without *bhajans*, you lose the diamond"—suggests that knowledge results from the renunciant *bhakti* practice of singing *bhajans*. Recall, from Ganga Giri's discussion of knowledge as light, her view that the stars and planets themselves produced their own light by means of singing *bhajans*. Her comment makes explicit that *bhajans* (i.e., sadhu *bhakti*) serve as the basis of revelatory knowledge, which brings about an extraordinary life of singing *bhajans*. Within this framework, devotion is more than just a bridge to liberating knowledge. It is also a function of knowledge, and hence simultaneously, the goal and purpose of asceticism. Singing this *nirguṇī bhajan* helps Ganga Giri to craft asceticism as a *sant bhakti* path of liberating knowledge and as a path of life. And because it leads to immortality, renunciant *bhakti*, as the sadhus say, "is a difficult path."

"Live as God Wants You to": Devotional Asceticism as Surrender

Most of the sadhus call themselves the "beggars of God." Their use of this motif indexes their perception that their lives are based on an attitude of complete dependence on the divine. Ganga Giri says, "I only have God and no one else. God is my support, so why should I fear [anything]?" When Ganga Giri talks about her life as a path of surrender, she sings the next *bhajan*, which she attributes to her mythic exemplum, Mira Bai. This is one of the few *nirguṇī bhajans* with a signature line at the beginning of the composition, rather than at the end:

Mira says: O Ranaji, live as God keeps you.
Some days there is halwā [sweet dish] and pūrī [fried bread] to eat;
Some days you have to go hungry.

O Ranaji, live as God keeps you.
Some days you have a pillow and mattress to sleep on,
Some days you have to sleep on the ground.
O Ranaji, live as God keeps you.
[Ganga Giri interjects this commentary into her performance]:
> *Whether [God] keeps us happy or unhappy, everything happens through [God's] support [ādhār]. This idea that, "I will do this, I will do that, I did this, I did that," is false. Nobody can do anything [without God's support]. Whatever God wants shall happen.*

[Returns to the bhajan]

Some days you have gardens to wander in.
Some days you have to live in the jungles.
O Ranaji, live as God keeps you.

Ganga Giri's understanding that *bhakti* involves an attitude of letting go of personal desires and living as God decides, "whether [God] keeps us happy or unhappy," is not an idea exclusive to *sant* teachings. To take an example, Ganga Giri defines asceticism through use of pivotal *Gītā* concepts like *tyāg* (the releasing of individual attachments to the divine). However, unlike the *Gītā*, Ganga Giri interprets asceticism à la *sant* understandings—as a renunciant *bhakti* path through which sadhus abandon their own ego-based notions, such as, "I do this and I do that," and instead, live in the manner that God intends for them. We notice, then, that both *Gītā* and *sant bhakti* frameworks converge in Ganga Giri's performance of asceticism.

Although Ganga Giri does not use the terms "surrender" and "dependence" in this *satsang*, she signals them in her commentary. More than three-quarters of the way into her performance she explains, "Everything happens through God's support... Whatever God wants [for his devotees] shall happen." The word Ganga Giri uses for what I translate as "support" is *ādhār*, which has corollary meanings of "base," "foundation," and "basis." Her employing this term suggests that she perceives her life in terms of her dependence on God. In other *satsangs*, Ganga Giri explicitly describes both her tradition of asceticism and that of the *sants* through means of the concept of dependence. She asserts that "[real] *bhakts* depend on God," implying in this statement what she makes explicit in her Mira *bhajan* performance: that God is the only real foundation, and thus, the ultimate supplier of everything in the universe. Ganga Giri's view that everything in life happens as God wills it to be approximates her understanding that her becoming a sadhu in this birth represents, in part, the influence of destiny—a divine directive. This concept indexes many of the sadhus' understanding of asceticism as a path of surrender and dependence.

Whenever Ganga Giri discusses the importance of dependence for asceticism, she almost always performs a song or story about Mira Bai. In doing so, she relates that Mira Bai, too, represents a beggar of God, a sadhu-renouncer who sacrificed everything in order to live not as the Ranaji wanted for her, but rather as God desired for her (DeNapoli, forthcoming). The Mira *bhajan* illustrates the idea of *bhakti* as surrender to and dependence on the divine through three different sets of images, each of which contrasts material bounty with material lack. One image compares eating *halwā* and *pūrī*, foods symbolic of material wealth, with having nothing at all to eat; another distinguishes between sleeping on a comfortable pillow and mattress and sleeping on the ground; and the third image contrasts residing among beautiful gardens with living in the jungle. All of these images represent popular tropes in *nirguṇī sant* literature (Lorenzen 1996), and Ganga Giri seems to understand them as promoting not only a *bhakti* attitude of dependence on God, but also an ascetic attitude of detachment (*vairāg*) from material things (e.g., food, beds, pillows, gardens), and more broadly, from the illusory and impermanent material world itself. In the discussion preceding her *bhajan* performance, Ganga Giri says,

> Nothing lasts forever. Sometimes there's no oil; sometimes there's no ghee; sometimes there's no flour. Even if you wanted [these materials] to last, they wouldn't. This is what happens [in life]. Like, these big businesses start, but they, too, don't last. Even the billionaires lose their money someday. Everything [in the world] comes to an end.

As with surrender and dependence, Ganga Giri does not explicitly speak about detachment. Nevertheless, this notion remains embedded in her comments on the impermanence of material world. She invokes detachment in her statement that "[n]othing lasts forever... Everything comes to an end." But she makes this comment not so much to teach that the material world is illusory and impermanent, but rather to explain that, whether a king or a pauper, devotees never know what God has planned for them in this life. "Whatever God wants shall happen," Ganga Giri says.

"Live as God Keeps You": Barfani Baba's Version

I recorded another version of this *bhajan* from Barfani Baba at his ashram on October 18, 2005. While their songs share the same refrain, the contents of the song texts are quite different. Unlike Ganga Giri's version, Barfani Baba's *bhajan* lacks a signature line, and he himself does not attribute the composition to any *sant*. Nonetheless, Barfani Baba's performance of this *bhajan*, like Ganga Giri's, underscores the *nirguṇī bhakti* themes of surrender and dependence.

Live as God keeps you
Say the name of Ram from your mouth and serve the Lord.

You are never alone,
The beloved Ram is always with you.
Whatever [Ram] has written [in your destiny],
Whether it be meditation, loss, or profit,
Endure everything.
Live as God keeps you.
Live as Ram wishes, and leave all your wishes behind.
Keep the relationship with Ram,
And break all other relationships.
Keep doing the satsang of Ram with the sadhus,
And put the colors of Ram over each and every limb of your body.

Live as God keeps you.
If you shall be proud, you'll not find your honor.
If you shall be proud, you'll not find your honor.
It shall be however Ram likes.
Let go [tyāg] of all the fruits [phalyā] and take Ram's name from morning till night.

Live as Ram keeps you.

This is one of the only *nirguṇī bhajans* I recorded from the sadhus that has the word *tyāg* in the text, a concept to which Ganga Giri tacitly refers in her Mira *bhajan* sing. Before he sings this *bhajan*, Barfani Baba obliquely discusses surrender and dependence by speaking about the personality differences between children and adults. He suggests that whereas children depend on others for their happiness and well-being, adults seek to control every aspect of their lives through their actions. Barfani Baba puts the issue like this: "Their work gives them *rotīs* [lit., "bread," but meaning, more broadly, food and shelter], but it takes them further from God." As Barfani Baba indicates, the problem with thinking, to use Ganga Giri's phrase, "I do this, I do that," is that no one really controls anything. Rather, God controls everything. The solution is for devotees to become like children (in their attitudes) and surrender to God's wishes, despite whatever God decides as the outcome of their lives.[28] "As long as we remain [like] children, God will keep us as [he] pleases," Barfani Baba explains. The *bhajan* reiterates what Barfani Baba teaches his devotees in the *satsangs* in which I attended—to depend on God for everything. Although neither he nor his *bhajan* explicitly mentions "surrender" or "dependence," the context of both his teaching and his oral performance makes it clear that Barfani Baba, like Ganga Giri, sings this *bhajan* in order to emphasize that these virtues are essential for devotional asceticism.

"Chant Prabhu's Name and Whatever is Spoiled Shall be Improved": Singing Bhajans as Transformative

A sixth *nirguṇī* theme that the sadhus highlight in their performances of asceticism has to do with the repetition (*nāma-jāpa*) of God's name as powerful and transformative. Ganga Giri performs the following *bhajan*, which she attributes to Kabir, as a means to articulate this view.

Whatever of yours is spoiled [bigaḍā huā] shall be improved [sudhar jānā].
Meditate on Hari, my friend.

Whatever of yours is spoiled shall be improved.
Chant the names of Prabhu, my friend.
Anka[29] *crossed over, Banka crossed over, Mira Bai crossed over,*
And the butcher, Sadankasai, crossed over.
Anka crossed over, Banka crossed over, Sadankasai crossed over,
The prostitute [gaṇikā] who taught the parrot [to say "Ram Ram"] crossed over.
And Mira Bai crossed over.

Meditate on Hari, my friend.
Mira Bai crossed over.

Meditate on Hari, my friend.
Whatever of yours is spoiled shall be improved.
Chant the names of Prabhu, my friend.

Wealth, the world, treasures, and the bullock cart,
Time shall steal these away.
Wealth, the world, treasures and the bullock cart,
Time shall steal these away.
One never knows when Time shall sound his drum.

Meditate on Hari, my friend.
Whatever of yours is spoiled shall be improved.
Chant the names of Prabhu, my friend.
Do such a bhakti in your heart.
Serve [the Lord] and cultivate dependence [adhīntā] on him,
And you shall meet Raghurai [Ram].

Meditate on Hari, my friend.
Whatever of yours is spoiled shall be improved.
Chant the names of Prabhu, my friend.

Kabir has said: "Listen sadhus."
The sadguru has told us the truth.
Kabir has said: "Listen sadhus."
The sadguru has told us the truth.
The world lasts only four days.

Take the name of Ram.
Meditate on Hari, my friend.
Whatever of yours is spoiled shall be improved.
Chant the names of Prabhu, my friend.

After Ganga Giri sings this *bhajan*, one of her listeners, Dadaji (in whose guest house I was living at the time, and who deemed it necessary to gloss Ganga Giri's speech for my benefit), explains his understanding of the *bhajan*'s meaning: he offers that its message is that devotees who take the divine name "will never suffer." The three other female householders participating in this *satsang*, who have adult children and visit Ganga Giri on the days that they take the *darśan* of the deities at the nearby Mahakaleshwar (Shiv) Temple, make eye contact with Ganga Giri and wait for her to speak before making their own thoughts on the matter known. While Ganga Giri does not disagree with Dadaji's response, it becomes clear from the verbal exchange following his explanation that her purpose in singing this *bhajan* is to provide another message. Here is my transcription of their conversation:

[D]A[D]AJI: When you take the name of God, you will never suffer and your work [*kām*] will never be spoiled.

[G]ANGA [G]IRI: Whatever is spoiled becomes improved.

DD: OK, and even if something of yours is spoiled [e.g., your actions; your thoughts; or your speech], it will turn out good. This is the meaning of the *bhajan*...

GG: But you have to take *bhagwān* name with love. Take God's name with love.

DD: [Pointing to his heart] From here, from the *ātmā*, take the name of God with love. Do your work with love. God is watching from above. Then, your work will turn out well.

GG: And whatever of yours is spoiled will be improved.

This brief exchange shows that Ganga Giri understands the renunciant *bhakti* practice of singing or chanting the divine name, whether referred to as Hari or as Prabhu, as a powerful form of transformation. It not only protects devotees from suffering, as Dadaji suggests, but also transforms them, as Ganga Giri indicates, by purifying their minds and, hence, their actions. The word Ganga Giri employs to relate this idea is *sudhar jānā*, which means "to be improved," "to be set right," or "to be corrected." Implicit in her usage of the term is the corollary meaning of "to be purified" of negative thoughts and actions. The line in the *bhajan* about the prostitute (*gaṇikā*) who teaches the parrot to say "Ram Ram" (a popular story that Ganga Giri shares frequently in other *satsangs*), and the line about the butcher, Sadankasai, suggest that singing or repeating the divine name results in the practitioner "crossing over."[30] Both of these devotees earned their livelihoods by engaging in work that "spoils" or negatively affects them (i.e., the prostitute exchanges sex for money and the butcher kills animals). Yet by singing the divine name, they are able to improve "whatever of theirs is spoiled" (e.g., their minds, bodies, speech, or their work).

Ganga Giri's belief in the potential of even the mechanical repetition of the divine name to transform devotees intimates, as discussed earlier, an underlying ideology of *bhajan* singing (and repetitive chanting or *jāpa*) as an efficacious sadhu *bhakti* practice in its own right. In both *Gītā* and *sant* frameworks, action (*karm*) is thought to influence the mental, emotional, and physical makeup of individuals. Depending on its nature, actions both contain and transmit qualities or properties (*guṇas*) such as wisdom (*sattva*), passion (*rajas*), and ignorance (*tamas*) to their actors (Marriott 1991). Accordingly, primarily wisdom-based actions bring about the qualities of truth and understanding; passion-based actions effect passion or lust; and ignorance-based actions produce ignorance, darkness, or lethargy in the minds and bodies of individuals. Just as devotees "spoil" themselves through their negative actions, they also improve themselves through their positive actions. In these *bhakti* frameworks, along with meditation on the divine (*dhyān*), repeating the divine name (e.g., Ram, Hari, or Prabhu) is also considered one of the most powerful actions by which devotees transform their psycho-physical defects.

Devotees like the prostitute and the butcher can, therefore, change not only themselves, but even a difficult situation, by repeating or chanting the name of God "with love" from the heart. Mira Bai's *bhakti* empowered her to emerge unharmed from the Rana's multiple death plots. Recall, from Ganga Giri's narrative in Chapter 3, that the Rana sent a bowl of poison disguised as milk to Mira, through a servant girl. Even though Mira drank the milk, as Ganga Giri emphasizes, "absolutely nothing happened to her," because Mira's *bhakti* to Krishna, which she enacted by singing her *bhajans* and holding *satsang* with sadhus and *sants* "from every caste," made it possible for her to escape from the hardships she experienced at the Rana's hands.

But the practice of repeating the divine name with love creates more than personal transformation. Most importantly, it also enables devotees to "cross over" the ocean of existence (*sansār*). Ganga Giri says that by "grabbing" (*pakaḍnā*) the divine name, devotees cross their "boats," or souls (*ātmā*), over the world of existence (*bhavsāgar*) and, in effect, "meet" God, an experience she describes as *mukti* or *mokṣ* (implying union with, rather than complete dissolution into, the divine). As Ganga Giri observes, "if you hold the name tightly [in your heart], you will cross over. But if you let it go, your boat will drown." We notice here that Ganga Giri's *bhakti* language again approximates the *sant* rhetoric as featured in her *nirguṇī bhajans*—songs which, like this *bhajan*, often legitimate the idea of the power of the divine name by listing the devotees (Anka, Banka, Mira, and so forth) who encountered God through such practices.[31]

By singing this *bhajan*, Ganga Giri legitimates her view of the transformative power of chanting the divine name and instills in her devotees the belief that God is the only permanent reality and truth behind the ever-changing *sansār*. The world, despite its appearance, is merely *māyā*. The *bhajan* relates this idea in the lines, "[w]ealth, the world, treasures, and the bullock cart, Time shall steal away." Time, as Ganga Giri makes explicit, constitutes Yamraj, the Lord of Death. Whereas anything that is of the material world belongs to Death, the *ātmā* belongs to God. Thus, "nothing lasts forever," because the property that defines the inherent nature of *sansār* is that of impermanence. The *bhajan* further attests to this crucial renunciant point in two of its verses: "One never knows when Time shall sound his drum" and "The world lasts only four days."[32]

Conclusions: Negotiating Multiple Perspectives of Vernacular Asceticism

Why do the sadhus sing *bhajans* to God? There are many reasons. They sing because they perceive this practice as efficacious for the current *kali yug*. Their descriptions of singing *bhajans* reveal an ideology of its performative efficacy, in which three foremost themes are embedded: *bhajans* are powerful and transformative; *bhajans* represent a symbolic currency of exchange between sadhus and householders, and between *bhakts* and *bhagwān*; and, finally, *bhajans* serve as a kind of *sevā* to God in the form of humanity. Most importantly, singing makes sadhus powerful and creates them as authentic practitioners. Equally significant, by singing *bhajans*, the sadhus understand that they forge connections with God and with those whom they serve as God.

Another reason the sadhus sing *bhajans* is because, as this chapter has shown, it performs their views of asceticism as a celebratory and community-based experience of singing with others, which is the superior way to experience God as love. For the sadhus, "love is what God is," and they access, as well as help others to access, God through *bhajan* singing. The *bhajans* that the sadhus sing are those drawn primarily from the *nirguṇī sant* poetry. Singing *nirguṇī* songs, the sadhus say, exemplifies *sant sannyās*, and by singing these *bhajans* the sadhus convey the idea that sadhu and *sant* identities are equivalent. The sadhus further say that *nirguṇī sant bhajans*, in particular, possess the precious and powerful *brahma-jnān* that *bhajan* singing not only releases into the universe for the benefit of the world, but also develops into the ascetic power of *tapas*. Much like the stories they tell and the texts they recite, singing *bhajans* allows them to place their *sannyās* within the more fluid context of *sant* devotional religiosity. In the process of singing, the sadhus construct their asceticism as a "very difficult" and "valuable" path to God. They also relate that it is as valid a form of *sannyās* as the kind portrayed in the classical texts.

To that extent, the sadhus' perception of *bhajan* singing as *tapasyā* illustrates their creative reconfiguring of the Vedic/Brahmanical model of *sannyās* in a manner that prioritizes the values, concerns, and experiences that are important to them as women and renouncers. While the revelatory knowledge that the sadhus attribute to singing *bhajans* recalls the classical emphasis on *tapas* as (strictly) a knowledge-producing practice, the sadhus define what *tapas* means and how it works within a new context of *sant bhakti*. From where these sadhus stand, *bhajan* and *tapas* "are the same." Crafting *tapas* in this way, they recast its dominant meaning through *sant bhakti* to accentuate the ideas of love and relationship implied by *bhajan*.[33] Their emphasis on *bhajan* as *tapas* refocuses how *sannyās* is seen, from an external lens to a lens positioned from within, and validates women's views. This inside view allows them to navigate competing visions of asceticism and create a tradition that complements Brahmanical *sannyās*.

Thus, in their devotional sings, the sadhus make explicit, as Meredith McGuire describes in her book-length study of religion-as-lived in the United States, that "[vernacular] religious traditions are hardly fixed or deterministic. People can create new... practices, adapt old ones, and ignore those traditions that are not... useful in their lives" (2008, 61). The sadhus' rhetorical practices perform the diversity of vernacular asceticism in South Asia and the hybridity of paradigms and resources—textual and phenomenological—that shape what *sannyās* is all about and how it is lived on the ground. The interpretive congruencies between the sadhus' devotional model and the textual model of *tapas*, no doubt, suggest the relevance of both "classical" and "vernacular" frameworks for asceticism as practiced in Rajasthan. Nevertheless, unlike the orthodox view that distinguishes between *bhajan* and *tapas*, the female sadhus see these concepts as identical. Accordingly, the power produced by *tapas* is constitutive of both *bhakti* and *jnān*: both love and detachment. Rather than heat, *bhakti*, together with salvific knowledge, serves as the ultimate and underlying source that fuels the powerful transformation, both mental and physical, their singing *bhajans* helps to create. And singing, as these sadhus say, is what "real" sadhus do.

Conclusion

"Meeting and Parting in the Melā *of Life"*

VERNACULAR ASCETICISM IN RAJASTHAN

Meeting is good, but parting is painful. It is hard to say goodbye.

—GANGA GIRI MAHARAJ

THIS BOOK HAS sought to answer the question, "What kind of *sannyās* might female sadhus in Rajasthan imagine and create by singing to God?" Using the categories of experience and practice that the sadhus themselves emphasized, I have argued that they construct a celebratory, relational, *satsang*-centered—and, considering the carnival metaphor—*bhakti* form of *sannyās* as they sing. Their practices interrogate the dominant Brahmanical notion, which, as I have shown, depicts a type of *sannyās* that has often determined how renunciation is discussed in academic and popular discourse. The female sadhus perform their rhetoric of renunciation as a means to create a different kind of *sannyās*, one that calls for developing a model of renunciation beyond the one represented in and by the mainstream imagination. By recasting *sannyās* as singing *bhajans*, the female sadhus constitute what I have characterized in this book as devotional asceticism as an alternative to Brahmanical *sannyās*. Moreover, as they stretch the dominant definitional parameters of the phenomenon through their rhetorical practices, the sadhus define not only *what* counts as *sannyās*, but also *who* counts as a sadhu. In their view, "Real sadhus sing to God."

Although there are excellent analytical frameworks that interpret *sannyās* through the lens of a maternal ethos (cf. Khandelwal 2004), the renunciation that the sadhus bring to life through the vernacular practices analyzed in this book shifts the discourse on *sannyās* beyond the Brahmanical model in a new way. I have suggested that, in the practices of the sadhus, singing *bhajans* and *sannyās* are not mutually exclusive categories. Rather, they combine in a new configuration in the construction of the phenomenon of vernacular asceticism as practiced, interpreted, and understood "on the ground" in Rajasthan. What is more, in comparison to the dominant Brahmanical model of *sannyās*, I have argued that the sadhus' vernacular practices construct a female sadhu tradition of asceticism. While my access to and contact with male sadhus was more limited than it was with female sadhus, the research I conducted with the male sadhus suggests that *bhakti* means something different to them than it does to the female sadhus.[1] Several of the male sadhus recognized and discussed the importance of *bhakti* for their *sannyās*. These sadhus told me that without *bhakti*, *sannyās* is "difficult," because *bhakti* teaches them ways in which to approach, and therefore to experience, God both within and as themselves.[2] Nevertheless, to these sadhus, *bhakti* represented more of a tool that allowed them to experience the ultimate objective of self-realization as liberation, rather than an end in itself—that is, *bhakti* functions as a stepping stone on the sadhu path, rather than defines what *sannyās* is about.

And yet, as I have shown, for the female sadhus, not only are *sannyās* and (sadhu) *bhakti* "the same thing," but so are *sannyās* and *bhajan*. Singing creates *sannyās*. Thus, while the male sadhus spoke about the significance of *bhakti* for *sannyās*, they did not conceive and articulate *bhakti* as central to, or definitive of, vernacular asceticism in the way that I observed with the female sadhus. Unlike their female counterparts, the male sadhus neither defined singing as *sannyās*, nor were they devotional to the extent that the female sadhus' were in their practices.

In her study of Jain female asceticism in Rajasthan, Anne Vallely has similarly discussed that, while she had more contact with the nuns than with the monks, it was conspicuous to her that "not only do monks display their devotion to a lesser degree, they narrate their lives less in terms of *bhakti* than do the nuns" (2002, 214). Vallely explains, "Their language is not saturated with idioms of surrender and devotion to the same degree [as the nuns' language]...Although all ascetics are encouraged to interpret their lives through a framework of *nivrtti marg* [asceticism]...the nuns juxtapose the framework of *bhakti* alongside that of *nivrtti* to a much greater degree than do the monks" (214). Vallely further states that "[t]he monks freely admit that devotion forms an important part of their ascetic lives, but they did not provide it the same centrality as did the nuns in their 'public' narrative accounts to me" (2002, 281, note 17).

Apart from their gendered understandings of *bhakti*, while the *bhakti*-oriented male sadhus recognized and referred to singing, storytelling, and textual recitation as *bhakti*, the male sadhus neither characterized these practices as *tapas*, nor associated them with *tapasyā*. In contrast, in the female sadhus' views, these practices performed *sannyās* and were thought to be as powerful as those practices featured in the dominant model of Brahmanical renunciation, such as fasting, penance, and meditation. At the same time, when the male sadhus talked about *tapas*, they often implied the Brahmanical masculine model of the concept in that, to them, *tapas* had to do with practices that effect the production of heat in the body-mind, which, in turn, manifests in the form of extraordinary spiritual power. The female sadhus, however, described their practices as *tapas*, which enables them to create *bhakti* and *jnān*—that is, love and detachment instead of heat—in the body-mind complex. On the whole, my research with sadhus in Rajasthan indicates that devotional asceticism, in the contexts described in this book, illustrates a gendered model of *sannyās*, because the female sadhus conceived of *sannyās* as radical *bhakti*, and equated these concepts with singing *bhajans*. Whether we compare the female sadhu tradition to the mainstream imagination, or to the practices of the male sadhus discussed in this book, the broader implication of my data is that female *sannyās* is more devotional than male *sannyās*.

Creativity, Ambiguity, and Power in Rajasthani Sadhus' Sannyās*-as-Lived*

Folklorist and religion scholar Leonard N. Primiano has identified creativity, ambiguity, and power as signal characteristics of vernacular religion (2012, 387). He notes, "Because…vernacular performances, whether verbalized or physically executed, are able not only to protest but also to confirm or create a surrounding environment, culture, or society, vernacular religion too can thus represent and express the interests of both the rich and the poor, the disenfranchised and the powerful" (388). This book has contributed another category to Primiano's hermeneutic of vernacular religion, that of the "text," by showing that in the practices of the female sadhus, performing texts (in this case the *Tulsi Rāmāyan*), and reworking their parameters beyond the written word or physical book in performance provides a means for the sadhus to perform power and legitimacy. The practices analyzed in this book have shown that the sadhus relate the concerns, values, and ideals that orient their everyday female worlds as they construct a *sannyās* that is fluid and flexible and weaves together into a vibrant tapestry the sometimes conflicting, sometimes complementary, multiple paradigms of Brahmanical *sannyās*, *sant bhakti*, divine intentionality elaborated via *karm*, *kartavya*, and *bhāgya*, and caste and gender ideologies. Constructing *sannyās* as a synthesis of various cultural systems is neither new nor unique to the Rajasthani sadhus, as I suspect religious minority groups in South Asia and elsewhere around the globe have been building their worlds by means of bricolage for a long time (cf. McGuire 2008; Orsi 2005; Primiano 1995). And yet, the kind of *sannyās* that these sadhus create brings them to the center of the phenomenon, instead of marginalizing them to the periphery or eclipsing their concerns, as is the case with most exclusive and elite expressions of renunciant religiosity.

But vernacular asceticism also contains perplexing and paradoxical ambiguities that arise and become articulated in the very processes of its performance. Citing South American liberation theologian Michael Candelaria (1990, 2), Primiano observes that "Vernacular religion is 'stubbornly ambiguous'" (2012, 387). That is, vernacular religiosity "communicates two or more separate and conflicting meanings" (Primiano 2012, 387), on account of its peculiar relationship to the more prescriptive or dominant "forms of power . . . as contestation to that power" (ibid). The negotiating or adapting function characteristic of vernacular religion, which features its inherent flexibility, produces ambivalence at the levels of message and meaning (McGuire 2008, 53).

A prime example of this pattern in vernacular asceticism is evident in the sadhus' exclusive ethos of caste ambivalence, discussed in Chapter 4. As minorities in the more global institution of *sannyās*, and as individuals outside the norm (and normative expectation) of householding, the sadhus utilize several strategies in performing their rhetoric of renunciation to legitimate their unusual position as female renouncers. It seems to me that legitimation and ambiguity are closely interlinked in vernacular asceticism. The former (a relationship to forms of power) appears to lead to the latter (the result of the contestation of that power struggle). Besides use of ideologies of exceptionalism (i.e., God chose the sadhus as God's representatives for the radical path of *sannyās* because they were special) or specifically gender exceptionalism (i.e., women make better sadhus than men because love, sacrifice, and suffering are the unique innate qualities of the female constitution) examined in Chapters 2 and 3, respectively, one of those strategies involved the claim that high-caste sadhus are mentally and physically better equipped to fight for God on the "battlefield of *bhakti*," as they possess the well-born traits that make being a ("real" or "good") sadhu possible. In the practices of the high-caste sadhus, "battlefield of *bhakti*" functioned as an idiom for *sannyās*, and thus for singing *bhajans*. As discussed in Chapter 4, the sadhus distinguished between two types of *bhakti*: sadhu *bhakti* and householder *bhakti*. The former was seen as a supreme and rigorous *bhakti*, whereas the latter was viewed as a generic *bhakti*. That distinction reinforces caste ambivalence. This ethos also undercuts gender distinctions in vernacular asceticism, as expressed in Rajasthan.

Sadhus like Sad Giri, however, interrogate such dominant and upper-caste exclusivist notions. Born into the low-caste Khatik (butcher) community, she has argued that the relationship between singing *bhajans* and caste is essentially irrelevant as a way to contest the power hegemonies of *sannyās* -as-lived in Rajasthan. Singing *bhajans* attributed to Mira Bai, and telling stories of her own exceptionalism, have enabled Sad Giri to distinguish herself as an authentic sadhu by putting the focus on what sadhus do with their lives, instead of what their caste status is (or is not). Her controversial practices of living in the same domicile as her *natal* family and operating a *satsang* business, for which she earns substantial cash income beyond what sadhus could ever hope to achieve through donations alone, have led other sadhus to question the sincerity of her intentions. But Sad Giri has moved past the various cultural barriers of caste, gender, and ritual purity that others have put in front of her by locating her authority in her vernacular practices. She, like most of the female sadhus, suggests that her power and prestige rest in, and are constituted by, singing to God.

Thus, constructive practice creates the sadhus' power, as well as supplies the means through which they exert, to use Keller's (2002) term, "instrumental agency" and navigate their authority in vernacular asceticism. By taking seriously Khandelwal's argument that renunciation is not equivalent to Brahmanical orthodoxy, and that female renunciation constitutes "a site of undetermination" where "agencies slip through the structures" (Khandelwal 2004, 197), I have shown that the sadhus' vernacular practices of singing, storytelling, and textual recitation perform female creativity, agency, and power in *sannyās*. While I do not deny that female sadhus *appear* to transgress patriarchal norms and ideals by opting out of domesticity (Khandelwal 2004; cf. Khandelwal, Hausner, and Gold 2006; but cf. Vallely 2002), this book has nevertheless pushed the issue of agency and power in female *sannyās* beyond the seemingly "trangressive" act of renouncing the world. To my mind, arguments that link female agency to (what scholars tend to perceive as) transgressive activities imply an individualistic and voluntaristic notion of agency and power that the data documented in this book has sought to question. As Mahmood (2005) and Jassal (2012) have argued, the notion of transgressive female activity as agency associates women's capacities to act with neoliberal, Western models of resistance to, or subversion of, dominant patriarchal expectations (Knight 2011), which are built on the tacit assumption that agency leads to progressive social change for women (Keller 2002; Asad 1993).

As "instruments" receptive to divine intentionality, the sadhus' actions cannot be considered as signs of their making their own choices (or as their acting on their own wishes), but rather as the manifestations of divine will and action. The sadhus hardly see themselves as autonomous agents in the world. Instead, as "the peons of God," they believe that their actions bring about divine fate. They are only doing what God intends them to do. Also, their divinely willed actions do not, as the ethos of caste ambivalence suggests, alter dominant power hegemonies. Hence, though they act in the world, the divine, cultural, or societal structures impinging on the sadhus' everyday actions prevent us from making the problematic assumption that they act alone (agentively) and on their own (autonomously). According to the sadhus, the goal is to align their behaviors (and will) with divine will. To that extent, the practices that the idiom of singing *bhajans* brings to light as vernacular asceticism themselves *act* as the vehicles through which individual and divine subjectivities combine in the construction of self and the enactment of instrumental agency. But just as significant, singing *bhajans* performs more than the sadhus' capacity to act constructively because or in spite of overarching power forces, human and otherwise; it also demonstrates their capacity to interpret in meaningful ways the practices they draw on to build their worlds. By grounding agency in constructive practice, I have contended that the sadhus' performances neutralize perceptions of their *sannyās* as trangressive by enabling them to disclaim personal agency, invoke specific female models and experiences as an alternative to normative renunciant paradigms, and craft themselves as traditional.

With respect to the first issue, the sadhus disclaim the agency implied in their becoming sadhus by constructing *sannyās* as the product of God's decision. In this framework, the sadhus validate their uncommon lives and make it difficult for those who might otherwise object to their *sannyās* and the unusual freedom of movement it allocates to women to argue with them, for who wants to take issue with God's decision? The sadhus' agency disclaimers help them to work within the cultural constraints of a predominantly patriarchal system that undermines, and at the extreme, denies female autonomy and agency, and to push back at that system, without completely (or intentionally) subverting normative gender paradigms or compromising others' perceptions of their authenticity (Ortner 1996). By conceptualizing *sannyās* through such disclaimers, the sadhus empower themselves to maneuver the gendered ambiguities and contradictions inherent in their positions and to exercise agency and power. Both the male sadhus and the female sadhus in my field study maneuver gender, agency, and power, but in different ways, and they stretch the meanings of gender norms and roles as they do so.

Another way that the female sadhus exert agency is by using gendered models of devotional asceticism in their vernacular practices as an alternative to the dominant Brahmanical model of *sannyās*. Their use of regional examples of female *sants*, like Mira Bai, Rupa Rani, Shabari Bai, and Karma Bai, narratively constructs a genealogy of female *sannyās* in Rajasthan, and more broadly, in Northern India. Most of the sadhus, regardless of the castes they were born into, explicitly trace the phenomenon of female *sannyās* in Mewar to the Rajasthani princess-turned-sadhu Mira Bai. What is more, most of these sadhus locate themselves (and their practices) in Mira's lineage, explaining that "lady" sadhus have been able to renounce because of her "grace." Even as these and similar statements make apparent the myriad institutional, social, and familial difficulties that women endure in their becoming sadhus, they also index that Mira Bai posthumously initiates female sadhus into her tradition of *sannyās*. In the view of the majority of these sadhus, Mira's example and influence authorizes their asceticism. It is also important to note that while the male sadhus do not, as I expected, draw on Mira Bai's model to represent *sannyās,* some of them recognize and, at times, extoll her *bhakti* and bravery, and attribute the phenomenon of female *sannyās* in Rajasthan to her extraordinary example.

From this perspective, the sadhus' claims to a gendered genealogy of vernacular asceticism make it possible to categorize renunciant authority and exercise receptive agency as female practitioners. At the same time, their example beckons the question: Might other female sadhus use alternative (in the sense that I have proposed in Chapter 3) gender models to generate genealogies of female *sannyās* through which means they, too, exercise power and authority? This important issue has yet to be discussed in the literature on female renunciation. Nevertheless, the implications of this study are that "traditional" female examples or scripts help sadhus to imagine and express constructively their individual traditions as an alternative to orthodox *sannyās*, and that they legitimate their authority through use of gendered models.

Finally, this book has argued that female agency and power in *sannyās* are intertwined with the sadhus' self-representations as traditional. The sadhus create themselves as traditional by situating, via performance, their *sannyās* in the (non-Brahmanical) tradition of *sant bhakti*. The sadhus' drawing on *sant* paradigms is significant in its implication that sadhus possibly construct themselves in relation to ideologies that lie beyond the (expected) parameters of renunciation. While it is generally accepted among scholars that the Brahmanical traditions regarded the *sant* movements as heretical on account of their vehement refutation of (the importance of) gender, caste, and class in the worship of God,[3] the sadhus do not perceive *sant bhakti* as necessarily anti-Brahmanical or as anti-traditional. For sure, creating their vernacular asceticism on what may have been perceived to be the heterodox *bhakti* religiosity of the *sants* distinguishes the sadhus in this study as unorthodox by dominant Brahmanical standards. To these sadhus, however, *sant bhakti* is consistent with orthodox *sannyās*: though their ideals and values differ, both *sant* and renunciant traditions envision spiritual freedom from the destructive grip of ignorance, from the fear of death, and therefore, from the endless cycle of existence through experience of, or identification with, the divine. Both traditions further view a nameless and formless God as the ultimate and most important goal, even though they disagree on how to get there.

In their use of *sant* paradigms and practices, the sadhus neither overturn nor deny the validity of the ideals and values associated with Brahmanical *sannyās*. Instead, they create their asceticism as complementary to the standard classical model. Furthermore, there is no reason to suppose that their self-representations as traditional constitute simply a rhetorical attempt to avoid being perceived as heretical or nontraditional by their male counterparts, or more generally, by a patriarchal society that, as we learned in Chapter 2, nonetheless suspects and respects female renouncers.[4] It goes without saying, however, that none of the sadhus with whom I worked want to be seen (or known) as heretical either by other sadhus or by householders in their local and translocal communities. For these sadhus, their positive reputations and, relatedly, respected statuses are intimately linked to, as well as sustained by, their being perceived as traditional women. Therefore, by constructing themselves and their *sannyās* as relatively consistent with Brahmanical *sannyās*, the sadhus make a tradition and an institution that has brought power, authority, prestige, and status predominantly, if not exclusively, to men fully their own, and more importantly, that they do so by reconceptualizing *sannyās* as singing *bhajans*.

The Polythetic Nature of Vernacular Asceticism in Contemporary North India

The model of vernacular asceticism that this book has proposed through analysis of the practices associated with the idiom of singing *bhajans* widens the parameters of *sannyās* as a heuristic category of analysis. To use Jonathan Z. Smith's (1982) terminology, as a "polythetic" or multi-textured classification, vernacular asceticism pushes back at the problematic conceptual distinctions between, among others, *sannyās* and *bhakti*, intellect and emotion, detachment and engagement, self and body, and this-worldly and other-worldly.[5] Vernacular asceticism as sadhus live it in Mewar consists in the mixing and modulating of all these seemingly dichotomous, yet individually signal, concepts in the construction of a new model and theoretical possibility.

But the vision of vernacular asceticism developed in this book derives directly from the ideas and experiences that are evoked every day through the sadhus' practices emplaced in *satsang* contexts. At every juncture in this study, the sadhus themselves have taught us that reciting the Tulsi *Rāmāyan* from memory is at once a devotional and a meditational experience—or, as in Ganga Giri's case, that recitation of select verses in the *Bhagavad Gītā* performs her idea of the differences in sadhus' natures and individual capacities, while also constituting the worship of *bhagwān*. That singing a *bhajan* serves humanity with love *and* detachment. That *satsang* symbolizes the threshold between God's world and that of humans, where sadhus foster and nurture human-divine connections. Finally, that liberation does not require either denial of or release from the body, but occurs as "peace" in one's heart-mind. From these various angles, the sadhus' vernacular performances allow them to interpret and live *sannyās* as singing *bhajans*. Moreover, when recast as singing *bhajans, sannyās* helps the sadhus to realize their instrumental agency and autonomy without it being perceived as threatening to the dominant patriarchal order. Their associations of *sannyās* and singing *bhajans* (and other categorical binaries) at the level of constructive practice, therefore, makes vernacular asceticism a powerful and emergent space for constituting female agency, power, and authority in their everyday worlds and lives.

In conclusion, the portrait of female vernacular asceticism that I have constructed in the foregoing pages by shining light on the practices of Ganga Giri, Tulsi Giri, Chetanananda Swami, Shiv Puri, Santosh Puri, Sharda Puri, Pratap Puri, Jnan Nath, Maya Nath, Kesar Giri, Sad Giri, and Devi Nath reveals women who are thoughtful and determined. Who love and are loved by their devotees—familial and nonfamilial, Indian and foreign. Who immerse themselves in their practices out of a passionate love for God and, as the sadhus highlight, an intense concern for the world. Who carefully negotiate gender and authority as female minorities in the mostly male-dominated institution of *sannyās*. And, whose *sannyās* complements and coexists with the male traditions. Like Mira Bai, Shabari, Rupa Rani, and Karma Bai, these sadhus experience singing as empowering, and their shared conceptualizations of *sannyās* as singing make it possible for them to exert their power and constitute their status in a tradition mainly created by and for elite men. In constructing *sannyās* as singing, the sadhus perform their *sannyās* as a distinctly female expression and build their identities. Furthermore, in singing to God, the sadhus make the gendered concerns that structure their lives a central issue without doing away with the prescriptive patriarchal ideals that also shape and define their worlds.

Notes

INTRODUTION

1. Henceforth, I refer to Mrinalini Tara as Tara.
2. In Hinduism, the right hand is considered to be ritually pure, as the left one is used for cleaning oneself when one goes to the toilet.
3. The *rudrākṣ* tree is associated with the god Shiva.
4. For a discussion on the *Rāmcaritmānas*, see Chapter 7.
5. Ramchandraji (Ram) is the hero of the *Rāmāyan* narrative traditions, thought to be an incarnation of Vishnu.
6. Classic Hindu cosmologies imagine time in terms of four ages (*yug*), each of which lasts a specific number of millions of years. The ages, from best to worst, are: *Satya Yug* (age of truth), *Treta Yug*, *Dwapara Yug*, and *Kali Yug* (age of degeneration). According to a number of cosmologies, after the end of the *Kali Yug*, the cosmos is destroyed, and after a period, starts anew with the *Satya Yug*. These cycles, therefore, are cyclical and support the widespread Hindu notion of reincarnation (*sansār*).
7. India's independence was formally declared on August 17, 1947. The reign of Congress probably signals the early 1960s.
8. This practice is known more commonly as *nāma-jāpa* (recitation of the divine name).
9. *Sansār* in the Hindu traditions denotes the idea of birth, death, and rebirth in the cycle of existence.
10. As Knight discusses, Bauls can be either Hindu or Muslim, and they challenge socially conservative views of caste and gender hierarchy (2011, 5–9).
11. It is difficult to find statistics available on Hindu sadhus. The information I cite comes from Khandelwal (2004), Gross (2001), and Narayan (1989).
12. As Khandelwal discusses (2004), the Dashanamis and Naths are only two of three competing Shaiva forms of renunciation in South Asia. A third form constitutes the Lingayats, which are a minority group specific to the state of

Tamil Nadu, South India. I mention only the Dashanamis and Naths because these are the forms that predominate in contemporary North India.

13. Khandelwal (2004) makes a similar observation in her ethnographic study of female Hindu renouncers in north India. These renouncers, too, appeared to construct eclectic and inclusive renunciant religiosities.
14. My data supports Khandelwal's (2004) observations that female varieties of *sannyās* are generally eclectic, because *sannyās* exhibits what she refers to as "a site of undetermination" (Khandelwal 2004, 43).
15. In this section, I do not give a literature review of this material. For readers interested in a review of this literature, see my article, "Beyond Brahmanical *Sannyās*: Recent and Emerging Models of Female Hindu Asceticisms in South Asia," in *Religion Compass* 3 (2009): 1–19.
16. It is also fair to say that so-called real sadhus, i.e., detached sadhus, have no concern for others' perceptions of their legitimacy, and that to be concerned with such worldly issues suggests one's attachment to the world.
17. *Sannyās*, as Olivelle (1975) discusses in connection with the term's original meaning, refers to the act of "throwing down" the ritual of fire, which symbolized the world of householding and domesticity.
18. As Khandelwal (2004) also points out, it is one of multiple paths to the divine.
19. As Olivelle (1992; 1996; 2011) discusses, in pre-classical Vedic ritual contexts, a man was considered a complete human being only to the extent that his wife performed the Vedic sacrificial rites with him.
20. See Olivelle (1993) for a discussion of the Hindu life stages (*āśrama*) under the classical system. I want to thank one of the anonymous reviewers of my manuscript for pushing me to clarify this point on what "mainstream" means.
21. The family often fought against my attempts to take my younger Brahmin "sister" with me, who at the time was unmarried. Whenever I went to see a sadhu other than Ganga Giri, who lived a kilometer from this family's colony, my Brahmin "father" felt he had to accompany me on my excursions. I experienced similar reactions from the Baniya family I lived with during the early stages of my research, in 2001 and 2003.
22. The Nath tradition, as a form of renunciant heterodoxy, is an exception. See Gross (2001).
23. But, as Khandelwal reminds us, the orthodox Dashanami order is not synonymous with *sannyās*, as its eclecticism on the ground attests. I shall have more to say about this issue later on in the Introduction.
24. In making this statement, I am not saying that women's domestic worlds are "private," but rather that dominant patriarchal constructions of gender assume them to be. See also Harlan's (2007) discussion on this issue, particularly her point that "private" and "femininity" are not synonymous categories.
25. Lakshmi represents a divine symbol of the Hindu idea of beneficence and (female) auspiciousness. Notably, she is always a married (and monogamous) goddess to her husband, Vishnu.

26. The *Laws of Manu* describes a Hindu law text and is part of a genre of texts known as the *Dharmaśāstras.*
27. See Olivelle (1993).
28. While female sadhus are not the only women who experience this tension, the context of this performance suggests that Shiv Puri speaks specifically about them, and thus I limit my comments to them.
29. Rajputs are a high-caste community, related to the Kshatriya *varna.* See also Chapter Four for a detailed discussion of caste status and its concomitant purity/pollution rankings in classical Hindu thought.
30. The Tulasi *mālā* is commonly used by Vaishnava sadhus.
31. See also Kinsley's (1981) discussion on a generic conception of *bhakti* as an alternative to marriage for women.
32. Karen Pechilis Prentiss (1999) also observes in her analysis of the poems of *bhakti*-poet saints from Tamil Nadu's classical period that female saints, in particular, similarly drew on an unorthodox notion of *bhakti* to legitimate their unconventional lives of asceticism. Moreover, in her recent book about the earliest South Indian poet-saint of Tamil Nadu, Karaikkal Ammaiyar, Pechilis (2011) shows that this saint's asceticism also revolved around reworking notions of *bhakti* to Shiva.
33. The sadhus characterize Mira Bai as a *sant,* thus complicating the academic boundaries that divide the *bhakti* poet-saints into "*sagun*" and "*nirgun*" camps. See also Chapters 6 and 8.
34. Here, I am referring to the householders and the male sadhus with whom I spoke.
35. In this case, the householders and male sadhus with whom I conversed characterized Mira as a *sant.* But, it also seemed to me that they distinguished between a *sant* and a sadhu-renouncer, while the female sadhus did not.
36. See Ojha (1981); Teskey Denton (2004).

CHAPTER 1

1. Ganga Giri's statement recalls the provocative title of Ann Gold's (1992) book, *A Carnival of Meeting and Parting,* which is an oral epic performance of the tale of the renouncer-king Gopi Chand. See also Chapter 4 for a discussion of this text and Ganga Giri's performance of it.
2. In their sociological study of itinerant *bhakti*-oriented sadhus, Miller and Wertz characterize their practices as "a 'folk' version of the ascetic tradition" (1996, 60). While these scholars recognize "the wide range of ascetic styles" in the state of Bhubaneshwar, East India, where they conducted fieldwork, they also assume the dominant Brahmanical model against which lived multiplicities are measured (60).
3. Smita Tewari Jassal (2012) similarly discusses that the predominantly low-caste women with whom she worked did not answer her questions with analytical statements, but rather with songs. These women performed their

interpretations of gender, caste, and power structures that constricted their life options through their songs.

4. *Bhakt* translates as devotee.
5. See Flueckiger's *Gender and Genre in the Folklore of Middle India* (1996), 22, for a helpful schematic of the components of the communicative act, and pages 21–23 for her discussion of performance as a method of analysis.
6. Meena Khandelwal similarly concurs in her discussion of studies of Hindu women's lives that focus on their discursive statements rather than their practices. See Khandelwal (2004), 200.
7. One particular woman whom I met through the sadhus, Laksman Pura Mataji, wore white clothing and lived in her eldest son's house. Unlike the female sadhus (i.e., women who have taken initiation into a renunciant tradition) who are the focus of this book, Laksman Pura Mataji did not take initiation into *sannyās*, and yet the sadhus considered her as a sadhu like themselves.
8. In his study of ideas of abortion in Japanese Buddhism, William Lafleur (1994) also invokes the notion of bricolage to understand Buddhists' lived practices that interrogate the more mainstream Buddhist representations.
9. Primiano defines the concept as follows: "Vernacular religion is, by definition, religion as it is lived: as human beings encounter, understand, interpret, and practice it. Since religion inherently involves interpretation, it is impossible for the religion of an individual not to be vernacular" (1995, 44).
10. In her explication of the concept, Flueckiger says: "Amma's healing room represents a level of popular, non-institutionally based Islamic practice... what I have called 'vernacular Islam'—...to remind us that "universal Islam" is lived locally. Here, on the ground, vernacular Islam is shaped and voiced by individuals in specific contexts and in specific relationships, individuals who change over time in social, economic, and political contexts that also shift. To study vernacular Islam... is to identify sites of potential fluidity, flexibility, and innovation in a religious tradition that self-identifies as universal and is often perceived to be ideologically monolithic" (2006, 2).
11. In Sufi Islam, *pīr* describe a Muslim religious teacher. A *pirānimā*, in the standard parameters, describes the wife of a *pīr*. As Flueckiger shows, Amma pushes back against the dominant conceptual parameters for *pirānimā*, as she takes on disciples and teaches them about her healing practice.
12. The concept of lived religion has been employed in a number of recent theoretical works on the subject; Orsi (2005) and McGuire (2008) are two excellent examples.
13. In using this phrase, I have been influenced by my mentor, Joyce Flueckiger, who constantly pushed students in her graduate seminars at Emory University to rethink the parameters of "what counts" in the academic study of religion.
14. McGuire makes a similar statement about lived religion (2008, 54).

15. I use Jonathan Z. Smith's (1978, 289–309) concept of utopian religion to mean religious movements whose mapping strategies (i.e., how they conceptualize their place in the world) emphasize transcendence. Renouncer traditions illustrate an excellent example of utopian models of religion.
16. Instead of the utopian, I promote a "locative" (Smith 1978) model of vernacular asceticism. See also DeNapoli (forthcoming), "The Freedom of Wandering, the Protection of Settling in Place: Gendered Symbolizations of Space in the Practices of Hindu Renouncers in Rajasthan," in *The Changing World Religion Map*, ed. Stan Brunn (Dordreht, Netherlands: Springer Publications).
17. See Cenkner 1995 [1983]. The four monastic centers are established in Badrinath (North India), Dwarka (West India), Puri (East India), and Rameshwaram (South India).
18. Shankar, however, performs the *pūjā* rites in the temples established to Shiva, in his form as Bholenath (lit., "innocent Lord").
19. Maya Nath also said that they tried to break into her ashram, but she kept a sickle with her and was prepared to "cut off their heads" if necessary. Since that initial theft, other attempts have been made to rob Maya Nath's ashram.
20. See also Khandelwal, Hausner, and Gold (2006).
21. Carans traditionally worked as historiographers, poets, and geneaologists for kings and feudal lords. As Manvendra himself told me, his late father, Ashiya Ranchor Singh, who used to be the director of the Bharatiya Lok Kala Mandal, Udaipur's folk art and cultural center, had worked with American scholar Lindsey Harlan, as well as with a number of French and English scholars. Manvendra has also worked with Lindsey Harlan.
22. This ethnographic practice of soliciting commentary, as Dundes puts it, "from the folk," exhibits the practice of oral literary criticism (cited from Narayan 1995, 244). Expanding on Dundes' insights, Kirin Narayan (2003) observes that "scholars generally have interpreted song texts as representing the subjectivity and emotions of a generic...woman in a particular regional context. Songs thus become textual *objects* on which general theoretical statements about women can be based rather than the lived *practices* of reflective subjects" (24).
23. See, for example, Flueckiger (2006); Hausner and Khandelwal (2006); Orsi (2005); Pintchman (2005); Maggi (2004); Sawin (2004); Lamb (2000); Abu-Lughod (1993); Behar (1993); Lawless (1998); see also Gluck and Patai (1991) for the ethical dilemmas and political implications of ethnographic research.
24. The exception to this pattern was when either a female sadhu or I was out of station. In my case, I traveled to Jaipur and Delhi to meet with my institutional advisor, in Jaipur, and with my funding research institute, the American Institute of Indian Studies (AIIS), in Delhi, every eight to ten weeks. Also, occasionally AIIS sponsored academic conferences, which I would also attend.
25. Shortly before I departed India to return to the United States in 2006, Ganga Giri bequeathed me with three *rudrākṣ* beads, which she placed on a thin, red

rope to form a necklace (*mālā*). She told me that she was giving me these beads so that I would remember her as my guru, and so I would never forget that I am her *celī*.

26. One female sadhu I had been working with while living in Jaipur on the AIIS Hindi language program wanted me to become a formal member of her "blood family [*khun kā riśtā*]" by marrying her younger brother. This female sadhu was elder to me only by a decade. Trying to mask my shock at her question, I asked this sadhu why she wanted me to marry her brother. Her response was that not only did she want to create a "world family," but she also felt that I would make a great sister-in-law, and thus, acceptable companion for domestic and international travel.
27. After referring to me as their *pardesi celī*, sadhus like Tulsi Giri would say, "for *bhagwān*, there's no *desi* [national] or *pardesi* [foreign], only the *ātmā*."
28. In addition to the sadhus, the host families with whom I lived held similar expectations about my remaining single and celibate throughout my research activities.
29. Most of the female sadhus assumed that I would become a sadhu like them eventually.
30. Many Indians had difficultly pronouncing my name, and soon people started calling me "Internet," instead of Antoinette. I asked people to call me "Anita" instead, which they liked very much, saying "it's a good Indian name."
31. Not all the sadhus, of course, had heard about the event. But, listening to my rendition of the tale, many of them were quite confident that a "girl with good *sanskārs* [traits] like me" would not do such a thing anyway. Most of the sadhus advised me not to worry about what had happened and to continue with my research.
32. The Alwars describe a classical (ca. sixth–ninth centuries) movement of *bhakti* devotees in South India who worshipped Vishnu and who composed poetry to this deity (see Prentiss 1999; Pechilis 2011; Narayanan 2003). Similarly, the Nayanars consisted of Shaiva devotees of the early *bhakti* movements of South India, and are responsible for the development of bhakti in medieval South India (Prentiss 1999; Pechilis 2011; Rodrigues 2006).
33. They sponsored a number of *satsangs* at their home, for the guru of my host father, and for the sadhus with whom I became close, like Ganga Giri and Tulsi Giri. The family, including myself, prepared large meals for the sadhus in these gatherings, and they usually lasted a whole day.
34. *Samādhi* describes the process in which a sadhu leaves his or her physical body and unites with the divine. That is one connotation of the term. Another is the notion of the memorial shrines in which sadhus are buried. Because of the power they are perceived to have, even after their physical deaths, sadhus are not cremated (most Hindus cremate their dead), but rather are buried in the ground, so that people are able to access their spiritual power.

35. Most of the sadhus believed that I was an Indian in my last life and that we knew each and "sang *bhajans* together," and promised in that life to sing *bhajans* together in this life.
36. King Karan is thought to have been the half-brother of the Pandava Brothers, born of the Queen Mother Kunti.
37. In the dominant model, sadhus should neither wear gold, nor touch money.
38. Ganga Giri's King Karan story performance also suggested that giving money to sadhus is a wrong form of "currency" exchange, and that sadhus would much prefer to receive food (or the materials to make it), since they are not supposed to touch money. See Chapter 8.
39. In 2001, there were only three Internet cafes, located primarily in the "old City," that is, along Lake Palace Road. The number of Internet cafes in the city itself, however, has exploded, with there being over a dozen or so cafes at the time of this writing.
40. In addition to Café Coffee Day, Udaipur city has Café 0294, which is named after the city's telephone code, and Café Namaste.
41. McDonalds, Kentucky Fried Chicken, and Domino's Pizza have penetrated into Jaipur, the capital of the state, located in northeast Rajasthan.
42. These temples are no longer active religious sites, but primarily serve as tourist attractions in the city.
43. Ann G. Gold insightfully writes: "Any study of Rajasthani attitudes concerning release and renunciation should... remain cognizant of warrior ideals... Many of the most important village deities, as well as innumerable minor ones, find the source of their divinity on the battlefield" (Gold 1988, 25).
44. Another ascetic, Pabuji, was also from a warrior (*kṣatriya*) caste. Though the female sadhus did not perform his songs or stories, Pabuji is considered to be a popular warrior-hero in Rajasthan, and bards sing his songs and tell his stories as part of the epic performance of Pabuji throughout the region. See Smith (1991).
45. Deryck O. Lodrick explains that, although Rajasthan is consistently identified by its inhabitants as "the land of Rajputs," Rajputs actually make up only 5.6% of the population (2001, 18).
46. As Lodrick points out, "It was this romantic picture of a noble, feudal aristocracy presented in Tod's *Annals and Antiquities of Rajasthan*... that became part of the British consciousness, and subsequently came to dominate British views of Rajputs and of Rajasthan" (2001, 10).
47. According to the self-representation of Sisodiya Rajputs, the Sisodiya dynasty is descended from the Surya Vamsh, or Sun-God. See Harlan (1992). See also Chapters 4 and 5.
48. Some of the sadhus mentioned this legend in their discussions of the founding of the Udaipur/Mewar.

49. Singhal's *Udaipur: The City of Lakes* is a pamphlet-sized book I purchased from the local folk museum, Bharatiya Lok Kala Mandal. It is widely sold in bazaars throughout Udaipur, and many Mewari householders whom I met recommended this book to me in order me to get a sense of local representations of Mewari history.
50. Several of the sadhus told me that numerous sadhus had joined Rana Pratap's army to fight against Akbar's army.

CHAPTER 2

1. The *Kumbh Melā* is India's most famous, month-long ceremonial gathering; male and female sadhus from different Hindu sectarian traditions come from all over the Indian subcontinent to participate in this festival. It occurs every twelve years at different sacred sites throughout India. Householder disciples of the sadhus also participate in the festivities, and many householders set up vending and food sites, or feeding kitchens, for the sadhus.
2. See also Lisa I. Knight's (2011) discussion of the female Baul singers with whom she worked. Through analysis of their oral narratives, Knight similarly argues that Baul women distinguish themselves as clever, which, in their view, constitutes a defining trait of being a Baul.
3. Munchaleshwar Mahadev is an epithet for the deity Shiva. It translates as the "mustached god," as Shiva is often imaged with a moustache.
4. Literally, "you." *Āp* is how one addresses one's elders or those with higher social status.
5. *Tū* also means "you." However, the speaker uses this form to address children or those who occupy a lower social status.
6. See, for example, Prasad (2007); Flueckiger (2006); Yamane (2000); Raheja (2003); Gold and Raheja (1994); Abu-Lughod (1993); Behar (1993); Etter-Lewis (1991); and Lawless (1988).
7. See, for example, Khandelwal, Hausner, and Gold (2006); Khandelwal (2004; 1997; 1996); Sarah Lamb (2000); Gross (2001); Ramdas Lamb (2008; 2002); Miller and Wertz (1996).
8. See John D. Smith's (2009) discussion in the Introduction of his abridged translation of *The Mahahbarata*.
9. According to citations of census data by both Gross (2001) and Khandelwal (2004), female Hindu sadhus comprise approximately 10–15% of the ascetic population on the Indian subcontinent.
10. My translation of *kartavya* is based on the meanings attributed by the female sadhus whom I interviewed. A standard definition of the term can also be found in R. S. McGregor, *Oxford Hindi-English Dictionary* (Oxford: Oxford University Press, 1993).

11. *Guru Pūrṇimā* is one of the most important religious holidays in India. It literally means "on the full moon (*pūrṇimā*), worship the guru." Devotees and disciples gather at the ashrams or religious hermitages of their gurus to pay them respect and to worship them as the form (*rūp*) of God. Many Indians believe that the guru is the human embodiment of God, and only through the guru does one get to God. The day that I went to visit Tulsi Giri at her guru's ashram, several hundred devotees had already started setting up their tents and food kitchens (*bhaṇḍāra*) for the upcoming holiday.
12. Lawless (1988) similarly discusses that the female Pentecostal preachers with whom she worked disclaim their individual agency by attributing their own public position of power and authority to God himself. As Lawless argues, the narrative theme of God calling a woman to become a pastor constitutes what she calls as a "ritual disclaimer" by which they, in turn, exert spiritual authority. See Lawless, *Handmaidens of the Lord: Pentecostal Women Preachers and Traditional Religion* (Philadelphia: University of Pennsylvania Press, 1988), 76.
13. Kashi, also known as Varanasi or Benares, is one of the oldest and most renowned cities in the North Indian state of Uttar Pradesh. Besides being considered by Hindus, Buddhists, and Jains as one of the holiest cities in India, Kashi is located on the banks of the sacred Ganges (Ganga) river. Sadhus often make pilgrimages to the city as a form of penance in order to purify themselves in this river. Some sadhus also settle permanently in Kashi and establish ashrams and other institutions as centers of religious learning and practice.
14. The word "tiffin" is commonly used in Indian English and, in this context, means the (usually stainless steel) container in which individuals pack their lunch or dinner. In Ganga Giri's description, her guru, Gauri Giriji, stores large amounts of food for the disciples at his ashram. The three-tiered tiffin here signifies the idea that different types of food were stored in different parts of the tiffin. For instance, rice, vegetables, and mixed-lentil soup (*dāl*) would be stored in different compartments of the tiffin to prevent the food from mixing together.
15. See also McGregor, *Oxford Hindi-English Dictionary*. For the English term "to find" I am using the definition provided in the *Random House Webster's Unabridged Dictionary*, 2nd edition (New York: Random House Reference, 2001), 719.
16. In the February issue of *Religion Dispatches*, an academic blog dedicated to discussing the theme of religion in contemporary Western cinema, Paul Courtright analyzes the incredibly successful film that has received ten Oscar nominations, *Slumdog Millionaire*. According to Courtright, destiny constitutes a popular religio-cultural theme through which the narrative of *Slumdog Millionaire* is framed and interpreted. As Courtright explains, "destiny is a broadly shared Indian cultural perspective." Courtright's sophisticated analysis of *Slumdog*

underscores that destiny hardly denotes passivity in an Indian context. In Courtright's words: "Being written—destiny—is not the same as passive acceptance. Jamal's [main character] sense of destiny does lead him to resignation; it energizes him." Courtright's observation equally applies to the female sadhus with whom I worked. Their understanding of their becoming sadhus enables their agency, not passivity. That is, by interpreting their asceticism through means of the traditional category of destiny, the female sadhus situate their lives within a religious framework that enables them to exercise agency and authority as female sadhus. See Courtright "Life as a Game Show: Reading *Slumdog Millionaire*" *Religion Dispatches* (2009), http://www.religiondispatches.org/archive/politics/1137/life_as_a_game_show%3A_reading_slumdog_millionaire/. I thank Paul Courtright for recommending this blog to me (personal communication, February 21, 2009).

17. See Tessa Bartholomeusz (1996) for a comparison with Theravadin Buddhist renouncers.
18. In stating my questions to the sadhus, I used the term *sannyās* for renunciation. This was the term I heard the female sadhus use the most in their descriptions of their own renunciant lives.
19. My suggestion about the power of the female sadhus' devotion, or *bhakti*, to God stems from Lawless's apt observation that "[r]eligion makes women brave" (1988, 82). Her thesis, while based on the patterns she analyzed in the women preachers' "life stories," is also applicable to the lives of the sadhus, for whom devotion to God makes them brave.
20. Pechilis's book, however, interrogates the notion that Karaikkal Ammaiyar was unquestionably female. See Pechilis (2011).
21. See DeNapoli, "'Nobody can be like Mira!': How Alternative is Mira Bai's Model of Alternative Femininity? The Challenge of Contemporary Female Hindu Ascetics in Rajasthan," in *Mira Bai*, edited by Nancy M. Martin (Oxford: Oxford University Press, forthcoming).
22. I borrow this phrase from Lawless (1988). The female sadhus' use of these narrative themes to construct themselves as "exceptional" (Khandelwal 2004, 21) and as different mirrors some of the ways the Pentecostal women preachers whom Lawless describes underscored in their stories what she calls "a perception of difference" in order to validate the "living script," that is, their religious lives as preachers (Lawless 1988, 69–72).
23. Ethnographic studies on women's renunciation in South Asia have emphasized the similarities more than the differences between the everyday worlds of female sadhus and householders (Khandelwal, Hausner, and Gold 2006; Khandelwal 2004; Teskey Denton 2004; Gutschow 2001; Bartholomeusz 1996; but cf. Vallely 2002). Following the insights of Walker Bynum's thesis (1987, 1992), many of these scholars contend that female sadhus' religious roles reflect continuity with their biological and social roles. By pointing out the ways

in which the female sadhus construct a perception of themselves as different from women in general, I do not mean to suggest that this perception translates as a gendered difference in their daily social roles. On the contrary, my point is that, while female sadhus and householders continue to perform similar social roles in terms of food preparation and living either with or close to their families, whom the sadhus regard as "disciples," the sadhus nevertheless understand that their renouncing the world in order to dedicate themselves to God makes them different from "ordinary" women, with whom they happen to share the same gender.

24. It is important to note that *bhakti* traditions are usually seen as promoting more "feminine" attitudes than the Dashanami and Nath traditions, in which the Rajasthani female sadhus I worked with were initiated. The female sadhus' use of duty, destiny, and devotion are gendered narrative strategies to the extent that, in *bhakti* frameworks, they promote a feminine attitude toward the divine.

CHAPTER 3

1. In Indian traditions, suffering constitutes a multivalent concept with various implications in the different philosophical and theological systems of thought in Hinduism, Buddhism, and Jainism (see the essays in Tiwari 1986). And, in the Hindu traditions of renunciation, the standard view of suffering is that of the mental pain and sorrow that arise from being trapped in an illusory and impermanent world. Renouncer traditions promote the goal of *mokṣ*, or liberation from the cycle of existence, as the ultimate means to escape and end human pain and suffering. However, to think that this is the only way in which traditions of renunciation and *sannyās* understand the nature and meaning of suffering would be shortsighted. Suffering is not simply that which is bad and should be avoided; rather, from the dominant perspective of renouncer traditions, including those of yoga, suffering is to be understood in order to acquire inner spiritual transformation.
2. According to Rajagopalachari's translation of this story, the sage Mandavya "spent his days in penance and the practice of truth," on account of which he achieved "strength of mind and knowledge of the scriptures." See C. Rajagopalachari, *Mahabharata* (Bombay: Bharatiya Vidya Bhavan, 1994), pp. 38–40.
3. Khandelwal shows, in her analysis, that while text-based Brahamanical *sannyās* touts the insignificance of gender for renunciation through use of rhetoric such as "there is no gender in renunciation," in fact, "renunciant discourse and practice are not only highly gendered but also gendered feminine. Sannyasa imagines itself as ungendered, hypermasculine, and maternally feminine" (2004, 192).
4. More specifically, the *bhakti*-poets analyzed by Hawley, in addition to those associated with Mira Bai, are Narasi Mehta and Pipa Das. See Hawley, "Morality

Beyond Morality in the Lives of Three Hindu Saints," in *Saints and Virtues*, ed. John Stratton Hawley (Berkely: University of California Press, 1987), pp. 52–72.

5. Ann Gold has pointed out the ways in which these Rajput norms of female gender, particularly that of concealment through *pardā*, can be manipulated, and have been used by Rajput and other high-caste women in a manner that gives them freedom, not restriction, and allows them to move in public (male) spheres without transgressing gender norms (Gold and Raheja 1994). Restrictions such as remaining sequestered in "female" space, the *zenāna*, or the home, while perhaps more applicable to royal and noble Rajput women, are not followed by the village Rajput women who, out of economic necessity, have to work outside their homes (Harlan 1992). In my fieldwork, I encountered many village Rajput women, devotees of the female sadhus, who concealed themselves by means of the edges of their saris (*ghūṇghaṭ*) when in mixed-gender contexts, but who removed their veils when they were in the company of only other females.
6. Hawley suggests that the *bhakti* saints Mira Bai, Narasi Mehta, and Pipa Das, for example, "present a *dharma* of their own, an ethic based on certain qualities of character and communal identification that are not quite ignored but certainly obscured in the teaching of traditional *varnāśramadharma*. In effect they present to the readers a new version of dharma, a bhakti dharma" (1987, 53).
7. Shiv Puri's disciple, that is, her daughter-in-law, who also serves as a *pūjārīṇī* of the temple, joined in the *bhajan satsang* a few times when she came to distribute water or tea, or to retrieve her eighteen-month old daughter from Shiv Puri's lap.
8. Importantly, Harlan discusses that *sat* is not an exclusively female quality (Harlan 1992, 124).
9. Narsi Mehta, as Neelima Shukla-Bhatt discusses, is one of the most influential *bhakti* poets of Gujarat, and is believed to have lived in the early fifteenth century (ca. 1414–1480).
10. As with Rupa Rani, there is a dearth of scholarly literature available on the historicity and life of the female *bhakts* Karma Bai. I have been able to find a scholarly reference to her life in the "Glossary of Devotees" section in David Lorenzen's monograph, *Praises to a Formless God* (1996), in which he briefly describes that Karma Bai was "a devotee of the god Jagganath of the city of Puri," and that she fed God every day "with little concern for ritual purity" (Lorenzen 1996, 266).
11. As the female sadhus explained, *khīnch*, a Rajasthani term, constitutes a sweet dish, similar in its consistency to *khīr*, another Indian sweet dish, but made as separated dishes with corn, millet, and wheat instead of rice.
12. This Karma Bai story shares thematic features with the oral tale of the Jungli Rani ("Queen from the Jungle" or "Uncivilized Queen"), analyzed by Ann Grodzins Gold (1994). In this story, because of her devotional power, the Jungli

Rani becomes accused by the King's other jealous wives, and by the King himself, of "dangerous magic." Gold explains, "her devotion [to the Sun God] is perceived as dangerous [because] [i]t fosters independence from, rather than submission to, familial demands—whether natal or marital" (161). But, as Gold points out, the Jungli Rani's devotional power hardly constitutes an example of dangerous magic, on the basis that she does not use her power for selfish or harmful means, but rather to create auspiciousness for her own family. In this tale, as well, the Jungli Rani's reputation as an auspicious queen becomes redeemed in the eyes of the King.

13. Grace Jantzen (1997) also discusses the ways the medieval Christian female saints used their divine visions, in which they received spiritual power from God (and Jesus), as a means to subordinate, albeit obliquely, male ecclesiastical authority to female spiritual power.
14. Both the sadhus and their audiences consisting of other sadhus and householders told me that the milieu in which the *sadhus* and *bhakts* lived represents the glorious *Satya Yug*.
15. Although Shiv Puri invokes Mira's example to account for the existence of Rajput sadhus, the other sadhus from non-Rajput communities (36% of the women came from other castes), also found inspiration in Mira's model and positioned their *sannyās* in her lineage.
16. While there are various versions of the discourse of modesty in South Asia, it traditionally requires women to stay within the parameters of the home and, in cases where women have to leave the home, to travel outside of its bounds in the protection of male kin or older female kin; to live under the rule of their male guardians; to adopt purdah (veiling) in their dress habits; and to remain quiet and aloof in the company of men, consanguineal kin, and strangers. See Knight (2011); Gold and Raheja (1994); Wadley and Jacobsen (1986); Wadley (1994); and Wiser and Wiser (2000).
17. As Knight (2011) says, Baul women have to straddle two conflicting (and competing) discourses: namely those of "good Baul" and "good Bengali woman." The good Baul evokes ideal notions of the wandering male mendicant who plays his one-stringed *ektara*, and popular ideas of a sexually promiscuous person. In contrast, the good Bengali woman stays home, lives under the authority of her male kin, and is sexually monogamous. Thus, to be a good Baul implies being a "morally loose" woman, whereas being a good woman suggests being a fraudulent Baul.

CHAPTER 4

1. On the legends of Bappa Rawal and Maharana Pratap Singh, in particular, see Lindsey Harlan (1992; 2003); L.P. Mathur (1988); and James Tod and William Crooke, vol. 2 (2010 [1920]).

2. Maharana Udai Singh (ca. fifteenth century) is thought to be the founder of the erstwhile capital of Udaipur, and is the father of Maharana Pratap Singh.
3. Haldigathi literally means, "yellow/reddish-hill," an epithet given to commemorate the battle that the Rajput army, under Maharana Pratap Singh (ca. sixteenth century), fought against Akbar's Mughal army, in order to protect the Sisodiya dynasty from being taken over by Mughal forces. The place where that battle was fought is known as Haldigathi.
4. My use of the term "dominant" here follows M. N. Srinivas's explication of the concept, in which "dominant" means that caste or class group with the most prestige and the social power to shape a society's cultural practices, norms, and institutions on the basis of its concerns and values. The ability of a dominant class to shape culture also leads to the corollary process that scholars have called "universalization," in which the concerns of the dominant class are seen as normative. The prestige and power associated with the (royal) Rajputs creates this caste group as the dominant class of Mewar. See M. N. Srinivas, *The Cohesive Role of Sanskritization and Other Essays* (Delhi: Oxford University Press, 1989).
5. Heesterman's analysis of the *pre-classical* Vedic ritual suggests that the Kshatriya, or more globally, the patron of the sacrifice, becomes through the sacrificial ritual a brahmin. While this idea may reflect the intentions of the predominantly Brahmin Vedic writers, my data in connection with vernacular asceticism in Mewar suggests that the relationship between Brahmin and Kshatriya is markedly different—the opposite, in fact. More specifically, my data indicates that the high-caste Brahmin sadhus' constructing of the ideals of *sannyās* through use of dominant Rajput virtues and characteristics illustrates the process by which Brahmin sadhus create themselves as ideal Rajputs, in order to increase the prestige of their caste status.
6. The phrase attributed to Ramananda is cited in Lutgendorf (2007), 82: "Do not ask about anyone's caste or community; whoever worships the Lord belongs to him." The phrase that I heard seems to play on the logic of the irrelevance of caste in the idiom attributed to Ramananda. The Hindi phrase I heard from the sadhus and householders alike goes like this: "*jāt nā puccho sādhu kī; puch līјiye jnān.*"
7. The term "Naga" refers collectively to warrior-sadhu, and the many forms of *sannyās*—Vaishnava, Shaiva, and *sant*—have their own Naga branches.
8. In the practices of the sadhus with whom I worked, the concept of "*samādhi*" refers to the guru's liberation from the physical body and the worldly plane of existence at the time of his or her death.
9. A telling counterpoint is discussed in Gold (2001). Citing the work of Shastri (1978, 53), Daniel Gold discusses that a disciple of Dadu Dayal, by the name of Sundar Das the Younger, is "matter-of-factly" remembered and recognized

in the hagiographical literature of the sect as a "Khandelwal *baniyā*" (Gold 2001, 251).

10. Texts in the *Saṃnyāsa Upaniṣads* state that the ideal sadhu internalizes the five sacrificial Vedic fires within himself in the form of his breath, and through renunciant penance performs the ritual sacrifices to the gods. See Olivelle (1992, 3–112).
11. See Robert Lewis Gross (2001 [1992]) for an extended discussion on the orthodoxy associated with the Shankaracarya Dashanami orders of *sannyās*.
12. *Akhāḍhā* literally means "gymnasium," and signifies the martial character of *sannyās* as practiced in early medieval and premodern India (i.e., between the thirteenth and nineteenth centuries, approximately); see Lutgendorf 2009, 79–82; Hausner 2007, 39, 78–880; Gross 2001; Bayly 1999, 64–96. In this way the term connotes that ashrams functioned as places for martial training in times of war.
13. Meena Khandelwal (2004) similarly discusses that, in her field work experience, the householders and sadhus whom she met also engaged in distinguishing between "real" from "fake" sadhus. According to Khandelwal, these distinctions are not at all dichotomous categories for the female sadhus with whom she worked.
14. The Gopichand epic, as documented, translated, and analyzed by Ann Gold (1992; 1991; 1988), constitutes the moving story of a "reluctant" sadhu, who, despite his sadhu status, remains woefully attached to his former identity as king, and his former life of wealth and comfort. It details the trials that Gopichand faces on account of his worldly attachments. The epic that Gold documents was performed by Nath bards in Ghatiyali district, eastern Rajasthan.
15. Ganga Giri refers to *Bhagavad Gītā* as *Gītājī*, that is, "revered *Gītā*."
16. In other conversations, Tulsi Giri has identified her *jātī* as Nagda Brahmin, which means that her *jātī* and Ganga Giri's *jātī* are different.
17. Personal communication with Manvendra Singh Ashiya, May 17, 2012. I also witnessed, during my fieldwork in Rajasthan, that the villagers who come for ritual purposes to the temple that Ganga Giri's daughter and son-law, also Goswami Brahmins, manage at their residence, address them both, or the son-in-law in particular, as "purohitji."
18. Sadhu communities are thought to have their householding branches, like the Gosains and Naths, for example. See Ann Gold and Daniel Gold (1984).
19. I mean Vaishnava and Shaiva *sannyās* here.
20. High-caste Hindus usually cremate their dead, the ashes of which are immersed in the sacred Ganges River in Haridwar. If Hindus are not able to trek to Haridwar, they may also journey to regional places that are associated with the Ganges. In Rajasthan, for instance, Ann Gold worked with Rajasthani Hindu pilgrims who journeyed to the sacred site of Pushkar, in order to immerse

their dead relatives' ashes, because its waters signified a regional form of the Ganges.

21. See also Hausner (2007).
22. See also Carstairs's (1967) riveting study of high-caste Rajputs in Rajasthan. In his study, Carstairs documents the transcription of an interview with a noble Rajput by the name of Sri Rajendra Singh, who took to a renunciant-like life (he did not formally take initiation), and legitimated his decision to live as a quasi-sadhu by invoking the notion that Rajputs represent ideal sadhus because of their inner proclivities to protect and honor their religion. Despite his quasi-*sannyās* vows, Rajendra Singh continued to drink alcohol and party in typical Rajput fashion.
23. The Rajput name Singh expresses this lion symbology.
24. The *janeu* represents the ritual string worn by the twice-born and signifies their right to learn and study the *Vedas*.
25. The Brahmin *varna* is commonly portrayed as nonviolent and peaceful. However, historical evidence from the late Mughal and early colonial periods suggests otherwise. In the eighteenth and nineteenth centuries, some Brahmin communities took to a life of paid soldiering under the new rule of the Marathas or Peshwas, who led successful insurgencies against the Mughals. Changing social values often preceded changes in Brahmin caste roles. See Bayly (1999, 74).

CHAPTER 5

1. The story of the *Rāmāyan*, as the tribal sadhu discussed in this chapter tells it, comes later in this discussion.
2. The Hindi terms are *guru-bhāī* (brother) and *guru-bahen* (sister).
3. *Ling* here represents an iconic form of Shiv. Icongraphically it appears as a phallic-like stone or symbol, signifying the masculine, generative qualities of creation. The *ling* is commonly shown as immersed in the female generative organ, the *yonī*, as illustrative of the combination of masculine and feminine powers in the creation of the world.
4. In classical Hindu mythologies it is thought that Shiv requested Ganga (the goddess of the sacred Ganges river) to make her descent through his locks in order to prevent the destruction of the world.
5. The *jyot* (light) describes that part of the *pūjā* ritual in which the worship lamp used during the culmination of the ceremony, known as the *ārtī* lamp, is lit and moved in a clockwise direction in front of the images of the deities being worshipped. In this case, Chetanananda's story indicates that she performed *jyot* to Eklingjī's image.
6. The reference to the *Gītā pāṭh* here describes Chetanananda and Prakashananda's hiring of a Brahmin priest to recite the *Gītā Sār*. An incredibly

popular ritual text in northern India, the editors of the *Gītā Sār*, a publication of Gita Press, explain that the text constitutes a distillation of the "essence" of the teachings of the *Bhagavad Gītā*.

7. *Havan* is a term that describes the Hindu ritual practice of offering vegetarian substances (e.g., ghee, flowers, milk, honey) into a sacrificial fire. The practice, while Vedic-based in origin (it is thought to be related to the Vedic *yajña*), was invoked and reinvented in the nineteenth century by Hindu reformists, such as Dayananda Saraswati, who sought to return Hindus to their Sanskritic origins. *Havan* rituals are popular forms of worship in the Brahmo Samaj and Arya Samaj communities throughout India and the Indian Diaspora. *Havans* typically downplay the use of images in worship, because of the argument that, unlike popular Hinduism, Vedic rituals used no icons.
8. As Harlan points out, Idar is located in modern-day Gujarat. It is believed that Guha came from Gujarat into southern Rajasthan and, through his military achievements, established his kingdom in Mewar. The evidence documented in Sharma et al. (*Rajasthan through the Ages*) also suggests that Guha and his clan may have originally been Brahmins, and later had their caste status changed to Rajput on account of the clan's military prowess and successes.
9. G. Morris Carstairs (1967) concedes this dominant viewpoint of his orthodox Hindu informants. He says that "Thefts were extremely common" in the Bhil communities of Mewar (127).
10. The literary versions are scant on this detail.
11. This narrative construction of Shabari's life appears in Kalyan's "*Bhakta Caritānka, 'Bhaktamatī Shabarī,'*" *Kalyan* 26 (1952): 292–296. Kalyan has issued another publication of the *Bhakta Caritānka*, in its fortieth issue, and the Shabari narrative corresponds in this issue to pages 316–320.
12. The exception to the representation of Shabari as low-born is the *Kalyan* journal (no. 26) in which the editor, Hanuman Prasad Poddar, explains that Shabari was actually from a high caste, and that because her name was Shabari, people assumed she was a low-status tribal Bhil; see p. 296.
13. The temerity of Shabari that Chetanananda constructs in her narrative practices recalls the assertive and vigorous image that fieldworking women in south India construct in their singing practices. See Velcheru Narayana Rao (1991) and Smita Tewari Jassal (2012).

CHAPTER 6

1. Bholenath is a name for Shiv, and is a very common epithet (lit., "the innocent Lord") for Shiv in Rajasthan.
2. This chapter is based on a paper I presented at the University of Wisconsin, Madison, Annual South Asia Conference, for a panel that I co-organized with

Susan Dewey, entitled "Strategies for Hope, Strategies for Survival," on October 22, 2011.

3. I only learned of Maya Nath's heart attack and *bhaṇḍāra* for the establishment of her *mūrtī* at her *samādhi* shrine two days after I arrived in Udaipur, during my visit with Tulsi Giri at her ashram.
4. *Jalebīs* are a fried sweet formed in the shape of a wheel and made with wheat flour. The outside of the sweet is drizzled with sugar syrup.
5. See also Ann Grodzins Gold (forthcoming), "Carving Place: Foundational Narratives from a North Indian market town," in *Place/No Place: Spatial Aspects of Urban Asian Religiosity*, ed. Joanne Waghorne (submitted to ARI-Springer series on Asia—a joint project between Springer publications and the Asia Research Institute of the National University of Singapore).
6. Ann Gold made this comment to me in a personal communication via email, August 2, 2012.
7. A *laḍḍū* is a sweet made in the form of a ball consisting of gram flour, sugar, and dried fruits.
8. See also DeNapoli (forthcoming), " 'Nobody Can Be Like Mira!': How Alternative is Mira's Alternative Model of Femininity? The Challenge of Contemporary Female Hindu Renouncers in Rajasthan," in Mira Bai, ed. Nancy Martin (n.d.).
9. Mahmood's analysis, however, suggests that agency is equivalent to autonomy. In a critical essay on the notion of complex agency, and the ways that Vedic texts may provide insights into more nuanced representations of the concept, Laurie L. Patton makes an important differentiation between agency and autonomy, and argues that scholars often erroneously conflate the two categories. The distinction Patton makes between agency and autonomy is explained later on in this chapter.
10. On the Ramdevra pilgrimage and shrine, see Ann Gold (2001) and Marzia Balzani (2001).
11. Sad Giri's idea of there only being "two" colors parallels the statements of other women in unusual positions of ritual and religious power, who see the universe as consisting of only two genders. See Flueckiger (2006).
12. Here, male sadhus and female sadhus of the same or similar caste status eat together. The sadhus' eating of the main meal provides the most conspicuous practice of caste exclusivism in *sannyās*-as-lived in Mewar.
13. I am grateful for the discussion on the idea of complex agency that Laurie Patton and I had in New Delhi on June 18, 2012.
14. Khatiks typically consume meat.
15. These are the terms Sad Giri uses in her descriptions of the divine.
16. Sex here refers to the idea of gender. Many Indians with whom I spoke, householders and sadhus alike, speak about gender through use of the term "sex." For a discussion of the idea of gender in Hinduism, see Vasudha Narayan (2003).

17. Many of the sadhus were born at the turn of the twentieth century.
18. This version of the legend I present here was told to me by Manvendra Singh. It represents a reconstruction of what I wrote in my field notes.
19. See also Ann Grodzins Gold (forthcoming), "Carving Place: Foundational narratives from a North Indian Market Town."
20. I am indebted to Ann Gold for encouraging me to rethink my earlier claim (and assumption) that Sad Giri's redefining of Khatik identity through practices that emphasize respectability was illustrative of her turning herself into a Brahmin.
21. As Gold points out, though, the Jahazpur Khatiks had a small Bheruji temple. Bheruji is usually associated with the Goddess, and his temples are frequently constructed near the Goddess' temples.
22. I should say here, as Gold makes clear, that one of the allies in the Khatiks' construction of their Satya Narayan temple was a Brahmin by the name of Ram Prasad. Because of the support he gave to the Khatiks, people in the local community began referring to him, in a derogatory fashion, as Ram Prasad Khatik (Gold forthcoming, 12).
23. Exceptions to the rule would be the extremely heterodox Aghori sadhus, who are thought to eat meat, drink liquor, and engage in Tantric ritual practices. See David N. Lorenzen (1985).
24. Like most of the female sadhus, Sad Giri does not practice veiling in her *sannyās*.
25. Ann Gold told me that she was not at all surprised that I met a Khatik sadhu in Mewar, as she had similarly encountered a Tantrik Khatik sadhu during her fieldwork with the Jahazpur Khatiks. Personal communication via email, August 2, 2012.
26. The groundbreaking work of cultural anthropologist Susan Dewey similarly shows the ways in which topless dancers in upstate New York, who engage in different forms of sex work, support dominant political ideologies that do not benefit them as a means to craft their own uniqueness apart from women in similar professions. See Dewey (2011).
27. Of course, Sad Giri, again, presents an exception to this norm, of which she remains overtly aware.

CHAPTER 7

1. The restructuring of Hinduism and its values in the early and middle nineteenth century by neoliberal, elite, educated Bengalis like Ram Mohan Roy, who started the Brahmo Samaj movement (in addition to his own publishing company), is a notable exception. The (male) leaders of the Brahmo Samaj saw female education as integral to uplifting Hinduism from its perceived

deteriorated state, and thus supported programs to educate women and widows.

2. In comparison to other states, Rajasthan still has the lowest literacy rates in the country.
3. See Hess (1987a) and Hawley and Juergensmeyer (1988).
4. Several of these male householders told me that I should consider relocating to Haridwar or Rishikesh, where I would surely find educated female sadhus who "know" something about *sannyās*.
5. The idea of an informal guru, as I heard it used, means that Ganga Giri serves as a teacher of knowledge and devotion to the other female sadhus, even though she did not give them *dīkṣā*, or initiation into renunciation. Many of the other female sadhus called Ganga Giri their "*dādā*-guru," meaning their "grandfather guru." This term was used as a sign of love and affection by the other female sadhus, and was not meant to absolve Ganga Giri of her femaleness.
6. Several of the female sadhus with whom I worked had their birth names tattooed on their arms as children. This practice was done, as I was told, so they can show (literate) others proof of identity.
7. In its Sanskritic and literary forms, the text is spelled as *Rāmāyaṇa*. In this essay, however, the spelling of the text appears as *Rāmāyan*, and reflects the vernacular Hindi-language pronunciation of the text as I heard it from the female sadhus I worked with. In Hindi the final "a" vowel is dropped.
8. Graham also explores the oral dimensions of scripturality as most significant in the formation of a relationship with the text; the "intensely personal engagement of a community with its sacred text," by means of hearing, singing, or chanting it, brings about scripturality (1993, 162).
9. Holdrege (1996) and Griffiths (1999) respond to and advance beyond Graham's theory of scripturality as the oral/aural functions of the written sacred text. As Holdrege explains, "the category of scripture needs to be further exploded and the very notion of textuality implicit in the concept reexamined" (1996, 5). In this essay I attempt such an "explosion" of the category of scripture which Holdrege signals through examination of the rhetorical (textual) performances of the female sadhus as a case study and a contribution of an alternative model of scripturality in the field of religious studies.
10. Martin S. Jaffee (1998) makes a similar observation: "Graham's book focuses squarely on the concept of scripture as textual tradition and enriches it through selected case studies of its oral dimensions" (Jaffee 1998, 225).
11. As Lamb (2002; 2008) observes, the Ramnamis are a Hindu sectarian movement consisting of both sadhus and householders, who worship the divine in the form of the deity Ram (or Ram and his wife, Sita). The Ramnami sadhus, more specifically, are also part of the Ramanandi sadhu tradition, which is traced to the medieval Vaishnava *bhakti* saint, Ramanand, and which hence represents a Vaishnava tradition of *sannyās* (a tradition in which Vishnu or

his many "forms" are worshipped as primary. See Gross (2001) for a historical discussion of Ramanand and the Ramanandis). Importantly, Ramanandi sadhus make up at least half of all sadhu traditions in India (a statistic that is sorely overlooked in academic studies of South Asian *sannyās*). In arguing that the female sadhus' tradition of devotional asceticism represents a nonorthodox and vernacular alternative to the dominant Brahmanical textual model of *sannyās*, I do not mean to imply that Brahmanical *sannyās* is the dominant form of *sannyās* practiced "on the ground" in the Indian subcontinent.

12. Not only do Ramanandi sadhus create a nonorthodox form of *sannyās* in comparison to the more orthodox Brahmanical textual model through their practices, but also, as Lamb suggests (2002), the Ramnamis, as a North Indian movement, create a nonorthodox form of Hinduism vis-à-vis Brahmanical Hinduism through their rhetoric and practices.
13. While *mahārāj* is a masculine noun that literally means "great king," most of the sadhus whom I observed in *satsang* use this word as a title to address each other in general, regardless of their gender. Not only sadhus, but householders, too, address sadhus through use of the respectful term *mahārāj*, by which they implicate underlying cultural perceptions of sadhus as religious virtuosi. While it may seem unusual for female sadhus to address themselves as well as one another with grammatically masculine terms, this does not suggest that these women perceive themselves as men or as masculine. On the contrary, the female sadhus continue to see themselves as women, even though, as some have told me, they no longer do the work typically associated with women (cf. DeNapoli 2009a; 2009b; see also Khandelwal 2004). Moreover, sadhus' and householders' use of the title *mahārāj* to refer to sadhus captures the underlying associations made between sadhus and kings, and to this extent, the underlying perceptions of sadhus as a class of powerful beings. It is also important to state here that both sadhus and householders also address female sadhus specifically in a strictly feminine way by calling them "Mātājīs" or "Māīrām," both of which mean "holy *mother*." See Khandelwal (2004) for a discussion of the ways the communities of female sadhus with whom she worked were also addressed as Mātājīs.
14. In the context of narrating her life story, Ganga Giri told me on several occasions that she was born on the day of *Rām Nāvami*. This detail adds an important framework to Ganga Giri's personal narrative of *bhagwān* and destiny as determinants of her renunciant life, and of the time of her birth as indicative of high spiritual status. This interpretive framework enables Ganga Giri to construct herself as special in the eyes of God, legitimating not only her own public position of spiritual authority as a female sadhu but also her individual renunciant "life choice." At the same time, this detail makes her relationship to the *Rāmāyan* more special.
15. The *samputṭ* is also a term used by the sadhus.
16. This translates as "Victory to Lord Rama and Sita."

17. Personal communication with Ramdas Lamb, July 17, 2009.
18. That *bhāv* is understood to produce intimacy, communion, and relationship between devotee and deity is an idea present in Shakta traditions as well. As cited in McDaniel (1989), the Shakta Tantrika saint Ramakrishna Paramanhansa equated *bhāv* with a state of divine relationship. In his words: "Do you know what a bhav is? Establishing a relationship with God and keeping it bright before our eyes at all times" (McDaniel 1989, 98).
19. In addition to *dohā* and *caupāī*, there are *soraṭhā* meters. As Lutgendorf explains, "A *soraṭhā* is a *dohā*'s mirror image: two lines each divided into eleven and thirteen beat segments" (Lutgendorf 1991a, 15).
20. The *Rāmāyan* recitation performances of the female sadhus present a striking counterpoint to the Chhattisgarhi women's temple *Rāmāyan maṇḍalī* performances discussed by Flueckiger in which, "the written, 'literate' verses [of the Tulsi *Rāmāyan*] are reshaped by the infusion of materials from an accompanying oral tradition" (1991b, 54).
21. See also Flueckiger 1991b in which she argues that women's informal *maṇḍalī* groups in Chhattisgarh involve their use of *bhajans*, with which they expand the boundaries of the Tulsi *Rāmāyan* beyond the written text. Flueckiger explains that the women identify most of the *bhajans* performed in the *maṇḍalī* with Tulsidas's written text.
22. In the views of most of the female sadhus, memorization not only indicates whether or not devotees know a text "by heart," but is also an expression of devotion.
23. This phrase translates as "Victory to God."
24. In Sanskrit, the word *kartavya* literally translates as "what is to be done," implying both individual and cosmic duty and responsibility; it is used in both standard and colloquial Hindi to denote "duty." The sadhus used *kartavya*, rather than the word *dharm*, to indicate personal or cosmic duty to God; however, when I asked them whether or not they distinguish between *kartavya* and *dharma* (the latter term is often used in the classical texts for "duty," and which the sadhus pronounce as *dharam*), they told me that these words "mean the same thing [*ek hī bāt hai*]."
25. Because sadhus are thought to exist outside of the caste system altogether, some scholars have insisted that they have no individual or otherwise cosmic duty (*dharma*) to perform in the world (cf. Dumont 1960; Olivelle 1975). According to the model of renunciation illustrated by the Brahmanical texts he analyzes, Olivelle proposes the idea of a "negative *dharma*" for sadhus and characterizes their lives in terms of "the negation of the *dharma* of life-in-the-world" (1975, 80). But see Vail (2002), who convincingly challenges Olivelle's thesis.
26. The classical Brahmanical idea of duty as that which "must be done," as action prescribed on the basis of a person's gender, caste, and life stage

(*varnāśramadharma*), and which must be carried out because it is what society (and God) expect in order to fulfill dharma, is illustrated in the *Bhagavad Gītā*. See Patton's translation (2008).

27. It is, however, necessary to point out that sadhus have participated in militaristic forms of social service. They have been recruited by kings to fight in wars, and they have formed their own militias to protect minority movements. See van der Veer (1988) and Gross (2001); see also Harman (2013).
28. See the work of Khandelwal (2004) and Barrett (2008) for the ways in which sadhus in other parts of North India understand *sevā* as worldly involvement and incorporate this value into their individual practices of *sannyās*.

CHAPTER 8

1. Take, for instance, the Ram *bhajan* that Tulsi Giri sings in Chapter 7. She classifies that *bhajan* as a "guni" or "saguni" *bhajan*, meaning a song that describes the qualities and characteristics of a specific deity. While the sadhus like to sing *guṇī bhajans*, they also say that *sant bhajans* have more power than the *guṇī* kind, because *sant bhajans* focus on worshipping God without qualities or traits. See also the discussion on *bhajans* as symbolic currency of exchange later on in this chapter and the section on *bhajans* as resources in vernacular asceticism.
2. Most of the sadhus have discussed the idea of the Four Yugas, or ages, which consist of the Satya, Treta, Dwarpara, and Kali. Whereas the Satya Yug is considered to be the ideal age of perfection and wisdom, the Kali Yug is understood to be the age of evil and destruction. Many of the sadhus agree that while *bhakti* is difficult to practice in the Kali Yug, *bhajans* (and/or *kīrtan*) are one of the most productive *bhakti* practices for devotees in this age. For more information on the Four Ages as discussed in the *Purāṇas*, see Dimmitt and Van Buitenan (1978). On the relationship between *bhajan* and *kirtan* in classical Sanskrit texts and vernacular religiosities across India's geographical landscape, see Guy Beck's "Kirtan and Bhajan," in *Brill's Encyclopedia of Hinduism*, edited by Knut Jacobsen et.al, http://referenceworks.brillonline.com/entries/brill-s-encyclopedia-of-hinduism/kirtan-and-bhajan-COM_2040060?s.num=0&s.q=kirtan.
3. The *mahārāṇā* Fateh Singh was the great-grandfather of the current *mahārāṇā* (in title) Arvind Singh. Ganga Giri began many of her legends about Bhole Nath by framing this as a conversation between the sadhu and Fateh Singh. In listening to Ganga Giri's telling of these legends, I was reminded of the Hindi-language legends about the relationship between the Moghul emperor Akbar and his famous court minister Birbal.
4. See Kalidasa's *Kumārasambhava*, a Sanskrit poem on the birth of Kumara, where such fan imagery is plentiful.

5. I am indebted to Laurie Patton for our conversations about *bhajans* as symbolic currency, and owe my own thinking about the sadhus' understandings of *bhajans* to Patton's discussion about *mantras* as forms of currency of exchange in her essay (1996a).
6. Like many sadhus I knew, Barfani Baba claimed to be 108 years of age.
7. Vasundara Raje was the prime minister of Rajasthan while I was conducting my fieldwork in Rajasthan between 2004 and 2006.
8. For example, I observed Ganga Giri make a similar performance of the uselessness of wealth when she was invited to dinner at Jagdish's house. As she was leaving the family's home, my Brahmin host mother approached her to give her money. Ganga Giri, however, said, "No, no. I don't need anything. I have your love. I have the love of this family." Then, she accepted the money and placed it in a blouse hidden beneath her ochre-colored shirt.
9. I often heard householders and sadhus refer to greedy sadhus in a derogatory manner as "svadhus," implying sadhus who think only of themselves instead of others. Most of my collaborators who used this term indicated their own perceptions that sadhus should (ideally) remain detached from material needs and concerns and serve others.
10. The sadhus' understanding of *bhajan* singing as *sevā* approximates the view of a female Baul sadhu with whom Kristin Hanssen (2006) worked. According to Hanssen, Tara Devi, a married Baul sadhu, seems to understand *bhajan* singing as a type of spiritual transaction through which means she exchanges her life (*prān*) in service to humanity. By doing so, she (hopes to) receive donations from patrons for economic support. For Tara Devi, singing *bhajans* enables her and her husband to earn a living (since sadhus do not work). See Hanssen (2006).
11. Susan S. Wadley and Bruce W. Derr discuss that, in their field research in the village of Karimpur, North India, they similarly discovered Hindu villagers' notions of eating sins with removing "bad" karma. See Wadley and Derr, "Eating Sins in Karimpur," in *India through Hindu Categories*, ed. McKim Marriott (New Delhi: Sage Publications, 1990), 131–148.
12. He explains, "[T]*apas* is both process and product. Through *tapas* one generates *tapas*. Through a 'heated effort' (*tapas*) one generates heat (*tapas*)....The fact that *tapas* is both process and product is most evident when *tapas* assumes the form of ascetic activity. It refers then to the 'heated effort' of such asceticism but also to the 'magical heat' which that effort produces" (Kaelber 1989, 2–3).
13. Sondra Hausner (2007) explains in her ethnography of sadhu life in North India and Nepal that she met a female sadhu who made similar associations between *tapas* and truthful speech (Hausner 2007, 173).
14. Ibid.
15. This discussion would not have evolved were it not for the astute insights of one of the anonymous reviewers of my manuscript. This careful reader pushed

me to consider that *bhajan* and *bhakti* may not be "the same" for the sadhus, as I had assumed, and to think through the implications of this distinction for vernacular asceticism.

16. Karen Pechilis's book *Interpreting Devotion: The Poetry and Legacy of a Female Bhakti Saint of India*, shows that the earliest (and perhaps first female) *bhakti*-saint Karaikkal Ammaiyar, in Tamil Nadu's classical period (ca. seventh century), also described her *bhakti* to Shiva with words like "precious" and "difficult." See Pechilis (2011).
17. The *sant vāṇī* were communicated through two different genres. One genre was the recited *dohā*, a short, rhymed poem with a refrain, and the other was the sung lyric known as the *pad/śabd*. Most of the sadhus' *bhajans* consist of *pads* (that is, *sant* poems set to a particular melody) or *rāg*. For a discussion on the sant *dohā* (and *pads*) as vehicles for the transmission of *nirguṇī* teachings, see Schomer (1987, 61–90).
18. Based on her examination of the standard collections of *sant* poetry attributed to Kabir, Dadu, and Rajjab (also known as the Dadu-panthi texts), Schomer identifies ten major themes in *sant* teachings: (1) the greatness of the *sadguru*; (2) separation; (3) the greatness of the *sants*; (4) *satsang* (the companionship of the *sants*); (5) supplication; (6) heroism; (7) admonition; (8) *māyā* (illusion); (9) *man* (the mind); and (10) faith. These themes appeared not only in the three standard collections of the Dadu-panthi texts, but also in popular versions of these collections. See Schomer (1987, 76–77).
19. *Sant* conceptualizations of God as *nirguṇī* coincide with the Upanishadic notions of *brahman* as *ātmā*, and with Advaita Vedanta interpretations that the individual *ātmā* dissolves into the Supreme *brahman* at the moment of realization. See Vaudeville (1987, 26).
20. According to the "Four Ages" text from the *Viṣṇu Purāṇa*, whenever *dharma* declines (due to the loss of truth or wisdom in the universe), Viṣṇu incarnates in the world in a particular form (Krishna, Ram, the boar, the fish, and so forth) in order to destroy evil and restore righteousness. Many of the texts from the *Viṣṇu Purāṇa* make this claim. See *Classical Hindu Mythology: A Reader in the Sanskrit Puraṇas*, Dimmitt and Van Buitenen, ed. (1978).
21. In the composition of their poetry, the *sants* borrowed imagery and concepts heavily from the *Purāṇas*. See Lorenzen (1995; 1996).
22. Dwarka is a popular pilgrimage city in the North Indian state of Gujarat, Jamnagar district. It is considered to be one of Krishna's dwelling places, and thus, the place where Mira united with Krishna.
23. Vrindavan is also a popular pilgrimage town in the North Indian state of Uttar Pradesh, Mathura district. It is considered to be the birthplace of Krishna and the place where, up until the time she left for Dwarka, Mira resided while she was living as a sadhu.

24. Whenever I asked the sadhus if they saw themselves as contemporary Mira Bais, almost all of them responded along the lines of: "Mira was Mira. No one can be like her." Nancy Martin discusses a contemporary group of holy women who identify themselves as Mira Bai and who are identified as Mira by their families who are coming to terms with their choices. See Martin (2007); personal communication with Martin on February 20, 2009; see also DeNapoli (forthcoming), "Nobody can be like Mira."
25. See A. K. Ramanujan (1999b, 270); see also Ramaswamy (1997) and Kinsley (1981).
26. According to Henry, the Jogi mendicants from whom he collected his *nirguṇī bhajans* were householders, and not ascetics, as many of the villagers had assumed (the villagers thought that since their repertoires had consisted of purely *nirguṇī* and philosophical *bhajans*, that the singers themselves had been wandering ascetics). The Jogi caste is a community of weavers from Uttar Pradesh and is believed to be descended from the Nath panthis. For this reason, many wandering Jogis sing the *bhajans* of Kabir and the Naths. See Henry (1988; 1991).
27. Lorenzen uses the text as sung by Abul Hassan, one of Henry's collaborators, and which appears in Henry's monograph, *Chant the Names of God* (1988).
28. The idea that adults should become like children before God is a popular idea in *nirguṇī sant* literature. See Schomer (1987).
29. In some of the *nirguṇī bhajans* Lorenzen discusses, this name appears as "Ranka" instead of as "Anka." See Lorenzen (1996).
30. For brief discussions on the prostitute and Sadankasai see Lorenzen (1996), "A Glossary of Devotees," 268.
31. Lorenzen makes a similar observation about the ways that *nirguṇī bhajans* legitimize their *bhakti* claims by listing famous historical *sants*, such as Kabir, Nanak, Dadu, and Mira Bai, and mythological devotees, like Prahlad, the butcher, and the prostitute, who also achieved liberation from the world through the means of their *bhakti*. He states, "When the authors of hagiographical songs [i.e., songs that praise the *bhakti* accomplishments of earlier *sants* and devotees] make an appeal to the examples of these and other saints, they are grounding their texts on the historical authority and witness of those who discovered the Truth for themselves" (Lorenzen 1996, 156).
32. In his examination of ten *nirguṇī bhajans* performed by different wandering male Jogis, Henry suggests that the recurrent motif of "four days" represents the four *āśramas*, or life stages, of the student (*brahmacārin*), the householder (*gṛhasth*), the forest-dweller (*vanaprasth*), and the renunciant (*sannyāsin*). See Henry (1995).
33. See Khandelwal (2001) for a discussion of the Brahmanical model of celibacy as hydraulics.

CHAPTER 9

1. Elaine Lawless (1988) makes a similar claim about Pentecostal male preachers and female preachers. Though she worked primarily with Caucasian, female Pentecostal preachers and pastors, Lawless compares the sermons of the women she met with published accounts of the sermons of African American male preachers, and finds that men and women not only highlight different themes in their sermons, but, when they do emphasize similar themes, they also understand them in different and gendered ways. See Lawless (1988), 111–143.
2. I emphasize here that the views expressed by these male sadhus on the importance of *bhakti* for their asceticism were atypical in comparison to most of the male sadhus who discussed their lives and practices with me. The few *bhakti*-oriented male sadhus I knew suggested that the purpose of their asceticism was to experience themselves in constant relationship with the divine. In contrast, the majority of the male sadhus understood the goal of their asceticism in terms of absorption of the individual soul (*ātmā*), into the *paramātmā* ("*ātmā paramātmā se līn hō jānā*"), and of the dissolution of all superficial distinctions between the *ātmā* and *paramātmā*. This shared view parallels dominant Brahmanical renunciant visions, according to which the nature and purpose of asceticism is to become absorbed into Brahman, the substratum of existence. Since the ultimate purpose of their asceticism is to become God, rather than to experience oneself in relation to God, most of the male sadhus do not emphasize the importance of *bhakti* for asceticism, an approach that implicitly pivots on seeing oneself in relationship to the divine.
3. In contemporary India, as others have observed, *sant* rhetoric continues, to some extent, to be perceived as heterodox, and has been a source of power by which disadvantaged groups and communities incite change and development in the subcontinent. See Lorenzen (1995) and Mukta (1997).
4. Grace Jantzen makes a similar observation about Christian female mystics of medieval Europe. See Jantzen, *Power, Gender and Christian Mysticism* (1997).
5. In documenting the devotional orientation of three male (Vaishnava) renouncers in Bhubaneshwar (Orissa), India, Miller and Wertz (1976) classify their renunciation as "non-intellectual," implying that devotion makes their asceticism "emotional" and thus non-intellectual.

Select Bibliography

Abbot, Justine E., trans. 1985 [1929]. *Bahiṇā Bāī: A Translation of Her Autobiography and Verses* (with a Foreward by Anne Feldhaus). Delhi: Motilal Banarsidass.

Abbot, Justin E., and Narhar R. Godbole. 1999 [1933]. *Stories of Indian Saints: Translation of Mahipati's Marathi Bhaktavijaya*, parts I and II. Delhi: Motilal Banarsidass.

Abrahams, Roger D. 1968. "Introductory Remarks to a Rhetorical Theory of Folklore." *Journal of American Folklore* 81: 143–158.

Abu-Lughod, Lila. 1993. *Writing Women's Worlds: Bedouin Stories.* Berkeley: University of California Press.

Allocco, Amy L. 2013. "From Survival to Respect: The Narrative Performances and Ritual Authority of a Female Hindu Healer." *Journal of Feminist Studies in Religion* 29(1): 101–117.

Alter, Joseph. 1994. "Celibacy, Sexuality, and the Transformation of Gender into Nationalism in North India." *Journal of Asian Studies* 53: 45–66.

——. 1997. "Seminal Truth: A Modern Science of Male Celibacy in North India." *Medical Anthropologist Quarterly* 11(3): 275–298.

Appadurai, Arjun, Frank J. Korom, and Margaret A. Mills, eds. 1991. *Gender, Genre, and Power in South Asian Expressive Traditions.* Philadelphia: University of Pennsylvania Press.

Asad, Talal. 1993. *Genealogies of Religion: Discipline and Reasons of Power in Christianity and Islam.* Baltimore: The Johns Hopkins University Press.

Babb, Lawrence. 1983. "Destiny and Responsibility: Karma in Popular Hinduism." In *Karma: An Anthropological Inquiry*, eds. Charles F. Keyes and E. Valentine Daniel, 163–181. Berkeley: University of California Press.

——. 1984. "Indigenous Feminism in a Modern Hindu Sect." *Signs* 9(3): 399–416.

——. 1986. *Redemptive Encounters: Three Modern Styles in the Hindu Tradition.* Berkeley: University of California Press.

Bacchetta, Paola. 2002. "Hindu Nationalist Women: On the Use of the Feminine Symbolic to (Temporarily) Displace Male Authority." In *Jewels of Authority: Women and Textual Tradition in Hindu India*, ed. Laurie L. Patton, 157–176. New York: Oxford University Press.

Baker, James N. 1993. "The Presence of the Name: Reading Scripture in an Indonesian Village." In *The Ethnography of Reading*, ed. Jonathan Boyarin, 98–138. Berkeley: University of California Press.

Balfour, Henry. 1897. "Life of an Aghori Fakir." *Journal of the Anthropological Institute* 26: 340–357.

Balzani, Marzia. 2001. "Pilgrimage and Politics in the Desert of Rajasthan." In *Contested Landscapes: Movement, Exile and Place*, ed. Barbara Bender and Margot Winer, 211–224. Oxford: Berg.

Barrett, Ronald L. 2008. *Aghor Medicine: Pollution, Death, and Healing in North India*. Berkeley: University of California Press.

Bartholomeusz, Tessa J. 1996 [1994]. *Women Under the Bo Tree: Buddhist Nuns in Sri Lanka*. New York: Cambridge University Press.

Bauman, Richard. 1977. *Verbal Art as Performance*. Prospect Heights, IL: Waveland Press.

——. 1986. *Story, Performance, and Event: Contextual Studies of Oral Narrative*. Cambridge: Cambridge University Press.

——. 1989. "American Folklore Studies and Social Transformation: A Performance-Centered Perspective." *Text and Performance Quarterly* 9 (July): 175–184.

——. 1992. "Performance." In *Folklore, Cultural Performances, and Popular Enterta inments: A Communications-Centered Handbook*, ed. Richard Bauman, 41–49. New York: Oxford University Press.

Bauman, Richard, and Joel Sherzer, eds. 1974. *Explorations in the Ethnography of Speaking*. Cambridge: Cambridge University Press.

Bayly, Susan. 1999. *Caste Society and Politics in India from the Eighteenth Century to the Modern Age*. Cambridge: Cambridge University Press.

Beck, Brenda E. F. 1983. "Fate, Karma, and Cursing in a Local Epic Milieu." In *Karma: An Anthropological Inquiry*, ed. Charles F. Keyes and E. Valentine Daniel, 63–82. Berkeley: University of California Press.

Beck, Guy. 2011. "Kirtan and Bhajan." In *Brill's Encyclopedia of Hinduism*, ed. Knut Jacobsen, Helene Basu, Angelika Malinar, and Vasudha Narayanan. http://brillonline.nl/entries/brill-s-encyclopedia-of-hinduism/kirtan-and-bhajan-COM_2040060. Accessed October 30, 2013.

Behar, Ruth. 1993. *Translated Woman: Crossing the Border with Esperanza's Story*. Boston: Beacon Press.

Bell, Catherine M. 1997. *Ritual: Perspectives and Dimensions*. New York: Oxford University Press.

——. "Performance." In *Critical Terms for Religious Studies*, ed. Mark C. Taylor, 205–224. Chicago: University of Chicago Press.

Bell, Sandra, and Elisa Sobo, eds. 2001. *Celibacy, Culture, and Society: The Anthropology of Sexual Abstinence*. Madison: University of Wisconsin Press.

Bhakta Caritānka (*"Bhaktimatī Śabarī"*). 1952. "Fortieth Issue." Ed. Hanumanprasad Poddar. *Kalyan* 26: 316–320. Gorakpur, UP: Gita Press.

Black, Brian. 2007. *The Character of the Self in Ancient India: Priests, Kings, And Women in the Early Upaniṣads.* Albany, NY: SUNY Press.

Blackburn, Stuart, Joyce B. Flueckiger, Peter J. Claus, and Susan S. Wadley, eds. 1989. *Oral Epics in India.* Berkeley: University of California Press.

Blackburn, Stuart, and A. K. Ramanujan, eds. 1986. *Another Harmony: New Essays on the Folklore of India.* Berkeley: University of California Press.

Bloomfield, Maurice. 1924. "On False Ascetics and Nuns in Hindu Fiction." *Journal of The American Oriental Society* 44: 202–242.

Borland, Katherine. 1991. "'That's Not What I Said': Interpretive Conflict in Oral Narrative Research." In *Women's Words: The Feminist Practice of Oral History*, eds. Sherna Gluck and Daphne Patai, 63–76. New York: Routledge.

Bourdieu, Pierre. 1991. *Language and Symbolic Power.* Ed. John B. Thompson, trans. Gino Raymond and Matthew Adamson. Cambridge, MA: Harvard University Press.

Boyarin, Jonathan, ed. 1993. "Voices Around the Text: The Ethnography of Reading at Mesivtah Tifereth Jerusalem." In *The Ethnography of Reading*, ed. Jonathan Boyarin, 212–237. Berkeley: University of California Press.

Bowman, Marion, and ÜloValk, eds. 2012. "Introduction." In *Vernacular Religion in Everyday Life: Expressions of Belief*, 1–19. London: Equinox Publishing.

Briggs, Charles L. 1988. *Competence in Performance: The Creativity of Tradition in Mexicano Verbal Art.* Philadelphia: University of Pennsylvania Press.

Briggs, George Winston. 1938. *Gorakhnatha and the Kanphata Yogis.* Delhi: Motilal Banarsidass.

Bronkhorst, Johannes. 1998. *Two Sources on Indian Asceticism.* Delhi: Motilal Banarsidass.

Burchett, Patton. 2009. "Bhakti Rhetoric in the Hagiography of 'Untouchable' Saints: Discerning Bhakti's Ambivalence on Caste and Brahminhood." *International Journal of Hindu Studies* 13(2): 115–141.

Burghart, Richard. 1983a. "Renunciation in the Religious Traditions of South Asia." *Man* 18(4): 635–653.

——. 1983b. "Wandering Ascetics of the Ramanandi Sect." *History of Religions* 22(4): 361–380.

Bynum, Caroline Walker. 1986. "Introduction: The Complexity of Symbols." In *Gender and Religion: On the Complexity of Symbols*, ed. Caroline Walker Bynum, Stevan Harrell, and Paula Richman, 1–22. Boston: Beacon Press.

——. 1986. "'...And Woman His Humanity': Female Imagery in the Religious Writing of the Later Middle Ages." In *Gender and Religion: On the Complexity of Symbols*, ed. Caroline Walker Bynum, Stevan Harrell, and Paula Richman, 257–288. Boston: Beacon Press.

——. 1987. *Holy Feast and Holy Fast: The Religious Significance of Food to Medieval Women*. Berkeley: University of California Press.

——. 1992. "Women's Stories, Women's Symbols: A Critique of Victor Turner's Theory of Liminality." In *Fragmentation and Redemption: Essays on Gender and the Human Body in Medieval Religion*, 27–52. New York: Zone Books.

Carrithers, Michael. 1979. "The Modern Ascetics of Lanka and the Pattern of Change in Buddhism." *Man* 14(2): 294–310.

——. 1989. "Naked Ascetics in Southern Digambara Jainism." *Man* 24(2): 219–235.

Carstairs, G. Morris. 1967. *The Twice-Born: A Study of High-Caste Hindus*. Bloomington: Indiana University Press.

Cenkner, William. 1983. *A Tradition of Teachers: Śankara and the Jagadgurus Today*. Delhi: Motilal Banarsidass.

Chapple, Christoper Key. 2008. "Asceticism and the Environment: Jainism, Buddhism, and Yoga." *Cross Currents* 57/4 (Winter): 514–525.

Chauhan, Brij Raj. 1967. *A Rajasthan Village*. Delhi: Vir Publishing House.

Clifford, James, and George E. Marcus, eds. 1986. *Writing Culture: The Poetics and Politics of Ethnography*. Berkeley: University of California Press.

Courtright, Paul. 2009. "Life as a Game Show: Reading *Slumdog Millionaire*." *Religion Dispatches* (February 20, 2009): http://www.religiondispatches.org/archive/culture/1137/life_as_a_game_show__reading_slumdog_millionaire. Accessed October 30, 2013.

Coburn, Thomas. 1984. "Scripture in India: Towards a Typology of the Word in Hindu Life." *Journal of the American Academy of Religion* 52(3): 435–459.

Crapanzano, Vincent. 1980. *Tuhami: Portrait of a Moroccan*. Chicago: University of Chicago Press.

Daniel, Sheryl B. 1983. "The Tool Box Approach of the Tamil to the Issues of Moral Responsibility and Human Destiny." In *Karma: An Anthropological Inquiry*, ed. Charles F. Keyes and E. Valentine Daniel, 27–62. Berkeley: University of California Press.

——. 1991 [1980]. "Marriage in Tamil Culture: The Problem of Conflicting 'Models.'" In *The Powers of Tamil Women*, ed. Susan Wadley, 61–92. Syracuse: Maxwell School of Citizenship and Public Affairs.

Daniel, E. Valentine. 1983. "Karma: The Uses of an Idea." In *Karma: An Anthropological Inquiry*, ed. Charles F. Keyes and E. Valentine Daniel, 287–300. Berkeley: University of California Press.

David, Kenneth. 1991 [1980]. "Hidden Powers: Cultural and Socio-Economic Accounts of Jaffna Women." In *The Powers of Tamil Women*, ed. Susan Wadley, 93–136. Syracuse: Maxwell School of Citizenship and Public Affairs.

Dazey, Wade H. 1993. "The Role of Bhakti in the Dasanami Order." In *Love Divine: Studies in Bhakti and Devotional Mysticism*, ed. Karel Werner, 147–172. Surrey, UK: Curzon Press.

de Certeau, Michel. 1984. *The Practice of Everyday Life*. Trans. Steven F. Randal. Berkeley: University of California Press.

DeNapoli, Antoinette E. 2008. "Write the Text Letter-by-Letter in the Heart: Non-literacy, Religious Authority, and Female Sadhus' Performance of Asceticism through Sacred Texts." *Postscripts: The Journal of Sacred Texts and Contemporary Worlds* 4(3): 3–40.

——. 2009a. "'By the Sweetness of the Tongue': Duty, Destiny, and Devotion in the Oral Life Narratives of Female Sadhus in Rajasthan." *Asian Ethnology* 68(1): 81–109.

——. 2009b. "Beyond Brahmanical Asceticism: Recent and Emerging Models of Female Hindu Asceticisms in South Asia." *Religion Compass* 3(5): 857–875.

——. 2010. "'Crossing over the Ocean of Existence': Performing 'Mysticism' and Exerting Agency by Female *Sadhus* of Rajasthan." *The Journal of Hindu Studies* 3(3): 298–336.

——. 2011. "Performing Materiality through Song: Hindu Female Renouncers' Embodying Practices in Rajasthan." *Nidan: International Journal for the Study of Hinduism* 23 (December): 5–36.

——. 2012. "Performing a Rhetoric of Renunciation: An Exploration of Female Hindu Renouncers' Vernacular Practices in North India." *Memphis Theological Seminary Journal* 50: http://mtsjournal.memphisseminary.edu/vol-50-1/performing-a-rhetoric-of-renunciation-an-exploration-of-hindu-female-renouncers-vernacular-practices-in-north-india. Accessed October 30, 2013.

——. 2013a. "Vernacular Hinduism in Rajasthan." In *Contemporary Hinduism*, ed. P. Pratap Kumar 97–113. Bristol, CT: Acumen Publishing.

——. 2013b. "Real Sadhus Sing to God: The Religious Capital of Devotion and Domesticity in the Leadership of Female Renouncers in Rajasthan." *Journal of Feminist Studies in Religion* 29(1): 117–133.

——. Forthcoming. "The Freedom of Wandering, the Protection of Settling in Place: Gendered Symbolizations of Space in the Practices of Hindu Renouncers in Rajasthan." In *The Changing World Religion Map*, ed. Stan Brunn (Dordrecht, Netherlands: Springer Publications.)

——. Forthcoming. "'Nobody can be like Mira!': How Alternative is Mira Bai's Model of Alternative Femininity? The Challenge of Contemporary Female Hindu Ascetics in Rajasthan." In *Mira Bai*, ed. Nancy M. Martin (New York: Oxford University Press.)

——. Forthcoming. "Speaking Shadows to Light: Vernacular Narrative as Vehicle for Rajasthani Female Sadhus' Voicing Vulnerability and Violence." In *Women and Religion in the World Series: Women and Asian Religions*, ed. Zayn R. Kassam (Santa Barbra, CA: Praeger).

Denton, Lynn Teskey. 1991. "Varieties of Hindu Female Asceticism." In *Roles and Rituals for Hindu Women*, ed. Julia Leslie, 211–231. Delhi: Motilal Banarsidass.

——. 2004. *Female Ascetics in Hinduism*. Albany, NY: SUNY Press.

Dewey, Susan. 2011. *Neon Wasteland: On Love, Motherhood, and Sex Work in a Rust Belt Town*. Berkeley: University of California Press.

Dimmitt, Cornelia, and J. A. B. van Buitenen, eds. 1978. *Classical Hindu Mythology: A Reader in the Sanskrit Puraṇas*. Philadelphia: Temple University Press.

Dobe, Timothy. 2010. "Flaunting the Secret: Lineage Tales of Christian Sannyasis and Missionaries." *History of Religions* 49(3): 254–299.

——. 2011. "Dayānanda Saraswatī as Irascible Ṛṣi: The Personal and Performed Authority of a Text." *Journal of Hindu Studies* 4(1): 79–100.

Doniger, Wendy. 1991. "Fluid and Fixed Texts in India." In *Boundaries of the Text: Epic Performances in South and Southeast Asia*, ed. Joyce Burkhalter Flueckiger and Laurie J. Sears, 31–42. Ann Arbor: Center for South and Southeast Asian Studies, University of Michigan.

——, trans. 1981. *The Rg Veda: An Anthology*. New York: Penguin.

Dumont, Louis. 1960. "World Renunciation in Indian Religions." *Contributions to Indian Sociology*. The Hague: Mouton and Company.

——. 1980. *Homo Hierarchicus: The Caste System and Its Implications.* Chicago: University of Chicago Press.

Egnor, Margaret. 1991 [1980]. "On the Meaning of Śakti to Women in Tamil Nadu." In *The Powers of Tamil Women*, ed. Susan Wadley, 1–34. Syracuse: Maxwell School of Citizenship and Public Affairs.

Erndl, Kathleen M. 1993. *Victory to the Mother: The Hindu Goddess of Northwest India in Myth, Ritual, and Symbol*. Oxford: Oxford University Press.

——. 1997. "The Goddess and Women's Power: A Hindu Case Study." In *Women and Goddess Traditions in Antiquity and Today*, ed. Karen I. King, 17–38. Minneapolis, MN: Fortress Press.

——. 2007. "The Play of the Mother: Possession and Power in Hindu Women's Goddess Rituals." In *Women's Lives, Women's Rituals in the Hindu Traditions*, ed. Tracy Pintchman, 149–158. Oxford: Oxford University Press.

Erdman, Joan. 2001. "Becoming Rajasthani: Pluralism and the Production of *Dhartī Dhorān Rī*." In *The Idea of Rajasthan: Explorations in Regional Identity*, vol. 1, ed. Karine Schomer, Joan Erdman, Deryck O. Lodrick, and Lloyd I. Rudolph, 45–79. New Delhi: Manohar Publishers.

Falk, Nancy Auer, and Rita M. Gross, eds. 2001 [1989]. *Unspoken Worlds: Women's Religious Lives*, 3d ed. Belmont, CA: Wadsworth Publishers.

Feldhaus, Anne. 1982. "Bahina Bai: Wife and Saint." *Journal of the American Academy of Religion* 50(4): 591–604.

Findly, Ellison Banks. 1985. "Gargi at the King's Court: Women and Philosophical Innovation in Ancient India." In *Women, Religion, and Social Change*, ed. Yvonne Y. Haddad and Ellison B. Findly, 37–58. Albany, NY: SUNY Press.

Flood, Gavin. 2004. *The Ascetic Self: Subjectivity, Memory and Tradition.* New York: Cambridge University Press.

——. 2008. "Asceticism and the Hopeful Self: Subjectivity, Reductionism, and Modernity." *Cross Currents* 57/4 (Winter): 481–497.

Flueckiger, Joyce. 1991a. "Genre and Community in the Folklore System of Chhatisgarh." In *Gender, Genre, and Power in South Asian Expressive Traditions*, ed. Frank Korom, Arjun Appadurai, and Margaret Mills, 181–200. Philadelphia: University of Pennsylvania Press.

——. 1991b. "Literacy and the Changing Concept of the Text: Women's Ramayana *Maṇḍalī* in Central India." In *Boundaries of the Text: Epic Performances in South and Southeast Asia*, ed. Joyce B. Flueckiger and Laurie J. Sears, 43–60. Ann Arbor: Center for South and Southeast Asian Studies, University of Michigan.

——. 1996. *Gender and Genre in the Folklore of Middle India*. Ithaca: Cornell University Press.

——. 2006. *In Amma's Healing Room: Gender and Vernacular Islam in South India*. Bloomington: Indiana University Press.

——. 2007. "Wandering from 'Hills to Valleys' with the Goddess: Protection and Freedom in the Matamma Tradition of Andhra." In *Women's Lives, Women's Rituals in the Hindu Tradition*, ed. Tracy Pitchman, 35–54. Oxford: Oxford University Press.

Flueckiger, Joyce B., and Laurie J. Sears. 1991. *The Boundaries of the Text: Epic Performances in South and Southeast Asia*. Ann Arbor: Center for South and Southeast Asian Studies, University of Michigan.

Ghurye, G. S. 1953. *Indian Sadhus*. Bombay: Popular Prakashan.

Gill, Kaveri. 2010. *Of Poverty and Plastic: Scavenging and Scrap Trading Entrepreneurs in India's Urban Informal Economy*. New York: Oxford University Press.

Gluck, Sherna Berger, and Daphne Patai, eds. 1991. *Women's Words: The Feminist Practice of Oral History*. New York: Routledge.

Goffman, Ervin. 1974. *Frame Analysis: An Essay on the Organization of Experience*. Boston: Northeastern University Press.

Gold, Ann Grodzins. 1988. *Fruitful Journeys: The Ways of Rajasthani Pilgrims*. Berkeley: University of California Press.

——. 1989. "The Once and Future Yogi." *Journal of Asian Studies* 48: 770–786.

——.1991. "Gender and Illusion in a Rajasthani Yogic Tradition." In *Gender, Genre, and Power in South Asian Expressive Traditions*, ed. Frank Korom, Arjun Appadurai, and Margaret Mills, 102–135. Philadelphia: University of Pennsylvania Press.

——. 1992. *A Carnival of Parting: The Tales of King Bharthari and King Gopi Chand as Sung and Told by Madhu Natisar Nath of Ghatiyali, Rajasthan*. Berkeley: University of California Press.

——. 2000a. "Counterpoint Authority in Women's Ritual Expressions: A View from the Village." In *Jewels of Authority: Women and Textual Tradition in Hindu India*, ed. Laurie L. Patton, 177–201. Oxford: Oxford University Press.

——. 2000b. "From Demon Aunt to Gorgeous Bride: Women Portray Female Power in a North Indian Festival Cycle." In *Invented Identities: The Interplay of Gender,*

Religion, and Politics in India, ed. Julia Leslie and Mary McGee, 203–230. New Delhi: Oxford University Press.

——. 2001. "Jātrā, Yātrā, and Pressing Down Pebbles: Pilgrimage Within and Beyond Rajasthan." In *The Idea of Rajasthan: Explorations in Regional Identity*, vol. 1, ed. Karine Schomer et. al, 80–109. New Delhi: Manohar.

——. 2003. "Outspoken Women: Representations of Female Voices in a Rajasthani Folklore Community." In *Songs, Stories, Lives: Gendered Dialogues and Cultural Critique*, ed. Gloria Goodwin Raheja, 103–133. New Delhi: Kali for Women.

——. Forthcoming. "Carving Place: Foundational Narratives from a North Indian Market Town." In *Place/No Place: Spatial Aspects of Urban Asian Religiosity*, ed. Joanne Punzo Waghorne.

Gold, Ann Grodzins, and Daniel Gold. 1984. "The Fate of the Householder Nath." *History of Religions* 24(2): 113–132.

Gold, Ann, and Gloria G. Raheja. 1994. *Listen to the Heron's Words: Reimagining Gender and Kinship in North India*. Berkeley: University of California Press.

Gold, Daniel. 2001. "The Dadu-Panth: A Religious Order in Rajasthan." In *The Idea of Rajasthan: Explorations in Regional Identity*, vol. 2, ed. Karine Schomer et. al, 242–264. New Delhi: Manohar.

Gonda, Jan. 1961. "Ascetics and Courtesans." *ALB* 25: 78–102.

Graham, William A. 1993 [1987]. *Beyond the Written Word: Oral Aspects of Scripture in the History of Religion*. Cambridge: Cambridge University Press.

Griffiths, Paul. 1999. *Religious Reading: The Place of Reading in the Practice of Religion*. New York: Oxford University Press.

Grima, Benedicte. 1991. "The Role of Suffering in Women's Performance of Paxto." In *Gender, Genre, and Power in South Asian Expressive Traditions*, ed. Arjun Appadurai, Frank J. Korom, and Margaret Ann Mills, 81–101. Philadelphia: University of Pennsylvania Press.

Gross, Robert L. 2001 [1992]. *The Sadhus of India: A Study of Hindu Asceticism*. Jaipur: Rawat Publications.

Gutschow, Kim. 2004. *Being a Buddhist Nun: The Struggle for Enlightenment in the Himalayas*. Cambridge, MA: Harvard University Press.

Hallstrom, Lisa Lassell. 1999. *Mother of Bliss: Ananadamayi Ma (1896–1982)*. New York: Oxford University Press.

Hanssen, Kristin. 2006. "The True River Ganges: Tara's Begging Practices." In *Women's Renunciation in South Asia: Nuns, Yoginis, Saints, and Singers*, ed. Meena Khandelwal, Sondra L. Hausner, and Ann Grodzins Gold, 95–124. New York: Palgrave Macmillan.

Harding, Sandra. 1987. "The Curious Coincidence of Feminine and African Moralities: Challenges for Feminist Theory." In *Women and Moral Theory*, ed. Eva Feder Kittay and Diane T. Meyers, 296–316. Stony Brook, NY: Rowman and Littlefield.

Harlan, Lindsey. 1992. *Religion and Rajput Women: The Ethic of Protection in Contemporary Narratives*. Berkeley: University of California Press.

——. 1995a. "Women's Songs for Auspicious Occasions." In *Religions of India*, ed. Donald Lopez, 269–280. Princeton: Princeton University Press.

——. 1995b. "Abandoning Shame: Mīra and the Margins of Marriage." In *From the Margins of Hindu Marriage: Essays on Gender, Religion, and Culture*, ed. Lindsey Harlan and Paul Courtright, 79–99. New York: Oxford University Press.

——. 2000. "Heroes Alone and Heroes at Home: Gender and Intertextuality in Two Narratives." In *Invented Identities: The Interplay of Gender, Religion, and Politics in India*, ed. Julia Leslie and Mary McGee, 231–251. New Delhi: Oxford University Press.

——. 2003. *The Goddesses' Henchmen: Gender in Indian Hero Worship*. New York: Oxford University Press.

——. 2007. "Words that Breach Walls: Women's Rituals in Rajasthan." In *Women's Lives, Women's Rituals in the Hindu Tradition*, ed. Tracy Pitchman, 65–84. Oxford: Oxford University Press.

Harman, William. 2013. "The Militant Ascetic Traditions of India and Sri Lanka." In *Contemporary Hinduism*, ed. P. Pratap Kumar 245–256. Bristol, CT: Acumen Publishing.

Hausner, Sondra L. 2006. "Staying in Place: The Social Actions of Radha Giri." In *Women's Renunciation in South Asia*, ed. Meena Khandelwal, Sondra L. Hausner, and Ann Grodzins Gold, 124–138. New York: Palgrave Macmillan.

——. 2007. *Wandering with Sadhus: Ascetics in the Hindu Himalayas*. Bloomington: Indiana University Press.

Hawley, John Stratton. 1986. "Images of Gender in the Poetry of Krishna." In *Gender and Religion: On the Complexity of Symbols*, ed. Caroline Walker Bynum, Stevan Harrell, and Paula Richman, 231–256. Boston: Beacon Press.

——. 1987. "Morality beyond Morality in the Lives of Three Hindu Saints." In *Saints and Virtues*, ed. John Stratton Hawley, 52–72. Berkeley: University of California Press.

——. 2005. *Three Bhakti Voices: Mirabai, Surdas, and Kabir in Their Time and Ours*. Oxford: Oxford University Press.

Hawley, John Stratton, and Mark Juergensmeyer. 1988. *Songs of the Saints of India*. New York: Oxford University Press.

Heath, Shirley Brice. 1982. "Protean Shapes in Literacy Events: Ever-Shifting Oral and Literate Traditions." In *Spoken and Written Language*, ed. Deborah Tannen, 91–117. Norwood, NJ: Ablex Publishing Corporation.

Heesterman, J. C. 1964. "Brahmin, Ritual, and Renouncer." *WZKS* 8:1–31.

——. 1985. *The Inner Conflict of Tradition: Essays in Indian Ritual, Kingship, and Society*. Chicago: University of Chicago Press.

——. 1988 [1982]. "Householder and Wanderer." In *Way of Life: King, Householder, and Renouncer: Essays in Honour of Louis Dumont*, ed. T. N. Madan, 251–272. Delhi: Motilal Banarsidass.

Henry, Edward O. 1988. *Chant the Names of God: Musical Culture in Bhojpuri-Speaking India*. San Diego: San Diego State University Press.

——. 1991. "Jogīs and Nirgun Bhajans in Bhojpuri-Speaking India: Intra-Genre Heterogeneity, Adaptation, and Functional Shift." *Ethnomusicology* 35(2): 221–242.

——. 1995. "The Vitality of the Nirgun Bhajan: Sampling the Contemporary Tradition." In *Bhakti Religion in North India*, ed. David N. Lorenzen, 232–252. Albany, NY: SUNY Press.

Hess, Linda. 1987a. "Kabir's Rough Rhetoric." In *The Sants: Studies of a Devotional Tradition of India*, ed. Karine Schomer and W. H. McLeod, 143–166. Delhi: Motilal Banarsidass.

——. 1987b. "Three Kabir Collections: A Comparative Study." In *The Sants: Studies of a Devotional Tradition of India*, ed. Karine Schomer and W. H. McLeod, 111–142. Delhi: Motilal Banarsidass.

Hess, Linda, and Shukdeo Singh, trans. 2002. *The Bijak of Kabir*. Oxford: Oxford University Press.

Hitchcock, John T. 1959. "The Idea of the Martial Rajput." In *Traditional India: Structure and Change*, ed. Milton Singer, 10–17. Philadelphia: American Folklore Society.

Holdredge, Barbara. 1996. *Veda and Tora: Transcending the Textuality of Scripture*. Albany, NY: SUNY Press.

Hymes, Dell. 1975. "Breakthrough into Performance." In *Folklore: Performance and Communication*, ed. Dan Ben-Amos and Kenneth S. Goldstein, 11–74. The Hague: Mouton.

Jain, Pankaj. 2011. *Dharma and Ecology of Hindu Communities: Sustenance and Sustainability*. Burlington, VT: Ashgate.

Jain, Pratibha, and Sangeeta Sharma. 2004. *Honor, Status, Polity*. Jaipur: Rawat Publications.

Jantzen, Grace. 1997 [1995]. *Power, Gender and Christian Mysticism*. New York: Cambridge University Press.

Jakobson, Roman. 1960. "Closing Statement: Linguistics and Poetics." In *Style in Language*, ed. T.A. Sebeok, 350–373. Cambridge, MA: MIT Press.

Jassal, Smita Tewari. 2012. *Unearthing Gender: Folksongs of North India*. Durham, NC: Duke University Press.

Kaelber, Walter. 1989. *Tapta Marga: Asceticism and Initiation in Vedic India*. Albany, NY: SUNY Press.

Kane, P. V. 1968. *History of Dharmaśāstra: Ancient and Medieval Religious and Civil Law in India*, 2d rev. ed. Poona: Bhandarkar Oriental Research Institute.

Karp, Ivan. 1987. "Laughter at Marriage: Subversion in Performance." In *Transformations of African Marriage*, ed. David Parkin and D. Nyamwaya. Manchester: Manchester University Press for the International African Institute.

Karp, Ivan, and D. A. Masolo, eds. 2000. *African Philosophy as Cultural Inquiry*. Bloomington: Indiana University Press.

Keller, Mary. 2002. *The Hammer and the Flute: Women, Power, and Spirit Possession.* Baltimore: The Johns Hopkins University Press.

Kelting, M. Whitney. 2001. *Singing to the Jinas: Jain Laywomen Maṇḍal Singing and The Negotiations of Jain Devotion.* New York: Oxford University Press.

——. 2009. *Heroic Wives: Rituals, Stories, and the Virtues of Jain Wifehood.* New York: Oxford University Press.

Kendall, Laurel. 1988. *The Life and Hard Times of a Korean Shaman: Of Tales and Telling Tales.* Honolulu: University of Hawaii Press.

Keyes, Charles F., and E. Valentine Daniel, eds. 1983. *Karma: An Anthropological Inquiry.* Berkeley: University of California Press.

Khandelwal, Meena. 1996. "Walking a Tightrope: Saintliness, Gender, and Power in an Ethnocentric Encounter." *Anthropology and Humanism* 21(2): 111–134.

——. 1997. "The Ungendered Atma, Masculine Virility and Feminine Compassion: Ambiguities in Renunciant Discourses on Gender." *Contributions to Indian Sociology* 31(1): 79–107.

——. 2001. "Sexual Fluids, Emotions, and Morality: Notes on the Gendering of Brahmacarya." In *Celibacy, Culture, and Society*, ed. Elisa J. Sobo and Sandra Bell, 157–179. Madison: University of Wisconsin Press.

——. 2004. *Women in Ochre Robes: Gendering Hindu Renunciation.* Albany, NY: SUNY Press.

——. 2009. "Research on Hindu Women's Renunciation Today: State of the Field." *Religion Compass* 3/6 (December): 1003–1114.

Khandelwal, Meena, Sondra L. Hausner, and Ann Grodzins Gold, eds. 2006. *Women's Renunciation in South Asia: Nuns, Yoginis, Saints, and Singers.* New York: Palgrave Macmillan.

King, Ursula. 1984. "The Effect of Social Change on Religious Self-Understanding: Women Ascetics in Modern Hinduism." In *Changing South Asia*, ed. Kenneth Ballhatchet and David D. Taylor, 69–83. London: School of Oriental and African Studies.

Kinsley, David. 1981. "Devotion as an Alternative to Marriage in the Lives of Some Hindu Women Devotees." In *Tradition and Modernity in Bhakti Movements*, ed. Jayant Lele, XX–XX. Leiden: Brill.

Kishwar, Madhu, and Ruth Vanita, eds. 1989. "Women Bhakta Poets." *Manushi* 50–52 (January–June).

Kishwar, Madhu, and Ruth Vanita, eds. 1989. "Modern Versions of Mira." *Manushi* 50–52 (January–June): 100–101.

——. 1989. "Poison to Nectar: The Life and Work of Mirabai." *Manushi* 50–52 (January–June): 74–93.

Klostermaier, Klaus K. 1994. *A Survey of Hinduism.* Albany, NY: SUNY Press.

Kolff, Dirk H.A. 1990. *Naukar, Rajput, and Sepoy: The Ethnohistory of the Military Labor Market in Hindustan, 1450–1850.* Cambridge: Cambridge University Press.

Knight, Lisa I. 2006. "Renouncing Expectations: Single Baul Women Renouncers and the Value of Being a Wife." In *Women's Renunciation in South Asia*, ed. Meena

Khandelwal, Sondra Hausner, and Ann G. Gold, 191–222. New York: Palgrave Macmillan.

——. 2011. *Contradictory Lives: Baul Women in India and Bangladesh*. Oxford: Oxford University Press.

Kothari, Komal. 2001. "Musicians for the People: The Manganiyars of Western Rajasthan." In *The Idea of Rajasthan: Explorations in Regional Identity*, vol. 1, ed. Karine Schomer, Joan Erdman, Deryck O. Lodrick, and Lloyd Rudolph, 205–237. New Delhi: Manohar Publishers.

Kratz, Corinne. 1994. *Affecting Performance: Meaning, Movement, and Experience in Okiek Women's Initiation*. Washington, DC: Smithsonian Institution Press.

——. 2000. "Forging Unions and Negotiating Ambivalence: Personhood and Complex Agency in Okiek Marriage Arrangement." In *African Philosophy as Cultural Critique*, ed. Ivan Karp and D. A. Masolo, 136–174. Bloomington: Indiana University Press.

——. 2001. "Conversations and Lives." In *African Words, African Voices: Critical Practices in Oral History*, ed. Luise White, Stephan Miescher, and David Cohen, 127–161. Bloomington: Indiana University Press.

Lamb, Ramdas. 1991. "Personalizing the Ramayana: Ramnamis and Their Use of the Ramcaritmanas." In *Many Ramayanas: The Diversity of a Narrative Tradition in South Asia*, ed. Paula Richman, 235–256. Berkeley: University of California Press.

——. 1994. "Asceticism and Devotion: The Many Faces of Ram Bhakti in the Ramananda Sampraday." *Journal of Vaishnava Studies* 2(4): 127–146.

——. 2002. *Rapt in the Name: The Ramnamis, Ramnam, and Untouchable Religion in Central India*. Albany, NY: SUNY Press.

——. 2008. "Devotion and Reincarnation as Factors in Hindu Ascetic Practices." *Cross Currents* 57/4 (Winter): 578–590.

——. 2011. "Sadhus, Sannyasins, and Yogis." *Brill's Encyclopedia of Hinduism*, ed. Knut Jacobsen, Helene Basu, Angelika Malinar, and Vasudha Narayanan. http://referenceworks.brillonline.com/entries/brill-s-encyclopedia-of-hinduism/sadhus-samnyasis-and-yogis-COM_9000000039. Accessed October 30, 2013.

Lamb, Sarah. 2000. *White Saris and Sweet Mangoes: Aging, Gender, and Body in North India*. Berkeley: University of California Press.

——. 2003. "The Beggard Mother: Older Women's Narratives in West Bengal." In *Songs, Stories, Lives: Gendered Dialogues and Cultural Critiques*, ed. Gloria Goodwin Raheja, 54–75. New Delhi: Kali for Women.

Lawless, Elaine. 1988. *Handmaidens of the Lord: Pentecostal Women Preachers and Traditional Religion*. Philadelphia: University of Pennsylvania Press.

Leslie, Julia. 1991a. "A Problem of Choice: The Heroic Sati or Widow-Ascetic." In *Rules and Remedies in Classical Indian Law*, ed. Julia Leslie, 46–61. Leiden: Brill.

——. 1991b. "Introduction." In *Roles and Rituals for Hindu Women*, ed. Julia Leslie, 1–13. Delhi: Motilal Banarsidass.

——. 1991c. "Śrī and Jyeṣṭhā: Ambivalent Role Models for Women." In *Roles and Rituals for Hindu Women*, ed. Julia Leslie, 107–127. Delhi: Motilal Banarsidass.

——. 1991d. "Sutee or Satī: Victim or Victor?" In *Roles and Rituals for Hindu Women*, ed. Julia Leslie, 173–192. Delhi: Motilal Banarsidass.

——, ed. 1991e. *Rules and Remedies in Classical Indian Law*. Leiden: Brill.

Levering, Miriam, ed. 1989. *Rethinking Scripture: Essays from a Comparative Perspective*. Albany, NY: SUNY Press.

Lévi-Strauss, Claude. 1966. *The Savage Mind*. Chicago: University of Chicago Press.

Llewellyn, J.E. "The Autobiography of a Female Hindu Renouncer." In *Religions of India in Practice*, ed. Donald S. Lopez, Jr., 162–172. Princeton, NJ: Princeton University Press.

Lodrick, Deryck O. 2001. "Rajasthan as a Region: Myth or Reality?" In *The Idea of Rajasthan:Explorations in Regional Identity*, vol. 1, ed. Karine Schomer, Joan Erdman, Deryck O. Lodrick, and Lloyd Rudolph, 1–44. New Delhi: Manohar Publishers.

Lorenzen, David N. 1995. *Bhakti Religion in North India: Community, Identity and Political Action*. Albany, NY: SUNY Press.

——. 1996. *Praises to a Formless God: Nirguṇī Texts from North India*. Albany, NY: SUNY Press.

Lutgendorf, Philip. 1991a. *The Life of a Text: Performing the Rāmcaritmānas of Tulsidas*. Berkeley: University of California Press.

——. 1991b. "The Secret Life of Rāmcandra of Ayodhya." In *Many Rāmāyaṇas: The Diversity of a Narrative Tradition in South Asia*, ed. Paula Richman, 217–234. Berkeley: University of California Press.

——. 1991 c. "Words Made Flesh: The Banaras Ramlila as Epic Commentary." In *Boundaries of the Text: Epic Performances in South and Southeast Asia*, ed. Joyce B. Flueckiger and Laurie J. Sears, 83–104. Ann Arbor: Center for South and Southeast Asian Studies, University of Michigan.

——. 2000. "Dining Out at Lake Pampa: The Shabari Episode in Multiple Ramayanas." In *Questioning Ramayanas: A South Asian Tradition*, ed. Paula Richman, 119–136. Oxford: Oxford University Press.

——. 2007. *Hanuman's Tale: The Messages of a Divine Monkey*. New York: Oxford University Press.

Madan, T. N. 1988 [1982]. *Way of Life: King, Householder, and Renouncer: Essays in Honour of Louis Dumont*. Delhi: Motilal Banarsidass.

Maggi, Wynne. 2004. *Our Women are Free: Gender and Ethnicity in the Hindukush*. Ann Arbor: University of Michigan Press.

Mahmood, Saba. 2005. *Politics of Piety: The Islamic Revival and the Feminist Subject*. Princeton, NJ: Princeton University Press.

Marriott, McKim. 1991. "Constructing an Indian Ethnosociology." In *India through Hindu Categories*, ed. McKim Marriott, 1–40. New Delhi: Sage.

Marriot, McKim, and Ronald B. Inden. 1977. "Towards an Ethnosociology of Indian Caste Systems." In *The New Wind: Changing Identities in South Asia*, ed. Kenneth David, 227–238. The Hague: Mouton.

Martin, Nancy. 1997. "Mīrābāī Inscribed in Text, Embodied in Life." In *Vaiṣṇavī: Women and the Worship of Krishna*, ed. Steven J. Rosen, 7–46. Delhi: Motilal Banarsidass.

——. 1999. "*Mīrā Janma Patrī*: A Tale of Resistance and Appropriation." In *Religion, Ritual, and Royalty*, ed. N. K. Singhi and Rajendra Joshi, 227–261. Jaipur: Rawat Publications.

——. 2000a. "Mirabai in the Academy and the Politics of Identity." In *Faces of the Feminine in Ancient, Medieval, and Modern India*, ed. Mandakranta Bose, 162–182. Oxford: Oxford University Press.

——. 2000b. "Mirabai and Kabir in Rajasthani Folk Traditions: Meghwal and Manganiyar Repertories." In *The Banyan Tree: Essays on Early Literature in New Indo-Aryan Languages*, ed. Mariola Offredi, 391–418. Delhi: Manohar Press.

——. 2003. "North Indian Hindi Devotional Literature." In *The Blackwell Companion to Hinduism*, ed. Gavin Flood, 182–198. Malden: Blackwell Publishers.

——. 2007. "Rajasthan: Mirabai and Her Poetry." In *Krishna: A Source Book*, ed. Edwin Bryant, 241–254. Oxford: Oxford University Press.

Mathur, L. P. 1988. *Resistance Movement of Tribals in India: A Case Study of the Bhils of Rajasthan in the 19th Century*. Udaipur, India: Himanshu Publications.

McDaniel, June. 1989. *The Madness of the Saints: Ecstatic Religion in Bengal*. Chicago: University of Chicago Press.

——. 1995. "A Holy Woman of Calcutta." In *Religions of India in Practice*, ed. Donald S. Lopez, Jr., 418–425. Princeton, NJ: Princeton University Press.

——. 2007. "Does Tantric Ritual Empower Women? Renunciation and Domesticity among Female Bengali Tantrikas." In *Women's Lives, Women's Rituals in the Hindu Tradition*, ed. Tracy Pintchman, 159–176. Oxford: Oxford University Press.

McGregor, R. S., ed. 1993. *Oxford Hindi-English Dictionary*. Oxford: Oxford University Press.

McGuire, Meredith B. 2008. *Lived Religion: Faith and Practice in Everyday Life*. New York: Oxford University Press.

McKean, Lise. 1996. *Divine Enterprise: Gurus and the Hindu Nationalist Movement*. Chicago: University of Chicago Press.

Miller, Barbara Stoler, trans. 1986. *The Bhagavad Gita: Krishna's Counsel in Time of War*. New York: Bantam Books.

——. 1998. *Yoga: The Discipline of Freedom: The Yoga Sutra Attributed to Patanjali*. New York: Bantam.

Miller, David M., and Dorothy C. Wertz. 1996 [1976]. *Hindu Monastic Life: The Monks and Monasteries of Bhubaneswar*. Delhi: Manohar.

Mines, Diane P. 2007. *Caste in India*. Ann Arbor, MI: Association for Asian Studies.

Mohanty, Chandra Talpade. 1991. "Under Western Eyes: Feminist Scholarship and Colonial Discourses." In *Third World Women and the Politics of Feminism*, ed. Chandra Talpade Mohanty, Ann Russo, and Lourdes Torres, 51–80. Bloomington: Indian University Press.

Monier-Williams, Monier. 1976 [1899]. *Sanskrit-English Dictionary.* New Delhi: Munshiram Manoharlal.

Mukta, Parita. 1997. *Upholding the Common Life: The Community of Mirabai.* Delhi: Oxford University Press.

Nanda, Serena. 1999. *Neither Man nor Woman: The Hijras of India,* 2d ed. Belmont, CA: Wadsworth Publishing.

Narayan, Kirin. 1989. *Storytellers, Saints, and Scoundrels: Folk Narrative in Hindu Religious Teaching.* Philadelphia: University of Pennsylvania Press.

——. 1994. "Women's Songs, Women's Lives: A View from Kangra." *Manushi* 81: 2–10.

——. 1995. "The Practice of Oral Literary Criticism: Women's Songs in Kangra." *Journal of American Folklore* 108 (429): 243–264.

Nayaran, R. K. 1958. *The Guide.* New York: Viking Press.

Narayana Rao, Velcheru. 1991. "A Rāmāyaṇa of Their Own: Women's Oral Tradition in Telegu." In *Many Rāmāyaṇas: The Diversity of a Narrative Tradition in South Asia,* ed. Paula Richman, 114–136. Berkeley: University of California Press.

Narayanan, Vasudha. 1997. "Renunciation and Gender Issues in the Śri Vaiṣṇava Community." In *Asceticism,* ed. Vincent L. Wimbush and Richard Valantasis, 443–458. Oxford: Oxford University Press.

——. 1999. "Brimming with Bhakti, Embodiments of Shakti." In *Feminism in World Religions,* ed. Arvind Sharma and Katherine K. Young, 25–77. Albany, NY: SUNY Press.

——. 2003. "Gender in a Devotional Universe." In *The Blackwell Companion to Hinduism,* ed. Gavin Flood, 569–587. Malden, MA: Blackwell Publishers.

O'Flaherty, Wendy Doniger. 1973. *Shiva: The Erotic Ascetic.* Oxford: Oxford University Press.

Okely, Judith. 1989. "Defiant Moments: Gender, Resistance, and Individuals." *Man* 26: 3–22.

Olivelle, Patrick. 1975. "A Definition of World Renunciation." *WZKS* 19: 75–83.

——. 1978. "The Integration of Renunciation by Orthodox Hinduism." *Journal of the Oriental Institute* 28: 27–36.

——. 1981. "Contributions to the Semantic History of Saṃnyāsa." *Journal of the American Oriental Society* 101(3): 265–274.

——. 1986. *Renunciation in Hinduism: A Medieval Debate,* vol. 1: *The Debate and the Advaita Argument.* Vienna: University of Vienna Institute for Indology.

——. 1990. "Village vs. Wilderness: Ascetic Ideals and the Hindu World." In *Monasticism in the Christian and Hindu Traditions,* ed. Austin Creel and Vasudha Narayanan, 125–160. Lewiston, NY: Edwin Mellen.

——, trans. 1992. *Saṃnyāsa Upaniṣads.* Oxford: Oxford University Press.

——. 1993. *The Āśrama System: The History and Hermeneutics of a Religious Institution.* New York: Oxford University Press.

——. 1995. "Ascetic Withdrawal or Social Engagement." In *Religions of India in Practice*, ed. Donald S. Lopez, Jr., 533–546. Princeton, NJ: Princeton University Press.

——, trans. 1996. *Upaniṣads*. Oxford: Oxford University Press.

——. 1998. "Deconstruction of the Body in Indian Asceticism." In *Asceticism*, ed. Vincent Wimbush and Richard Valantasis, 188–210. Oxford: Oxford University Press.

——. 2004. "Rhetoric and Reality: Women's Agency in the Dharmaśāstras." In *Encounters with the Word: Essays to Honour Aloysius Piers*, ed. Robert Crusz, Marshal Fernando, and Asanga Tilakaratne, 489–505. Colombo, Sri Lanka: Ecumenical Institute For Study and Dialogue.

——. 2007. "On the Road: The Religious Significance of Walking." In *Theatrum Mirabiliorum Indiae Orientalis: A Volume to Celebrate the 70th Birthday of Professor Maria Krzysztof Byrski, Rocznik Orientalistyczny*, 173–187.Warsaw: Dom Wydawniczy Elipsa.

——. 2011. *Ascetics and Brahmins: Studies in Ideologies and Institutions*. London: Anthem Press.

Ojha, Catherine. 1981. "Feminine Asceticism in Hinduism: Its Tradition and Present Condition." *Man in India* 61(3): 254–285.

——. 1985. "The Tradition of Female Gurus." *Manushi* 31(1): 2–8.

——. 1988. "Outside the Norms: Women Ascetics in Hindu Society." *Economic and Political Weekly* 30: WS34–36.

——. 2011. "Female Ascetics." In *Brill's Encyclopedia of Hinduism*, ed. Knut Jacobsen, Helene Basu, Angelika Malinar, and Vasudha Narayanan. http://brillonline.nl/entries/brill-s-encyclopedia-of-hinduism/female-ascetics-COM_9000000011. Accessed October 30, 2013.

Oman, J. C. 1905. *The Mystics, Ascetics, and Saints of India*. London: T. Fisher Unwin.

Orsi, Robert. 2003. "Is the Study of Lived Religion Irrelevant to the World We Live in?" *Journal for the Scientific Study of Religion* 42/2 (June): 167–174.

——. 2005. *Between Heaven and Earth: The Religious Worlds People Make and the Scholars who Study Them*. Princeton, NJ: Princeton University Press.

Ortner, Sherry. 1996. *Making Gender: The Politics and Erotics of Culture*. Boston: Beacon Press.

Patai, Daphne. 1991. "U.S. Academics and Third World Women: Is Ethical Research Possible?" In *Women's Words: The Feminist Practice of Oral History*, ed. Sherna B. Gluck and Daphne Patai, 137–154. New York: Routledge.

Patton, Laurie L. 1996a. "Myth and Money: The Exchange of Words and Wealth in Vedic Commentary." In *Myth and Method*, ed. Laurie L. Patton and Wendy Doniger, 208–244. Charlottesville: University Press of Virginia.

——. 1996b. "The Fate of the Female *Ṛṣi*." In *Myths and Mythmaking in India*, ed. Julia Leslie. London: Curzon Press.

——, ed. 2002a. *Jewels of Authority: Women and Textual Tradition in Hindu India*. Oxford: Oxford University Press.

——. 2002b. "Mantras and Miscarriage: Controlling Birth in the Late Vedic Period." In *Jewels of Authority: Women and Textual Tradition in Hindu India*, ed. Laurie L. Patton, 51–66. Oxford: Oxford University Press.

——. 2004. "'When the Fire Goes Out, The Wife Shall Fast': Notes on Women's Agency in the Asvalayana Gryha Sutra." In *Problems in Sanskrit and Vedic Literature*, ed. Maitreyee Despande, 294–305. Delhi: New Indian Book Center.

——. 2007. "The Cat in the Courtyard: The Performance of Sanskrit and the Religious Experience of Women." In *Women's Lives, Women's Rituals in the Hindu Tradition*, ed. Tracy Pintchman, 19–34. Oxford: Oxford University Press.

——, trans. 2008. *The Bhagavad Gita*. New York: Penguin Books.

——. 2012. "The Enjoyment of Cows: Self-Consciousness and Ritual Action in the Early Indian Gṛyha Sūtras." *History of Religions* 51(4): 364–381.

——. Forthcoming. *Grandmother Language: Women Sanskritists in Maharashtra and Beyond*. Albany, NY: SUNY Press.

Pauwels, Heidi. 2011. "Rathauri Mira." *International Journal of Hindu Studies* 14(2-3): 177–200.

Peacock, James. 1984. "Religion and Life History: An Explanation in Cultural Psychology." In *Text, Play, and Story: The Construction and Reconstruction of Self in Society*, ed. Edward Brunner, 9–116. Washington, DC: American Ethnological Society.

Pearson, Anne M. 1996. *Because It Gives Me Peace of Nind: Ritual Fasts in the Religious Lives of Hindu Women*. Albany, NY: SUNY Press.

Pechilis, Karen, ed. 2004. *The Graceful Guru: Hindu Female Gurus in India and the United States*. New York: Oxford University Press.

——. 2011. *Interpreting Devotion: The Poetry and Legacy of a Female Bhakti Saint of India*. New York: Routledge.

——. 2013. "Illuminating Women's Religious Authority through Ethnography." *Journal of Feminist Studies in Religion* 29(1): 93–101.

Pedersen, Kusumita P., ed. 2008. "Asceticism Today." *Cross Currents* 57/4 (Winter): 478–480.

Phillimore, Peter. 2001. "Private Lives and Public Identities: An Example of Female Celibacy in Northwest India." In *Celibacy, Culture, and Society*, ed. Elisa Sobo and Sandra Bell, 29–46. Madison: University of Wisconsin Press.

Personal Narratives Group. 1989. *Interpreting Women's Lives: Feminist Theory and Personal Narratives*. Bloomington: Indiana University Press.

Pintchman, Tracy. 2005. *Guests at God's Wedding: Celebrating Kartik among the Women of Benares*. Albany, NY: SUNY Press.

——, ed. 2007. *Women's Lives, Women's Rituals in the Hindu Tradition*. Oxford: Oxford University Press.

Potter, Karl. 1986. "Suffering in the Orthodox Philosophical Systems: Is there Any?" In *Suffering: Indian Perspectives*, ed. Kapil Tiwari, 1–11. Delhi: South Asia Books.

Prasad, Leela. 2004. "Conversational Narrative and the Moral Self." *Journal of Religious Ethics* 32(1): 153–174.

——. 2007. *Oral Narrative and Moral Being in a South Indian Town*. New York: Columbia University Press.

Prentiss, Karen Pechilis. 1999. *The Embodiment of Bhakti*. New York: Oxford University Press.

Primiano, Leonard N. 1995. "Vernacular Religion and the Search for Method in Religious Folklife." *Western Folklore* 54(1): 37–56.

——. 2012. "Afterword: Manifestations of the Religious Vernacular: Ambiguity, Power, and Creativity." In *Vernacular Religion: Expressions of Belief*, ed. Marion Bowman and Ulo Valk, 382–394. Sheffield, UK: Equinox Publishing.

Proudfoot, Wayne. 1985. *Religious Experience*. Berkeley: University of California Press.

Raheja, Gloria Goodwin. 2003. "Introduction: The Paradoxes of Power and Community: Women's Oral Traditions and the Uses of Ethnography." In *Songs, Stories, Lives: Gendered Dialogues and Cultural Critique*, ed. Gloria G. Raheja, 1–22. New Delhi: Kali for Women.

——. 2003, ed. *Songs, Stories, Lives: Gendered Dialogues and Cultural Critique*. New Delhi: Kali for Women.

Rajagopalachari, Chakravarti, trans. 1994 [1951]. *Mahabharata*. Bombay: Bharatiya Vidya Bhavan.

Ramanujan, A. K. 1973. *Speaking of Siva*. Harmondsworth: Penguin Books.

——. 1989. "Talking to God in the Mother Tongue." *Manushi* 50–52 (January-June): 9–14.

——. 1991. "Toward a Counter-System: Women's Tales." In *Gender, Genre, and Power in South Asian Expressive Traditions*, ed. Arjun Appadurai, Frank J. Korom, and Margaret Ann Mills, 33–55. Philadelphia: University of Pennsylvania Press.

——. 1999a. "Men, Women, and Saints." In *The Collected Essays of A. K. Ramanujan*, ed. Vinay Dharwadker, 179–294. Oxford: Oxford University Press.

——. 1999b. "On Women Saints." In *The Collected Essays of A. K. Ramanujan*, ed. Vinay Dharwadker, 270–278. Oxford: Oxford University Press.

——. 1999c. "Varieties of *Bhakti*." In *The Collected Essays of A. K. Ramanujan*, ed. Vinay Dharwadker, 324–331. Oxford: Oxford University Press.

Ramaswamy, Vijaya. 1997. *Divinity and Deviance: Women in Virasaivism*. Delhi: Oxford University Press.

Reynolds, Holy B. 1991 [1980]. "The Auspicious Married Woman." In *The Powers of Tamil Women*, ed. Susan Wadley, 35–60. Syracuse: Maxwell School of Citizenship and Public Affairs.

Richman, Paula. 1986. "The Portrayal of a Female Renouncer in a Tamil Buddhist Text." In *Gender and Religion: On the Complexity of Symbols*, ed. Caroline Walker Bynum, Stevan Harrell, and Paula Richman, 143–165. Boston: Beacon Press.

——, ed. 1991. *Many Rāmāyaṇas: The Diversity of a Narrative Tradition in South Asia*. Berkeley: University of California Press.

——, ed. 2000. *Questioning Ramayanas: A South Asia Tradition.* Oxford: Oxford University Press.

Roberts, Michelle Voss. 2008. "Flowing and Crossing: The Somatic Theologies of Mechthild and Lalleśwari." *Journal of the American Academy of Religion* 76/3 (September): 638–663.

Rodrigues, Hillary. 2006. *Introducing Hinduism.* New York: Routledge.

Robinson, Sandra P. 1985. "Hindu Paradigms of Women: Images and Values." In *Women, Religion, and Social Change*, ed. Yvonne Y. Haddad and Ellison B. Findley, 181–216. Albany, NY: SUNY Press.

Rosaldo, Michelle Zimbalist. 1974. "Woman, Culture, and Society: A Theoretical Overview." In *Woman, Culture, and Society*, ed. Michelle Zimbalist Rosaldo and Louise Lamphere, 17–42. Stanford, CA: Stanford University Press.

Rudolph, Susanne Hoeber, and Rudolph, Lloyd I. 1984. "The Political Modernization of an Indian Feudal Order: An Analysis of Rajput Adaptation in Rajasthan." In *Essays on Rajputana: Reflections on History, Culture, and Administration*, ed. Susanne Hoeber Rudolph and Lloyd I. Rudolph, 38–78. New Delhi: Concept.

——. 1987. *The Modernity of Tradition: Political Development in India.* Hyderabad: Orient Longman.

Samuel, Geoffrey. 2010 [2008]. *The Origins of Yoga and Tantra: Indic Religion to the Thirteenth Century.* Cambridge: Cambridge University Press.

Sangari, Kumkum. 1990. "Mirabai and the Spiritual Economy of Bhakti." *Economic and Political Weekly* 25(27): 1464–1475.

Saunders, Jennifer B. 2005. "Leaping Across the Ocean: Narrative in a Transnational Hindu Family." PhD diss., Emory University.

Sawin, Patricia. 2004. *Listening for a Life: A Dialogic Ethnography of Bessie Eldreth through her Songs and Stories.* Logan: Utah State University Press.

Sharma, Dasaratha, ed. 1966. *Rajasthan through the Ages: A Comprehensive and Authentic History of Rajasthan.* Bikaner, India: Rajasthan State Archives.

Schechner, Richard, and Willa Appel. 1990. *By Means of Performance: Intercultural Studies of Theatre and Ritual.* New York: Cambridge University Press.

Schieffelin, Edward L. 1998. "Problematizing Performance." In *Ritual, Performance, Media*, ed. Felicia Hughes-Freeland, 194–207. New York: Routledge.

Schomer, Karine. 1987. "The Dohā as a Vehicle of Sant Teachings." In *The Sants: Studies in a Devotional Tradition of India*, ed. Karine Schomer and W. H. McLeod, 61–90. Delhi: Motilal Banarsidass.

Schomer, Karine, Joan Erdman, and Deryck O. Lodrick, eds. 2001. *The Idea of Rajasthan: Explorations in Regional Identity*, vol. 1. New Delhi: Manohar.

Schomer, Karine, and W. H. McLeod, eds. 1987. *The Sants: Studies in a Devotional Tradition of India.* Delhi: Motilal Banarsidass.

Sered, Susan Starr. 1992. *Women as Ritual Experts: The Religious Lives of Elderly Jewish Women in Jerusalem.* New York: Oxford University Press.

Sherma, Rita D. 2000. "Sa Ham—I am She: Woman as Goddess." In *Is the Goddess A Feminist? The Politics of South Asian Goddesses*, ed. Alf Hiltebeitel and Kathleen Erndl, 24–51. New York: NYU Press.

Sherzer, Joel. 1987. "A Discourse-Centered Approach to Language." *American Anthropologist* 289(2): 95–309.

Shohat, Ella. 2001. "Area Studies, Transnationalism, and the Feminist Production of Knowledge." *Signs: Journal of Women in Culture and Society* 26(4): 1269–1272.

Shukla-Bhatt, Neelima. 2003. "Nectar of Devotion: *Bhakti-rasa* in the Tradition of Gujarati Saint-Poet Narasinha Mehta." PhD diss., Harvard University.

——. 2007. "Performance as Translation: Mira in Gujarat." *International Journal of Hindu Studies* 11(3): 273–298.

Shukla, Sonal. 1989. "Traditions of Teaching: Women Sant Poets of Gujarat." *Manushi* 50–52 (January–June): 62–73.

Sinclair-Brull, Wendy. 1997. *Female Ascetics: Hierarcy and Purity in an Indian Religious Context*. Surrey, UK: Curzon.

Smith, John D., trans. 1991. *The Epic of Pābūjī: A Study, Transcription, and Translation*. New York: Cambridge University Press.

——, trans. 2009. *The Mahabharata*. New York: Penguin.

Smith, Jonathan Z. 1982. *Imagining Religion: From Babylon to Jonestown*. Chicago: University of Chicago Press.

——. 2004. *Relating Religion: Essays in the Study of Religion*. Chicago: University of Chicago Press.

Smith, Wilfred Cantwell. 1963. *The Meaning and End of Religion: A New Approach to the Religious Traditions of Mankind*. New York: Macmillan.

Srinivas, Mysore Narasimhachar. 1962. *Caste in Modern India and Other Essays*. Bombay: Asia Publishing House.

——. 1989. *The Cohesive Role of Sanskritization and Other Essays*. Delhi: Oxford University Press.

Tambiah, S. J. 1988 [1982]. "The Renouncer: His Individuality and his Community." In *Way of Life: King, Householder, and Renouncer: Essays in Honour of Louis Dumont*, ed. T. N. Madan, 299–320. Delhi: Motilal Banarsidass.

Tedlock, Dennis. 1983. *The Spoken Word and the Work of Interpretation*. Philadelphia: University of Pennsylvania Press.

Thapar, Romila. 1982. "Householders and Renouncers in the Brahmanical and Buddhist Traditions." In *Way of Life: King, Householder, and Renouncer: Essays in Honour of Louis Dumont*, ed. T.N. Madan, 273–298. Delhi: Motilal Banarsidass.

Tod, James. 2010 [1920]. *Annals and Antiquities of Rajasthan*, 3 vols. Edited with an Introduction and Notes by William Crooke. New Delhi: Motilal Barnasidass.

Tulsidas. *Śrī Rāmcaritmānas*. With Hindi translation and commentary by Hanuman Prasad Poddar. Gorakhpur: Gita Press Publications.

Tweed, Thomas A. 2006. *Crossing and Dwelling: A Theory of Religion*. Cambridge, MA: Harvard University Press.

Vallely, Anne. 2002. *Guardians of the Transcendent: An Ethnography of a Jain Ascetic Community*. Toronto: University of Toronto Press.

——. 2006. "These Hands are not for Henna." In *Women's Renunciation in South Asia: Nuns, Yoginis, Saints, and Singers*, ed. Meena Khandelwal, Sondra L. Hausner, and Ann Grodzins Gold, 223–246. New York: Palgrave Macmillan.

Vail, Lise F. 2002. "Unlike a Fool, He is Not Defiled: Ascetic Purity and Ethics in the Samnyāsa Upanisads." *Journal of Religious Ethics* 30: 373–397.

van der Veer, Peter. 1987. "Taming the Ascetic: Devotionalism in a Hindu Monastic Order." *Man* 22(4): 680–695.

——. 1988. *Gods on Earth: Religious Experience and Identity in Ayodhya.* New York: Oxford University Press.

Vanita, Ruth. 1989. "Three Women Saints of Maharashtra." *Manushi* 50–52 (January–June): 45–61.

Vaudeville, Charlotte. 1987. "*Sant Mat*: Santism as the Universal Path to Sanctity." In *The Sants: Studies in A Devotional Tradition of India*, ed. Karine Schomer and W. H. McLeod, 21–40. Delhi: Motilal Banarsidass.

Wadley, Susan S. 1980. "The Paradoxical Powers of TamilWomen." In *The Powers of Tamil Women*, ed. Susan Wadley, 153–167. Syracuse: Maxwell School of Citizenship and Public Affairs.

——. 1983. "*Vrats*: Transformers of Destiny." In *Karma: An Anthropological Inquiry*, ed. Charles F. Keyes and E. Valentine Daniel, 147–162. Berkeley: University of California Press.

——, ed. 1991 [1980]. *The Powers of Tamil Women*. New Delhi: Manohar Publishers.

——. 1994. *Struggling with Destiny in Karimpur (1925–1984)*. Berkeley: University of California Press.

Wadley, Susan S., and Bruce W. Derr, 1990. "Eating Sins in Karimpur." In *India through Hindu Categories*, ed. McKim Marriott, 131–148. New Delhi: Sage Publications.

Wadley, Susan S., and Doranne Jacobson. 1986. *Women in India: Two Perspectives.* New Delhi: Manohar.

Wilson, Liz. 1996. *Charming Cadavers: Horrific Figurations of the Feminine in Indian Buddhist Hagiographic Literature*. Chicago: University of Chicago Press.

Wiser, William, and Charlotte Wiser, eds. 2000. *Behind Mud Walls: Seventy-five Years in a North Indian Village*. Berkeley: University of California Press.

Yamane, David. 2000. "Narrative and Religious Experience." *Sociology of Religion* 61(2): 171–189.

Young, Serenity. 1994. "Gendered Politics in Ancient Indian Asceticism." *Union Seminary Quarterly Review* 48(3/4): 73–92.

Zubko, Katherine. Forthcoming. *Fluid Gestures: Alternative Bodies of Devotion in Bharata Natyam*. Lexington Books.

Index